Finally, let us say something about Mr. Santos's post-prison future. On the basis of the work he has already done, we regard Mr. Santos as a writer and very eminent policy analyst in the field of sentencing and corrections. We also welcome his great wisdom about the most needed and feasible improvements in reentry practice and programs. We therefore hope to have him work with us in a number of roles, including teaching guest classes in our course at Stanford Law School and serving as a research collaborator on key projects with both faculty and students.

Joan Petersilia and Robert Weisberg
Professors of Law
Co-Directors of the Stanford Criminal Justice Center

* * * * * * *

Michael Santos has been extraordinarily successful in devoting his prison years toward both self-improvement and highly beneficial public service through his publications that are used to educate students throughout the country about imprisonment and the criminal justice system. I am not aware of any prisoner who has been more impressive in confronting his misdeeds and then undertaking a single-minded, successful effort at self-improvement over a period of many years beginning with his very first days in the federal prison system.

Christopher E. Smith, J.D., Ph.D.
Professor of Criminal Justice
Michigan State University

* * * * * * *

Michael Santos has used his time in prison in an exemplary fashion, educating himself and contributing to the community at large by his book and other writings while being a force for order and development within the prison community; he has demonstrated deep and sincere regret for his criminal conduct, and by his writing he has done his best to minimize the evil he did as a young man; he has prepared himself to make a serious contribution by scholarship to the federal prison system; he has satisfied a group of thoughtful and otherwise disinterested persons that he will lead a lawful and contributing life.

Norval Morris,
Professor of Law and Criminology
The University of Chicago

* * * * * * *

I have been impressed by your ability to read and master complex studies. I have been even more impressed by your ability to think and write dispassionately about subjects that are obviously of great and immediate import.

John J. DiIulio, Jr.
Professor, Princeton University

* * * * * * *

I have noticed over the years that we listen to some people because of what they have to say, and that we listen to others because of where they have been. I listen to Michael Santos for both reasons.

J. Colin Harris
Professor of Religion and Philosophy
Mercer University

* * * * * * *

Mr. Santos has been truly rehabilitated during his incarceration. Upon entering prison, he chose not to blame others for his fate and not to become a troublemaker. Instead, he chose to change—to work diligently to develop his knowledge and to alter his beliefs and approach to life. His efforts and accomplishments have been rather extraordinary.

Francis T. Cullen, Ph.D.
Distinguished Research Professor
University of Cincinnati

* * * * * * *

Michael Santos is unique. It is indeed unusual for a prisoner to earn both a Bachelor of Arts (Mercer University) and a Master of Arts (Hofstra University) while incarcerated. In addition, Michael took Ph.D. work under my direction. His articles have appeared in scholarly journals and textbooks. Michael believes that he must "earn his freedom."

George F. Cole, Ph.D.
Professor Emeritus
The University of Connecticut

* * * * * * *

Mr. Santos has channeled his fine mind and abundant energy into academic work of excellent quality. His personal and academic achievements while incarcerated convince me that Michael Santos has become a serious and intellectually sophisticated man who has great potential for doing good as well as doing well. His life and skills give promise of his becoming a significant figure in the campaign against the illegal drug trade and an influential role model in dissuading young people who might have thoughts of engaging in it.

Alfred Cohn, Ph.D.
Professor of Psychology
Hofstra University

* * * * * * *

Michael Santos' record of citizenship while incarcerated, both to the prison community and to the larger community, has been exemplary and extensive. As much as I admire his educational and behavior achievements, I must admit that I am perhaps more astonished by his accomplishments in the arena of citizenship, where positive contributions by an inmate are so much harder to come by.

Dr. R. Bruce McPherson,
University of Illinois

For more information on products and services that Michael offers to help others understand the criminal justice system, or to reach their highest personal potential, visit:

www.MichaelSantos.com

EARNING FREEDOM

Conquering a
45-Year Prison Term

Michael G. Santos

EARNING FREEDOM

Conquering a 45-Year Prison Term

Michael G. Santos

APS Publishing
855 Lakeville Street
Petaluma, California 94952

ISBN: 0983134081 / 978-0-9831340-8-4

For information visit
www.MichaelSantos.com
Michael@MichaelSantos.com
(707) 206-4127

Appreciations

First and foremost I thank God for bringing me hope and for opening opportunities that I could seize as I made my way through 9,145 days in prisons of every security level.

I'm grateful to my parents, Julio Santos and Frances Sierra. They had to endure the pain and humiliation of losing a son to federal prison, yet their support never wavered. I'm grateful for the love I received from all of my family, including my sisters, Julie and Christina, and my grandparents, Pat and Lois. I regret that bad decisions I made as a younger man have separated me in so many ways from family, especially the lives of my nieces, Isabella, Camilla, and Sophia, and my nephew, Zachary.

I'm grateful to the many mentors who came into my life to educate and inspire me. My first mentor, Dr. R. Bruce McPherson, from the University of Illinois, Chicago, and his wife, Carolyn, accepted me into their life as if I were family. Many mentors from academia followed thereafter, including Dr. Norval Morris from the University of Chicago; Dr. George Cole from the University of Connecticut; Dr. Todd Clear from Rutgers University; Dr. John DiIulio from the University of Pennsylvania; Dr. Marilyn McShane from the University of Houston; Dr. Mary Bosworth from Oxford University; Dr. Frank Cullen from the University of Cincinnati; Dr. Colin Harris from Mercer University; Dr. Joan Petersilia from Stanford University; Dr. Sam Torres from California State University, Long Beach; Dr. Tara Gray from the New Mexico State University; Dr. Alfred Cohn, from Hofstra University; and Dr. Bill Ayers, from the University of Illinois at Chicago, Dr. Jim Sutton, from California State University, Chico; Dr. Tom Kerr, From Ithaca University; Dr. Dana Hubbard, from Cleveland State University; Professor Kay Harris, from Temple University. These professors inspired me to believe that I could play a role in contributing to society, despite my lengthy imprisonment.

Carol Zachary and her husband Jonathan Axelrod, along with their children Zach and Tristan, gave me a model of community leadership that I strive to emulate and prove worthy of having received. I am grateful to the many friends who have come into my life, providing generous financial resources that sponsored my work along the way: Nick and Nancy Karis; Terry and Ann Karis; Norman Zachary; Gary Chern; Bob Brennan; Geoffrey Richstone; Lee and Melodee Nobmann; Greg Reyes; Jau-Yang Ho, The California Wellness Foundation; David and Judy Hager. I thank professionals from the literary community who assisted efforts to bring my work to market, including Dr. James Schiavone, Ben Sevier, Sabra Horne, Suzanne Stasczak, Peggy and Steve Urie, and Jonathan Harbaugh.

I feel indebted to Justin Paperny and Brad Fullmer, friends who believed in the vision I expressed and worked with me to convert it into a reality. Along with them, I thank Ken Mayer, Josh Mukai, and Kathleen Hays, each of whom played an essential role in launching the Michael G. Santos Foundation.

I am grateful to Jonathan Solovy, Tom Hillier, and Anthony Bisceglie. They are outstanding lawyers who invested thousands of hours in an effort to advance my release date.

Closest to my heart, I express my undying appreciation to my loving wife, Carole Santos. She came into my life and agreed to serve this sentence alongside me. Carole brings me strength, inspiration, and a reason to continue the climb.

Freedom, for me, is a life with Carole, wherever we are.

Michael G. Santos
December 1, 2012

To My Loving Wife

Carole Santos

Foreword

Joan Petersilia
Adelbert H. Sweet Professor of Law
Stanford University

I am writing to introduce Michael G. Santos. Over the past several years, I have become friends with (and a great admirer of) Michael, who was just released on August 13, 2012 after serving 25 consecutive years in federal prison for distribution of cocaine. There were no weapons and there was no violence involved with his case and he had never been incarcerated before that arrest. Nevertheless, the judge imposed a 45-year sentence.

Michael is unusual in that he became quite a scholar while behind bars–earning degrees and writing several books. As someone who has studied the prison system for more than 30 years, I find myself at a total loss for words when I get phone calls from convicts, parents, or family members asking questions like:

- How do I prepare for going to prison?
- What will my day be like in prison?
- How can I help my son or daughter adjust to prison and prepare for release?
- Will my son or daughter ever be able to get a job after prison?

I now have the perfect answer for all of those questions: just read Michael Santos's books! Michael writes beautifully and intelligently about some of the most complex issues of our time. He writes about the lifelong implications that accompany poor decisions he made as a young man and he tries to persuade others to think beyond the thrill of the immediate moment.

I highly recommend Michael Santos's books. His

experience gives us a unique knowledge of how to use time for reflection and preparation for release. Mr. Santos is not embittered by his prison experience but rather is trying to use this experience to inform those who need to understand what life is like behind prison bars.

If we listen to him closely, we may well understand why America's experiment with mass incarceration has failed. That would be good for those who think "what goes on in prisons stays in prisons." Mr. Santos teaches us that "what goes on in prisons eventually comes back to communities." We should all pay heed to his experience and recommendations for system change. I highly recommend this book to anyone interested in prison reform and community justice.

Joan Petersilia, Ph.D.

Table of Contents

Section I—*Veni*: I Came

Section II—*Vidi*: I Saw

Section III—*Vici*: I Conquered

...I Came

Chapter One: 1987-1988
Months 1-12

I can feel the DEA agents waiting. I don't know where or when they'll strike, but I know they're near. I've never been arrested before, and I'm scared. My wife, Lisa, sits next to me in our Porsche convertible, clutching my hand. We've only been married five months. She's a glamorous South American blonde who looks spectacular in her form-fitting designer clothes, better still in a bikini. With her beside me, I feel powerful. I've built my life on extravagance and appearances, and Lisa completes the image I want to project. She's five years older than I am and I always try to appear strong for her–man enough for her. I don't want her to see my fear, but inside I'm shaking.

Shadowy forces feel like they're closing in, but I don't have a grasp on what's coming. Instinct, intuition, a sense of impending doom keeps crowding my consciousness. This high-flying life is about to change. I can feel it.

Lisa and I have just left Miami where I learned from Raymond, a well-known criminal lawyer I've had on retainer, that a grand jury in Seattle just indicted me on drug trafficking charges. Raymond said that my arrest was imminent and that the criminal charges I'm facing could include the possibility of decades in prison. After hearing that unsettling news, I followed his instructions and gave him my diamond-faced Rolex to hold. Then I told Lisa how to make arrangements for his $200,000 fee.

After leaving Raymond's office, I drive us toward the Rickenbacker Causeway that leads to Key Biscayne. Despite my attorney's warning, I'm going home. He convinced me that a huge difference existed between an indictment and a conviction. By paying Raymond all the money I've got to fight the case, I'm hoping for a fresh start from the mess I've made of my life. I've been miserable for months, knowing that I needed to make a change.

* * * * * * *

We arrive at the entry into Key Colony, the private oceanfront community on Key Biscayne where Lisa and I live. The security guard raises the gate and I drive the Porsche forward. We make eye contact, and I sense resentment in his phony smile as he waves us through. I'm half his age, and for the past year I've driven through this gate every day in my flashy sports car with Lisa beside me, wearing a gold watch that cost more than he would make in a year. Today he's sporting a smug grin. Maybe I'm paranoid. No, I shake my head as I accelerate through the gate and turn right. My gut roils with a subconscious awareness that I'll never drive through this tropical paradise again.

I park in the garage beneath Botanica, the building where we live. Lisa and I walk arm-in-arm to the elevator, not speaking. I'm alert, watching, expecting the feds to rush me at any second. With heightened senses, I'm acutely aware of the salty ocean air filling my nostrils. My stomach churns as I push the elevator button and we ascend.

The elevator door slides open and we step onto the top floor. An open breezeway with palm trees and lush, tropical vegetation on either side leads to our apartment.

There they are, in front of us. The three men wearing dark blue jackets wait, eyeing me as I approach.

"Are you Michael Santos?"

"Yes."

In an instant, I see three guns aiming at my head.

"Freeze! Put your hands out where we can see them!" One of the agents then begins to recite my Miranda rights.

I comply with their orders. Lisa steps away from me, gasping. One agent clasps my hands behind my neck as he searches me for weapons, though I've never carried a gun. Then he lowers my arms, pulling them behind my back. I hear clicking and feel cold metal as he slams handcuffs over my wrists. When the agents see that I'm not resisting, their tone becomes less hostile. They begin to question me and, following Raymond's instructions, I refuse to answer.

"I want my attorney present before I say anything." I'm embarrassed that Lisa sees me so helpless, so impotent in the grip of authority.

"Do you want to say good-bye to Lisa?"

I cringe at the familiar way her name rolls off the agent's tongue, and I realize I'm really being taken away.

"Michael!" Lisa's tortured cry echoes across the breezeway. "Michael! What should I do?"

I don't turn around. To see her face would only prolong the agony of the moment. One agent is in front of me. I'm sandwiched between the other two and I feel hands gripping the chains of my handcuffs. I keep walking with my head down, humiliated.

* * * * * * *

It was 1987 and I was 23. For nearly two years I'd been the leader of a small group that distributed cocaine in Seattle. The scheme wasn't sophisticated. Those at the core of our little enterprise were my classmates from Shorecrest High School, in the North Seattle suburb of Lake Forest Park. Sensing a huge market for cocaine among Seattle's young professionals, I joined my friend Alex in a partnership to capitalize on it.

I found suppliers in Miami. My friend John and his girlfriend, Lori, drove the drugs across the country and delivered them to Tony in Seattle, who stored them in his apartment. Alex coordinated deliveries to customers using Loren and Rico as local drivers.

The shallow layers of people separating me from the actual cocaine fed my delusions that I wasn't really a drug dealer. Instead, I liked to think of myself as an entrepreneur. To the extent that I thought about it, I provided a simple service. No weapons. No violence. My friends and I only sold to consenting adults, so I equated our actions to those who supplied speakeasies during prohibition. It was my way of glamorizing the scheme to camouflage the severity of potential consequences.

The government, of course, saw things differently. Ronald Reagan occupied the White House and he was ramping up the "War on Drugs." I may have previously seen myself as a businessman, but riding through the streets of Miami in the back seat of a black Ford LTD with my hands locked behind my back, in the custody of DEA agents, left no doubt that I was in big trouble. I thought of Lisa. I thought of my parents. I wondered if my attorney, Raymond, could really get me out of this mess.

* * * * * * *

"So, what's up? Did you think you could run from us forever?" The two agents in the front seat switch to a friendlier approach. The driver has carrot-red hair, styled with a flattop and military fade. His partner looks hip, wearing feathered brown hair that he holds in place with his stylish sunglasses. They try to engage me in conversation, but I'm silent, deep in thought as I stare out of the tinted windows at the glass-faced, high-rise buildings of downtown Miami.

"Talk to us," the driver pipes in. "This may be your last chance to save yourself."

I'm mute, afraid, sensing that I've reached a pivotal moment.

"Alex and Tony have given us plenty already. Who're you tryin' to protect? This is the time," the driver speaks with authority. "No one knows you've been busted but us. Your pals cut sweetheart deals, left you hangin' in the wind. Take us to your suppliers and I'll turn this car around right now."

"You don't have much time." The other agent stares at me, tempting me, trying to persuade me. I can tell that he isn't much older than I am. "Once we move forward, you're booked, game over. Speak up now and you'll be able to go home to that pretty little wife of yours."

I don't say a word. It's not that I feel an allegiance to any criminal code. As crazy as it sounds, I don't even consider myself a criminal. It's simply that escaping problems by betraying others doesn't appeal to me as much as the chance for total vindication. Raymond suggests we can win through a trial, and I'm swinging for the fences, going for it. I cling to those hopes, but I'm also conflicted because a deep shame seeps through me. For years I've been telling lies, though I'm yet not ready to confront the reality of who I am, of what I am. I desperately want to resume a normal life and spare myself the humiliation of having to admit that I'm a drug dealer.

As the DEA agents urge me to confess everything, I think about Lisa. I've come to define myself through material possessions, and she is my trophy. I live a fantasy life with her, locked in a constant struggle to mask my shallowness. Cooperating with the DEA and informing against others to spare myself would show weakness, implying that I lacked the wits and enough power to resolve the situation. It wouldn't be the forceful image I've worked so hard to project. I remain silent, sealing my fate.

* * * * * * *

I've never been to prison, nor have I been locked in custody before, but I did have a previous problem with the law. In high school, I organized a sports gambling pool. When one student couldn't pay up he offered to settle the debt with a stereo he stole. I accepted. A few months later, when police officers caught him in another theft, he told the officers that he gave the stereo to me. That led to my conviction for receiving stolen property. When I confided in my father about the problems of the stolen stereo, he stood by my side. For my sanction, a judge ordered that I pay $900 in restitution and that I fill out a form for a probation officer each month for nine months. We concealed the incident from my mother and sisters, not wanting to worry them.

* * * * * * *

In the back of the DEA car, I think about how my arrest is going to devastate my family. I'm now in a predicament that's going to expose the deceitful life I've been living and I'm humiliated, yet I still can't bring myself to come clean because I've got too much invested in the lies I've already told. In choosing this path, with Raymond fighting my battle, I've got to go all the way.

* * * * * * *

My father was a Cuban immigrant. Together with my American mother he built a contracting company in Seattle and provided well for our family. We lived in a beautiful five-bedroom home that sat on several acres in Lake Forest Park. A stream with waterfalls ran through our front yard, with a thick forest behind the house. My parents worked hard to provide my two sisters and me with every advantage, to prepare us for success, grooming me to lead the family company.

My father took pride in operating heavy equipment, pouring concrete, and creating work of lasting value. His company specialized in public works, installing highway lighting and traffic signal systems. My dad was an old-country kind of guy, and he aspired to teach me a strong work ethic. But I resented pulling wire and carrying pipe. I especially dreaded working on weekends or during summers when my friends were waterskiing on Lake Washington. Even though I worked by my dad's side from the time I was six, I couldn't see myself doing physical labor, not for the long term. I wanted the good times my friends enjoyed.

After graduating from high school with mediocre grades, I maneuvered my way out of the field and into the office, wanting to wear clean clothes and to position myself close to the money. With high expectations, my parents gave me the position of vice president, despite the fact that I lacked the maturity to wield the responsibility such a title implied. They trusted me, and I exploited their confidence in my abilities.

I've always been driven by the pursuit of money and possessions, with a sense of entitlement, wanting more than what my parents gave. Their friends were professionals and business owners, people whose influence and style impressed me.

The family business was small when I joined it full-time after graduating from high school, employing only a few electricians. My dad worked alongside them to install illumination and electrical systems while my mom kept the books. The company remained free of debt and afforded us a comfortable life, though it wasn't enough for my tastes. To me, bigger seemed better.

Rather than studying and working through a four-year apprenticeship program to earn the state licenses I would need to assume control of the business, I thought of ways to expand without having to dirty my hands. I could always hire people with the necessary licenses and reasoned that my energies were better spent on increasing revenues.

I joined trade organizations and socialized with other contractors. Those relationships led to collusion, bid rigging, and other violations of state contract laws. My parents didn't object too strenuously as the company's annual revenues increased from hundreds of thousands to millions of dollars. To finance the growth, I persuaded my parents to sign agreements that required them to pledge their home and assets as collateral for higher credit lines with banks, suppliers, and bonding companies. Within three years I convinced my parents to expand the company from one of boring stability into a leveraged business with more than 50 employees. My dad could oversee jobs across the state while I acted as the big man, schmoozing with people and working with numbers that impressed me.

* * * * * * *

Greed was a sinister enticement, clouding my judgment. My friend Alex had been supplementing his income by selling cocaine. Since I had unencumbered access to money from our family's business, I proposed a scheme to Alex that would finance bigger coke deals and allow us to work together. I was 21, and the prospect of a quick score seemed harmless, too good to pass up.

Taylor, a mutual acquaintance of ours, agreed to supply us with several kilos of cocaine. For our first transaction I pulled cash from the company account to pay Taylor on the morning of delivery, and Alex contacted customers to sell the cocaine during the same day. By late afternoon Alex gave me back the money to reimburse the company's account. The deal left Alex and me with tens of thousands in profits.

All went as planned until the following day, when a maid discovered more than $100,000 in Taylor's hotel suite and reported it. Hotel management contacted the Seattle police who seized the money. When Taylor tried to claim it, the police required an explanation. "Just give us a receipt that shows how you received the currency and you can have it," the officers told him.

Taylor called me at work to explain what happened and he asked for my help. "I'll give you 20 percent if you can provide a receipt that will get me the money back."

"Thirty percent," I countered.

Since I'd withdrawn a substantial amount of cash to finance the transaction, I had a plausible explanation, or so I thought. We concocted a story that we were going to use the money to establish a leasing company. I then brought Taylor to the high-rise office tower of our company's attorney, and hatched a plan to bamboozle him into helping us retrieve the money. I had an excellent relationship with Geoff, who was a partner in the firm. Since I'd worked with the attorney before, I assumed he would simply make a few phone calls and resolve the complication.

Taylor and I sat facing Geoff across his polished cherry wood desk. His office overlooked the mid-rise buildings of South Seattle and Puget Sound.

"I gave the money to Taylor so that he could make a cash offer to purchase construction equipment from a contractor who was going out of business." Geoff listened patiently to my story, but in his eyes I saw skepticism.

Lying, I fabricated a story, telling him that Taylor and I were then going to lease the equipment back to my father's company. Supposedly, we would rely upon the leases to collateralize a bank loan to reimburse the company.

"Is your dad a part of this new venture you're launching?"

I still remember the doubt in Geoff's voice from his first question.

When I told him that I'd made this deal on my own, Geoff nodded, then turned his interrogation to Taylor, who sat across the polished desk as if he were an accomplished businessman there to consult on a corporate merger rather than seek help to retrieve a duffle bag full of cash.

"And where do you live?" Geoff's question was direct.

"I keep an apartment in The Grosvenor House." Taylor answered.

"That's on Queen Anne, isn't it?"

"That's right." Taylor didn't yet realize that he was out of his depth.

"About five minutes north of downtown?" Geoff persisted.

"Yes."

"So you keep an apartment in the city." Geoff nodded, holding a finger to his temple as he rocked in his chair.

"I do."

26

"Then help me understand why you'd take a hotel room a few blocks away from where you live. More to the point, why would you leave so much cash in a hotel room while you went to the gym for a morning workout?"

Taylor stumbled through Geoff's penetrating questions. I remember squirming in my chair, knowing the meeting was a disaster. The longer we sat there, the more I realized how foolish I'd been to think that I could manipulate a skillful attorney with lies.

Geoff said he'd make some inquiries with the police and call me later with a plan. I walked out of the office feeling sick to my stomach, knowing that I'd permanently destroyed my reputation. I wouldn't have the courage to face Geoff again.

"Are you alone?" Geoff asked when he reached me in the car later that afternoon.

"Yes." I was driving north on Interstate 5 toward the company office. Rain drizzled on the black Bronco I drove.

"Taylor isn't with you?" He sounded concerned for my welfare.

"No, I'm alone."

"I'm going to ask you some questions and I want you to answer honestly. Okay?"

"Of course." I knew what was coming.

"Does your father know about this money?"

"No."

"Did you give that money to Taylor?"

"No."

"Does that money really belong to you?"

"No."

"I didn't think so. Michael, I want you to listen very carefully to me. I'm speaking to you as a friend and as your attorney. You have a brilliant future with your father's company in this city. But I smell drugs with Taylor. I want you to run as far away from him as you can. He is a cancer and he will destroy you. Do you understand?"

"Yes. You're right. I'm sorry I brought him to your office."

"That's okay. We'll keep our meeting today between us."

Despite his kind tone, I sensed that I'd irretrievably lost

27

his respect. I hung up, humiliated. Taylor had created his own problem by leaving his money in a hotel suite while he exercised. By intervening I made Taylor's problems my own; there wasn't any way for me to erase what I'd done or re-establish trust with Geoff.

Instead of running away from Taylor as Geoff advised, I did the opposite. I abandoned my responsibilities and obligations to our family business. My poor judgment had forced my hand, I thought. With the irrevocable damage I'd done to my reputation I left Seattle for Miami, intending to earn a few million by becoming a coke dealer.

* * * * * * *

And that's how the scheme began that led to where I sit now, locked up. I'm a prisoner of the Drug Enforcement Administration, on my way to places unknown.

* * * * * * *

The driver turns into an office complex and parks. The third agent, the one who searched me and cuffed me during the arrest, parks a separate, identical car beside us. I exit the car with one agent holding the chain of my handcuffs behind my back. I'm like a dog on a leash, being walked into what I presume is a field office.

Once inside, the agents begin to process me. They unlock my handcuffs so I can hold a nameplate beneath my chin while one of the agents photographs my head. Another leads me to a station for fingerprinting. They invite me to cooperate again, to talk with them in exchange for a reprieve from jail. Last chance. The ship is sailing, fading away on the horizon, but I'm not onboard.

Disgusted with my refusal to spill the information they're trying to coerce from me, an agent leads me to a room the size of a broom closet and locks me inside.

"Get used to it." He warns, tossing the words over his shoulder as he walks away.

I'm alone in the tiny room. A bench extends the length of one wall. I sit, elbows on my knees, head in my hands. I've been immersed in a scheme of selling cocaine for nearly two years and now it's come to this. Although I'm not ready now, I'll soon have to answer to the world for the lies I've been living.

I knew my parents suspected something. My mother even accused me once, crying about how she didn't want to lose her son to prison. I tried to console her while simultaneously stonewalling her questions about why I had moved to Miami, about why I wouldn't provide her with a phone number or an address. My irresponsible choices broke her heart long ago.

With arms folded across my chest, I stare at the floor, leaning my back against the cold brick wall. I'd like to ask forgiveness, to take my lashes and start fresh, but instead I cling to Raymond's assurances that I'll prevail if I simply tough it out.

With stress and the bright lights exhausting me, I lose track of time, though I'm sure that more than an hour has passed. My head aches and I'm dizzy.

Finally an agent opens the door. "Cuff up!"

He slaps the cuffs around my wrists and locks them behind my back again. The agents take me outside to their car. They unlock and open the back door, then press me inside. I don't know where I'm going but I presume I'm about to see the inside of a jail.

We drive a short distance and turn into the parking lot of a complex enclosed by double rows of chain-link fencing. Coils of glistening razor wire loop through the tops of the tall gates and many more coils of wire lie stacked atop each other on the ground in the wide space of no-man's land between the fences. No one could escape without cutting himself to shreds.

It's hot and humid outside. Sweat forms under my arms, across my chest and back as I step out of the air-conditioned car. The agents march me toward the entrance of the Metropolitan Correctional Center, Miami. Prison guards from a control center press a button to unlock the heavy steel door electronically and I hear the click of the dead bolt. A guard from the Federal Bureau of Prisons wearing gray slacks, a white shirt, and maroon tie accepts manila folders handed over by the agents escorting me. They exchange words, though my mind goes blank and I can't comprehend their conversation. When the guard searches me, looks in my mouth, inside my ears, and tugs on the handcuffs to ensure they're secure, it's clear that I no longer share a common humanity with them.

The guard leads me inside a series of gates that roll behind us, locking me deeper inside the prison. I spend interminable hours in holding cells, sometimes alone, sometimes with other prisoners. I complete forms declaring that I don't suffer from health issues or require medication. Then I stand for photographs and more fingerprints–my life as a federal prisoner has begun

I exchange my brown alligator skin loafers and matching belt, linen slacks, and a silk dress shirt now reeking from sweat, for elastic-waist khaki trousers, a white t-shirt, and blue canvas slip-on deck shoes. Without my clothes I feel my identity slip away. It's ten at night when I receive a roll of sheets, a blanket, and towel. Then I descend into my first housing unit.

The rectangular building is a two-tiered shell of concrete and steel with hundreds of sullen prisoners loitering in the common areas. Some of the men stare at me. While walking through the riffraff inside, I'm struck by the level of noise.

My thoughts wander. Who are these people? What did they do? Can I handle myself in a fight with them? I see a line for the telephones and make my way through the crowd. When my turn comes I call Lisa.

Prisoners crowd around on all sides as I press the phone against one ear while holding my finger inside the other to silence the noise. Lisa's voice reminds me of all that I'm missing. I mask my emotions, trying to appear stoic. Between her sobs she tells me that Raymond told her I have a court date scheduled in the morning. "I'll be there," Lisa promises. "Your mom is coming with me."

"You told my parents?" My question comes across more like an accusation. I've lost control over the moment of truth, and it bothers me that I'll have to confront them.

"I had to. Raymond said he wanted to show that you have family support. Your mom wants to talk to you."

During my 18 months as a drug dealer in Miami, the family business collapsed, devastating my parents financially and emotionally. I've repressed the guilt that my reckless ambition caused the business to fail, but it surfaces again with my confinement, and it's heavy. My parents salvaged the assets they could and relocated to Miami, where my father's family lived.

Their marriage didn't survive the disruption and my mother now lives with my younger sister in a Miami Beach condo. The stable family and household where my two sisters and I had grown up were in shambles, only a memory.

"Don't worry, Mom," I say in an attempt to ease her distress after Lisa connects us. "I didn't do anything and I've got the best lawyer in Miami. You'll see. He's going to clear me of all this nonsense."

"Oh, Michael...your father and I are so worried." My mother sobs between her whispered words. "What have you done?"

"Nothing, Mom. I swear. I didn't do anything. You'll see. My attorney is going to clear all this up. Give it time. We just have to trust him."

"What are we supposed to do? What are we supposed to say? I can't believe this is happening!"

My time on the phone ends, not with a good-bye, but when a guard presses a switch to disconnect the call. He marches me to my room and locks me inside.

* * * * * * *

"*¿Que Onda?*" Another man is locked in the same cell. Cuban, I presume from his accent. He stands by a waist-high metal locker in boxer shorts, staring at me. He looks like a thug. We're the same height, though he is heavier, with more fat than muscle. Crudely drawn tattoos look like chicken scratches across his arms and torso.

I nod.

"*¿De donde eres?*" He wants to engage me.

"I don't speak Spanish."

"What is you, white?" He speaks in English this time.

The man's question bothers me. I think of myself as an American, un-hyphenated by ethnicity. "I am what I am."

"I thought you was Cuban."

"My dad's Cuban."

"So why the fuck you don't speak Spanish?"

"I speak English." I'm ready for this guy's challenge, if that's what he wants.

"Where you from?"

31

"I'm from Seattle."

"You a cop?"

I stare at him, wondering why he would ask such a ridiculous question when I'm locked in a prison cell, wearing prisoner's clothing. "Hey dude, what is it you want?"

"I'm sayin', muthafucka come up in my house, lookin' Cuban but think he white, gotta ask if you's a cop."

"I'm not a cop. I was arrested today. I'm going to court tomorrow."

"You's arrested?" He mocks me. "Where'd they bust you?"

"Key Biscayne."

"Oh, so you got paper."

"Paper? What are you talking about?"

"Money, muthafucka, you got money!"

"Why are you so interested in who I am? Who are you?"

"You up in my cell, bitch. Don't be axin' me no muthafuckin' questions."

"What are we doing here? Are you looking for a fight or what? It's late, I'm tired, and I've got to go to court tomorrow. But I've got all you can handle if that's what you want."

He sizes me up. "You ain't no snitch is you?"

"I'm done talking to you."

"Okay. That's good. Don't talk. That's you bunk, white boy."

The hostility in the cell surprises me. What's this about? I walk to the steel rack against the wall, unroll the mat, and stretch the sheet across it. I climb up without using the sink or the toilet, too exhausted for more confrontation. I turn on my side and stare out of a narrow vertical window. It's no more than six inches wide, but I can see outside. Spotlights shine on crabgrass, steel fences, and razor wire. I watch as a guard drives a white pickup slowly around the prison's perimeter and I fade into sleep.

It's an anxious sleep, and when I wake, I stare out the window, with tears filling my eyes. The man below me stinks. I miss Lisa's perfumed skin, her hair, her body. This is going to destroy us. My only hope is Raymond. He has to free me from this nightmare. I wipe my watering eyes and drift back into sleep.

A guard unlocks the door and yells my name into the cell. His voice bounces off the concrete walls and startles me from a dead sleep. I jump down from the rack and he orders me to dress for court. I'm still wearing my khakis and the t-shirt. Feeling beaten and exhausted, I slide into the canvas shoes and accompany the guard out of the cell. He slams the steel door behind us and uses a formidable key to lock the dead bolt.

I walk with other prisoners through the same door I entered last night. We join a throng of more than 100 men and the guards herd us into caged bullpens. The noise makes my head throb as I stand shoulder to shoulder with scores of angry prisoners. A clock on the wall shows that it isn't yet three, which explains why I feel exhausted. I can't believe court begins this early.

One by one, the guards call us out of the cage to change into our clothes. When I receive the mesh bag with my name on it, I see my clothes balled together at the bottom of the bag, ruined, my shoes on top of the shirt.

"The belt is missing," I tell the guard.

"What?" He growls.

"My belt is missing," I repeat.

"Let's see here." The guard grabs a processing form from the bag and scans down the boxes. "Don't show that you was wearin' no belt when you checked in."

"What do you mean? Of course I was wearing a belt. It was brown, alligator skin, matching my shoes."

"Form don't say nothin' 'bout no belt. Now get the fuck dressed and quit pussyfootin' around. Next thing you're gonna tell me is that you ain't got no panties."

I know that I stink, and my clothes are damp, which will add to the disaster of this day, my first as a prisoner.

As soon as I dress, a guard leads me back to the bullpen. My legs ache from standing. Hours pass. At six, the guards begin calling us out in groups of two. They shackle my ankles, wrap a chain around my waist, weave handcuffs through the front of the chain and then lock my wrists in place. The chains are heavy on my body. Secured, we march awkwardly out toward waiting transport buses.

"You don't like the chains," one guard taunts while

sucking on a cigarette, "quit selling drugs."

I have a window seat on one of the three packed buses that maneuver through morning rush hour in Miami. I peer through the spaces between vertical steel bars and a tinted window, looking at the faces of other drivers–people leading responsible lives. Legitimate work is something I haven't done since turning my back on responsibilities at my father's company.

We drive past the tollbooths that lead across the bay to Key Biscayne. I see the sign touting Key Biscayne as "The Island Paradise" and I'm overcome with sadness. My neck cramps as I try to wipe the tears on my shoulder. I may have a court date, but my gut tells me I won't be sleeping in my bed tonight.

The driver maneuvers our bus into an underground garage beneath the Federal Building. Guards march us through doors that lead to a series of adjacent bullpen cages. Still chained, we squeeze in like animals in a chute heading for slaughter. I don't understand this system, and I hate all that is happening. I'm trapped. Worse yet, I'm strangely uneasy about surrendering my fate to Raymond.

Paco, one of my cocaine suppliers, introduced me to Raymond. Paco praised him as one of the best lawyers in Miami, and when I visited his office, I was influenced by its opulence. I admired the photographs of Raymond smiling in victory with well-known organized crime figures. They stood victoriously outside a courthouse after beating federal racketeering charges. The press clippings convinced me I had to have Raymond on my team. Even though I wasn't expecting any legal problems, having a top-notch attorney on retainer made sense. I agreed to pay him tens of thousands in cash just in case.

* * * * * * *

"Santos. Santos. I need Michael Santos." I hear a guard yelling my name.

"I'm in here." I press my way through the crowd to the front of the cage.

"Let's go." He unlocks the gate for me to step out. After locking the cage behind us, he walks me to a tiny cubbyhole of a conference room for defendants to meet with their attorneys. I see Raymond sitting on a stool waiting for me. I notice immediately that he wears my Rolex.

"How're you holding up, Sport?" He greets me as if we're partners in a tennis match.

"I'm okay. A little tired." I'm embarrassed that Raymond sees me unshaven and in wrinkled, sweat-stained clothes.

"Did they treat you okay in there?"

"I don't know. It's loud, crowded. I haven't been able to think about anything but getting out of this nightmare."

"Have you eaten?"

"I can't eat." I shrug my shoulders. "They passed out bologna and white bread. Mine's still in the bag."

"You've got to eat," he says, trying to encourage me. "I need you strong through this."

"I need *you* strong," I counter, feeling weaker than I hope I show. "How long am I going to be in here?"

"We're trying to get you out on bond this morning. Lisa and your mother will meet me here at nine. I brought your watch for Lisa. If you were wearing it when they arrested you, they'd have seized it."

"Why does my mom have to be here?"

"This is a first appearance. We're going to enter a plea of not guilty to the charges. Then I'll ask the judge to let you out on bond. I need your mother and Lisa here to show that you've got community ties."

"You mean they're going to let me out?" For the first time, a sense of hope begins to surface through my despair.

"I'm sure going to try."

Raymond can see that I need something to pick up my spirits. He's like the baseball coach trying to encourage a little leaguer in a slump. "You need to toughen up. We'll make a good case. You don't have an arrest record. There aren't any allegations of violence or weapons. You've got family support."

"How much will it cost?"

"We need to talk about that, Sport," Raymond says as he leans back against the wall. "You've been charged with operating a Continuing Criminal Enterprise. It carries a possible life sentence. If the judge agrees to bond, it's going to be high.

What can we offer the court?"

"What do you mean, a life sentence?" Fear overtakes me. "For what? What's that mean?"

Raymond holds my wrist, trying to steady my nerves. "Don't worry. We talked about this. It's only the beginning. The government always overcharges." He dismisses the concern with a wave of his hand. "You've got to trust me, leave this to me. For now we've got to have a plan for the bond request so we can get you out of here. What kind of assets can you pledge?"

"I don't have anything." I'm embarrassed to admit that my whole life is a charade. "I told Lisa to get everything we have for you."

"What do you mean?" Raymond squints at me, disbelieving. "You didn't put anything away?"

I scratch my head, and then I rub my face in shame. "I bought some property in Spain from Paco. He hasn't given me the title yet. Lisa was supposed to talk with him yesterday about getting the money back so we could finish paying you. That's all I have."

I sense Raymond's incredulity and sinking respect as he scratches his head.

"How about your parents? What can they put up?"

"I don't have anything, Raymond. Let's just think about beating these charges, not the bond."

"How much is Lisa bringing me today? We need money to beat this thing, Sport."

"She has about a hundred grand. Paco will give her the rest and she'll pay you off."

"Tell me about this property. What's it worth?"

"A couple hundred thousand. Paco owes it to me from a deal we made that never went through. We've been waiting for him to transfer the title, but after we left your office yesterday, I told Lisa to get a hold of him and pull together whatever cash he could return immediately."

Raymond shakes his head in disbelief. "I can't believe you don't have anything set aside. How do you own a watch like this with no money?"

I feel like I'm eight-years-old. Totally deflated, I sink deeper into my chair.

"Don't worry." Raymond begins to recover. He can see that his questions about my finances are pushing me into a dark hole. "We'll be okay. I'll talk with Paco about this property. I've got to get into the courtroom."

The guard lets Raymond out and leads me back to the cage. I don't understand the talk about a life sentence. Why a life sentence? Also, Raymond's slightly veiled disdain for my financial situation troubles me. I'm not prepared for any of this, not emotionally, not physically, and certainly not intellectually. I'm totally in Raymond's hands. I feel nauseous, unsettled, but I dismiss the instinct that I should plead guilty and cut my losses. I've got to trust Raymond.

* * * * * * *

When the guard leads me into the courtroom I see Lisa and my mom. They hardly know each other and my mom has never accepted Lisa as a part of my life. Yet in that courtroom they hold each other, one supporting the other as I sit at the defendant's table beside Raymond. We can't talk, but I nod before turning away to face the court.

To steady myself I study the ornate courtroom–the elaborate paneling, the carvings in heavy wood, the high ceiling and podium. The room invokes a sense of majesty and ceremony. Prosecutors sit at a table to my left. To them I'm a nonentity, just another criminal. The judge considers arguments that I can't comprehend. I feel foolish, ill equipped to grasp the significance of all that is happening. The only words that register with me are possible life sentence. They resonate through my mind. Why? I see the judge's forehead crease when he stares down at me.

"There will be no bail for this defendant." The judge slams the wooden gavel on the podium after he rules.

This must be the longest day of my life. Federal marshals lead me back to the crowded bullpen. I'm dejected, thinking of my mom and Lisa tearfully embracing each other. The packed cage doesn't faze me as I press my way to a rear corner and slouch to the filthy concrete floor. My back rests against the evenly spaced steel bars and I drop my head to my knees.

These threats of a life sentence feel real, so much more real than Raymond has prepared me to cope with mentally. I

37

don't have enough money to fight this battle or to support Lisa. I need to get out of here, but I don't know how.

When I return to the prison, guards assign me to a different housing unit than I slept in last night. I'd been in a classification unit, though I didn't know anyone was evaluating me. This is a strange environment, where guards order me to specific locations, expecting me to comply without question. I'm now in Coral Unit, and I must sleep in a room with six other prisoners about whom I know nothing. Everyone snores as I climb onto my rack, still in my clothes. This time I don't have a window.

* * * * * * *

It's my third day in prison and a counselor approves me to receive visitors. I call Lisa and ask her to come. "Did Raymond give you my watch?" I ask, my entire identity wrapped up in my possessions. When she tells me that he did, I ask her to bring it.

"Can you wear a watch like yours in there?"

"I don't want to keep it here. I just want to feel it on my wrist again." I need some physical remembrance of the life I lived only 72 hours ago. We all wear white t-shirts and khaki pants. As much as I want to hold Lisa, I also want the other prisoners to see her beside me.

Within minutes of her arrival guards reprimand me for kissing her. They cite rules permitting a brief kiss at the start and end of each visit. If I kiss her again, they warn, they'll terminate my visiting privileges for one month. We sit on metal chairs at a round, Formica-topped, white table. I listen as Lisa describes the fallout from my arrest. Her mother is urging her to leave me though she pledges her undying love. The thought of her abandoning me strikes another jolt to my vanishing confidence.

"What about Raymond?" I ask, and inquire whether she paid him.

"I gave him the money. He's working through the property deal with Paco. They've already talked."

"You mean he wants the money *and* the property? That's worth way more than the $200 thousand he wanted!"

"I don't care. You can always make more money. I just

want you home."

I tell Lisa about my time inside. We have a law library and I've read scores of legal cases during the few days I've spent here. I may only have a high school education, but I understand what I read. The government has charged me with operating a Continuing Criminal Enterprise. Those law books describe the charges as the "kingpin statute." To convict, the government has to prove that I managed five people who participated in drug deals involving significant amounts of money. I know I'm guilty.

"Maybe I should plead guilty," I suggest to her. By pleading guilty early in the proceedings, I understand that the government might reduce the charges, or agree to a lighter sentence. The cases I've read suggest that if a jury convicts me, I'll receive a long sentence, maybe life.

"Are you crazy?" Lisa doesn't want to hear my reasoning. "We're not pleading guilty to anything! They didn't catch you with anything. Raymond told me this would happen, that you'd want to break down. He told me to keep you strong in here."

"If I plead guilty I could probably get a 10-year sentence."

"And what am I supposed to do for 10 years? You're my husband and I need you home."

"I wouldn't serve 10 years. There's parole and good time. I'd probably be home in three years or something."

"Michael, they didn't catch you with anything."

"No, but Alex and Tony are testifying against me."

"No one is going to believe them. They were caught in the act, with cocaine."

"Baby, I'm just saying we should think about pleading guilty, cutting our losses. This charge accuses me of being the boss. The government doesn't have to catch me with anything. Prosecutors only have to prove that I supervised others who sold cocaine."

"Who do you think you are, Al Capone?" Lisa laughs, mocking me. "This place is just playing with your mind. Where's my strong husband?" She reaches over to hold my hand and I look at the guard to see if he's watching. "We have to trust in Raymond. He says we can win and that's what we're going to do."

I'm still uneasy when our visit ends and I return to the housing unit. Later, I hear a guard's voice paging me over the loudspeaker to report to the visiting room again. Raymond has come to see me. We sit in a small conference room reserved for attorney-client visits. Raymond tells me that Lisa described my fears about the trial and he asks how I'm holding up. I want to appear unshakable, as if I can handle this struggle, though I know I'm in deep, way over my head. I tell him what I've read in the law books–about all the people serving life sentences for the same charges as mine.

"I don't want you reading those books," Raymond admonishes me. "They're just going to mess with your head and cloud your thinking. Those guys didn't have me representing them. They may have had shoddy lawyers for all we know. Besides, those books only show the losers. They don't publish the cases about the defendants who beat the pants off the government. That's what we're going to do."

I need that expression of confidence that we can prevail. "What am I supposed to say when people ask about my case?"

"If you have to say anything, tell them you've been wrongfully charged with a crime and that you will vindicate your name through a trial. I need you strong," he repeats, with an authority that bolsters my spirits. "This is my business and I'm the best in the world at what I do. Let me try this case."

Raymond forewarns me that the U.S. marshals will transfer me from Miami to Seattle. He promises to send copies of briefings he will file with the court, and says that he will fly to Seattle to prepare the case a few times before the trial begins.

"When are we going to trial?"

"We go to trial when *we're* ready, Sport." Raymond conveys the message that we're in control and that he has a strategy to deliver my acquittal. He urges me to stay strong while he determines the most advantageous time to try the case. Raymond insists that I not ask questions about what he is planning and insinuates that he has tactics he can't share with me. I leave our meeting feeling optimistic, wondering if Raymond is bribing the judge. That must be the reason he needs so much money.

* * * * * * *

Thanks to Raymond's heads-up, I'm not surprised the following morning when the marshals transfer me in chains on the vans, buses, and airplanes they reserve for prisoner transport. I'm held over in Oklahoma and Arizona prisons before arriving in Seattle. When the marshals book me into jail, I'm among several other men–most of whom are friends and now my co-defendants. They'll stand trial with me for playing a role in distributing the cocaine I sent from Miami.

Since moving to Miami more than a year ago, I isolated myself from the day-to-day activities of the trafficking scheme. From afar I could limit my role to logistics, coordinating with suppliers to ensure that the local distributors had enough coke to meet their demand. This strategy, I convinced myself, would ensure that I'd never face problems with the law. Yet here I sit, locked in the same jail with many of those who worked with me.

In the Miami prison I felt alone, totally new to confinement. The shock, together with the ominous possibility of a life sentence, wreaked havoc on my mental state. But in Seattle my tension lessens, even if I am locked in jail. I miss Lisa, of course. My father returned to Seattle when I was transferred here, and my sister Julie lives nearby. They spend a few hours with me on each visiting day. They also accept my collect phone calls, allowing my delusions of innocence and release to continue.

I adjust to the rhythms of this particular jail, actually enjoying the time I'm spending with my codefendants and others who have an indirect relationship to my case. While we wait for our judicial proceedings they teach me card games and chess. One day my spirits lift when I spot David, a Colombian I've worked with before but haven't seen for nearly a year.

Even when we did see each other in the past, we didn't communicate much because David doesn't speak English. His role in my organization was to store cocaine that Rico would distribute in Seattle. When Rico began cooperating with the DEA, he led the agents to David and his stash house.

David pulls me to a corner of the jail and tries urgently to communicate a message. He whispers and takes precautions to

41

ensure others don't hear us. I can't understand him and our inability to communicate frustrates him. I try to bring a bilingual prisoner over to translate, but David stops me. This is a private matter, he insists. He borrows a Spanish-English dictionary. Finally, I get the message he's been trying to convey.

When the DEA agents arrested David, they didn't find eight kilograms of cocaine that he had hidden. I'd been out of the loop, unaware that eight kilograms existed until David told me. My understanding had been that the government seized everything when Rico began cooperating with them. David explains that he was holding that cocaine for the Colombian suppliers who had fled after the arrests. He wants someone to retrieve and sell it, though he doesn't know anyone in Seattle.

David proposes a solution to my immediate problem. If I can coordinate this transaction, he offers to split the proceeds. At current prices, eight kilograms of cocaine will bring more than $200,000. My cut will cover Lisa's expenses while I wait for Raymond to free me. From my perspective this isn't even a risk since I'm already facing trial.

I call Tom, Lisa's brother, and invite him to visit. In the past, I relied upon Tom as a courier to transport cocaine. Since we both want the best for Lisa, I trust him. The government charged Tom in my indictment, but the minor role he played in the conspiracy allowed him to remain free on bail during the judicial proceedings in Seattle. During our visit I explain what I've learned from David.

We visit in a tiny booth with a glass partition separating us. I show him a map that David has drawn for me. It feels as if I'm coordinating a treasure hunt from the jail. The potential life sentence no longer troubles me, as I've resigned myself to let Raymond handle the trial. My focus has switched to providing Lisa with more financial resources.

"There's nothing to it," I explain to Tom. He may be out on bail facing federal charges, but he, too, sees the opportunity. I instruct Tom to deliver the cocaine to Walt, one of my clients who wasn't I implicated in the indictment.

"Just pick up the eight kilos. Once you get it, call Walt and he'll sell it. Tell Walt I'll finance him. He can pay over time, without pressure. The whole thing shouldn't take more than an hour and we make a hundred grand."

I return to my housing unit, completely oblivious to the new crime I've just committed. During a phone conversation the following morning Tom says all is well. Within days Tom receives tens of thousands of dollars and sends Lisa what she needs. He rents a home near the jail and pays for Lisa to move to Seattle so she can visit while we await my victory and release.

"I knew you'd be able to handle this." She places her hand against the glass that separates us in the visiting room, smiling at me as if I'm a hero.

I'm visiting with Lisa whenever we're allowed, and there is something about providing for her that empowers me, even if my family doesn't like her. They don't understand, especially now that I'm in jail and still shutting them out by refusing to talk about my case. I'll make things right once Raymond frees me from these charges. For now I need to take care of Lisa. That's about all I can manage.

* * * * * * *

At 23, I'm younger than most of the prisoners around me. Raymond, my attorney, flies to Seattle whenever necessary. On visiting days, other prisoners see me with my striking wife. I walk with a swagger, filled with delusions that I'm quite the man about the cellblock. I play it up, enjoying the role of kingpin during those first few months in the Seattle jail, thinking that I'll soon be walking out victoriously, beating the feds.

I spend my first Christmas behind bars, and then I celebrate my 24th birthday in January 1988 with a Snickers-bar party for all the prisoners in my housing unit. The time in jail hasn't been bad, but only because I'm certain my liberty is coming. My mother continuously asks what I'll do once I get out. She has a hard time defending me to relatives and friends who inquire about my predicament. But I don't have an answer for her, as I haven't thought about anything besides beating the case. I'll think about the future later, I tell her, suggesting that she ignore what others say.

After five months of pretrial detention, I'm impatient, ready for the action to begin. The government doesn't have any tape recordings of me doing deals. Further, DEA agents didn't

43

catch me with any drugs or any money, and the people who've agreed to testify against me have self-interests in blaming me even though they were the ones caught with cocaine. I can't wait for Raymond to persuade the jury that I shouldn't be in jail.

Before the trial starts Raymond coaches me on the testimony I'll give. We sit for hours in a small conference room adjacent to my housing unit while he fires questions as if he's the prosecutor trying to rattle me.

"When you answer," he coaches, "look at the jury. Find a juror you like and talk directly to her. Speak clearly, without rushing your words. We need them to trust you, to believe that you're just like them."

I'm getting excited. It feels like we're approaching opening night and I've got star billing.

"Is the jury going to know how much time I'm facing?" The jurors would not convict me, I'm certain, if they knew I was facing a life sentence.

"We're not allowed to discuss the possible sentence. The trial is about determining guilt or innocence."

"Can I slip the possible sentence into one of my answers when I'm on the stand?"

Raymond pauses to consider my question. "Well I can't say anything about the sentence, but if you see an opportunity, take it quickly because the prosecutor will object in a hurry."

I'm ready the following morning when the marshals transport me from the jail to the courthouse.

* * * * * * *

The marshals escort four of us in chains through the working areas of the post office. I see postal clerks eying us suspiciously as they sort the mail into large bags while we wait for an elevator to take us to the courthouse. We walk into a bullpen. The marshals remove our handcuffs and chains before locking us in.

A few minutes later the marshals bring in Alex, my former partner. I recognize his voice when they lock him into an adjacent cage. We can't see each other, but once the marshals leave I hold onto the bars on the front gate and talk to Alex, disregarding the solid wall that separates us.

44

"How can you testify against me?" I ask him. "We've been like brothers." Alex graduated from high school two years ahead of me, but despite our age difference, we became close friends. After he introduced me to the money we could earn by selling cocaine, we became partners.

"I'm sorry." I could hear the humiliation in his voice. "It was too fast. When they caught me, I just got scared. I didn't know this would happen."

Alex began cooperating with prosecutors a year before my arrest, when DEA agents caught him with a kilogram of cocaine. In a plea negotiation that would limit him to two years in prison, he agreed to testify against me.

"Do you know that I'm facing a life sentence?"

"I heard." His voice drops, and I know the severity of sanction that I face weighs heavily on him.

"The government's case rests on your testimony." I try to manipulate not so much what Alex will say, but how he will say it. "It all rests on you. Either you can come across like some kind of star witness, or you can come across in a way that might make you look like a liar in the eyes of the jury. Just remember that you've already got your deal. If you fall apart under cross-examination from my attorney, the jury won't convict me."

"I got ya."

The seed I planted bears fruit. When Alex testifies before the jury, both on direct examination from the prosecutor and on cross-examination from Raymond, he seems totally untrustworthy. His testimony emboldens me, as I know Alex's stuttering and mumbling portray him as a less than credible witness, out to save his skin at any cost.

Later that evening I'm elated when I return to the jail, thinking that my friend came through. The government has been counting on his testimony, but now the prosecutors will have to present more compelling evidence if they want a conviction. In the following days, we have peaks and valleys, scoring well with some witnesses, not so well with others. All in all, I feel my acquittal nearing.

* * * * * * *

My hopes for release shatter during the second week of

the trial. When I return to the jail after court one evening, I call Lisa for our nightly conversation. While we're talking I hear aggressive male voices shouting in the background. Then the line goes dead. I dial the number again. Someone picks up the phone without answering. I hear a click followed by silence. Frantic now, I dial a third time. I haven't dispelled rumors in the jail that I'm a man of means, and I worry that some gang leader from the jail has orchestrated a home invasion or kidnapping. Finally, a male voice answers. When the operator announces my collect call, the call goes through.

"Hello, Michael." The man who answers takes a familiar tone, snickering.

"Who is this and what're you doing in my house?" I squeeze the handset of the phone in anger.

"I'm a special agent with the DEA," he taunts. "You'll find out soon enough why we're here."

"You're harassing my family because you're losing the trial."

The agent laughs at me. "I don't think that's the case," he says. Then, just before he hangs up, he adds that they've arrested Tom, Lisa's brother.

Minutes later, officers from the jail arrive to pull me out from the housing unit. They lock me between sally port cages that separate the unit from jail corridors and I crouch down in despair. My mind reels with questions. Worry torments me. Why would the agents invade Lisa's house? Why would the agent tell me they have Tom? My heart races like never before. Then I see a team of DEA agents enter the housing unit. They march past me and into my cell for an apparent search.

After the agents finish their ransacking, the guards lead me back into the housing unit and lock me inside. Adrenaline surges through my body, I can't sleep. When guards come for me in the morning, I'm pacing. They escort me to the bullpen for court transportation and I'm stunned to see Tom, Lisa's brother.

"What're you doing here?" I can't believe Tom is in jail. He's been free on bond since our initial arrest, sitting beside me at trial each day. I can't fathom what happened.

"I messed up." He doesn't look at me when he responds.

"What are you talking about? Were you home last night

46

when the DEA busted in on Lisa?"

Tom didn't even know that the DEA had been to the house. He tells me that the DEA arrested him yesterday afternoon following the court proceedings.

"Why did they arrest you? And why would the DEA bust in on Lisa?"

"I messed up." Tom repeats. He won't make eye contact. While sitting on the bench, rubbing his face and looking at the floor of the cage, he tells me what happened. Several months ago, just days after my arrest, when I instructed Tom to retrieve those eight kilograms of cocaine and deliver them to Walt, Tom decided to sell them on his own. One of his customers, it turns out, is a DEA agent.

"You mean you've been selling that cocaine this whole time on your own?" I'm angry to learn that Tom disregarded my specific instructions to deliver the cocaine to Walt.

Tom nods. "I thought I could make more money that way."

I close my eyes and shake my head. "Please tell me that you weren't storing the coke at Lisa's house."

"I didn't keep it there, but I stashed money under my mattress. I also gave Lisa some money I'd been paid by the guy who turned out to be the undercover DEA agent."

All I can think about is the possibility that Lisa has been arrested. I receive clarification a few hours later, when Raymond fills me in. He says the agents might charge Lisa with the crime of lying to a federal officer. When the agents were at the house, she told them that the money in her purse belonged to her, when in fact Tom had given her DEA-marked bills. At least she wasn't in custody.

Raymond urges me to snap out of my despair and focus on the final hours of my trial, which is my immediate problem. I no longer care about the trial or its outcome. The true severity of my problems has finally crashed down upon me. I've not only made a disaster of my own life, but of everyone else's, I want to give up, to die.

* * * * * * *

The jury returns its verdict, convicting me on every

47

count. Lies of innocence yield to the reality of my guilt. I have to accept that I'm facing a life sentence. Who cares? I don't know what's coming. Nothing matters. The government may charge Lisa with a felony and the thought of her in handcuffs rips me apart.

I ask Raymond to make some kind of deal with prosecutors, to tell them I'll accept a life sentence, a death sentence, I'll waive my right to appeal, anything, if the government will leave Lisa alone. He tells me the government hasn't even charged me in the case.

"Then tell them I'll confess. I arranged for Tom to receive those eight kilograms. They were part of the same crime I was just convicted of, but if I hadn't sent Tom, the coke would've stayed buried."

"I'm not going to do that. You're under duress. I don't want you cooperating. You haven't even been sentenced and you've got excellent prospects on appeal."

"I don't care about an appeal, I don't care about anything other than doing what I can to spare Lisa. She doesn't deserve this. Call the prosecutor. Tell him I'll confess."

"I won't do it."

Raymond doesn't want to involve himself with my talking to prosecutors. I don't understand his reluctance–it may be that he doesn't want me to reveal the counsel he has given throughout my ordeal, or he worries that I might divulge information about the property he received from Paco as part of his fee. I don't care. Raymond is not my priority. Wanting to do whatever I can for Lisa, I fire Raymond, telling him that I don't want him to represent me anymore.

I dial the prosecutor, Jerry Diskin, myself.

"Is this the same Michael Santos who testified that he didn't know anything about drug trafficking?" The prosecutor is mocking me.

"Look, Jerry," I say, "I was doing what my attorney told me I had to do. I'm sorry. I'll confess to anything you want, I'll give up my right to appeal, I'll accept any sentence you want to impose. Please, just don't put Lisa through this."

"I have some problems with what you're offering," the prosecutor puts me in my place. "Let me start from the beginning. First, don't ever call me Jerry. I'm a United States Attorney, Mr. Diskin to you. Do you get that?"

"Yes. I'm sorry."

"Second, I do not, I repeat, *I do not* want to speak with you unless it's through an attorney. Why are you contacting me instead of Raymond?"

"Raymond doesn't want me to talk with you. I don't want him to represent me anymore."

"Then I'll have the public defender send someone over. Don't contact me again. And for the record, let me respond to the offer you made. I don't need your confession. You're convicted, and you're facing a life sentence. Your appeal doesn't concern me. I don't know why you think I would want to talk to you."

Mr. Diskin is right, I realize. I breathe in deeply and exhale, trying to ease the pressure and anxiety squeezing my chest.

* * * * * * *

While lying on my rack, I think of all the ways I've disappointed and humiliated my parents. They never wanted the business expansion I craved. Throughout my childhood and adolescence, my parents worked hard, hoping to give my sisters and me privileges that they didn't enjoy growing up. They weren't college-educated people, but they loved us, and they built a life that provided our family with a beautiful home, new cars, regular vacations. I abused their trust and pushed them into decisions they would've never made without my influence. Ultimately, my greed led to the destruction of our family and their business. Then, when I saw a better opportunity to enrich myself by dealing cocaine, I abandoned them. My decisions destroyed my parents' prosperity, contributed to their divorce, and embarrassed my sisters.

My criminal decisions also humiliated my grandparents. They were devout Catholics who expected me to lead a moral life and make good decisions. The letters I've been receiving from my mother describe their disgust at my actions. I haven't had the courage to speak to them since my arrest. Instead, I've burdened my mom with the impossible task of defending me to them.

My mental anguish is relentless. I carry Lisa's picture in my hand trying frantically to think of anything that might save her. How can I persuade the government not to prosecute her?

Suicide feels so inviting. I think about another prisoner who did it using the blades from one of the plastic razors we're allowed to have in jail. While sitting in a toilet stall, he sliced his wrists and bled to death. That option appeals to me. It could be one way of reaching Mr. Diskin. If I'm dead, he may feel some sympathy for Lisa.

But killing myself would crush my parents and my sisters. Although I don't want to face the consequences of my actions, I know I can't allow these suicidal thoughts to continue. My dad urges me to be strong and through long letters that my mom writes, she shows that her support will not waver. Lisa, on the other hand, worries mostly about the fallout from my problems spilling over to her. During our daily phone calls, tormented by the possibility of going to prison she pleads with me to save her.

Boils erupt on my arms and legs as the stress I'm feeling manifests itself throughout my body. The egg-sized volcanoes of pus burn like hot acid under my skin, exerting unbearable pressure. Only a visit to the infirmary for an excision relieves the pain, though within hours of having one drained, more begin to fester and swell.

* * * * * * *

I've been in jail for six months and must languish through several more before my sentencing date. I don't know what the judge will impose, though I accept the possibility of a life sentence as being real. I'm not interested in playing cards or table games. I stay in my cell reading the Bible with hopes of finding solace, an anchor. The Scriptures help me resist a growing urge to end my life and strengthen me to hold on for another day. Although I want to identify with the agonies and loss described in the Book of Job, comparisons end there. Job, at least, wasn't beset with self-recriminations over acting stupidly and dishonestly. Knowing that decisions I made spawned my tribulations aggravates the continuous torment in my mind.

The marshals come for me again and drive me to the

courthouse. I meet Justin, my public defender who is there for my debriefing session with Mr. Diskin. Justin hasn't had an opportunity to review any court records or files pertaining to my predicament, though he knows a jury convicted me on numerous counts of high-level drug charges only days before. I haven't been charged with additional crimes and he doesn't understand my motivation for wanting to talk with the prosecutors.

"Look man," I tell him in the private room, "I'm responsible for everything. I'm the one who told Tom to pick up the eight keys. He may've sold them to the guy who turned out to be DEA, but I'm responsible."

"But you haven't been charged," Justin points out. "What do you hope to gain from this admission?"

"The government can do whatever it wants with me. But the prosecutors are threatening to charge Lisa with a felony. All I want is to take the punishment myself, whatever it is. Tell them to slam me with whatever, but to leave her alone."

The public defender shakes his head in resignation, knowing that I'm not ready to receive counsel. We walk to an adjacent courtroom to meet with the prosecutor. Justin sits beside me as I respond to Mr. Diskin's questions. His first question is whether I lied when I took the witness stand during my trial. I answer that I did, and he asks whether I understand that admitting to such lies exposes me to the additional criminal charges of perjury. I offer to accept any charges or sanctions the government wants to impose and then I plead with the prosecutor not to charge Lisa. Mr. Diskin smirks, unmoved.

The debriefing session lasts for an hour. In the end, Mr. Diskin tells me that I haven't revealed anything he doesn't already know.

"You're going to have to face the full punishment for your crimes." The prosecutor narrows his eyes as he lashes out at me. "And you may find yourself sitting at the defendant's table again, this time beside your wife."

The marshals drive me back to the jail. I'm completely spent, knowing that I'm powerless to protect Lisa. For weeks I lie in my cell, clutching my pillow, staring at the wall, catatonic with grief.

* * * * * * *

While I wait through long months leading to my sentencing date, I look for anything that will pique my interest. I stumble across a two-volume hardcover anthology called *A Treasury of Philosophy* in the jail's book cart. Hoping it might help, I begin reading. Even though I've never been a reader, the essays intrigue me. Since graduating from high school I haven't read a single book. Yet now, here I am, aching with thoughts tormenting my mind as I try to read philosophy in a jail cell.

Philosophy isn't a subject I've encountered before. I find a dictionary and begin a tentative step into another world, discovering that the essays in this anthology help to lessen my feeling of hopelessness. They give me new understanding of an individual's relationship to society. I begin to believe that maybe, over time, I can reconcile myself with my fellow citizens. This thought of redemption comes to me as I read the French philosopher Jean Jacques Rousseau, who defines the "social contract" and outlines each citizen's covenant with and responsibility to society. In breaking the law, I haven't been faithful to the social contract Rousseau described, but in reading his work, I begin to believe that I can make amends.

I read John Locke, whose essays on human understanding introduce me to the concept of the tabula rasa, or blank slate. Locke believed that everyone comes into this world without prior knowledge or innate ideas. Rather, everything a person sees, feels, tastes, and smells makes an impression, influencing who and what the person becomes. As Locke suggests, I learn from my experiences in society. In turn, those experiences spawn the values that guide my thoughts, my decisions, and my actions.

Thinking about Locke's philosophy, I rest the open book on my chest and stare at the ceiling of my cell while I clasp my hands behind my head. What made the lasting impression on my blank slate? What prompted me to think that earning money by selling cocaine would be a proper life choice? The questions deepen my introspection.

* * * * * * *

Unlike many of the men locked up with me, I had options. Had I chosen college, my parents would've supported my decision. But without worries about receiving a paycheck, I took the easy road. At 20, I persuaded my dad to pay me a higher salary than I deserved. He also leased a new black Bronco I could drive without concerning myself with expenses for gasoline, insurance, or maintenance.

If it wasn't economic necessity that drove me to crime, what was it? Maybe insecurity. I wanted others to see me as something more than what I was. Greed and a sense of entitlement drove my decisions. But underneath the flash I wasn't anything more than an insecure boy.

Where did my fixation with money begin?

My grandparents lived a moral life as hardworking Americans, and they showered my sisters and me with love from the time we were children. I should've learned more from them. Yet, I equated who I was with what I materially possessed, always wanting more.

In our household, we never spoke honestly about drugs. Although our parents harped about the wickedness of drugs, their admonitions didn't apply to the consumption of alcohol. They entertained in our home regularly and drinking was always a major component of any gathering. When my sisters and I discovered that two of our parents' close friends–one a prominent lawyer and the other a neurologist–had used cocaine, we confronted our parents. They made excuses. I still remember, vividly, how my mother tried to explain, telling my sisters and me that their friends snorted coke for health reasons.

Inconsistencies between what my parents said about drugs and alcohol with what I saw may have contributed to my perceptions on morality. Likewise, my parents' tolerance for bid rigging and collusion in the pursuit of contracts to advance our construction business couldn't help but influence my sensitivity to the law's relative importance to society.

My parents' lectures about honesty, integrity, temperance, and other virtues of good citizenship didn't make as firm an impression on me as the hypocrisy I saw. As far as I was concerned, certain activities might be illegal, but if they were committed without harming recognizable victims, then it was okay to shrug off or disregard those laws. My parents' reasoning differed dramatically from the principled approach Rousseau

53

taught in his essay on the social contract, a pact that bound all citizens.

* * * * * * *

As I move closer to my sentencing date, I begin to feel responsible for the crimes I committed. By contemplating the writings of John Locke, I start to appreciate the influences that shaped the young man I've become, and I accept that I have to change. I must "unlearn" the corrupting influences that led to my bad actions, and eventually, to my imprisonment.

When I pick up the *Treasury of Philosophy* again, I read an essay that describes the trial of Socrates and it slowly helps me accept the predicament I have created. Socrates was convicted for breaking an absurd law that prohibited the aristocratic classes from teaching the commoners. The Athenian tribunal sentenced Socrates to a self-induced death by poisoning for his crime. He waited patiently in jail for the date of his scheduled execution.

Many leaders of Athens loved and respected Socrates. Outraged at his sentence, they coordinated a plan that would allow him to escape punishment and live the remainder of his life in exile. Socrates refused the offer, explaining that his conscience would not permit him to sneak away, avoiding punishment for his actions. Reading about Socrates inspires me. As a lover of law and democracy, Socrates asserted that his honor would require that he carry out the sentence by drinking the poison that would kill him. In my eyes, that principled position reveals Socrates as a man of strength and courage. While waiting for the imposition of my sentence, I look to him as a role model for the type of thoughtful man I'd like to become.

With my Bible and the philosophy books, I live like a monk in my cell. The reading transports me to new worlds of thought and contemplation. I feel an unfamiliar maturity creeping into me, bringing hope. I write letters to my parents, my sisters, and every day I write to Lisa, promising to redeem my crimes by educating myself and using time in prison to prepare for a productive life upon release.

* * * * * * *

Seven months after my initial arrest, the government

indicts me with several new criminal counts. I accept these new charges and don't dispute the leading role I played in distributing eight kilograms of cocaine or my perjury during the trial. Lisa isn't named in the indictment, although the lawyers speculate that she'll later face criminal charges for lying to a federal officer.

My efforts to protect Lisa have failed, but prayer and philosophy inspire optimism. Rather than allowing forces I can't control–such as the sentence my judge will impose–to dictate my attitude, I begin to feel a spiritual strength building inside of me.

Prison will not destroy or define me. Rather, I make a commitment to define myself through my response to the sanctions I face.

* * * * * * *

I want to atone for my crimes. To make my statement public, I write to Stuart Eskenazi, a journalist who covered my trial for *The Tacoma News Tribune*. In the letter, I express remorse for my crimes and for the ways I acted after arrest. I pledge to find ways to make up for my wrongs during the decades ahead.

A few days later, Eskenazi comes to interview me in jail. I understand that audiences will be skeptical about my commitment to educating myself and to creating opportunities for positive social contributions. Still, I'm committed to begin anew. I feel myself turning the page on the decisions that brought me into confinement.

The front-page story that Mr. Eskenazi writes for the local paper does not influence my sentencing judge. After two separate hearings, he imposes consecutive sentences. In total, the judge orders that I serve a 45-year sentence and fines me $500,000 for my crimes.

"You will be an old man when you walk out of prison," the judge states flatly. "But you've earned it."

Chapter Two: 1988
Month 13

The court paid my public defender, Justin, to represent me after I cut ties with Raymond. Now that I've been sentenced, however, I'm without much access to legal counsel. Justin will prepare a direct appeal, but he won't be available to help me understand how to navigate my way through the 45-years I must serve. I don't even know what that means and I wonder whether the judge really intends for me to languish in prison for longer than I've been alive.

Unlike the federal time that I'm serving, most of the other prisoners in my housing unit at the county jail face problems with the State of Washington's criminal justice system. From those men I learn that all 50 states maintain their own criminal justice and prison systems, with different rules and legal codes. As a federal prisoner, I have little in common with them. Still, by listening to the more experienced prisoners around me I become familiar with concepts like "parole" and "good time."

The federal prison system is in transition, abolishing parole and significantly reducing the amount of good time possible. Since my convictions stem from crimes I committed prior to the date of the new law's enactment, I'm part of the old-law system where parole still exists. Still, the statute under which I stand convicted, "the kingpin statute," is one of the few crimes under the old law that doesn't qualify for parole eligibility. Of the 45-year sentence that my judge imposed, I've learned that I'm only eligible for parole consideration during the final two years of my sentence, the portion imposed as a consequence of my perjury conviction. Still, it's all very confusing to me and I don't know how many years I'll actually serve in prison.

To pass time I read legal books in the jail's law library. From those books I understand that a good-time provision under the old law authorizes prison administrators to reduce my sentence if I remain free of charges for disciplinary misconduct.

Still, according to calculations I make on a piece of lined writing paper, regardless of what I achieve in prison, I'll serve more than 26 years. That doesn't make much sense to me, as I didn't have charges of violence or weapons, and only consenting adults were involved in my crime.

The length of my sentence doesn't haunt me as much as Lisa's legal issues. She's now in Miami, where she receives more family support while her lawyer works through the best possible plea agreement. The entire situation is a mess I've created. I try to comfort her during our nightly telephone calls even though I'm powerless to protect her. Our only connection is on the phone, but the conversations we have don't seem to be enough.

I ask her to pray with me, but she always snaps back "I don't want to pray, Michael." It stings as if she's slapping me when she uses my name instead of a more endearing term. "You're supposed to get me out of this mess," she says.

"I'm trying, Lisa. I'm trying. No matter what happens though, we still have each other and with God's help we're going to get through this." I've never been religious, but during these traumatic times I find strength through prayer and I want her to join me.

"How?" she wails. "How do you think we're going to get through this if you're in prison and I'm in prison? How is God or prayer going to help us through that?"

"You're not going to prison, honey. God's not going to let that happen. I can feel it. The judge sentenced me to far more time than everyone else, and I'm sure he slammed me with all the time he intends to hand out in this case. It's over."

"That's not what my lawyer says," she argues through tears. "He told me I could get five years. Five years, Michael! I can't handle this. I can't go to jail!"

"Don't worry, Baby. It's not going to happen. I know it's not going to happen. At worst he'll sentence you to probation. I need you to pray, to have faith in God."

Lisa pauses on the phone, as if contemplating what she wants to say. "Raymond keeps calling me."

"Why is he calling you?"

"He calls because he's a pig, that's why. Last night he

asked me to come to his house for a soak in his hot tub. He said that a real man wouldn't have put me in the position you did."

The news sickens me. My former lawyer has taken everything I own and now he's trying to seduce my wife. My losses continue. With only one place to decompress, I return to my cell, my haven from madness, and I lie on my bunk, realizing that the sentence is only the start. There is still more pain to come, farther to fall.

I want peace but I can't escape the noise blasting through the cellblock. Rap songs blare from music television stations. There's also a continuous chatter from the scores of prisoners roaming purposely and posturing in the common area, along with loud exclamations and expletives from each of the table games. From my bunk I can see a haze of tobacco smoke that lingers beneath the ceiling. I feel close to the edge, uncertain whether I'll make it through without wrapping a noose around my neck or slicing an artery. Suicide seems so easy, so inviting.

My mom and Christina, my younger sister, are in Florida. The geographical distance that separates us is a relief. After all the lies I've told about innocence, I can't bring myself to face my family, especially my mother.

Through a telephone call I learn that my trial has brought my mom and Lisa's father together. His name is Hank. Although I've never met him I know that he shares a mutual grief with my mom, and that grief has led to a romance between them. My life has become an absurd soap opera.

"This is crazy," I tell Christina over the phone. "How can Mom get together with this guy? She's only been divorced from Dad for a year."

"Give her a break, Michael. She's lonely and sad. I'm glad she's found love. No one wants to be alone and you're no one to judge."

Christina's right. I shouldn't judge my mom, or anyone. I'm in jail and I don't even know my own family, just as the choices I made over the past three years resulted in my family not knowing me. "I'm sorry," I tell her. "I want Mom to be happy too. The news just surprised me, that's all."

"That's okay. It's kind of funny when you think about it. I mean, for one thing, Hank isn't anything like Dad. Besides that, when Mom and Hank marry, that means you'll be married to your own stepsister and Hank will be both your father-in-law and your stepfather. Just like you don't know Hank, none of us really know Lisa."

* * * * * * *

My father and my sister, Julie, wait through slowly moving lines to visit me in the jail. Julie is a year older than I am. She's totally independent and strong, holding our shattered family together as my conviction and sentence loom. Each weekend we visit through glass partitions, clutching telephone handsets as we cry in the booth.

"Tell me again, son. Why did you feel that you had to do this?"

The jail officers only allow me to spend 15 minutes in the booth, and when my father asks me these questions I press my hand against the glass to match his and cry.

"I'm sorry, Dad. I'm sorry."

"It's okay, Son. Don't cry. We're here for you." He's crying too, as is Julie. The sadness is hard to take, and at this stage, I don't know how it will end.

"We're here for you," Julie repeats. "Whatever you need, we're here for you. We just need you to be strong in there and to know it's going to get better."

"Santos!" The jailer yells in the booth. "Let's go! Time's up! I'm not telling you again. Move out!"

I pull my hand from the glass. Not wanting others to see my weakness, I rub tears from my eyes as I walk away. I'm going to ask my family not to visit anymore. Whenever I walk away from the visiting booth the devastation I've caused plays out in my mind. Those images come with pangs of guilt that linger like a dark cloud.

When I left the family my father was such a force. He was rough, a hard-working man who came to this country with nothing but ambitions to build a better life. While on a construction site, surrounded by heavy equipment, I could always find him as he yelled out orders to the men who worked for him. He and my mother wanted so much for me. I'm besieged by thoughts of what my conviction and long sentence

60

has done to my parents. My father steered a small boat across 90 miles of the Atlantic, braving Caribbean waters and the unknown to escape Castro's communism. But when I look in his tearing hazel eyes, see the new worry lines etched in his brow, or the way that his once black hair is turning white, I know he fears that I won't survive prison. In the night, he has told me, he wakes in a panic and suffocates with anxieties that news will come informing him that I've taken my life.

"Promise me you'll be strong enough to see this through," he pleads with me frequently over the telephone.

"Yes, Dad. I'm going to make it. I promise."

"Say it again!" He insists.

"I promise." My father has lost his life's work and his marriage and now his son. He's only 53-years old, yet he's tormented, blaming himself for the prison term I face. The guilt of it crushes me.

* * * * * * *

I struggle to understand the philosophies of Friedrich Nietzsche, Jean Paul Sartre, and Albert Camus. Existentialism centers on personal responsibility and I espouse the concept even though these writers reject the concept of God. I'm living hour-by-hour, and they sometimes feel interminable. Through prayers I find comfort, leaving me conflicted by the existentialists. I'm torn between embracing and rejecting them. Although I oppose their godlessness, I find their message about personal will empowering. Regardless of what social exposures influenced my judgments, values, and actions, my ego, greed and shortsightedness caused my problems. Neither prayer nor religion is going to fix my problems, but I feel a spiritual force moving me. Both prayer and the teachings of the existentialists convince me I can grow into the man I aspire to become.

* * * * * * *

It's late summer of 1988 when a jailer opens my cell door early on a Saturday morning. "Santos! Roll up!" He throws two plastic bags on the concrete floor. "Dump your personal belongings in one bag, pile your sheets and blankets in the other. Move out! Now!"

With my hands and legs in shackles I carry the bag filled

with letters from Lisa, her photographs, and a few books as I follow the jailer through a maze of corridors. He locks me in a holding cell with others. We don't wait long before the U.S. marshals take control and herd us like chattel into a transport van parked in the jail's basement garage.

My time in the county jail has come to an end.

"Can you tell me where I'm going?" I ask the driver of the van.

"You don't know?"

I shake my head while shrugging my shoulders.

"You'll find out when you get there."

We drive south on Interstate 5 and don't stop for several hours until we reach a landing strip at the Portland airport. After another hour in the van I see the plane's tires hit the tarmac and the landing precipitates movement. The marshals and other law enforcement officers emerge from separate vehicles donning black armor vests and gripping their assault rifles firmly while taking positions to guard the plane.

I remember going through this drill before, when some of these same marshals transported me from Miami to Seattle for my initial court appearances. I shrink into my seat, watching the drama unfold and waiting for the requisite but dehumanizing inspections before I board the plane to some unknown destination.

I look through the tinted window of the transport van and watch prisoners leave the plane, hobbling down stairs in chains, with marshals inspecting them as if they are a lower species. I think how differently events might have unfolded if only I had made better decisions after I stepped off that plane last year.

I can't blame anyone but myself for where I sit. My friends didn't testify against me out of malice and I don't begrudge them the evidence they provided against me. I miss them. We grew up as brothers and although we haven't spoken, I sense that they empathize with my plight. Without delusions of acquittal I too could've accepted responsibility for my crimes. I knew I was guilty, but rather than accepting responsibility and putting the past behind me, I fooled myself into believing that since I didn't touch the cocaine, prosecutors wouldn't be able to prove anything and a jury wouldn't convict me. Within days of stepping off that plane last year, I even orchestrated a cocaine deal from inside the jail.

The chains on my wrists, around my waist, and on my ankles feel heavy, but not as heavy as my guilt. From my understanding, I'll wear them for at least 26 years. Since I haven't been alive that long, it feels like an eternity.

"Where you headed?" A prisoner addresses me as I settle into the seat beside him on the airplane. He's older, about 35, but I'm guessing. He wears a goatee and I notice the flame tattoos on his forearms.

"To prison." I shrug.

"Which one?"

"They wouldn't tell me. Marshal said I'd find out once I got there."

"Prick. I'm sick of livin' like this, hate all these motherfuckers."

"Where're you going?"

"Lompoc."

"What's that?"

"Huh?"

"Lompoc, what's that?"

"Whud'ya mean, 'what's that?' Motherfuckin' joint, that's what it is. You green, just comin' in or something?"

"I've been in jail for a year. Now I'm on my way to prison."

"Go to trial?" His eyes suggest that he's testing me.

I nod. "Guilty on all counts."

"Drugs?"

"Cocaine," I answer.

"What'd they hit you with?"

"My sentence you mean? Forty-five years."

He whistled. "That's some heavy shit. You old law or new law?"

"I'm old law."

"At least you've got that goin' for ya. You'll be able to see the board after 10 years."

"No I can't. I've got a Continuing Criminal Enterprise, no parole."

My neighbor whistles again. "That's a bitch, young'n.

Been down before?"

I shake my head.

He whistles again. "Least they'll know you ain't no snitch. How old're ya?"

"I'm 24."

"You got an ol' lady?"

"I'm married."

"Cut that bitch loose. Can't be hangin' on to no woman when you're pullin' a 45 piece. Gotta be ready to do time, and can't do that with no woman on your mind."

"How long have you been in prison?"

"Eight motherfuckin' years. Got two more to pull 'fore the board's gonna cut me loose."

"What are you going to do when you get out?"

"Fuck if I know. I ain't thinkin' 'bout no streets. One thing you're gonna learn in prison, ain't no one out 'til they're out. Anything can happen. Best forget about them streets."

This guy paints a somber picture for me. We haven't even exchanged names and he has already advised me to give up on the world I once took for granted. He sounds so bitter, devoid of hope.

"What's it like to serve eight years in prison?"

"A motherfuckin' bitch," he admits as his head presses into the headrest and he closes his eyes. "Got the man breathin' down yer neck ever' day. Fuckin' family and friends from the streets desert ya. Parole board shittin' on ya. Board could'a let me out a year ago. Said I wasn't ready. Like they know what it's like to live in the pen. They gave me a date, got me walkin' on egg shells tryin' not to catch a shot 'til then."

"You mean a ticket?" I ask if he's referring to disciplinary infractions.

"You're in the feds, young'n. Better learn the lingo. Tickets is in the state joints. In the feds we call 'em shots and you can catch 'em for just 'bout any motherfuckin' thing."

"Like what?"

"Anything. Look at a bitch's ass, catch a shot for reckless eyeballin' and lose your parole date. Show up late for work, catch a shot for bein' outta bounds. Lose your date. Get caught with food from the kitchen in your locker, catch a shot for stealin'. It's all bullshit. Motherfuckers'll give you a shot for jackin' off. They don't want no one gettin' out."

He sleeps while I digest what he's told me.

* * * * * * *

The plane lands in Oklahoma. After stepping off I exchange my plane seat for a bus seat and a road journey to El Reno. I recognize the high fences, the coils of razor wire, the guards who drive in white vehicles continuously around the medium-security prison's perimeter to discourage escapes. I passed through the same gates on layover the year before, when I was being transported from Miami to Seattle for the trial. This is not new and I know what's coming: crowded bullpen cages, processing forms, fingerprinting, mug shots, and hours of standing before I get locked in a small cell with a stranger.

The cell house is an old design with long rows of sliding steel bars, the type from classic prison films, that clank when slammed into place. Midnight has long since passed by the time I climb onto the top rack. The prisoner on the steel bunk beneath me snores, oblivious to the putrid stench hanging in the cell or the oppressive late summer Oklahoma heat that suffocates me. Moonlight blends with the prison spotlights to cast a glow on the cracked concrete walls, just enough to illuminate the roaches that scatter along the edges of light.

Despite a restless night, I'm eager to explore the prison surroundings when I hear the guard crack the cell house gates open at six in the morning. I climb down and glance at the prisoner on the lower rack who sleeps with his pasty overweight belly and chest exposed, his hand in his shorts. Since I don't know the protocol of this new environment, I deliberate but finally resist the urge to use the stainless steel toilet or tiny sink next to the bunk.

Unwashed, I slide into blue slip-on canvas deck shoes and follow the herd of prisoners walking toward the tier's stairs. When I passed through this prison last year guards processed me. Then, hours later, in the middle of the night, they shackled and processed me out to continue my westward journey. I didn't have an opportunity to walk around. During the year I spent locked in the county jail, my freedom of movement didn't extend beyond the cramped quarters of the housing unit. I take in everything: the grass, the flowers, and the design of the buildings. It feels good to walk around.

The chow hall is a large, buffet-style cafeteria. I advance through the line, accept a pastry that a prisoner worker in white clothing places on my tray, and I fill a plastic cup with milk. It reminds me of my time in high school, except we're all guys and we're under the scrutiny of suspicious guards rather than bored teachers. I eat alone and then walk out to explore. It's early on a Sunday morning but the burning sun and high humidity trigger a sticky sweat that instantly dampens my armpits and trickles down the front and back of my torso.

I fall in behind a group of jive-talking prisoners walking with weight belts and exercise bags who head to the prison yard. After passing through a few gates and an unguarded metal detector I see the large track. Scores of prisoners work out on a massive outdoor weight pile. Three tennis courts to the left appeal to me; I played regularly when I lived in Key Colony and developed a decent game. I walk around the large oval track that circles the soccer and softball fields. Just when prison begins to feel like a park I see the stark, grim reminders that it's not a park at all: tall, double fences with endless coils of glistening razor wire separating them surround me in every direction.

The recreation area includes a gymnasium with a full basketball court. Floor-to-ceiling mirrors cover the walls of an adjacent indoor weight room. I watch as a beefed-up prisoner pumps out reps on the bench with four plates on each end of the bar. He's throwing up 405 pounds as if it's a broom handle. I've kept fit with thousands of pushups each week in the county jail and I wonder if I'll build such Herculean strength during the time I serve. I want to start at once.

"You be likin' them muscles, don'chu?" Another prisoner sneaks up next to me, flexing in his tank top and smiling with a lascivious grin exposing a mouthful of gold teeth. "Dat wha'chu need up in here, a real mans."

That's my cue to leave. Outnumbered and out of place, I walk out, lacking the courage to confront him for the insinuation he made. I'm not ready to take a stand.

"Don't be actin' like you don't like it now," he chuckles

behind me. "Daddy goin' see you later, belie' dat."

I'm younger than most of the other men. As I walk through the gates toward the library I'm conscious that my absence of tattoos and whiskers stand out. The encounter in the gym puts me on high alert and I realize that to survive in here I may have to battle more than the long sentence. To some prisoners, I probably look like the proverbial rabbit among wolves. Stay vigilant, I remind myself, as I open the doors to the law library.

I don't really know what I'm looking for, so I pick a random law book from a shelf and start flipping through the pages. The episode in the gym bothers me and I'm not able to concentrate. I pretend to read, though I only stare at lines of words that I don't absorb from the page. These encounters will happen again, and I'd better anticipate them. My response can't leave a doubt that I know the score and that I'm capable of defending myself.

But am I? Is this what I'm going to become? What options do I have when confronted with predators? I haven't been on a prison yard for two hours and someone has already mistaken me for a punk. I haven't been in a fistfight since junior high. Somehow prison doesn't seem like the kind of environment where fistfights settle confrontations and I can't envision myself picking up a weapon.

It's impossible to read with these worries muddying my concentration. I close the law book and walk out. Other prisoners in the corridor carry Bibles in their hands as they walk into a chapel. While in the jail I was comfortable praying alone, but now I need something to take my mind off the guy in the gym.

I sit in the back row and observe several prisoners working together to lead the service. Their level of preparation impresses me. It's clear that religion plays a central role in their lives and the congregation respects them, addressing them as Brother Tom and Brother Frank. When it's time to sing the men don't show any awkwardness or embarrassment. Some surprise me with the way they sing–eyes closed, arms and open hands stretching heavenward. With all their tattoos and goatees they strike me as being a bit over the top, both dramatic and comical.

I'm more self-conscious. Although I can embrace God's

presence in my life when I'm alone and silently praying for guidance, group prayer doesn't work for me. When the service concludes and several of the leaders approach with genuine warmth and invitations to participate in Bible study programs I thank them but decline and request a Bible to read on my own.

Following the chapel service I return to my cell where I catch the guy assigned to the rack below me. He's in his 40s and not particularly intimidating, standing barefoot in boxer shorts splashing water under his arms; it's a birdbath in the tiny sink. Still, I feel awkward as I stand outside the open gates of the cell.

"You the new guy?" he asks, sensing my apprehension about walking in on his personal routine.

"Yeah, got in last night."

"Well, you'd better come in. Count's about to start and you don't want to be out on the tier when those gates roll closed."

"Michael," I offer and stretch out my hand to shake.

"Buck," he responds and closes his hand into a fist. I realize he prefers to knock knuckles in greeting. "Where you headed?"

"What do you mean?"

"Next stop? Where you going?"

"Don't know, here I guess. I'm just starting out."

"You might be starting out, but it won't be here. This here's Oklahoma unit. Every swingin' dick in here's in transit, on the way to the next prison. If you were stayin' here, you'd 'a been in one 'a the permanent blocks."

"Well I don't know where I'm going then."

I set my Bible on the top rack as the cell gate rolls closed and locks us in. We hardly have any floor space. Buck sits on the lower rack.

"Have a seat," he gestures to the toilet. "Count won't be for a while. Where'd you come from?"

"Seattle." The quivers in my stomach settle when I realize that he's friendly. "I've been in jail going through trial for the past year," I add.

"Yeah I can see that you've got that jail skin color. No sunlight."

"This's been my first time walking outside since last

summer."

"You might 'a liked it this mornin', but by afternoon you'll be wishin' you was still in Seattle. Gets to be over a hun'erd degrees here, humid as a swamp."

"I felt it last night."

"The nights ain't bad. It's the late afternoons that'll bake you."

Buck and I pass the day together exchanging stories. He's serving a 20-year sentence for armed bank robbery. It's a crime that surprises me as I associate bank robberies with old westerns rather than crimes that people engage in today. He has spent the past four years at the United States Penitentiary in Leavenworth. The parole board has taken his good behavior into account and agreed to release him in two more years. Buck is transferring to a medium-security prison in Memphis where he expects to finish out his term.

"You can find out where you're going tomorrow," Buck tells me. "There'll be a counselor holdin' open house in the office downstairs. Tell him you're new and you want to know where you've been designated."

"Where's the best prison to serve time?"

"The best spot is them prison camps, but with 45 years you ain't going to no camp. Forget about that. You might go to an FCI since you ain't never been locked up before but there's a good chance, with a sentence like yours, you might be headin' to a USP."

As I lie on the top rack listening to Buck talk into the night I feel like a kid listening to ghost stories by the camp fire. The lights are out and a large fan at the end of the tier makes a rickety noise while it stirs the air. "What's the difference between an FCI and a USP?"

"Gonna see a lot more blood in the USP. Lot 'a the guys inside them walls ain't never gettin' out so there's pressure, somethin's always cookin'. Ain't a week gonna pass without some'n gettin' stuck, or some head bein' busted open with a pipe. Bloods always flowin' in a USP. FCI's is more laid back, like here."

"This place doesn't seem so laid back to me."

"What do you mean? What's not to like about this spot?"

I tell Buck about the morning encounter with the guy in the gym. Although I walked away, the remembrance of what was implied still unsettles me. I'm consumed with trying to figure out what to do if a predator approaches me again. A violent altercation isn't what I want but circumstances may force my hand.

"I wouldn't worry about anything here." Buck yawns and rolls over on the bunk beneath. "You probably won't be here but a minute. When you get to your next stop, that's when you need to act."

"How so?"

"Can't be lettin' the bulls come at you. Not less you want to start suckin' ever' dick in the pen." He laughs as if such a thing could be a joke. "Gotta take a stand. First thing you're gonna wanna get is a piece. Someone comes at you wrong, put holes in him, send him away leakin'. Do that once an' fellas'll get the message that you ain't no punk."

I know that I'll do what it takes to survive, but the penitentiary wisdom Buck dispenses doesn't sit well with me. "Did you have to stab people when you were at Leavenworth?"

"I had to get my respect, but things is different 'tween me and you. You ain't barely 20. I'm just sayin', that ain't but a baby in the pen. Guys is gonna try you more readily than they gonna try an older dude. Bulls is gonna try to get over on anyone that'll let 'em, but the younger guys who ain't got no backup gotta make 'emselves known quick. The gangs is getting real fierce in these parts."

"How'd they try to get over on you?"

"Couple 'a young dudes came at me thinkin' they's gonna get me to pay rent for livin' on the tier. I wasn't havin' it. I didn't have my piece with me at the time, so I just slow played like I was gonna pay. When they come to collect on store day I was ready. After I laid one out by smashin' him in the face with a mop ringer, they both got the message that they'd better find someone else to play with. Didn't have no more trouble after that."

"Weren't you thinking about your parole date or what would happen if you got caught?"

"Shit. When you's in the penitentiary it's livin' day by

day. Better not be thinkin' 'bout no release date or parole board or what the man's gonna think. All I'm thinkin' 'bout is one day at a time, gettin' through. A man's gotta do what a man's gotta do. You'll see."

Before drifting into sleep I think about Buck's advice. I'm hoping the counselor will tell me that I'll begin my term in a Federal Correctional Institution, an FCI, but my intuition tells me that I'm on my way to a USP, a high-security United States Penitentiary.

A few hours later I wake when a guard rolls the cell gate open. I'm hoping that he has come to take me on the next phase of this prison journey. No such luck. The guard calls for Buck. We wish each other luck, then he walks out. After the guard slams and locks the gate I lie awake for a while longer, intrigued by the roaches racing across the wall without apparent purpose.

Buck's advice troubles me because I can't see myself serving my sentence day-by-day. Living for the moment may be the conventional adjustment pattern but I don't want to forget about the world outside. There's got to be a way for me to make it through my sentence without violence. Join a church group? At least then I wouldn't struggle with loneliness, vulnerability. I hate this weakness that seizes me, and I've got to do something about it, but I don't know what.

Instead of getting up when the gates open in the morning, I doze on my rack. The solitude of the cell gives me space to think. I read the Bible while I wait for the counselor to arrive.

The Bible encourages me, though some of what I'm reading doesn't make sense with what I've come to believe about a forgiving God. The concepts of eternal damnation and one path to God aren't beliefs I can embrace, so I pray for guidance, acknowledging that neither Bible groups nor religious programs are going to carry me through this term.

I see the counselor and receive the confirmation I've been expecting. I'm on my way to the United States Penitentiary in Atlanta. I'll deal with it because I have to, because I don't have a choice.

"Can I make a phone call?"

"Three minutes," the counselor says without looking at me. "What's the number?"

The counselor dials the number I give for Lisa. When she answers, the counselor tells her that she has a phone call from a federal inmate. Then he passes me the handset and fixes his eyes on me. I want to wipe the phone clean, as if I can wash off the filth of prison.

"Hi, Baby."

I feel awkward talking to her with the counselor looking at me as he sits across the desk. To him I'm not a human being.

"Michael! I've been so worried when you didn't call. Are you okay? Where are you?"

I tell her that I'm on my way to a prison in Atlanta and that I'll be able to use the telephone once I'm there. When the counselor taps his watch, I tell Lisa I love her and promise to call again when I'm able.

Sadness makes me sluggish as I walk aimlessly from the counselor's office, thinking of Lisa's voice and remembering how wonderful it felt to hold her in my arms. I'm lost, without a clue of how I'm going to keep our marriage together. Not wanting to dwell on home, I head toward the law library. Feeling sorry for myself makes me vulnerable in a predatory population, which isn't good. I need a toehold and the strength to climb out of this hole.

* * * * * * *

The law books serve a purpose. Although I want relief from my sentence, the reality that I'll spend a long time in prison has begun to settle in. A year has already gone by since my arrest, so I'm not a beginner, and I know that many more years will pass before anything changes. I need a plan to make it through. The law books begin to help me understand more about the system that traps me. Like an endless riddle or puzzle, each paragraph I read steers me to other books for clarification.

Studying the law distracts me from misery. As with the philosophy books that helped me through the months in the county jail, the main lesson I learn from these studies is the depth of my ignorance. I berate myself for not having continued my education after high school.

"Looking for anything in particular?"

I don't know whether the man who stands beside my

table is a prisoner or a staff member. He's in his thirties, trim, with thinning blond hair, and I notice that he missed a spot shaving. He wears the khaki pants and white t-shirt of all prisoners, but he has an authority about him that confuses me with respect to his position or status.

"Just reading," I answer.

"Are you designated here or are you in transit?"

"I'm in transit, on my way to USP Atlanta."

"My name's Brett." He extends his arm with a clenched fist.

I introduce myself and tell Brett about my sentence. I'm trying to learn more about the system and about the Continuing Criminal Enterprise charge.

"Have you filed your appeal yet?"

"I have a public defender in Seattle who's putting the appeal together."

"If you've got a 45-year sentence you'd better get more than a public defender to write your appeal."

"Why? What's wrong with the public defender?"

Brett shrugs his shoulders. "It's not that there's anything wrong, it's just that they're overworked. They've got so many clients to worry about that they can't give too much attention to one appeal. You need someone who specializes in convictions like yours."

"What I need and what I have are two different things. I don't have any money to hire specialists. Besides, the last specialist I hired took me through the trials that got me my sentence."

"I've got a guy you should contact. He's a law professor in Indiana and he writes appeals for these kinds of cases. Once you settle in Atlanta you ought to write him. Tell him about your case and that you're on appeal. He might be able to help."

Brett's concern for my predicament seems genuine but I'm burned out with legal procedures. I don't even care about the appeal. The philosophy books I read helped me accept my guilt. Thinking about an appeal might put me on an emotional roller coaster. I don't want to live in denial anymore. My focus is on living the lessons I've learned from those great philosophers. I want to acknowledge that I'm responsible for what I did, and for what I am, and for where I am, and I want to begin to make decisions that will improve my character and my life.

"What about a Rule 35? Do you know anything about that?" I ask.

Brett laughs when I ask about a legal motion that I want to file for the judge to reconsider my sentence. I've read about the motion in the law books. Under the old law, defendants may file the motion after the conclusion of all appeals.

"Rule 35 is a joke," Brett tells me. "With a sentence like yours you better have something more up your sleeve than a Hail Mary."

"So you're saying no one ever gets relief from the Rule 35?"

"Rule 35 motion goes before the same judge who just saddled you with 45 years, Bud. Think he's going to reconsider the sentence? Better think again. If he wanted to give you less, he would have. That motion doesn't carry any weight. This system's about finality, and the only way to change a sentence is through the appeals court where three or more separate judges review the proceedings at trial."

The meeting with Brett is discouraging but I walk away with my resolve intact. I'm okay. I'm going to live through decades in prison, I tell myself, so I better accept it's reality and prepare my mind for what's ahead. I've already made it through the first year since my arrest.

A Rule 35–the legal motion that will petition my judge to reconsider my sentence–may be a "Hail Mary," as Brett mocked, but a prayer might be all I have. Before I can file the motion I must exhaust all my appeals. I'm not thinking about reversing my conviction. In fact, my experience through the judicial system has been misguided and I feel a little dirty because of it. I'm not going to contest my guilt any more. What I want is a do-over, an opportunity to accept responsibility and express remorse. Forget about winning on appeal, I tell myself. The only way to purge this overwhelming guilt is to atone.

Since procedure dictates that I can't file the motion for the judge to reconsider my sentence until my attorney exhausts all appeals, I write a letter to Justin, the attorney assigned to my case by the public defender. I urge him to focus on stalling for as long as possible. The object for me is not to win through some legal loophole, I explain. Instead, I want time to distinguish myself in prison. I don't know how I'm going to do that, but if Justin can succeed in delaying the process for a few years, I expect I'll find opportunities to demonstrate my remorse and my worthiness for reconsideration.

From what I've read of the law, timing is a critical factor. The established procedure requires that I file the Rule 35 within 120 days of the time that the final appeal affirms my conviction and sentence. After 120 days, the law precludes the judge from modifying my sentence. Before that time limit expires I need to show significant progress toward redeeming my crimes. I don't yet know how I'll reconcile with society, but I know the clock is going to start ticking when the appeals court makes its decision. I'd better be ready by then.

Returning to my housing unit, I notice a schedule for college classes posted on a bulletin board. The signs announce courses in English, math, history, and other subjects that could lead to a university degree. Earning a university degree would provide the kind of clear, compelling proof of my commitment to change, and with the news of its possibility, I find hope.

Judge Tanner would probably resist a motion to reconsider my sentence if nothing changes. Earning a college degree, however, would provide tangible evidence, showing discipline, character, and commitment. The choices I made that led to my conviction suggest such virtues were absent in my life, but earning a college degree might alter and soften the system's judgment against me. I don't know whether the penitentiary in Atlanta provides opportunities for collegiate study but the possibility encourages me.

* * * * * * *

I have a lot on my mind, and sleep isn't coming easily. The prison is a population of more than 1,500 men and I haven't crossed paths with the predator who tested me in the gym. Still, I know that confrontations will be a constant in prison. How am I going to handle them? If I'm to invest myself fully in building a string of accomplishments that will persuade the judge I'm worthy of reconsideration then I can't allow a single blemish on my prison record. Not one.

The trouble isn't with me. I can control my actions and behavior. Regardless of how I choose to serve my sentence, the real threat comes from how others choose to live in a high-security penitentiary. I won't be able to control the ways that others serve time, but as I experienced in the gym, the decisions of others could have an immediate impact on my life. I'll have to learn how to manage in this twisted environment.

But it isn't only my early adjustment and assessment of my environment that bothers me, as Lisa's predicament is still unresolved, troubling me. Her sentencing isn't scheduled until the fall, but the possibility of her imprisonment isn't something that I can totally dismiss. Everyone has a breaking point and her imprisonment could be mine. I've got to put this out of my mind, at least until her sentencing date comes closer. It's just too much to worry about for now.

The gate to my cell rolls open. "Santos!"

"Yes," I sit up from my rack instantly.

"Roll up!" the guard orders.

I'm on my way, with new anxieties. While locked in the county jail I read Homer's epic The Odyssey, describing Odysseus's 20-year journey home. My odyssey might take longer. I don't know. Moving forward helps, even if my fear of the unknown accompanies each step.

It isn't concern about conflicts with other prisoners that drive my anxieties. I'm 24 and I'm strong–confident that I can give as good as I get if it comes to fighting. But I don't want an altercation. I want to turn this page of my life, to start writing a new chapter. I need to think about how others will judge me by what is written from now on. Every decision I make will have more than immediate consequences, but those decisions will also dictate where I stand in months, years, and decades to come.

After marshals yank on my chains and manacles, I fall into line with others and hobble up the stairs into the airplane. It's already packed inside and by the time we take flight every seat is filled with hundreds of prisoners who deal with the crisis of imprisonment in his or her own way. Doubting whether any of them have a sentence as long as mine, I close my eyes and rest, wondering how many real killers are on board.

* * * * * * *

My ears pop as the plane descends and lands in New Orleans. We pass by hundreds of private jets and I realize that the airport is busy because the Republican National Convention is in town. President Reagan's second term is approaching its end and the news reports I've read suggest that Vice President Bush will prevail over Michael Dukakis in the fall election.

A massive dark plane catches my attention. The words "Forbes Capitalist Tool" decorate the plane's tail in large, bold letters, distinguishing the jet from smaller, white, sleeker models. The centers of corporate power and wealth have converged upon New Orleans to celebrate the anticipated new leadership of George H.W. Bush.

Only a few years ago I came of age and pulled a voting-booth lever for the first time. I considered myself an up and coming businessman, proud to vote Republican, for the party of business, for Ronald Reagan. That was before I considered selling cocaine, before the television series *Miami Vice*, or the big screen hit *Scarface*. Now I realize those glitzy shows influenced me. The fast boats, exotic sports cars, designer clothes, and incredibly seductive women presented an exciting image of cocaine trafficking.

As the marshals call names for prisoners to disembark I continue watching the fleet of corporate jets. Conservatives have won the marketing campaign of the 1980s, convincing me that they were the party of elites, the ruling class, and the group I wanted to join. Not understanding or caring about the broader implications of governance, I bought into the campaign propaganda painting "liberal" as a pejorative term, as a party of losers.

Although I'm not a scholar by any means, the concepts of liberalism and conservatism mean something different to me now that I've read essays by John Locke and Thomas Hobbes. Those essays convinced me that political parties and political thought dictate the direction of society. When I bought into the Republican theory of conservatism, without even knowing what it was, I rejected the liberal philosophy of John Locke that makes so much sense to me now. Yet as I stare out the window and look at those symbols of power, it's clear that the conservative philosophy of Thomas Hobbes prevails in the 1980s. I'm an outsider, no longer a man or citizen. I'm a prisoner, stripped of the delusions and pretensions I had about taking a shortcut to a life of comfort.

* * * * * * *

With the exchange of prisoners complete we leave the corporate jets behind and fly east. Eventually I deplane and board a bus with other prisoners. We ride through the busy streets of Atlanta and as I look at the glass-faced skyscrapers, the places of commerce, the people, I try to soak it all up, knowing I'm not going to see a big city for a long time.

My stomach churns as the bus speeds across a dip in the road. And then I see it. For the first time I stare through the window at the fortress that will hold me, a monster, with an intimidating façade and a 40-foot high concrete wall that encapsulates the penitentiary's perimeter. Coils of razor wire top tall metal fences that surround the outer wall as added protection against escape. Gun towers are evenly spaced about every 50 yards, standing ominously around the wall. I see guards inside–alert, at attention, with automatic rifles in their hands, watching as if our approaching bus carries enemy combatants. Perhaps that is the guards' perception of us.

We cross an intersection and turn into a semi-circular drive. The bus comes to a slow stop in front of the dramatically wide steps that ascend to a majestic entrance. The architects who designed this awesome edifice of granite blocks and steel intended to send a message of permanence, of finality. The penitentiary symbolizes something, but I don't know what. It might be justice, it might be vengeance, or it might be power. I don't know. As I sit on the bus looking at the penitentiary from the outside, I also perceive an absence of humanity. The guards wear matching outfits of gray slacks, white, long-sleeved, button-down shirts, and maroon ties. Those with an air of authority wear dark blue blazers and carry clipboards. Others surround the bus wearing navy blue windbreakers with large gold "BOP" initials on the back. Instead of clipboards they carry assault rifles.

When the guards complete their preparation one of them calls us to the front of the bus, individually. "Listen up! When you hear your name, stand and walk toward the front of the bus. Give me your registration number. Then step off and walk directly up the stairs and into the penitentiary. Look straight ahead and don't even think about trying to run. We will shoot."

Chains bind our ankles, more chains wrap around our waists, and handcuffs weave through the chains in the front to lock our wrists in place. Who could possibly run?

"Santos! Michael!"

When I hear my name, I stand and shuffle my way through the cramped aisle toward the front of the bus.

"Number!" The guard demands while comparing my face to the mug shot on his file folder.

"Number 16377-004."

"Date of birth?"

"January 15, 1964."

"Go!"

Passing inspection, I make my way off the bus and keep my eyes dead ahead. I don't know how I'm going to climb all those steps but I begin, taking it slowly as I advance through a gauntlet of armed guards. They stare at me through mirrored sunglasses and I know I'm being assessed. I make it to the top and follow the procession of prisoners through a series of metal gates. I'm inside the walls, walking into the penitentiary's main corridor, the belly of the beast, as another prisoner once famously called it. It's a stretch, longer than a football field, 20 yards wide. The marble floor is highly polished and buffed beige, surrounded by white concrete walls and steel side doors. This place is solid and eerily quiet. Our lumbering steps with dragging chains are the only sounds I hear. Other than those of us moving through, I don't see any prisoners.

We turn to the right and walk downstairs into a basement. The familiar series of cages await us. I march into the bullpen, part of the herd. Guards unlock our chains and we begin the interminable wait for the processing to begin. The gates finally lock with 42 of us inside. I sit on a fixed bench that runs along the wall, shoulder to shoulder with strangers in the cramped cage. Trying to understand these new surroundings, I feign indifference as I listen closely to the conversations around me.

"Yo, you's up in Lewisburg, back in '74?"

The large prisoner to my right isn't talking to me, but initiating communication with another prisoner who stands in front of us. I'm calculating the years as I listen; he's asking about another prison 14 years ago, when I was only 10.

"Dat's right," the man responds. He sounds suspicious, as if trying to figure out whether the man questioning him is friend or foe. Neither man looks as if he knows the concept of fear. The welts and scars on their skin tell me that prison, confrontation, and violence have become extensions of life for each.

"Used to run wit' Big Smoke and 'em?"

"Smoke's my dog, yo! Where you be knowin' Smoke from?"

With a mutual acquaintance established, genuine enthusiasm seems to replace the suspicion.

"Shee-it, Dog! I's up in da 'burg wit' you, D-block, Dog. I's da one split Tone Loke open, left his guts fallin' out all up in his hands outside da gym an shit." This guy's obviously proud of his reputation.

"Oh yeah, yeah, right. Used to be runnin' wit Big-O and shit." There is recognition between them.

"Dat's what's up, Dog." The two muscular men, both bald with goatees, bump fists.

"Where's you comin' from, Cuz?"

"Man I been on tour Dawg. Lockdown at Marion, few at Leavenworth, I'm comin' out 'a Terry Haute right now. How 'bout you? Where you been at, where you be comin' from?"

"Shee-it, I been out Lompoc, yo, kickin' it and shit." Then he turns to me. "Yo young'un, why on't you step off for a minute? Let the Big Dogs kick it."

It's not really a question. He's telling me to move, telling me that I'm irrelevant in this world. I'm an insect, a nonentity unless I choose, at a moment like this, to define myself as something different.

The prisoner would not have considered challenging a man he respected in such a way. But in my face, and in my eyes, and in my movements, he reads that I haven't yet earned respect in this world that is so unfamiliar to me.

In a split second I have to decide whether to stand my ground and follow consequences to their end, wherever they take me. I'm calculating at the speed of light, certain that my response can influence where I am in 10 seconds and in 10 years. The penitentiary requires aggressive force–instantly and without hesitation–for respect. But I don't aspire to have the penitentiary define me. It's much more important for me to earn respect outside of prison walls. So I stand to surrender the space I had on the bench. This isn't the time to assert myself. I'm my own general in my war and I need to choose which battles are worth fighting.

I'm learning, absorbing everything going on in this cage. Survival means more than fitting in to the penitentiary. I want out, but every step counts. Instinctively, I'm taking the first steps, but I'm walking across a high wire, a tightrope. Every decision I make determines whether the privilege of another step will come, or whether I'll begin a free fall to my demise. Deliberate, careful, calculated steps will lead to the other side.

I berate myself for having sat in the first place. This is not a game, this is life, and I can't allow my senses to dull. I must stay alert. Like an antelope crossing the plains of the Serengeti, I must use all of my innate intelligence to avoid succumbing to the perils that lurk here. And there are many. I can't forget that every movement, every choice, every word will influence what happens next. Had I not taken space on the bench the other prisoner would not have spoken to me, challenged me. I have to think, to ensure that every move has a purpose. I have to remind myself that I don't want to be "the man" in the penitentiary. I want to go home, and when I do go home, I want to go home ready to succeed.

I stand in the crowd, using peripheral vision, listening. The other prisoners are sturdier. I don't know whether the skulls and demons and gang signs indelibly inked on their arms, necks, and faces cloud my judgment, but these prisoners seem as if carved from material more calloused than flesh. Some, I gather from the chatter, serve sentences of life without parole. They accept the penitentiary as the last stop.

* * * * * * *

I move through the admissions process. Guards pass out administrative forms with question after question that I must answer. When it's my turn, I sit with various staff members who evaluate my responses.

I sit across a desk from a psychologist. "You've never been incarcerated before?" he asks. He's skeptical about the veracity of my response given the length of my sentence.

"I've been in jail for the past year but I've never been incarcerated before this arrest."

"And you don't have any history of violence?"

"No."

"No weapons, guns, knives, gang affiliations?"

I shake my head and tell him no.

He rests his elbow on the desk, using the back of his hand to prop up his chin as he evaluates me. He seems confused that I'm serving 45 years for a first offense without a history of violence or weapons. After a minute, he offers some advice. "Perhaps you should consider growing some facial hair."

The psychologist may mean well. Still, I consider his unsolicited advice an insult. Knowing that I'm out of my element, I acknowledge with a nod, swallowing my pride. My efforts at projecting a stern, no-nonsense disposition have failed. I take his comment as it was intended, an insinuation that my clean-shaven face could lead to unwanted attention from prison predators.

My next stop on the circuit of staff interviews is the office of a case manager. The gray metal desk looks as heavy as a tank and crowds the room. As he flips through pages of a file on his desk, I sense that the case manager isn't particularly concerned with my anxiety during these first hours in the penitentiary.

"Sit!" he orders, without looking up. "Which one are you? Santos?" He fingers the file in his hand.

"Yes sir."

"Habla Ingles?"

He emphasizes his American accent. The sneer in his tone suggests that he's trying to establish an air of superiority. The question annoys me because he is reading from a page of responses that I wrote in English. I don't like the insinuation that we're different, that just because of my name I'm not an American. But when he looks at me I only nod in response.

"Never been locked up before. Forty-five years. Out date 2013." He whistles after reading through personal identifiers from my file. "See ya, feel ya, wouldn't wanna be ya," he chants. "Any reason I can't put you in gen pop?"

"What?" I don't know what he's asking.

"Can you make it in general population?"

"What do you mean? Why couldn't I?"

"I'm asking you! Ever work for law enforcement?"

"No."

"Ever testify against anyone in a court of law?"

"No."

He flips through more pages in my file, considering my responses. "Why'd you leave this blank? Don't got no one who wants you?"

He asks why I didn't respond to a question about whom the prison should notify in the event of my death.

"I'm only 24. I'm not going to die in here."

"Fact is, no one walks into the pen thinkin' he's gonna die. Few months ago we had us a major disturbance inside these walls. Inmates took 90 officers hostage. No one s'pected that either. Shit happens. Now who you want me to call if something happens to you?"

The animosity in the interaction shakes me. His use of the word "inmate" sounds contemptuous, as if he suspects that I may have been in allegiance with those who rocked the penitentiary with violence during the disturbance. The tension differs from the transient nature of the jail and detention centers. A line exists between us and I'm on the wrong side of it. I give him Lisa's name but I'm too shaken at the moment to recall her address and phone number. I'll give him those details later, I say.

After finishing the admissions process I grab my roll of bed sheets, blankets, and a pillow, then I walk with six prisoners toward the housing units. We wait behind a locked gate that separates us from the main corridor. From the aggressive, hostile tone two of the other prisoners use toward staff members, I can tell that neither authority nor the threat of punishment faze them. One curses out an officer on the other side of the gate so thoroughly that the roles of power seem reversed, as the officer simply ignores the enraged prisoner who grabs and shakes the gate, screaming to be let out. I'm intimidated and I doubt the front I'm making at being cool convince anyone.

When an institutional loudspeaker blasts out an announcement for a scheduled "controlled movement," the guard finally unlocks the gate. With shaking legs and growing rings of perspiration beneath my arms, I walk with my bedroll toward A-cellblock just as the other guards unlock doors from all the housing units in the penitentiary. Hundreds of prisoners converge into the corridor at once. The frenetic movement reminds me of the Kingdome after a Seahawks game, with all the fans rushing toward the stadium gates at once.

The announcement may have called the movement "controlled," but the madness doesn't resemble control at all. Hundreds of prisoners charge in both directions, hastening through, shoulders bumping shoulders. I feel like a pinball as I bounce forward with the forceful momentum. While I'm trying to get to my housing unit for the first time, everyone else uses the main corridor to move to or from the recreational areas of the penitentiary.

"Man down, man down!" I hear guards yelling ahead of me. "Make a hole."

"Let da muthafucka die!" yells a voice from the crowd.

"Put 'im out his mis'ry."

Just before I reach the entrance of the A-cellblock I see the cause of the commotion. Two guards lean over to assist a prisoner bleeding on the floor. They clearly try to help him while fellow prisoners, apparently unmoved by compassion, keep walking toward their destinations. Suppressing a natural human instinct to look and to help I, too, step over the pool of blood and turn right into the housing block.

The housing unit guard sits at his station to the left. I pass him my identification card.

"Santos," he drones as he leans back in his chair. "I've got you in cell 517."

I'm on my own as I climb the stairs to the fifth tier.

Chapter Three: 1988-1990
Months 14-36

I'm assigned to A cellblock. It's a long, rectangular, hollow shell of a building with high ceilings similar to the Oklahoma housing unit I just left at El Reno. Pigeons fly around in the open space above. It's late summer and the oppressive heat, without air conditioning, makes me sweat. Burgundy tiles cover the floor. The beige, enamel-faced brick walls have been stained yellow from nicotine smoke that has accumulated over decades.

In the center of the shell, a freestanding metal and concrete structure reaches five stories high. Each tier supports a four-foot wide catwalk that wraps around the caged tower. Steel bars evenly spaced four inches apart enclose the side-by-side cells in the building's core, and metal mesh screens the catwalk. From the looks of it I suspect administrators ordered the screens as an afterthought to keep prisoners from throwing bodies off the walkways. This is going to be a tough place to live, but in my mind I'm getting ready for all the challenges that I expect to come.

As I climb the stairs I wonder how much blood has spilled on that tile floor below. I'm only carrying a bedroll–two sheets and a pillowcase wrapped inside a green woolen blanket–but apprehension weighs on me.

After reaching the top tier I walk toward my cell. Through the bars of the cells I see that four steel bunk bed racks accommodate eight prisoners in each cell. An open toilet is mounted against the wall at the back of the cell. There isn't any privacy, just a commode. As I continue down the long tier I pass an open shower area. It's just a huge vacant space laid out the same as a cell, but instead of sleeping racks it has five spigots sprouting from the far wall. I catch sight of four men soaping themselves beneath spraying water.

"See somethin' you like, young'un?" one of the prisoners jeers at me and I hear the others laugh. I keep walking, ignoring the taunt, eyes straight ahead with the bedroll in my arms as if it's a bundle of firewood. Near the tier's end I find cell 517. I walk through the open gate and I notice a small table to my left. One prisoner lies atop his rack with the newspaper's sports section absorbing all of his attention. I stand motionless and look around, wondering which bunk I should claim. Three top racks are empty.

"What's up?" The other prisoner finally notices me. He is in his 50's, fit, baldheaded, and sporting a goatee.

I nod. "My name's Michael Santos. I'm new, assigned here."

"Oh yeah? Where you from?" His interrogation begins.

"I grew up in Seattle, but I've been living in Miami for the past couple of years."

"How much time you got?"

"Forty-five years." The length of my sentence makes a statement. In here I don't need to feel ashamed of it. "Old law," I clarify.

The prisoner sits up from his rack, sets the newspaper aside. "How old're you?"

"Twenty-four."

He shakes his head. "Well, youngster, you got some trouble to pull. Welcome to the big house. Ever been locked up before?"

"I've been in jail for a year, been through transit. This is my first prison. How's it measure up?"

"Suits me just fine, but one spot's the same as another for me. Question is, and I gotta ask since you're in my house, how're you gonna get by? What're you into?"

"I don't know." I shrug. "I'd like to go to college if possible, study, work out, that's about it."

"You a doper?"

"What do you mean? I'm in here on drug charges."

"So is everyone else. What I wanna know is whether you get high."

"No."

"Gamble?"

"I don't have any money for gambling."

"That would only make things worse, but it don't answer my question. What I asked was do you gamble?"

I shake my head.

"Not into punks, right?"

"I'm married. No punks."

"Well that ain't gonna last, the marriage part I mean."

He stands, puts out his hand. "Name's McFadden. They call me Check. Long as you ain't with no dope, gamblin', or punks, you can set your stuff here." He taps the rack above his. "This here'll be your locker, and this is your chair. Got four other men who live here and we all do our part to keep the house clean. This here's the schedule." He points to a hand-drawn calendar on the wall with names of people on scheduled cleaning days. "You either clean up on your day, or you pay to have someone sweep and mop; Pancho next door has a cleanin' hustle. Most guys pay a pack 'a smokes a week. We keep it quiet here. You got visitors, take 'em outside the cell. Don't bring ye'r problems to the house, else you'll have new problems. With me. Lights out at nine. Can you live with them rules?"

"Sure. They sound fine to me."

"Okay. What else?" He scratches his chin while contemplating how much more he should tell me. "You lucked out as far as cells go. Everyone here knows what time it is. Ain't no snitches here, no one up in anyone else's business, and we like keepin' quiet. We've all been around a while and don't want none 'a that jitterbug foolishness 'round here. Got questions, ask. Got problems, like I said, don't bring 'em back to the house."

I set my bedroll on the rack and thank him for the welcome while I start tying the sheets around the mat. "Why do they call you Check?"

"Let me give you the first rule of prison. Don't ask no one 'bout his personal business, least not unless you got reason, like he's movin' into your house."

"Got it."

"You play chess?"

"A little. I learned in the county jail when I was waiting for trial."

"Any good?"

"Like I said, I just play a little."

"Well when you finish makin' your rack, sit on down and give it your best shot. I'll show you why they call me Check."

As Check demonstrates his mastery of the chessboard he gives me more rundown on the penitentiary and his prison experiences. He's been in since 1972, 16 years, and he looks forward to release on parole from a life sentence in another year. Check tells me the penitentiary is in transition. After the riot, administrators shipped all prisoners out in order to assess the damage and prepare for rebuilding. The first prisoners to repopulate the penitentiary transferred in from lower-security institutions as a clean-up crew. Those lower-security prisoners are now transferring out to make room for the high-security prisoners that penitentiaries are designed to hold. The men are coming in on buses each week from Lewisburg, Leavenworth, Lompoc, and other jails or prisons.

"This place is only halfway 'live now, but give it a few months and it'll be rockin' just like any other pen."

I've heard enough about the violence, the gangs, and all the nonsense of prison life. It doesn't interest me. I inquire about the routines, the day-to-day life inside. From Check I learn that all prisoners receive a job assignment for full-time work. I can either try to find my own job or the counselors will issue me a work assignment. Prisoners, I am learning, provide the labor to run the penitentiary. Some jobs, Check explains, don't require much more than attendance while others require full-time duty and overtime for those who want to earn a few extra dollars.

"When I was in El Reno I heard about a college program. Do they offer any college courses here?"

"Haven't heard nothin' 'bout school, but that ain't really my thing. If school's what y'er into, you need to go check things out for yerself. There might be somethin' you can do."

* * * * * * *

In an effort to control USP Atlanta's 2,500 prisoners, guards enforce rules that only allow "movement" from one area of the penitentiary to another within a ten-minute window at the top of each hour. Check explains that if I want to inquire about educational opportunities I need to request a movement pass from the unit officer, then wait in line for the corridor guards to unlock the doors and gates of the housing unit. He draws a map directing me to the library and suggests I go explore.

I maneuver through the crowds easily enough and find the library, though in comparison to what I saw at El Reno, it's disappointing. During the riot that erupted several months before, a number of buildings were destroyed. One of those was the penitentiary's main library. A new education building is under construction but, for the time being, the library and entire education department occupy the basement in the prison's old health-services building.

As I walk through I notice a man with a military haircut and wearing black, plastic-frame, government-issue glasses. He's wearing the same prisoner's khaki outfit as I wear, but he's sitting at a desk positioned inside the entry to one of the rooms and I'm assuming that he holds some kind of authority. Bookshelves line the walls, but for all I know, they may be off limits. The prisoner at the desk reads his law book, indifferent to my curiosity. I'm reluctant to interrupt him but since I don't want to appear disrespectful by ignoring his position and simply walking past, I introduce myself.

"Excuse me, Bud. My name's Michael Santos. I just got here and don't really know the layout. Is it okay if I walk in to see what kind of books are available?"

"Suit yourself," he mutters, never looking up.

Browsing through the bookshelves I notice row upon row of westerns, romance novels, and science fiction, but I'm looking for nonfiction and there isn't much. I'm encouraged to see two sets of encyclopedias. Although I never spent much time reading reference books I know there's a wealth of information in these two sets. All I'm thinking about as I walk around the bookshelves is how and what I'm going to study while I serve my sentence. I'm eager to start making progress in here.

The room I'm in is quiet though I hear people talking in adjacent rooms. "Wha'da ya like to read?" The clerk spins his chair around, all of a sudden interested in me.

"I'm just looking, trying to get a feel for the place."

"Won't be much here 'til the new library opens and that's about a year away. You can check out anything from these shelves, or you can order books from the interlibrary loan program. Takes about two weeks for those books to come. 'Sides that, Chandler's got a set 'a bestsellers, but you've got to check them out directly from him."

"Who's Chandler?"

"Supervisor of Education. His office is in back, down the hall and to the left."

"Is he the guy to talk to about getting a job in the library?"

"He's the one, HMFIC."

"What's that?"

"Head motherfucker-in-charge. Where you from?"

"Seattle. I'm just comin' in."

"Long ways from home. What's up? Why they got you way out here?"

"I was living in Miami when I got arrested. I guess that has me classified as being from the East Coast.

"How much time you got?"

"Forty-five years."

"With that kind of time, only thing you should be readin' is them law books. They're down the hall. You need to get some 'a that time off, bro."

"I don't know much about the law, but I know that I'm tired of fighting this case. I need something else besides appeals to carry me through."

"What're you a lame? Givin' up? Just plan on serving all that time?"

I shrug my shoulders. "I know I'm going to serve some of it. I'm thinking about the Rule 35, asking the judge for reconsideration. Ever hear of anyone catching a break from it?"

"Only snitches. Ain't no judge gonna reconsider the sentence he imposed less a dude starts rattin' out motherfuckers. This system's 'bout finality. You gotta fight if you want relief."

"That what you're doing?" I gesture to the open law books on his desk.

"Damn straight. Been fightin' every day since I came in. I always got somethin' goin' in the courts."

"Has it changed anything for you?"

"Look, Bro, that ain't the way to look at it. This system's

dirty, fed by lies and corruption. Know what I'm sayin'? We're in a war here, and it's our job to keep filin' paperwork, assailin' this system 'til it changes. Can't just give up. If everyone in the pen kept filin' in the courts, we could expose this system. That's the only way we're gonna change it."

"You're probably right." The tone of his voice and the way his fist clenches the pen reveal his passion. Although the argument doesn't make much sense to me, the last thing I want is a confrontation. "Like I said, I've just come in and I'm trying to find my way around this place. You obviously know a lot more than I do."

The clerk accepts my deference to his wisdom. "So you lookin' for a job in the library?" He leans back in his chair.

"I think so. I like the quiet, the time to study. Do they have college here?"

"The only classes here are for the GED and they're not much. Next year, when the new buildin' opens, they might start offerin' college courses, but there ain't no room now. This's kind of a self-service prison. You wanna find college courses, gonna have to look for them yerself. This might help," he reaches for a reference book on correspondence courses from the shelf beside him and hands it to me.

"Thanks a lot, Bud," I say in accepting the book. "This will help. Can I ask your name?"

"Keith, Bro."

I sit on one of the hard chairs at a table and read through every page of the guide to correspondence programs. This research leads me to a description of Ohio University that sounds perfect. Although I've never studied at the university level before I'm motivated to invest as much energy as possible in educating myself. From the description I learn that even though I may never step foot on a university campus, I can earn a four-year degree from a nationally recognized school.

The book explains that Ohio University accepts Pell grants, and as a prisoner I qualify for financial assistance that will cover nearly all tuition costs. I'm confident that my parents will pay whatever the Pell grant doesn't fund, as I know they want me to make the best use of my time and I can't think of anything better than to educate myself. I'm a little humiliated, at

24, to need financial support from my parents, especially after the flamboyant life I led before prison and the ruin I brought to my family's stability. Yet I know that I'll need help, and I'm going to ask for it.

After writing down all of the information about how to enroll, I walk down the hall toward the area where Keith said the Supervisor of Education keeps his office. On the way I look inside one room with side-by-side shelves of legal books on case law, statutory codes, and procedure manuals for filing in court. I see several tough-looking men working at tables with law books open in front of them, just as Keith was doing, and I wonder what level of skill these men have with regard to judicial proceedings. With all those hateful designs inked on their skin they don't impress me as being scholarly types.

I pass by another room where several men sit at tables typing on electric typewriters. They may be obsolete in the real world, but typewriters are as close as we're going to come to high-tech in here. In high school I excelled in typing class and I look forward to sharpening my skills. With books, a law library, typewriters, and pockets of silence, the library looks and feels like the right spot to begin my adjustment. I'm hopeful Mr. Chandler will hire me. The door's open to his office so I knock on the metal frame.

The makeshift office where Mr. Chandler's stationed suggests that he's in transition. He's got gray hair, bloodshot eyes, a rumpled brown suit, and an orange tie is knotted loosely around his fleshy neck. The lines etched in his face and the dot-sized pores that I can see from ten feet away suggest he might need a few drinks to make it through the day. Loose papers and boxes overflowing with files cover the floor, a couch, and even a windowsill. No clear pathway from the door to his metal desk exists, so I pause before stepping into the crowded work area. Non-matching binders stacked out of kilter dominate his disorganized desk. On the dirty-beige, concrete-block walls that surround him, Mr. Chandler has taped several papers, as if they're reminders or references. They're not the small post-it notes, but full-sized pages with either typing or handwriting in felt pen, and they flap against the wall because of the breeze from a desk fan. Mr. Chandler isn't an administrator, apparently, who believes that the tidiness of his work area reflects the sharpness of his mind. Maybe he doesn't care. When I knock he doesn't look up.

Instead he waves me in with his hand. I stand in the doorway, apprehensive and uncomfortable, observing the surroundings while I wait for his signal to speak. A newspaper is spread across his desk. Mr. Chandler is absorbed with the comic strips.

I shift my weight from one leg to the other. Why did he gesture me in if he doesn't want to be disturbed? Maybe he didn't, I wonder as I continue standing. No, I distinctly saw him raise his arm and wave me in with his hand. After several minutes, I begin to feel very foolish, as if I'm an inanimate object standing there.

"Would it be better if I were to return later?" I finally muster the courage to ask.

He puts his hand up, a stop sign, though he still doesn't look up. The phone on his desk rings and he answers. "Chandler," he says. "Uh huh, uh huh, okay." He hangs up, continues reading, and I continue standing.

"What is it?" he asks, finally, still looking down.

"Mr. Chandler, my name is Michael Santos and..."

"Okay Mr. Santiago," he interrupts me, mistaking my name. "What is it? Get to the point."

"I'm new here and I'd like to work in the library, if you would consider hiring me."

"Got a cop-out?" He asks for the standard inmate-request-to-staff form, one that I received from the clerk.

"Yes sir." I maneuver my way around the piles of books and stacked boxes to hand him my form requesting employment.

Mr. Chandler writes that I'm approved to work in the library and signs his name. "Hand it back to your counselor," he tells me, returning my cop-out. I'm evidently dismissed.

I return to the front desk in the library, grateful to have resolved the hurdle of a job search, knowing that I've settled a major issue of my adjustment. "Mr. Chandler hired me," I tell Keith, trying to suppress my pride and satisfaction at having conquered one hurdle of prison life. "I'm going to be working here, in the library."

"Don't get too excited. You're still in prison, Bro."

"Maybe so. But at least I'll have all the time I need to read, write, and study once I enroll in college. Have you ever heard of anyone completing the program at Ohio University?"

"Look, kid, like I said before, school ain't my thing. Far as I'm concerned, all that schoolin' does is make 'the man' look good. I ain't interested in makin' anything better in this system, or helpin' hacks look like they're educatin' fools in here. I'm at war here, tryin' to tear this system down. Only way I'm gonna do that is by beatin' 'em at their own game, with these here," he says as he points to the law books. "You'll learn that soon enough."

* * * * * * *

During my first weeks in the penitentiary I meet hundreds of men. Listening to them convinces me that it's best to keep a low profile, at least until I understand more about my environment. I don't even talk much with the other men assigned to my cell.

Just as Check told me on my first day, the men mind their own business and don't show much interest in building new friendships. They work in the prison's factory, manufacturing or repairing mailbags for the U.S. Postal Service. I catch the vibe—one of apathy rather than hostility. These men have no interest in talking with a young prisoner who shows enthusiasm about being hired to work in the library. Enthusiasm dies long before most men enter the inside of these walls, I suspect. It might reveal naiveté, which exposes vulnerability.

In the evenings I lie on my rack thinking about how I'm going to make it and realize that I'm at the start of a long journey. I block out the noise that comes in endless waves from outside the cell. More than 600 of the 2,500 prisoners in the penitentiary live in A cellblock, though their activities don't concern me as much as the thoughts about how I will walk out of prison when I'm released.

But I can't seem to focus. The papers I've received from the administrators confirm that my 45-year sentence brings a possible release in 2013. It's only 1988 and after one year as a prisoner I still can't grasp what it means to live another 25 in here. According to the counselor, case manager, and unit managers, a group of administrators collectively known as the "unit team," 25 more years is the best I can hope for, and that's contingent on my not receiving any disciplinary infractions that could result in my loss of good time. No amount of effort or accomplishment, the unit team assures me, will advance my release date.

Although I don't talk about my spiritual beliefs, I read the Bible every night. My resistance to religious services and organized prayer groups irritates the zealots, or "Bible thumpers," as they're known. That's of little consequence in the long run because my relationship with the Bible brings me comfort, guides me, and provides occasional relief from the deep sorrow gripping me. I read it lying on my rack or while sitting on a wooden chair in a corner I've claimed for myself between bookshelves in the library.

Sometimes I find parables that seem as if written directly to me. I must prepare—that is the message I receive from my readings. The message comes to me from verses in both the Old and New Testaments. I find the message in the story of Noah and the Ark; I read it in the parables of the wise and foolish virgins, as well as the parables of the talents described in the Book of Matthew. I must prepare.

I learn from my daily Bible readings that everyone has a responsibility to live God's plan, and that plan requires us to maximize the gifts we receive. I'm not convinced that I must fast, wear certain clothes, use prayer oils, face the sun at specific hours, or publicly claim that I'm saved, to come closer to God. The belief I begin to form is that I need to live as a good man, to develop the gifts God has blessed me with and to work toward the making of a better world.

My belief strengthens my spirit, improves my attitude, and gives me a positive outlook. Instead of looking at my sentence as a burden I begin to see it as a challenge, an opportunity to grow in ways I never would've without extreme adversity. To accept that my sentence may have a purpose not yet revealed requires that I have faith that God has a plan, one that will open opportunities, and trusting in God's plan gives me a sense that I can go on.

I want to convey these thoughts to Lisa, but she's slipping away. Her sentencing date approaches so I understand her lack of enthusiasm when I express my excitement about beginning correspondence studies at Ohio University. When she mocks my growing faith in God, I realize how the time and space of my sentence separates us. Despite my love for her, we're growing apart.

Telephone restrictions preclude me from talking with her more than once every few days. I can only use the telephone on the days that A cellblock is scheduled for access. On telephone days, a guard leads 15 of us at a time to a room with rotary-dial, wall-mounted phones, and I wait in line to use one of them. When it's my turn, I'm authorized to make one 10-minute phone call.

To avoid the frustration of the brief phone calls I write long letters to Lisa every day, expressing my love for her and sending promises I don't know how I'll keep. Whatever sentence she receives, I assure her that it's part of God's plan, one that will bring us closer together. Just before her sentencing date she travels to Atlanta to visit with me.

I'm in my second month in Atlanta and it's been six months since I've seen my wife, more than a year since we've held each other or even touched. I'm lonely for her, aching for her. Thoughts of Lisa have, at various times, strengthened and weakened me, inspired and depressed me. Now I'm going to see her, to hold her, to kiss her.

I iron my khaki pants and shirt with creases as sharply pressed as a military officer's uniform and, in order to show how much larger my biceps have grown through exercise, I fold up the short sleeves of my shirt. I'm ready and I'm eager. Today Lisa will fall in love with me again, just as she loved me before.

"Yo, young'un, who's comin' to see you?" Other prisoners inquire as they watch me peering through the window to see who's walking down the prison corridor.

"My wife's visiting me today." I'm enthusiastic, refusing to use the standard prison reference of "my ol' lady."

"Have a good one."

Soon after I hear my name paged a guard arrives to escort me from the housing unit. We walk through the wide, quiet, empty corridor on polished marble floors surrounded by high, white walls. The guard doesn't talk to me. The only sounds along the dreary walk are our footsteps, the sound of swinging handcuffs that hang from the back of the guard's thick leather belt, and the occasional static blasts from his radio. It's a long walk.

Instead of entering the visiting room the guard opens the door to an adjacent room, where another guard waits at a desk.

"Inmate Santos for a visit," the escorting guard informs his colleague before locking me in the closet-sized room.

The guard seated at the desk asks for my ID and begins writing the information in his logbook: my name, registration number, the time I arrived, and my visitor's name. "What are you waiting for?" he asks as I stand there, watching.

"Oh, can I go in?" I'm dehumanized, conditioned to ask permission for any movement as if I've been a prisoner all my life.

"You know the drill."

"What drill? This is my first visit."

"Strip!"

The order surprises me but I follow it without question. My main concern is getting to Lisa, though I'm careful to keep my clothes looking crisp and so I take extra time to fold my pants and shirt before I set them on the dingy floor.

"Everything," the guard says as I stand in my boxers and socks.

I've been through hundreds of strip searches but guards sometimes let me stand in underwear while they inspect me. Not this one. He's a stickler for detail and insists on seeing me naked. He orders me to lift my privates, bend over and spread. I comply as he directs, giving him the full view he wants, and then I dress. Finally, he authorizes me to enter the visiting room.

I walk down a few steps to a platform where two guards sit at a desk. The room is large, like a high school cafeteria with bright lights. Vending machines line the walls. It's packed with people engaged in hundreds of simultaneous, loud conversations. I don't see Lisa. One of the guards asks for my identification. He then patronizes me with questions on whether I understand the rules. Those rules may be designed for security reasons, but they strip people of dignity and contribute to the loss of community ties. I remember the rules from when I first saw Lisa in the Miami prison more than a year ago. They don't permit us to embrace during the visit, and limit kissing to the start and finish. The guard tells me where to sit and points me in the direction.

Finally, I see her. She sits in a row of plastic chairs along the wall and watches as I walk toward her from across the brightly lit room. My eyes lock with hers and memories flash of better times. I remember crowds parting as she held my arm while we walked through Las Vegas casinos; I remember drinking champagne and eating chocolate truffles with her at a dessert bar overlooking Central Park; I remember powering through deep blue, rolling waves of the Atlantic on my ocean racer, with her in a sequined string bikini, clinging to me. Those days are gone, never to return. I have repressed thoughts of Lisa's seductiveness, her magnetic sex appeal, but as I walk closer to her those feelings surge, inflaming all of my senses.

The year has taken its toll on me. With the total absence of a woman's touch, of affection, of physical warmth and release, an enormous urge rises in me. I'm oblivious to the hundreds of other people visiting in the room. It's as if I'm seeing Lisa in an airport terminal for the first time after a long trip abroad. Only she's not here to welcome me home. When she stands I want to devour her. Since we have just this one opportunity, I manage with a deliciously long, marvelous kiss.

"I still love you, Michael," Lisa says, holding me before we sit.

"And I love you," I respond while pulling her close. "We're made to love each other. I've told you that from the beginning. Our love is strong enough to carry us through anything, even imprisonment." I'm eager to say anything and everything that comes to mind with desperate hopes of holding on to her.

We sit side-by-side, as close as the stationary, hard plastic chairs will allow. We're close enough that I feel the soft skin of her arms touching mine, close enough that I can breathe in her perfume. The romantic euphoria of our first hour together doesn't last, however, as we can't avoid discussing the ugliness that has become our lives.

"How is it in here, really? Are you safe?"

"I told you, you don't have to worry about me. As long as we're together, I'm okay. My dad sent the money to the university, so I should receive my books and lesson plans soon. I've got a great job in the library. I'm exercising every day. I've got plenty of books to read. You're going to see how I turn this mess around. I'm going to leave here so much better than I am now, stronger and wiser. I'm going to make you proud."

"But what about me? What do you think is going to happen at my sentencing–and after? I can't live in a place like this!"

"Honey, nothing's going to happen." I comb my fingers through her blonde hair. "You didn't do anything that bad. You told a little lie about money. What's the big deal? The judge isn't going to put you in prison for that. People lie all the time. Every time someone gets pulled over for speeding, he lies about driving the speed limit. They don't put people in prison for that."

"But what if they do? What's going to happen then?" She grips her fingers into my hands. "I don't want to live in a place like this."

"It's not going to happen," I soothe. "Why don't you pray with me? When I pray, God gives me strength."

"Come on, don't start with that! What are you doing? Becoming a priest in here? Prayer isn't going to help me!" Lisa abruptly lets go of me and folds her arms across her chest in frustration.

"Yes it will, it helps me through every day."

"You got 45 years! Did prayers help with that?"

"Baby, don't talk like that. You have to trust in me, trust in God. It's going to get better."

"Sometimes I don't think I know you anymore. All you talk about is school, God, about how it's going to be better when you get out. Don't you get it? We're going to be old by then!"

"It's not going to be that long." I sit back in my chair, swallowing the harshness of her assessment.

"What about me? How am I supposed to live? Our money is running out."

"Why don't you get a job?"

"Doing what? What can I do? You want me to wait tables or something?"

"Don't worry, Baby. Let's get through your sentencing next week and put this mess behind us. I'll think of something."

Our visit may have begun with passion, but it ends with the cold reality that we don't have enough of anything to sustain us. We don't have enough money, enough maturity, or enough commitment. When visiting hours end she stands and we hold each other, but I know she's not coming back. Our parting kiss tastes like good-bye. As she walks away I'm more alone than I've ever been.

The following week Lisa is sentenced. After the scheduled time of her hearing I call my father, who accompanied her to lend support. He tells me that the judge sentenced her to serve five years on probation for her felony conviction of lying to a federal officer. I'm relieved. Thinking of Lisa enduring the handcuffs, the chains, the regular strip searches, orders, and daily indignities of confinement would have crushed me. I can handle prison, but I wasn't sure she could have, and if she were put inside my level of stress would've risen exponentially. At least I have that complication behind me. Now it's on to new challenges and complications that I expect to flow over the next 10,000 days.

* * * * * * *

Since the library is an open space where all prisoners can congregate freely, it serves as a kind of marketplace for hustlers and prisoners use it for more than checking out books or typing. They exploit it to hide weapons, drugs, and other contraband that they conceal in the drop ceiling or inside books they hollow out. Guards seize contraband they find, but since the library is a common area they can't punish an individual without further information, like a tip from a snitch.

I'll never become a source of such information, as I won't try to make my life easier at the expense of making someone else's life harder. Blood spills inside these walls. I'll survive by making decisions that ensure I don't have to hide from anybody and that no one has to hide from me. I want to live invisibly, to be "in" the penitentiary, but not "of" the penitentiary. I focus intensely on steps I can take that will lead me closer to home, that will prepare me for a productive life outside.

My own research and the inquiries I make of other prisoners convince me that only two mechanisms exist through which I can earn my way out. One is to ask my judge to reconsider my sentence using the formal legal proceeding known as the Rule 35 motion, but the strict time parameters of that rule limit me. Once the appeals court affirms my conviction and sentence–as I'm sure it will–the 120-day clock starts ticking. After that time elapses, my sentence becomes etched in stone. The only other mechanism, barring future legislative reform, is asking the president to grant relief through executive clemency.

The Ninth Circuit Court of Appeals will affirm my conviction and sentence within a year. What can I possibly accomplish in another year of imprisonment to persuade my sentencing judge that I'm a worthy candidate for relief, that I've earned freedom? It's not enough time and yet I've got to make something happen. Every minute that passes without my having a plan or making progress means that I'm losing ground. I feel like I'm a cartoon character, lying on a table with a swinging, spinning saw blade gradually dropping from the ceiling toward my exposed and extended neck.

Improving my situation will require support from people outside. Yet 40-foot walls hinder my ability to connect with society, frustrating me. I stare at library walls wondering how to distinguish myself from every other prisoner who wants a sentence reduction. I can't simply express sorrow or regret. I am deeply remorseful, though I understand the cynicism of the system. When I file my Rule 35, I'm expecting prosecutors to argue persuasively that I'm not at all remorseful but only want out.

I wrestle with the opposition I expect to face. Why do others think it so wrong that I want to advance my release date? I want out, but I also want to atone, to somehow reconcile with society. I aspire to show others that I'm earning my freedom. As I stare blankly at the books all around me I suddenly see the solution that will help me pierce these walls and connect with society: I'll write a book!

I may not know what I'm doing but the fact that I'm doing something, making progress, empowers me. For the first time I'm not sitting around waiting for outside forces to dictate my fate. Instead, I have a plan and that brings new energy, motivation, and inspiration. I'll write about how the romantic, swashbuckling images I had of coke traffickers seduced me into the trade. Reading my story will provide compelling reasons for others to avoid making the same choices. I'll express remorse openly and perhaps other young people will be dissuaded from breaking the law. The book should assist law enforcement by helping stop crime before it starts.

I've never taken a writing course or even written anything more substantial than short letters, but if I begin now and work on it every day, I can finish a book in time to generate support for my Rule 35. This project becomes my Hail Mary effort to begin a record of atonement.

Julie and her fiancé, Tim, are my strongest supporters. I write her and they agree to launch a nonprofit corporation to publish the book, which I title *Drugs and Money*. That way instead of selling the book we can donate it. A funding arm from the State of Washington offers financial resources for programs designed to improve community safety, and I write a grant proposal to fund our project. Julie submits the grant proposal through the nonprofit, and then she persuades those on the board of the grant committee to fund production of *Drugs and Money* with $20,000. It's a sufficient amount of funds to produce and distribute 2,000 books to schools, jails, and other organizations for at-risk adolescents. This community-service effort helps me reach beyond the penitentiary, build support, and begin making a contribution to society.

* * * * * * *

I hear my name being paged over the loudspeaker with an order to report to the Education building. I sit down at the desk where I write each day, and Mr. Chandler, the Supervisor of Education, approaches.

"Sanchez, why am I getting a package from Ohio University with your name all over it?" He is not happy.

I look up, surprised that he's upset and wondering what I did wrong. "I enrolled in a correspondence program, sir," I respond, not wanting to aggravate him further by correcting his mispronunciation of my name. "I wanted to study toward a college degree."

"Boy, don't you know I got half a mind to lock you up? Ain't no courses get ordered 'round here less they go through me. Who authorized you to enroll in college?"

"I didn't know I needed to have authorization."

"Don't you knows you's in the peniten'try! You better axe somebody! Can't be havin' no packages sent in here without auth'rization. Interferes with security of the institution."

"Sorry, sir. I didn't know that a package from a university could interfere with security. But I won't make that mistake again."

Mr. Chandler softens some with my contrite response. "What you doin' in here all day anyway boy?" He spreads the pages of longhand on my desk.

"Writing, sir, just trying to stay out of trouble."

"Well you 'bout found trouble, and you're lookin' at it. Now come on back to my office and get these here books 'fore I send 'em back and lock yo ass in da hole."

I stand and follow him down the center corridor, giddy as a boy on Christmas morning, ecstatic that my course work has arrived. I don't know why he was so angry, but it doesn't really matter now that he's agreed to allow me to proceed. When we enter his office I see the box from Ohio University open on his desk.

"This ain't nothin' but a lot 'a extra work for me."

"Thanks for helping, sir. I apologize for causing so much trouble."

He opens each book, inspects the binding, fans through the pages, then he passes the book over to me. I have courses in English, philosophy, algebra, and psychology. I thank Mr. Chandler again and return to the desk where I can begin to work with a new sense of purpose.

In my mind I'm no longer a prisoner. I'm 24 years old, about to endure my second holiday season in confinement, but I'm also on track for making real, measurable progress. I'm now a university student and an aspiring author. Others will soon have tangible results to gauge my commitment to atone.

* * * * * * *

It's 1988 and Vice-President George H.W. Bush is about to become America's 41st president. He talks about a thousand points of light and inspires me with his call for a kinder, gentler America. Yes! More compassion and understanding is exactly what I need, and I'm working feverishly to prove worthy of reconsideration.

With each passing month I feel the pressure. But I like having a reason to push through each day. My studies and writing goals necessitate a strict schedule and I train myself to function on less sleep. The cellblock rocks with constant noise and ceaseless disturbances, but with clearly defined goals I block out all distractions and become more skillful at carving out niches of time and space to study.

The tight schedule helps immensely, especially as my connection to Lisa becomes more and more tenuous. I'm proud of what I'm producing and for Christmas I send her copies of the assignments I'm completing. I also share the progress with my manuscript and I include photographs of the physique I'm building through strenuous weightlifting.

She's not interested.

When I write her to announce news of the grant Julie received to produce and distribute *Drugs and Money*, she asks how much money I'll be able to send her from those proceeds.

"Baby, I'm not writing this book for money," I try to explain over the telephone. "I've told you the plan. I'm working to come home. I have to build a record that shows I can contribute to the world, and that's what this book is for. We're using the money to produce it and distribute it so I can build support, so I can come home."

"I'm your wife, Michael. It costs money to live, and you didn't leave me with enough to be giving books away."

"I know, Honey. Listen, I thought you were going to find a job. Why don't you sell clothes? There's got to be some way for you to earn an income. You've got to support yourself until I

104

come home."

"When? In 25 years? Michael, this isn't working."

"Don't say that! We're married. Of course we can make it work. And it isn't going to be 25 years. That's ridiculous. The judge isn't going to let this sentence stand, not with all I'm doing. I'll be home in like eight years, maybe less." I feel her slipping away. "When are you coming to see me?"

"I told you already. My probation officer won't let me visit you."

"But for how long? How long until she lets you come visit me?"

"Five years, Michael! She told me that I'd never be able to visit you while I'm on probation and that I should divorce you."

"That's going to change. They can't keep us apart like this. We're married. You still love me, don't you?"

This is ending badly. I sense where it's heading, even though I'm trying to pull affection that should flow freely. To cope, I work harder.

* * * * * * *

It's early 1989 and I've turned 25. The time pressure intensifies every day, requiring that I deny myself sleep and activities that others rely upon as distractions from the pains of imprisonment. Table games won't carry me through.

When I read that President Bush is going to deliver his first prime-time news conference from the Oval Office I walk to a television room and watch the broadcast from the back of the auditorium.

The president looks dour. While seated in his high-backed chair behind his executive desk, President Bush holds up a clear plastic bag filled with cocaine. My spirits sink when I hear him tell millions of viewers that the War on Drugs is of paramount importance. Illicit drug abuse, he warns, threatens America as we know it.

Apparently the kinder, gentler America the president spoke about doesn't include compassion for prisoners–especially those who sold drugs. His message suggests Americans need an object to hate. The object of that hatred is drugs and everyone who has anything to do with them. He calls for vigilance, urges children to turn in their parents and announces that under his administration American law enforcement will have zero tolerance for drugs. He appoints William Bennett as a "drug czar," whatever that means.

As I lie on my rack, blocking out the noise that ricochets through the concrete and steel cellblock, I consider what our new president said. He actually clarifies the enormity of my challenge. I'm a convicted drug offender with a long sentence. As much as I want to earn support from my fellow citizens, from the prosecutor, and from my judge–the president has just told people in society that I'm not worthy of consideration. They shouldn't look beyond my conviction and sentence. I have to face the truth that others may never accept the efforts I'm making to atone. Zero tolerance. That's what President Bush calls for.

* * * * * * *

I wake with determination to work harder. Another prisoner tells me about a job in the prison factory's business office that may make it easier to write.

"It's a clerical job," the prisoner says. "If you get it, you'd have your own desk and access to a computer."

"Would they let me type my school assignments on the computer?"

"How the fuck should I know? Go fuckin' check it out for yourself."

Mr. Chandler signs my pass and I walk across the compound toward the business office. A morning controlled movement is in progress and a line of men wait their turn to pass through a metal detector. A prisoner in front of me walks through and the machine starts beeping.

"Take 'em off," the guard orders.

"Come on boss, you knows I done got steel-toe boots on. That's all that's settin' your joint off."

"Then it shouldn't be a problem. Now take 'em off and walk through again. Else you can strip down. Makes no difference to me."

The guard won't allow anyone to go through until he

clears the man in front of me. I rarely leave the library because of this obsession with security. But the prospect of a new job that would provide access to a word processor and my own desk makes the inconvenience bearable today.

When it's my turn I clear the metal detector without interference. I walk through two more sets of gates and I ride the elevator to the business office. The atmosphere differs from any other place I've been in the penitentiary. Instead of concrete and steel there are plasterboard walls, wooden doors with moldings, and carpeted floors soften the large, open room. Desks align neatly in aisles and rows. Prisoners wearing crisply pressed khakis sit behind them, absorbed in their work. Each desk has its own computer monitor and keyboard. I hear the buzzing of business machines, copiers, printers, and adding machines.

Yearning for my unrecoverable past, I walk through the open area toward the smaller offices in the back. I see the door marked "Transportation" and I knock. A woman looks up from her desk and greets me with a friendly smile.

"Good morning. My name is Michael Santos." I present her with my pass from Mr. Chandler. "I was told of a job opening for a clerk in the Transportation office. I'd like to apply."

"How much time do you have? Thirty years I hope."

"I have 45 years, Ma'am."

"Oh," she flinches. "I'm sorry, I didn't mean that. I was only asking because training a clerk takes a lot of time and I didn't want one of these short timers about to transfer out."

"That's okay. I'm enrolled in college and I expect that I'll be here for a long time."

"Have you ever worked in an office before?"

"Yes Ma'am. My father owned a contracting company and I worked in his offices."

"So you can type?"

"I type very well, at least 50 words per minute."

"Where do you work now?"

"I work in the library. Mr. Chandler is my supervisor."

"How's your disciplinary record? Do you have any shots? Ever go to the SHU?"

"No Ma'am, my disciplinary record is clear. I keep to

myself, stay out of trouble."

"Why are you in prison?"

"I sold cocaine." I say, knowing that I'll be answering this question for the rest of my life.

"And you got 45 years for that?"

"Yes Ma'am."

"Have you ever been in prison before?"

"This is my first time, and my last."

She nods her head, and for the first time since I've been in prison I feel genuine compassion from a staff member. "My name is Lynn Stephens. Watch the call-out for the job change. You've got the job." She smiles, and for that instant I'm a person rather than a prisoner.

As I return to the library I realize that I forgot to ask Ms. Stephens about time for schoolwork and whether I could use the word processor to type my assignments once I completed my office responsibilities. It doesn't matter. I'll find a way to make things work. The office environment cleansed away the filth of imprisonment and I want to spend my time there, in the company of Ms. Stephens. I sense it's the right place for me, away from gangs, confrontations, and cellblock pressures; away from the continuous hustling and scheming that take place in the library and other common spaces.

* * * * * * *

When the cell gates open at 6:00 a.m. I rush to the gym for my morning workout. A quick cross-training workout allows me to fit all my exercises in before 7:00. Then I return to the cellblock, shower, shave, and dress in my pressed khakis. Optimistic about my new job, I bring an envelope with photographs in case there's an opportunity to share pictures of my family with Ms. Stephens–I want her to know that I have a life outside of these walls.

"Good morning," she greets me when I walk in. Strangely, I'm a bit uneasy being in close proximity to a woman. The office we share is small, the size of a bedroom in a suburban house. Her desk sits immediately to the right of the door in the office's front corner. As her clerk I'll sit inside a U-shaped workstation in the back, diagonally across from her. Five paces separate us. I'm conscious of her perfume and try to keep my knees from bouncing beneath the desk.

"What we do here is coordinate all the paperwork for shipments that leave the factory," Ms. Stephens explains, describing my duties. "Each day the factory manager will send us a sheet with the number and type of mailbags that are ready for processing out. From that sheet you'll type these forms we call the shippers and make five copies of the documents for distribution to billing, quality control, the postal service, the shipping company, the factory, and our records.

I handle the sample of documents that she provides and know that I'm capable of keeping this busywork in order. "How many orders do we receive each day?"

"It's more like 15 each week. On some days you'll receive one or two orders; other days you may not receive any at all. Then you may receive four, five, or six all at once. It might take you a few weeks to get used to the system but you'll get the hang of it. As long as you stay on top of it and don't let the work pile up, you'll be fine."

"What am I supposed to do when I'm caught up? It doesn't sound like these duties will require more than a couple hours a day, if that."

"Let's just see how it goes. We've always got files to organize, envelopes to stuff, and copies to make. If you'd like to listen to the radio, tune into any station you'd like."

I catch on quickly to my duties: typing, copying, distributing, and filing. The small radio behind me only picks up the AM band. As I flip through the stations I settle in on talk radio, and I listen to an audacious political commentator named Rush Limbaugh. The show is gaining national popularity, I've read. Magazine articles describe Limbaugh as a self-indulgent, obese, college dropout who dumped his marriage but represents himself as a social conservative. Despite the hypocrisy between his personal life and his public life, he makes me laugh.

* * * * * * *

Lisa isn't responding to the daily letters I've been writing, and every time I'm finally able to call her, I walk away frustrated because she doesn't answer. It's been more than two weeks since I've heard from her. Premonitions chip away at me. I hurt from the emptiness and loneliness disturbs my sleep.

The prison's automated phone system only allows collect calls. A major drawback is that once I dial I can't hear what's happening on the other end of the line until someone pushes a digit to accept. When I dial Lisa's number I don't know whether the line is busy, no one is home, or the call simply doesn't go through.

I wonder what's going on, why she doesn't write, and where she is. I ache to tell her about my new job, about my progress with school, about the manuscript I'm writing, and about how much I miss her. I want to know about her life, how her job search is going. She must've found a job. She's probably working at the times that I call, but I wonder why she doesn't respond to my letters. I dream of the softness of her lips, but nightmares haunt me with images of her kissing someone else.

* * * * * * *

"Hey! How come you haven't been calling me? I've been worried about you." It's Julie, cheering me up with her loving enthusiasm when she accepts my call.

"I'm sorry. It's not so easy to use the phone here. I have to wait in long lines and I'm only able to dial one number once my turn comes up. Have you been getting the letters I've sent?"

"I'm so proud of you! You're doing great in there, with your schoolwork and the writing. I'm glad you've got a job you like."

"Everything's okay, but I haven't been able to talk with Lisa and I'm worried. Has she called you?"

"She wouldn't call me, you know that. Do you want me to patch you through on a three-way?"

"Would you? When I call her number I'm not getting through at all. I can't leave a message or anything."

"What's her phone number?"

I give Julie the number and wait for her to dial. She patches into the call when Lisa's phone starts ringing.

"I'm just going to wait until she answers. Then I'll put the phone down and you can talk as long as you want."

"Thanks, Julie. I appreciate your help."

My heart pounds and I bounce between excitement to

110

hear my wife's voice and apprehension over what she might tell me. But it's not Lisa who answers. It's a man's voice that picks up.

"I'm sorry," I say. "I must've dialed the wrong number."

"What's the number again?" Julie asks, after disconnecting the unknown party.

I give her Lisa's number a second time. "That's the number I thought I dialed. Let me try again."

The phone rings and I hear the same voice answer. "Who's this?" I ask.

"Who's this?" The man doesn't answer my question.

"This is Michael Santos. I'm calling for my wife, Lisa."

"Oh. Well, Lisa's not here. I'm Lisa's boyfriend and I live here now. Sorry to tell you this, but it's probably best if you don't call back. She isn't ready to talk with you."

I'm humiliated that this is the way I learn my marriage is over, and that my sister hears it along with me. Speechless, I hang up the phone, not even taking the time to thank Julie for making the call.

Blindly, I press through crowds of prisoners and find my way to the stairs, not caring who I push aside in my grief–a knife in the gut would be a welcome reprieve from the pain twisting through my heart.

Somehow I find my cell and fall onto my rack, smothering my face in my pillow. With the spirit of perseverance abandoning me, I squeeze my eyes shut to keep tears from falling. Everything inside of me feels broken. I hear my pulse pounding in my ears, feel it throbbing in my head. I'm having a hard time acknowledging that she's gone, that I've lost her. It's like a painful vise squeezing tighter and tighter, suffocating me and bringing doubts on whether I can climb through 24 more years of this pain.

Sleep doesn't restore my confidence. I crawl off my rack and sit on the metal chair to lace my dirty sneakers. Consumed with sadness, I walk down the stairs and pace, wondering why I should go on. I'm not able to summon the will or a reason to live. Lisa and I may've been growing apart, but at least I had the illusion of love. That's been shattered and I don't know what I'll do in here for decades.

I walk to the library, numb to everything but my pain, seeking solace from the stories of others who suffered. I search for books about Viktor Frankl, Elie Weisel, and other innocent people who confronted horrific adversity in concentration camps like Auschwitz and Buchenwald. I need to immerse myself in their stories. Although I've hit bottom, the inspiring literature of Jewish survival and courage shines a light down my psychological well, beginning to ease the tightness in my chest.

* * * * * * *

When I call home on May 27, 1989, I hear the news from Julie that Christina has given birth to a daughter, Isabella. I've known of Christina's pregnancy for some time, but I've been too wrapped up in dealing with the loss of Lisa and the challenges of my prison adjustment to grasp what that means. It's surreal to think of my younger sister as a mother, and to think of myself as an uncle.

Christina and I grew up very close as children. I have fond memories from our grade school years, and of bringing her fishing with me in a neighborhood stream. But I haven't seen her since my imprisonment. Now she's a mother, and trying to imagine her as a grown woman with a family of her own feels almost incomprehensible. Life is changing without my being a part of it. I hang up in tears, unable to suppress my mix of emotions. I'm happy for Christina, but also filled with sadness because I've missed Isabella's birth.

I need to walk around the track but that means waiting in line for a pass, then waiting in the crowd for the next scheduled movement to leave the housing unit. Instead, I head for my cell. There isn't anywhere I can console the ache I feel inside privately. As I lie on my rack with my head pressed into the pillow I can still hear Check and his buddy playing chess at the table. Dropping into self-pity, all I can think about is the isolation from my family. I'm a stranger, isolated from the family bonds that make life worth living.

How will society view me? If I were a free citizen today and encountered a man who had served more than a quarter of a century in prison, I'd have major preconceptions about him. I'd feel reluctant to accept him as a neighbor, a colleague, and certainly as a peer. Women, I expect, will think twice before dating a man who served time in prison. And if I'm not released until my late 40s, without a work history, savings, and a home, there's a strong likelihood that I'll never become a father and have children of my own. How could I?

It's too much. I have to break this up in my mind, take it in smaller increments, one chunk at a time. Otherwise it overwhelms and defeats me.

Where will I be in 10 years? That's what I should think about. What is the best I can become during the first decade of my imprisonment? My studies are going well and I've nearly completed the manuscript for *Drugs and Money*. I don't know what will happen with the Rule 35 motion once the time comes to submit the request for reconsideration of my sentence. But in 1997, after a decade in prison, if I stick to this plan I'll be an educated man. If I keep my focus I'll have a university degree and possibly a law degree. Those credentials will distinguish me from prisoners who thrive on hate and who rely upon weapons and gangs to empower themselves.

Still, I live amidst the weapons, the gangs, and the power struggles within my community of felons. With two years behind me I understand the politics of race, geographical origin, and anarchy. On the surface it looks as if whites mix with whites, blacks with blacks, and Hispanics with Hispanics. But that isn't the real story, as this culture is driven by influences that are far more complex.

I live in a society of deprivation, where policies extinguish hope. With years to serve, abandoned by their families, and severed of their previous identities, most prisoners give up trying to improve themselves. Instead, they ripen for rebellion. They form an anti-society culture with its own underground economy, values, and social structure. Mafia dons and gang leaders hold the top spots with snitches and child molesters at the bottom. Disruptive factions form and either scheme together or battle each other for power. In this society, where prisoners kill without remorse in an effort to increase their share of prison wealth and to protect their territory, my efforts to avoid 'prisonization' make me vulnerable. I can't outrun them but, by existing under their radar, I can evade them. I'm captain of my own metaphorical submarine, gliding stealthily beneath the waves and currents. My periscope is up but my strategy is to remain invisible, deep below the turmoil. It's working.

By waking at 5:00 a.m., when the other men in my cell are still asleep, I can use the toilet and wash in privacy. I use a small book light to read until 6:00, when a guard walks down the tier unlocking the gates. I'm first out of the cell and one of the few avoiding the chow hall to take advantage of early exercise. By 7:30 I'm at work, which is a reprieve from the tensions of the cellblock and yard.

My supervisor, Ms. Stephens encourages my academic pursuits. She authorizes me to study and type my assignments once I complete my daily work. When I leave the business office I report to the prison's hospital as a volunteer. Prisoners deemed at risk for harming themselves are kept under 24-hour surveillance, and I'm one of those on watch. This schedule allows me to avoid the other prisoners and to study. When I return to the cellblock at midnight the prison is quiet. I shower, climb to my rack above Check, and I sleep soundly for five hours. It's a routine I want to keep for the incomprehensible 24 years that I've still got to serve.

The pockets of solitude I've carved out give me peace, and I've become extremely productive. I'm on a tight schedule, always racing to exceed my expectations. I've completed my first quarter with Ohio University and I've enrolled in another full load of courses for the second quarter.

Besides taking correspondence classes through Ohio University, Mercer University has begun offering courses inside USP Atlanta, and I'm now enrolled as a full-time student in its program. One of the professors from Mercer, Colin Harris, takes time to mentor me. I'm busy, working hard to prove worthy of the trust placed in me. According to the timeline I've laid out, I should earn my undergraduate degree in 1992, and I intend to earn it with honors.

* * * * * * *

"Guess who I ran into at Safeway?" Julie asks in a carefully measured tone.

"Who?"

"Judy Murphy." She mentions the mother of one of my high school friends.

"Oh, how's Sean?"

My sister hesitates and then tells me that Sean died of leukemia.

It's tough news for me to take, as I liked and admired Sean. I ask my sister when he died.

"Just a few months ago. It struck him without warning. He was studying engineering at the University of Washington. He died during surgery."

When Julie hangs up I return to my cell and think about Sean. He was a friend of mine since junior high school. With the news of his death, I sit and think more about what I'm doing here. I face the wall in my cell, unable to muffle the hollering, laughing, and slamming of dominos on steel cellblock tables. Bad news from beyond prison walls keeps coming, and it will keep coming, and I must learn to accept it alone.

Sean and I hadn't spoken since high school graduation. He lived responsibly, a student-athlete, disciplined and respectful of others while I was living recklessly. I remember our friendship as kids and as teammates in football and baseball. It's hard for me to believe that I'm now in prison and his life has ended. Many more lives will end while I serve this sentence, maybe even my own.

I rest a pad on my knee so I can write to his parents, expressing my sympathy. Then I pledge that memories of Sean will inspire me to make better use of my life, to use every day working to become a better person. I don't know how Sean's parents will respond to my letter but I feel compelled to write it. For some reason, news of his death piles on more guilt. It brings feelings of nostalgia for high school, those earlier days before I thought of selling cocaine. I regret decisions I made and feel a colossal disappointment in what I've made of my life.

* * * * * * *

I want to reach beyond these walls and my chance arrives when Julie receives the grant money for printing 2,000 copies of *Drugs and Money*. She makes the trip from Seattle to visit me so we can plan our strategy to distribute the books.

"You've grown so much," Julie cries as we hug for the first time since my arrest, almost three years before.

"I told you I've been exercising every morning since I got here. Check this out." I flex my arms, showing off.

She admires my fitness but then looks around, disoriented with the prison experience. "What did that guy do to get in here?"

"Come on, let's not waste our time talking about anyone else. He probably sold drugs, like everyone else. I told you I'm a loner in here, I keep to myself."

"I can't believe you don't have any friends. How can you spend all your time alone?"

"I'm okay. I talk to a few guys from class, but life is different for me. I'm so busy with school that I can't take time for television, movies, or any of the craziness that goes on around here." I tell my sister about the hustle of brewing alcohol with fruit, sugar, and yeast, and how some prisoners pass through the monotony of confinement in a drunken stupor. "Others are into gangs, gambling, and drugs. I feel safest and most productive by sticking to myself."

"How do prisoners get drugs in here?" Despite my efforts to talk about the book, my sister persists in asking me about prison life.

"Through visits I guess, and some corrupt guards mule them in. I stay away from everything. That's one of the reasons I keep such a busy schedule, to avoid trouble."

While sitting across the table from my sister, I don't feel any shame at all. It isn't the same when my mother or father visits me. With them I feel empty inside and embarrassed that they see me in a place like this. Both my mom and dad want to hold my hand, pat my head, or assure me with words that things are going to turn out fine. But they're afraid for me. Their nervous gestures bring out my guilt from having put them through such misery. I've asked them to leave visits early, feigning exhaustion. In truth, sadness overwhelms me and all I want to do is disappear.

With Julie, on the other hand, I grin and laugh, happy to listen as she tells me about our younger sister, Christina, our parents, our niece, and her own engagement to Tim. Life continues regardless of my ordeal. I look at the clock, conscious that the minutes move so quickly, and wish the visit wouldn't end. With hundreds of other prisoners' family members visiting, it's loud in the room. We're eating sandwiches from vending machines and drinking sodas. Life feels almost normal. Even though she periodically breaks into tears, I'm not in prison when I'm with Julie. She's so sweet, telling me that she'd switch places with me if she could.

We talk about the many ways we're going to leverage all of the relationships we have in Seattle to attract media attention for the book. Drugs are becoming a bigger issue in society with President Bush's zero-tolerance programs and I feel strongly that the book I wrote could contribute to the solution. Through a story describing what happened to my friends and me, the book sends a message regarding the tragic consequences that follow drug trafficking.

Although I face considerable restrictions in promoting the book, Julie is free to speak on my behalf. She returns to Seattle and begins contacting jails, schools, and other institutions where the message in *Drugs and Money* can add value. With books to donate, Julie contacts local talk radio programs to promote the book and to secure invitations for me to participate in telephone interviews.

Conscious of the reprimand Mr. Chandler gave me for enrolling in college without first seeking his permission, I ask advice from my supervisor, Ms. Stephens. I want to know which staff member can authorize me to interact with the media. She directs me to Ms. Sheffer, the Warden's Executive Assistant, and Ms. Sheffer tells me that if representatives of the media want to speak with me over the phone, then I'm within my rights to converse.

*   *   *   *   *   *   *

"I'm locking you up," a lieutenant chastises me after paging me to his office.

"Why? What did I do?"

"Listen to this." The lieutenant plays a tape recording of a portion from an interview I gave to a Seattle radio station over the telephone. "You can't be giving no interviews on the radio from my institution. Where do you think you are? This is a federal prison! You're supposed to be serving time, not writing books and talking to the media."

"But I was only talking about the reasons people shouldn't get involved with selling drugs. I'm trying to send a positive message."

"Well I'm sending you to the hole to think about your positive message. Next time you'll think twice about what you're saying over my phone system and who you're talking to."

"But I asked permission from Ms. Sheffer before I made the call. She said I could talk with the media over the phone."

The lieutenant looks at me skeptically. "What? Ms. Sheffer said that? When?"

"Three weeks ago. My work supervisor told me she was the person I needed to speak to for permission, and she said it would be fine."

"Go back to your job," the lieutenant orders. "I'll get to the bottom of this. If you're lying to me, you're gonna be sorry."

I walk back to the business office, intimidated by my encounter with the lieutenant. Since I had permission, I don't think I'm in trouble, but the lieutenant's threat about the hole shakes me. From an isolation cell I won't be able to attend my classes with Mercer University, and if I can't complete my classes, the timeline I'm working toward to graduate in 1992 falls apart. I'm frustrated that the decisions of others have so much influence on my life.

Ms. Sheffer is waiting for me when I get back to my desk. With her shoulder-length blonde hair and form fitting designer clothes, she looks more like a babe than a prison official. Despite her attractiveness and the fragrance of her perfume, she talks tough, at least to me.

"From now on, if you're going to talk with the media, you coordinate it through my office." Ms. Sheffer scolds me while pointing her finger at me, ruining fantasies I've had about her, the kind that keep a young man alive. My confusion quickly leads to embarrassment.

"I'm sorry. I thought you said it was okay for me to talk over the phone."

"I only said that because I didn't think a member of the

media would accept your phone calls. It was my mistake, that's why you're not in the hole. But let's be clear, from now on you need to coordinate all media communications through my office."

When Ms. Sheffer walks out I'm left alone in the office with my supervisor. "You're really rocking the boat around here."

"I don't mean to. I'm just trying to build support outside."

Ms. Stephens shakes her head in doubt. "When you started here you said you wanted to keep a low profile, to stay out of trouble. Writing books and talking on the radio puts you on the front line, not exactly low profile."

"I meant I wanted to keep a low profile in prison. I still have to try and build support outside. I can't just give up, you know, I've got to try to make something more of my life than this."

"I just hope you know what you're doing. Most inmates want to avoid attention, but you're bringing the spotlight right to you. If you do anything wrong, all this attention is going to backfire."

Ms. Stephens makes clear that she thinks it would be best to focus on school and forget about media contacts. "Just remember," she chills me with an admonishment, "I can't protect you if the lieutenant decides to lock you up for an investigation."

Ms. Stephens means well. I know she cares for me, but she is a part of the system, and she knows a lieutenant can easily lock a prisoner away in a disciplinary cell for months at a time. If that should happen to me I wouldn't have access to school, to telephone calls, to exercise. She doesn't want me locked in a box. What Ms. Stephens doesn't understand is that I am locked in a box.

* * * * * * *

When a guard passes an envelope through the bars of my cell I'm surprised to see a woman's penmanship. The letter is from Susan, a girl I know from high school. She dated my close friend Rich, and her letter expresses support, telling me that she heard me speaking on a local radio interview.

I read Susan's letter a hundred times. The letter isn't suggestive, or with any romantic innuendo, but it's the only letter I've received from a woman since Lisa dumped me six months ago. I like holding the paper that left Susan's hands, wanting this connection to last. It makes me wonder how many years will pass before I kiss a woman again.

I write Susan a lengthy letter, telling her all about my schoolwork, my routine in prison, and the challenges I face in promoting my book. Although a romance is probably too much to hope for, I make it clear to her that I value her correspondence. I'm lonely, longing for ties to anyone beyond prison walls, especially a woman.

* * * * * * *

The next letter I receive isn't from Susan and it isn't nearly as pleasant. It is from my attorney, Justin, who informs me that the Court of Appeals has affirmed my conviction. The court's decision doesn't surprise me, but I've been hoping that the court wouldn't issue its ruling for another year, or better yet, not until I expected to earn my degree in 1992. Yet my hopes don't matter. It's 1990 and I know what this appellate decision means. The clock on the 120-day time limit for the Rule 35 has begun to tick.

I write the judicial motion for the Rule 35 from my desk at work. Through the request for my judge to reconsider the sentence he imposed I express remorse for the crimes I committed and accept that I will serve several years in prison as a consequence of my convictions. Yet I implore the judge to reserve his final judgment of me, explaining that I'm working to educate myself, to contribute to society, and to build a record that will demonstrate my commitment to atone and to prepare for a law-abiding life. As an offer of proof I include copies of my university transcripts, my stellar progress reports from prison administrators, copies of *Drugs and Money*, press clippings, and letters of appreciation that my work has already generated. The entire package fits in a large envelope and I submit it to the court without assistance from counsel.

I don't have to wait long before I receive the government's response to my motion. When I open the envelope my heart sinks as I read the prosecutor's passionate argument for the judge to let my sentence stand. He closes the three-page rebuttal with a sentiment so powerful in its denunciation of me as an individual, a fellow human being, that it takes all the wind out of me.

If Michael Santos served every day of his life in an all-consuming effort to repay society, and if he lived to be 300 years old, our community would still be at a significant net loss.

I read the prosecutor's response over and over. It eats at me, wakes me from sleep at night. He prepared the case against me for trial. He knows that I've never had a weapon and that I don't have a history or proclivity for violence. Here, in the prison, I live in the midst of dangerous men who truly threaten society, yet they serve sentences that are a fraction in length compared to mine. I don't understand why the prosecutor is so vehement in opposing my relief, or why his response drips with such venom. I'm sinking again, needing to tap into some type of inner strength before I sink back down into the abyss.

When the guard slides the next envelope–from the district court, my judge's chambers–through the bars of my cell, I need to lie down. It comes on Friday. Judge Tanner didn't require much time to dismiss my motion. He agrees with the prosecutor, and with his ruling, the sentence I serve is now final.

Chapter Four: 1990-1992
Months 37-57

Contractors complete the remodel of B cellblock and I join the 600 prisoners who were confined with me in A cellblock for our relocation. It's not far from the old housing block to the new one, just across the polished corridor. I climb the zigzagging metal staircase to the top unit, B-3 carrying all of my possessions. I have sneakers, t-shirts, sweats, khakis and toiletries bundled up and tied inside my blankets and sheets that I carry over my shoulder, like a hobo. The move lifts my spirits. It's a fresh start in a clean, new environment. Although I'm still in the same prison, the remodel replaces the hundred-year-old decaying building with modern plumbing, working lights, and air conditioning. The remodeled B cellblock brings an upgraded quality of life, much better than I've known for several years, and I'm learning to appreciate these incremental improvements.

In place of the old-style cages, the new housing unit features a different design. Solid steel doors enclose rooms, side-by-side, along the outer walls of the building. Community areas include an open rectangular area the size of a basketball court that prisoners call "the flats," located in the center, and a second-tier, mezzanine level. I smell freshly painted walls, but with costs and utility in mind, the builders left the bare concrete floors unfinished. Six single-stall showers at the far end of the unit offer an illusion of privacy. An annoying fire alarm blasts repeatedly, suggesting that contractors still haven't finished their work. Even so, I already like B cellblock better, which is good because I expect to remain here for several more years.

Prison counselors may have additional duties but, from a prisoner's point of view, their scope of responsibility is limited primarily to assigning work details, approving visiting lists, and assigning living quarters. I don't expect any counseling on how to cope with the inevitability of living for multiple decades in prison. I have to adjust on my own, and from the counselor's list,

I see that my next adjustment will take place in cell 616, on the top tier. I'm assigned to share that cell with a man in his late 30s who goes by the nickname Windward. The proper term is "room" rather than cell, as it has the steel door instead of bars. But since we're locked in, it's still a cell to me.

Windward is a native of Georgia and his speech has that slow southern twang, peppered with lots of "y'all's," that I've become familiar with over the past two years. Windward likes to say he is American by birth but Southern by the grace of God. He takes pride in his appearance, wearing his hair in a mullet–long in the back, feathered on top, and cut short above the ears–with long, sloping sideburns that he calls the "Georgia slant." His mustache curves down around his mouth, and he has a habit of twirling the long ends with his fingers when he talks.

Windward served a previous prison term for drug trafficking in a Georgia State prison. With that criminal conviction on his record he couldn't find a job, so he reverted to smuggling drugs. The Coast Guard intercepted his boat–which was loaded with 300 kilograms of cocaine–as he cruised through a channel somewhere in the Caribbean known as the Windward Passage. He pleaded guilty to an importation charge and his judge imposed a 20-year term. The name Windward became his handle. I won't mind sharing the cell with him, as he's not dangerous, and he's entertaining with his tall tales about thousands of female conquests.

Coordinating a schedule in our two-man room is easier than it was in the larger cell I previously shared with five men in A cellblock. I continue to work in the factory business office, attend school, volunteer on suicide watch whenever possible, and exercise. Windward's schedule is more relaxed. He's a unit orderly and he works the night shift, sweeping and mopping the floors while all other prisoners in the block are locked in their cells. Except for lockdown periods, Windward and I don't crowd each other in the tightly confined space of our closet-sized room. I have time alone to think, which is how I like it. But not everyone feels the same way.

Whenever violence erupts in the penitentiary the warden orders a lockdown and the claustrophobia drives Windward stir-crazy. Sometimes the lockdowns last for a day, sometimes for weeks. Although I miss the yard, I relieve stress with pushups or running in place when I'm not working on my independent studies. We don't have enough space for both of us to be on the floor at the same time, so while I read on my rack Windward paces four steps toward the door, peers out the window, turns, paces four steps toward the bunk, turns, and repeats this pattern over and over.

"Can't you relax?" I ask him.

"I hate being cooped up in here." Windward snaps as he continues to pace.

"You know what you need? A goal. Some self-direction, something to work toward, to fill your time."

"What I need is a woman, a fifth of Jack Daniels, and an ounce of good weed."

"That's what you want," I point out, "not what you need. There's a difference."

"Damn straight, and I know what I want," he tells me. "I want a woman, some good booze, and an ounce of good weed."

"It's better to focus on something to work toward, something they can't take away or stop." I'm no longer a novice at serving time, but I haven't yet learned how to restrain myself from dispensing unsolicited advice.

"Not again with all that dime-store psychobabble bullshit," Windward waves his hand at me, swatting away my suggestion as he would an annoying fly. "I told you once and I'm tellin' you one more time. All that schoolin' ain't fixin' to help you none. A convict once, Michael, a convict forever."

"That's giving up."

"That's reality, Son. Ain't nothin' matter here but time. Y'all can read all the books you want, but in the end ain't nothin' gonna matter. I done been there. You ain't tellin' me nothin' I don't know."

Windward expresses only two possibilities for his future. Either he will seduce and marry a rich woman, or he will earn a living with drugs again after release. He thinks I'm fooling myself with my aspirations of joining society. He's convinced that a prison record extinguishes all possibility for a legitimate life. It's like an echo, this recurring message of hopelessness, reverberating throughout the penitentiary. I refuse to buy it, refuse to accept that I can't create new opportunities and new directions for my life. Every day I renew my commitment to work toward something better. I'm planting seeds, knowing that those seeds will take many years before they take root and blossom. When they do, however, they'll provide for a better life than I've known and a better life than what others tell me I can expect.

I prefer not to have contraband in the cell, but I don't live here alone. The best I can do is get a promise from Windward that if guards find his stash during a shakedown, he'll take the heat. Still, I'm not deceived about the value of such promises and I worry. He assures me that he'll never keep home-brewed wine in the cell, or drugs, but I know he conceals a plastic shank inside a hole he hollowed in his mattress that he insists is necessary for protection. I have different perceptions on how to protect myself: I stay out of people's way and I mind my own business. I can control my decisions, but I can't tell anyone else how to live and I won't go sniveling to the counselor with a request to move because I don't like what Windward keeps in the cell. I have to roll with the realities of living inside a high-security prison.

"Rolling with it," however, is stressful because of the personal commitments I've made. I constantly visualize how I'll return to the outside world, and I'm not convinced that society as a whole would agree with my prosecutor's statement that 300 years of good deeds would not suffice to atone for my two years of trafficking in cocaine. Redemption may be as elusive as the Fountain of Youth, but I'm determined to minimize my exposure to problems that can block my efforts to find it.

I'm familiar with executive clemency, a power vested in the presidency by the Constitution. With the stroke of a pen, a president can commute a federal prison term. It's rare, as presidents build legacies by signing international treaties, or pursuing world peace, not by releasing prisoners. Still, striving to build a record that proves worthy of consideration for clemency gives me a purpose, something to work toward.

"What're you gonna do, walk on egg shells through your whole sentence?" Windward taunts, laughing at my aspirations.

"Don't you get it? No one cares what you do or what happens in here."

"Maybe not. But what do I have to lose by trying? Even if the president doesn't commute my sentence, if I earn real credentials, don't you think I'll have a better shot at success when I do get out?"

"It's just no way to serve time. You'll see."

Windward is right. It's the reason I never think of myself as serving time. I'm in a hole, a pit that is deep and dark, and I'm doing what I can to build a ladder that will allow me to climb out. I don't know how long it's going to take but I know that every rung I ascend to will make a difference in my future.

That's why I pay close attention to Mark as I sit in those Mercer University classes. He's in his mid-30s with an athletic build that is suited to his chosen sport of tennis; I never see him working out on the weight pile where I exercise every morning. He doesn't have tattoos and he's one of the few prisoners in here who keeps a clean-shaven face.

Mark may sit at the small desks in the same classrooms with other prisoners and me, but his vocabulary, eloquence, and knowledge distinguish him. It doesn't matter what course we're studying, whether it's literature, history, or economics, Mark articulates his thoughts with confidence. It's obvious our studies at Mercer are not his first university experience.

"In what ways does Jane Austen use irony in *Pride and Prejudice?*" Professor Higgins asks the class, but only Mark has answers. I don't even know what "irony" means.

"Who can help us understand the connection between the *Treaty of Versailles* and World War II?" Dr. Davis, our professor of history asks, looking for a class discussion. Mark is the only student capable of discussing the treaty's influence on the morale of the German people and the subsequent rise to power of Adolf Hitler.

"How does the economic system of Marxism differ from capitalism?" While the other prisoners and I shift in our seats and stare blankly at Dr. Watkins, our economics professor, Mark's hand shoots up. He offers an elaborate contrast between the theories of Adam Smith and Karl Marx, emphasizing the essential influences private property, competition, and free markets have had on advancing Western civilization, particularly that of the United States.

I want to express myself like Mark, intelligently, and with a style that shows I'm a man who understands the world and how it works. Knowing that I can learn from him, I introduce myself after class one day.

"You must've gone to college before," I observe.

"No, only in prison. Been taking classes here and there for the past seven years," Mark answers.

"Seven years? And you haven't graduated?"

"I hardly ever finish. A year hasn't passed when I haven't been hauled off to the hole for something or other. Sometimes I just drop the classes, bored with it all."

"Don't you want to earn a degree?" Seeing an obviously bright guy with such little ambition puzzles me.

"It's not that I don't want one. I just get caught up with the day-to-day living. Can't do much about it when I catch a shot for a dirty urine or get caught with a mug of pruno."

"Why don't you quit using drugs?"

"You sound like my ol' lady," he laughs.

"Yeah, I don't get that," I tell him. "It seems to me that someone as smart as you would understand the importance of having a college degree."

"If I get it, fine. If not, it doesn't make much difference."

"How is it that when you're in class you sound like a lawyer, but out here you sound like you don't care about anything?"

"When in Rome, do as the Romans," he laughs. "Truth is, I don't care. But in class I get tired of all those professors coming in here thinking we're all worthless."

"That's not how they see us. Most of us probably aren't as advanced as the students they teach on campus."

"I like letting 'em know I speak their language."

"I've noticed. Someday I hope to know as much as you."

"None of it's new. This stuff was drilled into me night after night at the dinner table growing up. Got turned off of education when the parents beat me over the head with it, telling me how crucial school was to my future. Fuck it. Started getting high instead, rockin' out with Led Zeppelin and Hendrix and the Stones."

"I wish I knew so much that I could simply turn my educational level on and off at will. It takes everything I have just to keep up with the class." I explain to Mark that I consider an education essential to my future and describe how I've structured my time inside to avoid the obstacles that block so many others.

"Doesn't that get old?" he asks.

"What?"

"All that goody-two-shoes bullshit, the rigidity, that structure. I mean, Dude, we've got enough people telling us how to live in here. I can't see how you'd want to put those kinds of demands on your time. I mean, let's be real. You've got enough time. It wouldn't hurt nothin' to let up a little."

"Yeah, I don't see it that way. I've got an opportunity to earn a degree right now. Who knows whether I'll have it tomorrow? I've got to seize the moment, then create something from it."

"Big deal. Let's say you finish all your classes and get your degree. What's next? You've still got more than 20 years to go."

"One step at a time. With a degree, I know I'll be able to open new opportunities. Maybe I can go to law school. I'll find something and I know the degree will help, especially if I can learn how to express myself as well as you. How did you build such an extensive vocabulary?"

Mark laughs. "You mean my 'grown up talk?' All you need to know in here is 'motherfucker.' Learn how to use that word as an adjective, noun, and verb. Drop as many motherfuckers as you can into every sentence, drop it into the middle of words, and you'll fit right in. Like I fuckin' said, when in Rome, fuck everyone else. Do as the motherfuckin' Romans." He laughs.

"I'm not trying to fit in here. This isn't my life and it'll never be my life. I'm serious. How did you develop such an impressive vocabulary?"

"I don't know. How did you learn the word window?"

"Really, I'm serious."

"I'm serious too. I learned the language that was spoken in my house. When I write home or to people outside, I communicate one way. When I'm in here I use the language of the pen."

From my pocket I pull a stack of index cards I carry with me. On one side I've written a word that I came across in a book, on the other side, the definition, the part of speech, and an example of the word in a sentence. "This is how I train myself to learn new words," I tell him. "It's a strategy I picked up after reading *The Autobiography of Malcolm X.* Whenever I'm waiting in line or whenever I have down time, I work through the flash cards. Test me." I toss Mark the stack.

"You're kidding. Man, you're fuckin' obsessed, intense!" He starts shuffling through the cards, looking at the words. "Immutable?"

"Immutable." I spell it. "Not capable of being moved or changed."

"Okay, that's pretty close. How about truculent?"

"Mean, a bad attitude, a truculent person is one who always wants to fight or battle."

"A lot of that in here. I don't even know this one. Tenebrous."

"Dark and gloomy."

"See, your vocabulary's good, just as good as mine." He passes the stack back to me. "Just keep reading."

"It's not the same. I'm learning the words and I'm able to use them in writing when I concentrate, but they don't come to me easily, or roll off my tongue naturally when I'm trying to express myself. That's what I want to learn."

"Well you need to reach out, to communicate with more people. All work and no play makes for a dull guy. You can't just live as a hermit in here. There's a word for you, *hermitage.*"

"I already know how to speak the language of this place. I'm trying to transcend this place, to leave here without everyone I meet knowing that I've spent my whole life in prison."

Mark considers me for a second, then he offers a suggestion. "I've got a friend you should write. He's a professor. My sister's always trying to straighten out my life and she introduced me to him."

"You're kidding! You have a friend who's a professor?" I can't believe this good fortune Mark offers so casually. I've been living in prison for three years, but books and learning have transported me out of here, at least in my mind. A university campus is like a mythical setting to me. Although I've been studying, accumulating credits, and building my transcript, I can't imagine a more personal connection to the university than communicating with an actual professor.

"He's from Chicago, but for now he's in Chapel Hill, at the University of North Carolina. We write every week."

"Is your sister a professor?"

"She's not a professor, but she's affiliated with the university. Bruce, my friend, heads the program she's with, some kind of renewal center for educators. Do you want to write him?"

"Do I! This is the best news I've had since I've come in. I'll write him tonight."

"Fine. Give me the letter tomorrow and I'll send it off with an introduction."

The next morning I give Mark the lengthy letter I want him to pass along to Dr. R. Bruce McPherson. It describes who I am, what I'm doing in prison, and how hard I'm working to educate myself. I try to express how grateful I'd be to learn from him through correspondence.

* * * * * * *

A week later I'm sitting on the lower rack when a guard flicks an envelope beneath my door. I lean over to pick up the envelope and read "University of North Carolina" on the return address. For a moment I just hold it in my hand, tracing my fingers over the embossed lettering and the university logo. The wreath signifies academia, and a charge of excitement runs through me. I'm a 26-year old man, yet I open the envelope with the same giddy anticipation as a child anticipating birthday money from his grandparents.

Dr. McPherson's letter expresses his enthusiasm to mentor me through my term, and he asks me to mail him the visiting authorization form. He also writes that I should soon receive a book he sent separately, from the university's bookstore. Wanting to share my good fortune I pass the letter to Windward for him to read.

"What's the big deal?"

"What do you mean?" Windward's indifference puzzles me. "He's a professor, and he wants to help me."

"Big fuckin' deal! What can he do? He's probably a fag."

"How can you say that? He's an educator, he has his own life out there, and he's offering to help me. Why would you insult him?"

"Don't cry, little guy," he mocks when he notes my offense at his dismissive response. "I'm just sayin', what the fuck can he possibly do for you? You've got to think about what people want, Dude. Why would he want to write someone he doesn't know? It don't make no sense."

Windward fits right in to the penitentiary culture. He not only accepts defeat for himself, he expects those around him to do the same. Nothing good comes with the prison experience. Therefore, any indication that someone may succeed in overcoming pessimism and despair threatens his belief in failure as the inevitable. Failure is comfortable to him, a real concept. Working toward anything different, or better, upsets his equilibrium.

"Give me back my letter." I'm learning that within this tenebrous environment my enthusiasm must be internal. Sharing victories, no matter how small, only breeds more sarcasm.

With the news of Bruce's interest in my life I instantly ascend ten rungs up my virtual ladder to freedom. If nothing else, his friendship will help lift me out of the caverns of ignorance where I dwell.

* * * * * * *

When my counselor, Mr. Skinner, receives Bruce's completed visiting form he calls my office supervisor, Ms. Stephens, with a summons for me to report to his office.

"Do you know a Bruce McPherson?" The counselor sits at his metal desk in his cubbyhole office reading from the visiting form that he holds in his hand. With greasy gray hair and a stained white shirt, his appearance, like his office, is a disorganized mess. The office stinks of stale tobacco and his body odor.

"Yes. He's a professor and he's helping with my school work."

"So you sent him this visiting form?" He flicks the form with his fingers.

"That's right."

"Well he's not getting in. I'm not authorizing him to visit."

The dehumanization continues. Prisoners have to ask permission for everything, and I'm accustomed to the apparent malevolent satisfaction some staff members get from denying requests. Still, this denial is more of a slap to my dignity than most because I'm convinced that I can grow through Bruce's mentoring.

"Can you tell me the reason?" I don't understand why the counselor won't authorize Bruce's request to visit.

"You didn't know him before you started serving your sentence. That's all the reason I need to deny him."

"But he's a *professor* and he's offering to help me, to teach me."

"I don't care if he's the Pope. We've got rules in here! We don't know why he's coming to see you, what you've got going on with him. Security of the institution, Son! In order to visit, rules say the relationship had to exist before your imprisonment."

"Counselor Skinner, I'm from Seattle. No one visits me. Bruce McPherson is someone who can guide me through my prison term. Can't you make an exception?"

"Go back to work. Give me your pass to sign." He's unwilling to listen any longer.

Dejected, I walk back to the business office. I sink into my chair and hold my head in my hands. Our country goes to war over supposed human rights violations, yet it feels to me as if such violations occur within the federal prison system every day of the year.

"What's wrong with you?" Ms. Stephens straightens a stack of papers on her desk as she senses my despair. "You look like you just got 45 years."

She's trying to lighten the mood in her caring way, but at this moment I want to grieve over all the indignities of being a prisoner, of having to ask permission for friendship and then being denied.

"Please. Not today."

"What happened?" she asks again, giving me her complete attention. I know that she wrestles at moments like these with the awkward balance of being a staff member, a part of the prison machine, and her natural tendency to empathize with another human being. We sit in the same office every day. We relate like two "normal" people, not as a prisoner and a staff member separated by some ridiculous ethos splitting our humanity.

Ms. Stephens knows about Bruce, and she has been totally supportive of my efforts to advance my education. The factory rules forbid prisoners from working on schoolwork, reading, or even writing personal letters during the workday, even though an efficient worker with good organizational skills can complete the daily responsibilities in two hours. She has intervened on numerous occasions to protect me from her colleagues who resent my studying on the job and using the office as my sanctuary. She nods her head when I tell her about Counselor Skinner denying Bruce visiting privileges.

"I need you to step outside for a minute so that I can make a phone call."

I leave to pace around the outer office. A dozen prisoners sit at their desks, sipping from stained coffee mugs and passing their time discussing the story dominating the news. I saw it over the weekend. Some crazed leader from Iraq, Saddam Hussein, ordered his military to invade a neighboring country, Kuwait. Talk radio listeners can't get enough of the story although the entire episode strikes me as being bizarre.

I grew up during a time when the United States was at peace. The thought of one country invading another seems like something from the dark ages. Yet the talk shows buzz with conversation about our national security being threatened by Hussein's aggression. Some commentators suggest that our country might go to war.

It doesn't make much sense to me, but a lot of the prisoners have been energized by this military action. They're speculating that if the United States goes to war opportunities might open up to parole prisoners into the military. Such a scenario seems plausible. I've read that during previous wars, like the Vietnam War, judges frequently offered offenders the choice of either joining the military or facing imprisonment. I'm not hopeful that changes will come for me, though this sudden shift in global events causes me to think about what else could take place in the world over the remaining 23 years that I must serve.

Shortly before I came in, President Reagan told Gorbachev to "tear down the Berlin Wall." I didn't know much about global politics then, but a unified Germany seemed absurd because I grew up learning about two completely separate Germany's, an East and a West. Then, just last year, the Berlin Wall came down, and just like that, Germany was unified. Soon thereafter, the Soviet Union crumbled ending the Cold War. When it happened I remember thinking that maybe America's ridiculous Drug War would end too.

According to all the business office chatter, though, we're moving dangerously close to a very hot war in the Middle East. I don't understand it, but I must admit I'm not nearly as interested in what's going on in the Middle East as the other prisoners. They're talking about the possibility of war with a lot more passion and enthusiasm than I can muster. Unlike most of them, I don't have a burning animosity toward the United States. In fact, I can't wait to leave prison and return to society, because where I'm living right now feels about as far away from America as a man can get.

I circle around toward my office. The walk has improved my mood. I've breathed, allowed my frustration to dissipate, and with all the speculation about war, I've reminded myself to keep the bigger picture in mind. Bruce's friendship and guidance isn't contingent on us visiting, and whether I'm allowed to visit or not, I'm going to make it. Although I constantly feel the dehumanizing culture of corrections, my attitude and deliberate actions to redeem myself restore my dignity.

I slip into the office and see Ms. Stephens busy at her desk. She's not on the phone, so I presume it's okay to walk in. Just to make sure, I ask.

She smiles and nods. "When you go back to the housing unit you'll see a new visiting list. I had a chat with Counselor Skinner and he told me that he would put the list on your bunk. Dr. Bruce McPherson has been approved to visit."

My face turns red as I thank her for her kindness, but I'm uneasy. It's troubling to me that I have to prostrate myself with requests for special interventions in order to find a friend, someone who can help guide these efforts I'm making to grow. It's patronizing, dehumanizing. Ms. Stephens saw that Skinner got to me, and it bothers me. After years in prison, these kinds of indignities aren't supposed to bother me, or at least I shouldn't let my aggravation show. "Sorry to have troubled you," I say.

"Don't be. Sometimes I'm embarrassed by this organization I work for."

I shrug my shoulders. "It is what it is, and by now I ought to be able to roll with it. But sometimes the pressure gets to me. Regardless of how hard I work, I'm always going to be a prisoner, indistinguishable from anyone else in here."

Ms. Stephens' elbows rest on the desk with her hands clasped beneath her chin as she listens to me openly, sympathetically. "Look. I can't imagine what you're going through inside, and there's not much I can do to help. I've been in this job for 12 years and I *do* see how hard you're working. Others might not see it, but I wouldn't go out of my way to help if I wasn't convinced that you're sincere. That's what I told your counselor and I'll tell anyone else who asks. It's not right that you're in here for so long."

My eyes water as she comforts me. I know Ms. Stephens is taking a position that the system discourages. As a staff member she isn't supposed to be personal with an inmate. The BOP motto for staff members is to be "firm but fair," and that means she is first supposed to consider my status as a prisoner. Fairness requires strict adherence to prison policy. If the policy states that prisoners cannot visit with people they didn't know prior to imprisonment, then fairness requires counselors to enforce the policy across the board. That's Counselor Skinner's position. It's the kind of oppressive rigidity that threatens to suffocate prisoners, every day, and I've endured a thousand days of it. I wonder how I'll make it through nine thousand more.

Regardless, I want to walk over and hug Ms. Stephens. Her concern validates me, restores a spirit and energy that imprisonment so effectively crushes. I cherish this moment and I'll remember it as further evidence that God is with me, always strengthening me with what I need along the way.

* * * * * * *

My schedule keeps me in the business office all day, in classes learning from professors in the evening, and on the suicide-watch tier late into the night. I'm more productive than I thought possible. I enjoy challenging myself by setting goals, writing them out, and sending them to family and friends with encouragement for them to hold me accountable. Reaching my goals is one thing, but empowering myself to exceed them is quite another. I'm obsessed with my personal records and with my daily journal, but only because I find them so effective in motivating me to reach milestones that others insist are beyond a prisoner's reach.

Not only am I accumulating university credits, I'm working through a formidable reading list. My understanding and enjoyment of the classics, such as Plato's *Republic,* Dante's *Divine Comedy*, and Dostoyevsky's *Brothers Karamazov,* are clear signs that I'm really learning. I summarize what I learn in book reports that I write and send to Bruce for his evaluation and comments. He returns them, bleeding with red ink, simultaneously broadening my education and awareness through his teaching and mentoring.

I didn't grow up in a home like Mark's, where both parents held advanced degrees and emphasized the importance of higher learning, but my parents taught me the importance of working hard. In an effort to demonstrate my commitment to making good use of my time inside, I'm applying extra effort. The more knowledge and writing skills I can develop, the better equipped I'll be to succeed when I'm released, to show that I've conquered imprisonment, because this system feels like it's designed to perpetuate failure.

My vocabulary is improving. The index cards I keep in stacks of 50 now number 1,000. By mastering words and definitions, my spelling has also improved, and when I respond in class, I express myself in the language of the university rather than the penitentiary. When I listen to NPR or read *The Wall Street Journal* my confidence rises with my understanding of words and concepts that used to baffle me. And whenever I have questions, I have the skills to find the answers.

Since I've charted the progress I want to make by 1997, the end of my first decade, I know exactly where I should be in 1992, at the halfway point. I also know where I'm supposed to be now, in 1991, only a year away from earning my undergraduate degree.

I'm exceeding my expectations with a schedule that keeps me racing to beat my timeline. Whereas the penitentiary rocks with violence and corruption scandals, I'm so absorbed with my work that news of the stabbings, beatings, and investigations into staff corruption are of little concern to me. I know how to stay under the radar.

I've determined that a bachelor's degree won't be enough to get me where I want to go. The judge's refusal to reconsider my sentence and the prosecutor's statement that 300 years of imprisonment wouldn't be sufficient for my punishment remains an ugly reminder of a judicial mindset that is unwilling to bend. I have to build a record that warrants consideration for a commutation of sentence, and the president is the only person who has the power to commute my sentence. I must work harder and achieve more.

When I conclude my shift on the suicide-watch tier in the hospital, I walk through the metal detectors, the gates, and the corridors that lead back to the cellblock. The guard unlocks my door and I enter. Windward's snoring is undisturbed as the deadbolt slams into place behind me, locking me inside.

I grab my pillow from the bunk and set it on the steel chair to use as a cushion while I sit, staring at the concrete floor. While trying to think, I'm distracted and I begin to count the beige concrete blocks that form the walls of my cell. Before snapping out of my reverie, I fantasize about bursting through these immutable walls.

* * * * * * *

I'm excited to see Bruce, my mentor. He's a bear of a man, big in every way, and through our correspondence we've built a friendship that has deepened. I look forward to our weekly exchange of mail and quarterly visits. He now lives in Chicago, having recently retired as a professor. He continues to use his immense talents, and he gives of his wisdom generously with hopes of making societal contributions through his teachings.

Bruce introduced me to his wife, Carolyn, who sometimes accompanies him on visits, and through correspondence I've met his daughter and sons. The bad decisions of my past don't matter to him. My efforts to become a good citizen define me in his eyes. He strives to round out my cultural education by exposing me to art, opera, and theater, and he often stresses the importance of fully investing oneself in the community. Although Windward and other prisoners here don't understand the motivations of a man like Bruce, I see joy in his expressions as he describes the experience of helping others reach their potential.

After the guards at the desk clear me, I walk down the stairs and through the aisles toward where Bruce sits. An aging athlete, he stands to embrace me and I notice his white hair is a little thinner than the last time we met, though his eyes still shine a brilliant blue. He played as an offensive lineman in college football and it's easy to see how his size and strength would've powered open huge holes for his running backs.

"How've you been?" I ask.

"I'm well," he tells me, then says that he heard from Mark. "He told me to send you his regards," Bruce says, embracing me.

"What's he doing?"

Mark was released from prison through parole. With the restrictions that prohibit felons from communicating with each other, I'm losing touch with him except for periodic updates from Bruce.

"He's working for a friend who owns retail clothing stores, doing well. A guy with his moxie always has a place in sales."

"No more school for him then? He's not going to finish his degree?"

"I don't think so. He's putting his life back together and his plans probably don't include much more classroom time."

"That's all I'm doing, putting in classroom time, and I'm grateful for every minute of it."

Bruce reaches over the table to tap my arms. "You're steady at the gym I see. How much are you benching now?"

I beam with pride. "I'm hitting 315 for triple reps, feeling stronger." I tell Bruce about my schedule, how I'm now working out twice a day, once before breakfast and a second time during the lunch hour.

"When are you eating?"

"I eat at work," I explain. "Avoiding the chow hall is still a priority for me. That's where the chaos in here begins, with the racial segregation and the politics, meaning which power group sits in which section. My parents and sisters send me money for commissary, so I buy packs of tuna, soups, other foods that I eat at work. Besides that, I can barter my writing or typing skills for sandwiches from guys who work in the kitchen. Great culinary experiences aren't my priority now."

Bruce nods his head and smiles. "What did you think of the Monet prints?"

To teach me about art Bruce sends postcards and magazine articles. He describes the great museums of the world and writes that he looks forward to walking through the Prado with me in Madrid, the Louvre in Paris, and the Art Institute of Chicago. He buys me subscriptions to *The New Yorker* and *Smithsonian*.

"When you get out I've got a whole world to show you. You can visit the Stratford Festival with Carolyn and me in Canada. We're there twice a year to celebrate the performances of Shakespeare plays."

"That's what I need to talk with you about. Getting out." My time in the visiting room is limited so I feel compelled to turn our conversation to something of more immediate importance. "I've got to be thinking about what I'm going to do after I graduate next year."

"How can I help?"

"Well, a lot's been on my mind, but I need other people to make things work. I can't succeed without your help."

"What's on your mind?"

I explain to Bruce why and how I need to build a coalition of support.

"Do you want help raising money to hire a lawyer?"

Bruce misses my point so I try to elaborate. "The people who become a part of my network must join me because they believe in me, like you. I'm not interested in buying support by hiring lawyers. What I need to think about is earning support, building new friendships and relationships with people who will support my efforts to earn freedom. I'm not trying to get out now, but I'm trying to position myself for 1997, when I'll have 10 years in."

"How should we start?"

"Well, one thing I need is support from someone inside the Bureau of Prisons."

I explain my relationship with Ms. Stephens and the ways that she has intervened for me on a local level to smooth out complications with her colleagues who block me from receiving library books and other resources I need for my education.

"What I need is the same kind of help from people who have national influence in the system. The obstacle is that I don't have any direct contact with them. The leaders of the BOP are all in Washington and to them I'm just another prisoner, a number. Ms. Stephens cares because she sees how hard I work, and she goes the extra mile to help me succeed. She believes in me, just as you do."

"How can someone in the BOP help you?"

"I'm not going to be able to make the progress I need from this prison. There's way too much violence here and it's getting worse. We're on lockdown at least once each week. I want to stay here until I earn my degree, but at some point after graduation I need to transfer, and I need to transfer to the best spot in the BOP for continuing my education. I'll need help to identify where that place is and then I'll need help getting transferred there when the time is right."

"So what're you thinking?"

"I read an article in an academic journal by Sylvia McCollum," I explain to Bruce. "She's the Director of Education for the entire Bureau of Prisons. Her article describes how she created a new policy that makes it mandatory for all federal prisoners who don't have a high school equivalency to participate in GED classes. I want to build a relationship with her, to get her support. But I can't just write her a letter because to her I'm simply another drug dealer in prison."

"That's not true," Bruce counters. He always sees the good in everyone and dislikes my cynicism. "She's going to see the record you've been building, your progress in college."

I shake my head, disagreeing. "It's not enough. The culture in this organization is one that trains staff members to consider prisoners as something less than human beings. She'll only see me as a prisoner, a drug dealer, scum. I need to do something more, something to distinguish myself. I was thinking that we could write an article, a response to her article from the perspective of a prisoner and his mentor. It should describe how the GED is one step toward preparing for release, but it's hardly sufficient. Men who leave prison should emerge with values, skills, and resources that will truly translate into success, and a GED isn't enough. The Bureau of Prisons should use incentives that will encourage more prisoners to continue their education with college or vocational training."

"And what're we going to do with the article? Send it to her?"

"That's how I need your help. Not only will we have to write the article, I need you to arrange publication. It would be one thing for me as a prisoner to write an article and send it to her. Big deal. On the other hand, if I were to write an article together with you and send it to her, that would carry more weight, more influence because not many prisoners cultivate mentorships with distinguished professors. But the best approach, I think, would be to write an article that we publish together, as the professor and the prisoner. That's one way I would stand out, one way that she would remember my name, see that I'm different."

Bruce nods his head and agrees to help. When he returns to Chicago, he promises to make inquiries at the various peer-reviewed academic journals to see what steps we must take to submit an article for publishing consideration. It's a process that will take several months, which suits my schedule well, as I need that time to finish my undergraduate work.

"What I also need," I tell Bruce before he leaves, "is a list of all the law schools in the United States. I need to start writing letters to see if any of the schools will allow me to earn a law degree through correspondence."

"So you're still set on law school?"

"I'm set on earning an advanced degree, something, anything more than a bachelor's. I'm going to need unimpeachable credentials that people respect, like yours."

Bruce is a role model and I'm eager to follow his leadership, to emulate his commitment to society. He told me how he and Carolyn were volunteering their time on weekends to help homeless people in a Chicago shelter write résumés that would facilitate their prospects for employment. Bruce and Carolyn give of themselves, without expectation for return or desire for recognition. Success for Bruce comes when his efforts lead to another person's independence or happiness. I'm determined to prove myself worthy of his generosity, of the trust and the investment he's making in me.

* * * * * * *

This hard plank of steel I'm lying on influences my thought process. I'm locked in this small room with another man who uses the toilet and flushes a few feet to the right of my head. What Bruce and Carolyn do to make life better for so many people gives me a different perspective on humanity. I know that my motivations lack the purity of Bruce's, as I'm so much more pragmatic. I want out, so there's always a selfish component to my actions, and that somehow cheapens them in my mind. I contemplate Maslow's Hierarchy of Needs, a concept I learned about in sociology. Until a man satisfies his most basic needs he can't evolve. My primary need is liberty, and decades may pass before I leave these walls. Everything I do up until then must prepare me for freedom. Perhaps when I'm free from concrete and steel I'll be able to emulate Bruce more completely. I want to live as that type of a good, kind man. But I don't know how to reconcile this desire to live with the kindness and generosity of spirit that Bruce exemplifies with the need for survival in a predatory environment.

My philosophy courses have broadened my perceptions, explaining man's purpose, his relationship to society, his quest for personal fulfillment and enlightenment. I've embraced lessons from Aristotle and Sun Tzu among others. Aristotle advises those who follow him "to know thyself," while Sun Tzu emphasizes that it is equally important "to know thy enemy."

Know thyself and know thy enemy. I wrestle with these thoughts. I know I *must* thoroughly understand my strengths and weaknesses. I *must* use every resource God has given me to become stronger and to grow. Likewise, I *must* understand my enemies. In my case, the enemies are a corrupting environment, demeaning perceptions, and ugly prejudices I will encounter in the decades ahead, perhaps for the rest of my life. Responsibility to triumph over a system that is designed to extinguish hope and to perpetuate cycles of failure rests with me. Solely.

* * * * * * *

I'm grateful that Bruce takes the time to visit the American Bar Association in Chicago. He sends me a package of information that includes addresses to every ABA accredited law school in the nation. All of the schools I've written to have responded with disappointing news that the ABA prohibits law schools from allowing students to earn law degrees through correspondence. But there's a sliver of hope that comes in a letter from Dr. Al Cohn, a professor at Hofstra University's graduate school.

Dr. Cohn wrote that my letter impressed the Dean of Hofstra's law school, and the dean forwarded the letter to him. Although Hofstra can't allow me to earn a law degree without attending school there, Dr. Cohn's letter indicates that he might consider waiving the residency requirement if I pursue a graduate degree. Hofstra has never admitted a prisoner before, he admits, but he admires my determination to educate myself. If I earn my undergraduate degree with an acceptable grade point average, propose an acceptable area of study in which I can specialize, and complete a probationary period of conditional admittance, he will waive the requirements of taking the Graduate Records Examination and on-campus residency. Wow! Dr. Cohn tells me that Hofstra will allow me to earn a master's degree if I meet those requirements.

I've read that roughly 30 percent of American adults have earned university degrees, but fewer than 15 percent have graduate or professional degrees. My aspirations are not to become a lawyer, necessarily, but to earn credentials that others respect. I'm certain that the higher my level of achievement, the more I'll be able to build a support network, one that will help me transition from prisoner to citizen.

As I contemplate Dr. Cohn's letter I can't help but think of Mick Jagger, the rock-and-roll legend. He sings that you can't always get what you want, but if you try sometimes, you just might find, you get what you need. I may not earn a law degree, but with the opportunity extended by Hofstra University I know that nothing is going to stop me from earning a master's degree.

* * * * * * *

I pass my fifth Christmas in prison. It's now 1992, I'm 28, and in only a few months Mercer University will award my undergraduate degree. This is a big deal for me. Out of more than 2,500 men locked inside USP Atlanta's walls, I'm the only one to receive a degree. In fact, Mercer hasn't awarded a degree to any prisoner since I've been in Atlanta.

I'm inspired by other men who used their knowledge and prison experience to make significant contributions, like Alexander Solzhenitsyn whose eight years in a Russian prison was followed by three years in exile. His hardship awoke his muse, resulting in such classics as *A Day in the Life of Ivan Denisovich* and his opus, *The Gulag Archipelago*, exposing readers from around the world to Russia's oppressive prison life.

Eight years, whether in Russian prison camps or the United States penitentiaries, is a long time. Through his literature Solzhenitsyn made monumental contributions to society and earned a Nobel Prize, and he *inspires* me. As crazy as it sounds, a seed is taking root, and I feel the bud of this thought that maybe, through hard work, I can transform the decades I'll serve in here into something positive. I've begun to accept that I may serve my entire sentence, and I need more examples like Solzhenitsyn's. Not knowing what I can do for 21 more years, I continue reading about other men who served long sentences.

One such prisoner was Nelson Mandela, the black South African activist locked in prison for 27 years by white authorities between 1962 and 1990. That length of time is comparable to what I may serve, and I take heart that multiple decades did not destroy Mandela. On the contrary, it strengthened his resolve, evidenced by his influence in ending the oppressive policies of Apartheid, and by the position he now holds as a world leader, revered throughout the international community.

* * * * * * *

I don't know what it means to be an intellectual like Solzhenitsyn or a leader like Mandela, but I know what it means to face decades in prison. I also know what it means to be a man, and recently I've met a woman who's reminded me of all I've been living without.

Her name is Sarah, and she's a lawyer. We met by chance two months ago when we were in the visiting room at the same time. My father had flown in just before Christmas to spend a weekend with me. Sarah was visiting another prisoner I knew. Under the pretense that I might need some legal advice I asked Sarah for her business card. Yet having lived for so long in an abnormal community of only men, I wanted a woman in my life more than I wanted to know anything about the law.

The dance of seduction begins when I write to her, initiating an exchange of letters. She writes back. At first the correspondence is bland, tame, harmless. Soon the letters between us grow in frequency and in complexity. They're handwritten now, not typed. I learn that she earned her degrees from NYU, that she contemplates starting her own law firm, and that she's 30. I also know that she named her cat Snuggles, that she rollerblades, loves aerobics, and is recovering from a broken heart. She's vulnerable. Through our exchange of letters, I'm coming to know Sarah the woman, and in my world, any connection with a woman is a gift.

Desire creeps into me, threatens me. I've been successful in repressing or ignoring these urges that have been dormant for so long, but now they keep me awake. I remind myself where I am, what I went through with Lisa, and the goals I'm working so feverishly to complete.

But another fever takes hold. Every day I ache for a letter from her, for something, any kind of sign that lets me know where this is going, how much I can escalate the heat. I don't remember what I wrote in the letter she should've received today, and like a teenager, I wonder whether I went too far, revealed too much. She must know what's going on with this exchange of letters, that I want her.

It's mail call and the guard just flicked her letter beneath my door. I see her stationary, her handwriting, and I pick up the envelope. She wrote her words yesterday, making it an exchange of three letters this week. I'm on her mind. In the words she chooses I catch some suggestive double meanings. My confidence grows. We're flirting and we both know it, and I want to see her again. I'm a man in the desert and she's my oasis.

I graduate next month. Mercer University is honoring me with a ceremony. I can't travel to the campus, so my commencement will take place inside USP Atlanta, in the chapel. A hundred other prisoners will participate, receiving GED certificates or certificates for completion of basic education classes. Even though I'm a class of one, I'm invited to speak as valedictorian. Mr. Chandler authorized me to invite two visitors, and I'm choosing my sister Julie and Sarah. If Sarah accepts it may be the sign I'm looking for, confirmation that the desire I'm feeling is mutual.

Vidi

...I Saw

Chapter Five: 1992
Months 58-62

Since I received the divorce papers from Lisa, my interactions with women have been limited to Ms. Stephens, my work supervisor, and Susan, my friend from high school with whom I've had an ongoing, friendly correspondence. But those relationships don't have any possibility for intimacy. This thing with Sarah is different. She lives in Atlanta, and her proximity causes me to fantasize that I could seduce her, make her my woman. Given the rules of this place, however, initiating physical intimacy will be a major challenge. Still, forced celibacy doesn't diminish my thirst for love or my desire for sex.

Thoughts of love have been on my mind for years. Another prisoner, Eugene Fischer, fed my hopes with a story about Orianna Fallaci, a world-famous journalist who loved a man who served time in a Greek prison for an attempted assassination. I wonder whether I could find a woman who would see me as a man and love me despite my imprisonment. I'm 28, and I refuse to give up on the possibilities.

Upon receiving the invitation to attend my graduation, Sarah surprises me by driving over to the penitentiary. I'm on a volunteer suicide-watch duty in the hospital, looking after a despondent prisoner, when I receive the call. While I study for final exams, the guard hollers my name from the other side of locked gates.

"Santos!" he yells. "Let's go!" I see him standing outside the gate, fumbling with the ring of keys hanging on a chain attached to his belt.

"What?" I have no idea what he's talking about.

"We've been paging you for 30 minutes. You're supposed to report to the visiting room."

"I didn't hear a page." I close my books and walk toward the guard.

"Leave the books. You're late. I've got to take you straight to visiting."

"Why?"

"Your attorney is here and she's been waiting. Didn't you know she was coming?"

"I didn't have any idea." The 15-minute walk takes me through a maze of gates and courtyards and metal detectors and corridors. With each step I'm thinking about Sarah. She's not on my visiting list, so I wonder how she got in. If she felt this urgency to see me, perhaps it's to tell me face-to-face that my invitation went too far and to clarify where we stand. Or maybe it's something else.

* * * * * * *

Some prisoners' families live near Atlanta and I hear the institutional loudspeaker page those men for visits regularly. Until this back and forth with Sarah began, my focus on school extinguished any longing to sit in the visiting room. Sarah's surprise visit breaks my routine. The strip search by an inquisitive guard doesn't even bother me.

After the full inspection I pull on my boxers and socks, step back into my khakis, tuck in my shirt, and lace my sneakers tightly before walking into the visiting room.

Since Sarah came as a lawyer, I'm directed past the stairs leading down into the general visiting room where hundreds of people sit beside each other under the scrutiny of guards and surveillance cameras. The guard instructs me to walk across the hall to one of the private conference rooms.

"She's in two," he says.

Through the narrow vertical window cut into the wooden door I see Sarah for the first time in three months, since that day she handed me her business card. For a second I pause to watch her. She's seated at a small table, absorbed with a stack of papers. Black designer sunglasses hold her long, honey-colored hair away from her face while she works. She's prettier than I remember. I knock, startling her. She looks over at me, smiles, and waves me in.

As I open the door she stands and quickly straightens her navy skirt. Suddenly we're face to face in a room half the size of my cell.

"Surprise!" she greets me as I close the door. Her perfume lingers in the air and I inhale the subtle, sweet fragrance.

"Wow! This is a surprise. How'd you get in without being on my list?"

"Lawyer privileges. I just flash my bar card. What took you so long to get here?"

I smile. "I didn't know you were coming."

"It's okay. I brought some work with me. How about a hug?" She opens her arms.

Her arms encircle me in a friendly gesture. I've been deprived of a woman's touch for almost 3 years and I load the gesture with a lot more meaning. I'm awkward, unsure if I should hold her slender waist or keep my hands high on her back. The embrace lasts a second, but in that second, through her silk blouse, I feel the warmth of her back on my hands and her breasts pressing into my chest.

"It's cozy," she says, looking around the small room. Some designer of prisons splurged by using two shades to paint the concrete walls—dark beige to shoulder height and a lighter beige up to the matching ceiling above. Its dreariness contrasts with Sarah's radiance. She moves the suit jacket she's folded over the back of the extra chair and we sit.

When she asks whether I've ever been in this part of the visiting room, I shake my head no, telling her that I hardly ever come to the visiting room. She nods, in empathy I think. "So you're graduating next month. Congratulations!" Her eyes shine as she leans back, pushing her fingers through her hair.

"I'm looking forward to the commencement ceremony. Did you get my letter inviting you to come?"

"I did. That's why I'm here."

"Uh-oh."

"What do you mean?"

"If you went to all the trouble of driving out here just to give me an answer, it probably means you can't come, or you won't come."

"No, not at all. I'd love to watch you receive your degree. It's just that you've expressed so much admiration for Bruce, and you wrote that they'd only allow you to have two visitors. Maybe you should invite him and your sister. I can visit you any time."

"Well Bruce will be on vacation, but I asked you because I want you here. Will you come?"

Our eyes lock as she smiles, nodding yes.

"Good, I want you to meet my sister, Julie. I've written to her about you."

"Really? What about?"

"Just that I've made a new friend and that we're corresponding. My sister and I are close. She worries about me, wants me to be happy."

"I understand. Sounds like you've got a great sister."

"Two great sisters," I say. "The best."

Sarah and I talk for three hours, discussing challenges I've faced, plans I'm making, and steps she's taking to open her own practice. Without a doubt, I'm relishing the electricity between us, feeling a connection that hasn't been a part of my existence for years. When I stand to leave we share a longer embrace, and she promises to return before my graduation. I'll hold onto this memory of her breasts pressing into my chest. It's been the best day since my confinement began.

* * * * * * *

I return to my cell and read. My brother-in-law, Tim, purchased a subscription to *The Wall Street Journal* for me last year. He's building a career as an investment real estate broker and he advises me to familiarize myself with finance. Appreciating his advice, I make a point of carefully reading each issue. Learning more about the stock market helps me understand how to value public companies and reading the *Journal* broadens my business education. Rather than following sports, I devote time to commerce every day, convinced that the education will make me more capable of contributing to any business that will employ me once I'm released.

I read an editorial in the *Journal* that upsets me. John DiIulio, a professor of politics at Princeton University, wrote a scathing article calling for society to build more prisons and urging administrators to manage them with tighter controls and fewer privileges. Wanting to provide him with a different perspective, I write him directly.

In my letter I express my disagreement with his premise, explaining why we don't need more prisons in America with tighter controls. Rather, we need strong, intelligent leadership to make better use of the prison resources we have. Instead of locking so many nonviolent people up and eradicating hope, I suggest administrators should implement policies that encourage prisoners to work toward educating themselves, reconciling with society, and earning freedom.

I explain to Professor DiIulio what I've seen during the five years I've served. Most prisoners give up while they serve time. Many join gangs, hustle drugs and weapons, or incite disturbances. Oppressive policies cause negative adjustments. Instead, we need policies similar to those in business that encourage people to contribute with meaningful incentives. I explain to the Princeton scholar that I strive to live as a model for such reforms, that I'm about to graduate from Mercer University and that I'll begin graduate school at Hofstra University in the fall. I conclude my letter by restating that by inspiring more prisoners to focus on preparing for release, prison leadership could better serve the interests of society by, among things, lowering recidivism rates.

Dr. DiIulio surprises me by responding to my letter. Even though I've never stepped foot on a campus, universities have become a big part of my life. Holding the heavy stock of the envelope and letterhead gives me a charge. Wow! Princeton University. It's one thing for me to write an unsolicited letter but quite another to receive a response. Through his letter he validates and honors me as a contributing citizen, as a man, not a prisoner. It's moments like these that inspire me to keep up the work of building my support network. I'm on the right path.

Dr. DiIulio agrees with all I expressed in my letter but says that the limitation of an op-ed piece doesn't permit him enough space to elaborate on all his thoughts. After informing me that he has published extensively on the subject of prison management, he offers to send books I can read and comment on. It is the beginning of another fascinating correspondence.

* * * * * * *

To broaden my education, Bruce insists that I read classic literature, especially the plays of William Shakespeare. He sent me a complete anthology. Although I'm not smart enough to find much value in the poetry, I've read every play and I enjoyed many. From Julius Caesar, a line stays with me:

There is a tide in the affairs of men, which taken at the flood, leads on to fortune; omitted, all the voyage of their life is bound in the shallows and in miseries.

In Dr. DiIulio's offer to correspond with me, I find a new opportunity to read critically and to challenge opinions with confidence. It's as if my tide has come in and the flood is leading to fortune. I feel it. If an Ivy League professor finds me worthy of his mentoring energies I'll have an incredible resource, another strong academic reference that will distinguish me from other prisoners.

* * * * * * *

May 12, 1992 is a day I've been working toward ever since guards processed me into USP Atlanta. I'm so excited. I feel as if I'm being released, and in a way, I am. I'm being lifted above a life of insignificance, distinguishing myself as a college graduate. It's a credential I'll carry for the rest of my life. A sense of liberty comes with this accomplishment, because regardless of how the prison system tries to direct me, I know where I'm going. I will leverage my degree to pry open new opportunities, and on this day, at least, I'm more than just a prisoner.

I wrote and rewrote a speech for the commencement ceremony, four single-spaced pages. For the past six weeks I've practiced my delivery at every opportunity and after hundreds of rehearsals I've committed each word, sentence, and paragraph to memory. I knew this day would have significance. Now that it's here, I'm glad I took the time to prepare. When it's my turn to speak I think I can stand onstage with confidence that the penitentiary is powerless to repress.

Immediately after the guards clear the afternoon census count I walk with a hundred other prisoners to the education building. The carefully scripted ceremony will begin at five in the chapel. Mr. Chandler and his subordinates have taken care to prepare and honor the dignitaries from Mercer University who will share the stage with Warden Stock and members of his executive staff. Although I want to impress those community leaders, mostly I'm eager for Julie and Sarah to see me.

The prisoners who've earned their GEDs cheer. During my speech I want to inspire them to continue their education, as I plan to do myself. We have a responsibility to change this system. The best way to bring change is to develop skills and credentials to ensure we emerge into society successfully, as well-educated citizens, ready to contribute. As a prisoner, I also want the Mercer administrators to leave with a clear understanding of the need for more educational opportunities in prison. And I want my speech to inspire everyone in the auditorium, especially my sister and Sarah.

Julie is 29 now, working as a young executive with an international cosmetics company. We've only visited a few times since I arrived in Atlanta. Her professional responsibilities, an active social life, and the geographical distance between us make traveling to Atlanta difficult. For years she has accepted my collect phone calls, sent me money to purchase goods in the commissary, and paid my educational costs. She is vested in every choice I make and I'm determined to show her that her trust and support are well placed. With Sarah, I have different motivations. I'm a man and I want a woman in my life.

The music opening our graduation ceremonies begins, and I walk at the head of the procession, leading all the graduates who are now in matching black gowns and caps with tassels. In the audience I see a dozen people I presume came from Mercer; Julie and Sarah sit in the front row. Dr. Colin Harris, one of my favorite professors, is on the stage with Jean Owens, Mercer's outreach program coordinator. Mr. Chandler sits beside them with the warden and several other staff members. I can't quit smiling, grateful for the recognition. I walk to the front row to take my seat.

As Mr. Chandler opens the ceremony with obligatory expressions of gratitude to the warden and other staff members, I exchange glances with Julie and Sarah. Then, we all bow our heads as Dr. Harris, Professor of Religion, gives the invocation.

Next, Jean Owens delivers the keynote, turning me crimson as she tells the audience about my work ethic and determination. She describes the bright future that opens with education. Using the catchy slogan to promote Michael Jordan's basketball shoes, Ms. Owens encourages those in the audience to "be like Mike," referring not to the basketball legend but to me, and she urges those in the audience to continue their studies.

I think I might have to excuse myself and find a bathroom, but when it's my turn to speak, I walk with assurance to the stage to deliver the valedictory address, all else forgotten. I feel so tall at the lectern, like I've just grown six inches. I turn to my left and thank those from Mercer University, then to my right to thank the prison staff, and then out at my audience of graduates, staff, and guests in the cushioned seats, thanking them for attending.

Without notes I deliver my speech that I've carefully rehearsed hundreds of times. Julie beams with pride in the front row, and I see Sarah grasp her hand. They've only just met, but in their support of me they've come together. Those 12 minutes on stage feel as if they're the most positively energizing of my entire life.

The audience gives a standing ovation. Even Warden Stock stands and gives me an affirmative nod when I look his way. Elated, I return to my seat, squeezing my sister's hand as I pass in front of her. The other prisoners and I then receive our diplomas. Mr. Chandler gives closing remarks and ends the ceremony in order to maintain the schedule. We don't have time for a reception. After all, this is a penitentiary. I'm the only prisoner with guests, and no allowance is given for further visitation. At least they were allowed to come for my memorable moment, and I'm in high spirits.

"You were awesome!"

"Send us a copy of your speech."

"I'm so proud of you."

Though it's involuntary, a smile stretches across my face as I walk between my sister and Sarah through the corridor. I stop at the entrance to B cellblock and, under the watchful eyes of the warden, I hug each of my guests and say good-bye.

* * * * * * *

I'm paged to the mailroom, and when I show up, Mr. Chandler is standing at the door. "Boy, all the years you done been locked up and you still ain't learned nothin'?"

I know this routine and I stand waiting for the head of the education department to continue his reprimand, though I don't have any idea what he's talking about or why he paged me to the mailroom.

"I done tol' you befo' 'bout havin' yo folk' send boxes to my depar'ment without axin' me 'forehand."

"Yes, I remember. I haven't had anyone send me any boxes."

"If you ain't had no one send no boxes, then why I gotta go through this mess lookin' through books that done come from Princeton University?"

A month has passed since my correspondence with Professor DiIulio, and when I wrote that I would welcome the books, I wasn't thinking about the mailroom rules. If books come from a publisher or bookstore in an envelope, we're allowed to receive them. For a prisoner to receive boxes, a staff member must provide advance authorization.

"Don't be standin' there with your mouth all hangin' open like you ain't know these is comin'. Letter's addressed to you."

"I thought the books would come in an envelope from the bookstore," I say in way of an apology and explanation. "I didn't know there would be so many."

"Who this Professa D'oolioo? You know 'im?"

"Not really. I just wrote him. He teaches at Princeton and writes books. He wrote that he would send me some books but I didn't know they would come like this."

"Boy you a real piece a work." He handles the books one by one and squints while reading the titles and flipping through the pages. "*Guv'nin' Prisons, No 'xcape.* This professa be writin' these books?"

"I guess so."

"What business you got readin' all these books 'bout prison. Ain't you know 'nough 'bout prisons yet?"

"I'm still learning, sir."

"I hope you done learnt 'nough to stay out." I sense Mr. Chandler likes me. My graduation from Mercer and the speech I gave during commencement put a positive spotlight on his department. His gruff demeanor doesn't intimidate me anymore because I know it's just his way.

"Well go 'head on then. Next time make sure you see me 'bout auth'rization."

Jubilant, I carry the box of books back to the business office where I work. Dr. DiIulio sent 17 books, two of which he authored. I sit at my desk and clear a space on the bookshelf behind me. Reading the books will help me build a relationship with him. I intend to write him about what I learn from each, and I especially look forward to reading the books that he wrote. My small personal library will provide ample research material as I begin my studies at Hofstra.

* * * * * * *

Since I can't earn an accredited law degree from prison I've had to think about what I can study. Although reading the *Wall Street Journal*, and studying the stock market and finance interest me, I don't want to pursue an MBA. Instead, after consulting with Bruce I propose to Hofstra that I study prisons and the people they hold. My Hofstra advisor is Dr. Al Cohn, Professor of Psychology and he approves of my plan. We establish an interdisciplinary curriculum, with studies in sociology, cultural anthropology, and psychology. To complete the program, Dr. Cohn and other Hofstra professors will evaluate my research reports and the lengthy thesis I must write to earn a Master of Arts degree.

The books from Dr. DiIulio give me a theoretical understanding of the functions prisons should serve in society:

1. Prisons should deter citizens from engaging in criminal behavior.
2. They should punish those who stand convicted of having committed crimes.

3. Prison terms should incapacitate those who serve them from committing additional crimes, at least during the term of confinement.

4. And prisons should rehabilitate offenders in an effort to help them return to society as law-abiding citizens.

After reading *Governing Prisons*, Dr. DiIulio's comparative study of management in three separate prison systems, I begin collecting information to write my first term paper on prisoner adjustments. The book leads me to several other books and inspires me to develop a questionnaire to conduct original, ethnographic research to be tested on my fellow prisoners. The resulting term paper, which I entitle "The Crusonian Prisoner," is accepted for presentation at an annual conference of the Academy of Criminal Justice Sciences in Chicago, boosting my self-confidence as a student.

Perhaps it's not surprising that my research leads to findings that differ from the distinguished Princeton professor. He calls for tighter controls in American prisons while my observations and experience convince me that administrators should run prisons like leaders run business. They should govern through the use of incentives rather than threat of further punishments. In a letter to him, I offer reasons to support my conclusions and I also send a copy of my academic paper describing the Crusonian prisoner.

* * * * * * *

"I want to kiss you." Sarah has come to visit five times since my graduation ceremony last month and our letters have become much more personal. Her lawyer privileges allow her to visit whenever she chooses, making the regularly scheduled visiting hours irrelevant. Today is Tuesday, not a visiting day, and it's early evening as I sit with her in one of the private rooms reserved for lawyers and law enforcement interviews. In these lawyer rooms, surveillance cameras do not monitor us. The guard sits at his desk, fifteen yards away on a platform and down a flight of stairs. The intensity of our gaze on each other tells us what we haven't previously expressed in words. I lean across the table when she says it.

"Kissing is something better done than said," I say as I sit back down, still savoring the sweet taste of Sarah's lips, the moist warmth of her tongue.

"You should send me a visitor's form so I can visit you regularly. I could have a problem alone in a room like this with you." She closes her eyes while gripping the edge of the table.

"But this is so much better to visit alone, privately."

"It's dangerous for me, the temptation. I could get into trouble for abusing privileges. The prison could deny me access."

I stand and take two steps toward the door to peer through the narrow window. "Come here. Look at this. The guard at the desk to our right can't come toward us without us seeing him climb the stairs, and the only other entry is from the corridor, requiring unlocking a door to the left. We're alone. I don't want to give up this privacy."

Sarah runs her manicured fingertips over her gray skirt as she stands and walks over. I surrender the window and move behind her. She looks down the hall to the right toward the guard's station and to the left toward the heavy steel door leading in from the main corridor. I'm directly behind her with both of my hands on her hips. With my face I push her hair to the side and I kiss her neck.

"Stop," she whispers while pressing her body back into mine.

"Watch. You can see the guard. Tell me if he moves." I continue kissing her, touching her, feeling her, moving with her. For this moment, right now, I'm not a prisoner. I'm a man, 28 and virile, alone with a woman for the first time in five years. My prison record doesn't matter, my goals don't matter, and my freedom doesn't matter. I'm not thinking about her professional standing. In the passion of this moment, neither is Sarah. The decades I must serve seem too far away. I need release, and Sarah is the woman who gives it to me.

When we return to our seats perspiration has glued my shirt to my skin. Sarah is disheveled but glowing.

"My God! What are we doing?" her smile belies a mixture of nervousness and exhilaration after the forbidden interlude.

"Nothing. We're not doing anything," I protest.

"You call that nothing? I could lose my license!"

"For what? As far as anyone is concerned, we're just a lawyer and a client in here. There isn't anything different now from when you walked in here, nothing different from any other time you've visited."

"Your shirt's wet. What are you going to say when you go back in?"

"It's hot in here. Just stay for a while longer, it'll dry."

"How do I look? Can you tell?" Her hands shake as she pulls a compact from her purse. She looks into the tiny mirror.

"You're sexy. I can't take my eyes off you."

She smiles and applies makeup. "You're going to get me in trouble."

Chapter Six: 1992-1995
Months 62-84

It's Thanksgiving, 1992, just before my sixth holiday season in prison. Despite the forbidden affair I've been carrying on with Sarah for the past six months, today she tells me that she needs to move on with her life. She understands the risks associated with our trysts and she's come to the conclusion that the stress would be too much to bear for another 21 years.

I've hardened emotionally, as I'm now familiar with the concept of loss. I've been expecting this moment, anticipating her good-bye since our first kiss. Grateful that it has lasted this long, I'm prepared to move forward.

* * * * * * *

"What's up? Did she finally dump you?" Windward asks, sensing my despondency when I return to the cell and drop to my rack without undressing.

"I told you she's my lawyer. That's it."

"And I told my judge that I thought it was flour I was bringin' in. What's that got to do with anythin'?"

"Can't you just be quiet?"

"Least you can do is tell me how it went down. No sense keep denyin' it. Ain't no hot young lawyer gonna keep visitin' a man in the joint 'less somethin's going on. 'Sides that, I smell her all over ya."

"She was trying to help with my case. That's it. Enough, just drop it."

Lying on my rack, ignoring Windward's irritating interrogation, I silently acknowledge that I knew Sarah would eventually disappear from my life. She was a wonderful, delicious respite from my all-male world, but now she's gone and despondency starts to settle in like a dense fog. Thoughts of women, family, and the normal life from which I'm separated rush in, squeezing me. I *have* to refocus, to push thoughts of Sarah out of my mind and block all hope of finding a woman to carry this burden with me. I'm going to focus on completing five years at a time, alone. I've got to reach 1997.

* * * * * * *

The people have elected William Jefferson Clinton the 42nd president of the United States. I closely followed the political coverage throughout the year. Julie even purchased a subscription to the *Washington Post* for me to keep abreast of politics. Now, on a sunny day in January 1993, I'm overwhelmed by my emotions, tears filling my eyes, as I watch Justice Rehnquist swear our new president into office.

"Why do you care so much who the president is when you can't even vote?"

In my sister's world the president doesn't play much part in day-to-day life and she doesn't grasp why I'm optimistic with this switch from Bush to Clinton. As a federal prisoner, I live under the restrictions of the Bureau of Prisons, an agency that needs major reform. I'm hoping that President Clinton or his attorney general will appoint a new director of this agency. I'm certain the change will bring more empathy, as the president's younger brother, Roger, served a federal prison sentence for nonviolent cocaine trafficking. Reform and liberalization of prison could well come under Clinton's leadership.

In preparation of a research report I'm working on for Hofstra I read about various progressive prison systems that President Clinton may consider. In Scandinavian countries citizens from local communities participate in panels designed to oversee and facilitate positive adjustments for offenders. Prisoners meet with "ombudsmen panels" at the beginning of their terms and together they work to establish clearly defined, individualized programs that prisoners may follow to reconcile with society and earn their freedom through merit. No similar program exists in our justice system, though under Clinton there's hope for change. Hope has been a mantra of Clinton's throughout the campaign, and if he wants to restore it for people in prison, he'll need a different kind of system.

Instead of a system that encourages offenders to embrace societal values, studies combined with my experiences convince me that our system has a dramatically different mission with dramatically different outcomes. It began to deteriorate in 1973, after Robert Martinson, a criminologist, published "Nothing Works." It was an influential study suggesting that regardless of what programs administrators initiated, people in prison were incapable of reform. Then Professor James Q. Wilson, a mentor of Dr. DiIulio's, published his widely quoted book, *Thinking About Crime*. In that book, Professor Wilson suggested that society ought to limit the functions of prisons to two goals: isolate and punish. I'd like to see a different approach, and under President Clinton's leadership, I'm hopeful for meaningful reforms.

Either way, I'm on my own, knowing that I must succeed in spite of external forces. The concepts of isolation, deterrence, and punishment don't concern me. I'm making daily progress by staying physically fit and putting in long hours of study toward my master's degree. Regardless of whether President Clinton appoints enlightened leadership to change the system or not, I'll continue to learn and grow. Neither the system of punishment nor anything else will block me from achieving the goals that I set.

Despite the rigid, punishment-based policies espoused by theorists like Martinson and DiIulio and endorsed by the BOP–policies that thwart my struggle to emerge as a capable and contributing citizen–I'm heartened to learn of leaders who embrace what I consider an enlightened system of justice. Some come from surprising places, like the United States Supreme Court.

In a 1985 commencement speech entitled "Factories With Fences," Former Chief Justice Warren Burger called for the graduating students from Pace University to reform America's growing prison system. Instead of perpetuating a system that simply isolates and punishes, Justice Burger urged changes within the system that would encourage prisoners to work toward "earning and learning their way to freedom."

Although eight years have passed since Justice Burger delivered his speech, the Bureau of Prisons has done little to implement his vision. I don't see any way to earn freedom. Through my work and achievements I want to become an example and a catalyst for change. I may not advance my release date, but *I will contribute,* and *I will lead a life of relevance.* I will show by example that self-discipline and education can lead a prisoner to emerge as a contributing citizen, and I will urge reforms that encourage others to do the same.

* * * * * * *

I'm inspired by what I've learned from *The Future of Imprisonment,* a book Dr. Norval Morris published in the 1970s. Dr. Morris wrote that prisons in an enlightened society should enable prisoners to rise to their highest levels of competence. His thoughts resonate with me so I write him. Thinking that he's still a law professor at Harvard, I send my letter of introduction to Cambridge. I want him to know that his work has touched my life, and I ask for his guidance going forward.

Several months pass before I receive his response. Administrators at Harvard forwarded my letter, as Dr. Morris moved to become the Julius Kreeger Professor of Law at The University of Chicago. He responded graciously to my letter, offering to advise me with my studies at Hofstra and throughout the remainder of my term. "I may be of particular help to you at times," he writes, "as I've known every director of the Bureau of Prisons, and the past three directors are close friends of mine. Count on my support if you run into any obstacles with your pursuit of education."

Dr. Morris's support boosts my spirits. To have distinguished academics like Professors McPherson, DiIulio, and Morris as mentors means that I'll have guidance from the same professionals who offer expert opinions to legislators and to the highest levels of prison administrators. The professors will have an interest in preparing me for release; I can trust in them to advocate for me if I need help.

Through our letters and phone calls, Dr. Morris and I become friends. He encourages me to call him Norval and introduces me to other leading American penologists. I begin to correspond with professors from across the United States, including scholars such as Leo Carroll, Todd Clear, Francis Cullen, Timothy Flanagan, Tara Gray, and Marilyn McShane. They all support my efforts and invite me to contribute to their work. As a prisoner who studies prisons from the inside and shares what he knows with the world of academia, I'm evidently unique. Dr. George Cole, an author and Chair of the Political Science Department at the University of Connecticut, pledges his support. We begin to build a close friendship.

Liberation seeps incrementally into my psyche with each of these relationships. I'm less susceptible to the hopelessness that pervades the lives around me. The woman I loved left me and I serve a sentence that is still measured in decades, but I've created a sense of meaning and I feel as though I'm making progress, which is the key to growth.

* * * * * * *

Bruce and I have completed our collaboration on "Transcending the Wall" about the importance of education in transforming prisoners' lives. He generously gives me credit as the first author but it is Bruce who coordinates publication in the scholarly, peer-reviewed *Journal of Criminal Justice Education*. As I told Bruce during our summer visit in 1993, our publication serves a pragmatic purpose.

"I need to start thinking about transferring from this penitentiary," I tell him during one of our visits.

"Are you feeling threatened?" he asks, on alert.

Bruce read about the violence at USP Atlanta in a *New York Times* article that cited it as one of the nation's most dangerous high security prisons. He's always concerned about my safety.

"My schedule keeps me away from trouble, but gang activity is more intense every day. It's violent, bloodshed every week. I think it's time to request a transfer."

"So what's stopping you?"

"I need more information. The thing is, when a prisoner asks for a transfer there's no telling where the BOP will send him. It's like playing roulette. I need to transfer to the most education-friendly prison possible."

"Can Norval help you?"

"He can help, and he said he would. The problem is that I don't know where to go. If I ask for a transfer the BOP will probably send me closer to Seattle, but being closer to home isn't as important as the preparations I need to make for when I get out."

"What do we need to do?" I always love Bruce's steadfast support, and I especially appreciate his use of the "we," meaning he's always on board to help.

"I need to find the best prison for educational programming, but not according to what staff members say. I need inside information from actual prisoners who serve time in the institutions."

Bruce doesn't understand why the prisoners' perspective is so valuable to me when I actively avoid close interactions with the penitentiary population.

I try to explain. "If someone were to inquire about educational opportunities here at USP Atlanta, the staff would discuss the basic programs. They would say that teachers, classrooms, and even college programs are available. But I'm the only prisoner out of 2,500 who's earned a degree here, and there's a reason for that. It's because, despite what staff members say, the atmosphere in here is oppressive and the policies in practice discourage us from pursuing an education."

"Yes, but you've gotten around the obstacles here. What makes you think that you won't get around them wherever you go?"

"The reason I make progress here is because I have support from Ms. Stephens, Mr. Chandler, and a few others. They let me create a schedule that allows me to avoid problems and gives me access to computers; they intervene when policies or staff members try to block me. When I get to the next prison I'm just another prisoner, and I'll be facing obstacles there like everyone else, including from BOP staff members that may resent me for striving to become something more. Those kinds of staff members throw up insurmountable barriers. I see them every day here, but this penitentiary has become as familiar to me as the back of my hand and I know how to get around in here. I need details and the up-to-date truth from prisoners about what goes on in other prisons. With that information I can decide where to request a transfer."

Our conversation evolves into a plan. Bruce writes a letter of introduction to Sylvia McCollum, the Director of Education for the entire Bureau of Prisons. He lists his credentials as a retired professor of education from Chicago and explains that for the past several years he has been mentoring me. He includes a copy of the article we co-authored, offering to travel to Washington to meet with Ms. McCollum and discuss contributions he might make to the Bureau of Prisons as a volunteer.

Had I written to Sylvia McCollum directly, it's unlikely that my letter would've reached her, or that I would've received a response. With Bruce as my emissary, on the other hand, I knew that I would have a better chance of receiving the data I was looking to find.

Bruce visited Ms. McCollum at her office in DC, at the Bureau of Prisons headquarters. She welcomed his offer to mentor other prisoners and even congratulated me through Bruce on the progress I've made. When he told her that he wanted to help others, Ms. McCollum encouraged him. She gave him clearance to visit any federal prison he wanted and instructed those who presided over education departments to accommodate him by arranging private meetings with the prisoners who were most active in education programs.

"I'm ready to begin my journey," Bruce tells me over the phone after describing his successful meeting with Ms. McCollum. "Where should I go?"

* * * * * * *

The research work pays off. With Bruce and Norval's assistance, I successfully coordinate my transfer after learning that the best prison for education is FCI McKean. It's wonderful news when guards inform me that I'm being transferred out of the United States Penitentiary and that I'm on my way to McKean.

"Santos. 16377-004." I respond to the guard who processes me in for transfer as he calls me forward.

He shakes my wrists to ensure the handcuffs are secure and then yanks on the chain around my waist.

"Whadda we got goin' on down here?" The guard pulls my pant legs out from between my skin and the steel bracelets locked around my ankles.

"I didn't get any socks, sir. The chains were digging into

my shins."

"Gonna have to live with it. Security first." He tightens the cuffs to ensure I don't pull the pant legs through again. Then he clears me.

I once read a novel by Wilbur Smith describing the horrific experiences of people who were locked in chains after slave traders captured them. The slaves were forced to walk across rough terrain to the ships stealing them from Africa. The descriptions sickened me when I read the novel and I'm reminded of them as I shuffle my way onto the bus. The steel rings once again cut into my skin, but by shortening my steps I lessen the pain.

My stomach churns despite three earlier trips to the bathroom. My body hasn't moved faster than my legs could carry it since 1988, the last time I was in a vehicle. Now, in the spring of 1994, I'm sitting on an uncomfortable seat in the prison bus that is about to transport me out of USP Atlanta. Diesel fumes from the engines make me nauseous as beads of sweat form on my forehead

It's been seven years since my arrest. I'm now 30-years-old, certainly a different man, though still a prisoner with a long, steep climb into more darkness.

I smile as I settle into the black vinyl seat, recalling how I engineered this transfer. With Norval's help the administrative obstacles to the transfer were insignificant. Bruce visited five prisons and spoke with several prisoners in each. Clearly, the news about the Federal Correctional Institution in Bradford, Pennsylvania, known as FCI McKean, suggested that it would be my best choice. The prisoners at McKean refer to it as "Dream McKean," with a progressive warden, Dennis Luther, who wholeheartedly supports educational programs.

Ordinarily the documented address of release residence in my case file would've prohibited my transfer to McKean. The BOP confined me in the Southeast region because of my arrest in South Florida, but my release address is Seattle.

"I can submit a transfer for you to FCI McKean," my case manager told me when I asked, "but I know the Region isn't going to approve it. You don't have a release address for that part of the country, and I know you'll either be sent to a prison in the West or another prison here in the Southeast."

"I don't care about being close to home. I've got too much time left to serve and McKean's the best spot to finish my education." I persisted with the request, knowing she wanted to help.

"Look, I support you and I'm going to submit you for McKean. I'm just telling you what's going to happen. Once I send the file to the regional office it's out of my hands, and no one in that office knows anything about you."

My case manager, Ms. Forbes, had attended my graduation in 1992 and helped me make arrangements with the mailroom to receive the books I needed from the Hofstra library. She supported my efforts but was honest in telling me what she thought would happen once she put forth my file for transfer. I existed only as a number in the system, and I understood that all consideration from staff at USP Atlanta would end with my transfer request.

After that conversation with my case manager I called Norval and explained the advantages that FCI McKean offered along with the challenges I would have in transferring. Norval said he knew the regional director and promised to call him on my behalf. That was two days ago.

When the bus engine begins to roar, I feel ready to leave. I've lived through six holiday seasons amidst prisoners serving multiple life sentences in the penitentiary. Transitioning to a medium-security prison means encountering less volatility and more optimism, I hope.

As I wait for the bus to roll along, my thoughts, curiously, turn to my eventual release. I submitted a petition for clemency about six months ago. It wasn't my intention to submit the petition until 1997, when I would've completed my first decade. But after discussing my plan with Norval, he convinced me on the merits of submitting the petition at once.

"These efforts take time and work," Norval explained, "and clemency is extremely rare, especially in this political climate. I don't see any advantage in waiting until 1997. You've earned one university degree and you're well on your way to earning a second. Draft a petition now and send it to me for review. I think you should get the process started."

With Norval's letter of support, I proudly sent my petition to the U.S. pardon attorney in Washington. That was more than six months ago. Whenever I've made an inquiry on the progress, I received form letters that say my petition is under review. I have no idea what will happen, if anything. I can't grasp the concept of 19 more years in prison. But I'm transferring from a high-security penitentiary to a medium-security FCI now, and I'm excited about the change of scenery, even if I'm still immersed in a population of more than 1,500 felons.

* * * * * * *

The air brakes sigh as the bus stops in front of the administration building of FCI McKean. As I look through chain-link fences separated by razor wire, I remember my first close look at a prison, back in 1987, when the DEA escorted me through the gates of MCC Miami. McKean has that same non-threatening feel of an office park. Without the impenetrably high concrete walls and gun towers of Atlanta, McKean looks almost welcoming, at least from the outside. I suppose the years have institutionalized me.

While hobbling off the bus I inhale the scent of evergreen trees. McKean is set in the midst of northwestern Pennsylvania's Allegheny Forest. I can't remember the last time I've been in such a natural setting, double, razor-wire topped fences notwithstanding. The cool mountain air makes me shiver, but I soak up the sight of trees, spring flowers, and distant rolling hills as I shuffle along in line with 22 other prisoners toward the processing area.

It's early afternoon by the time guards snap my photograph, fingerprint me, issue my bedroll and ID card. Rather than following the wide concrete walkways through manicured lawns toward my housing unit, I detour into the education department for a look and to introduce myself to the supervisor of education. I find Ms. Barto's office and knock.

"May I speak with you for a minute?"

She looks at my blue canvas shoes, my elastic-waist khaki pants, my dingy white t-shirt with 2XL written in black felt-tip marker on the upper left chest, and the bed roll I carry under my arm.

"Looks like you just pulled in."

"Yes. I just got here." From Bruce's description of her I knew to expect a sight different from Mr. Chandler. Ms. Barto is in her mid-30s, slender, with chestnut hair, gleaming white teeth, and blue eyes that sparkle. She has a welcoming smile that many prisoners, I'm sure, confuse with an invitation to flirt.

"Haven't you reported to your housing unit yet?"

"Before going there, I wanted to introduce myself and ask if you might have a job for me. My name is Michael Santos. I'm just transferring from USP Atlanta. You may remember my mentor, Dr. Bruce McPherson, who visited you and a few inmates here about a month ago?"

"Oh, you're Dr. McPherson's friend. He mentioned that you were going to try transferring here. I'm surprised you made it, and so quickly."

"I was lucky, I guess. I wanted to talk with you about an educational program I'm involved in, and I hope you'll help me with some special requirements."

"You're in correspondence school, right?" She remembers Bruce talking about me.

"I'm nearly finished with a program at Hofstra University. To complete it I'll need to make arrangements here so Hofstra's library can send the books I need to read. Besides those arrangements, I'm hoping you might have a job available that will provide access to a word processor."

With Bruce having paved the way before I arrived, Ms. Barto extends all the support I need, and there are no delays settling in at McKean. She assigns me to a job of tutoring other prisoners on their self-paced studies to learn word processing skills. She authorizes my use of the computer for school and coordinates with the mailroom to accept packages from Hofstra's library. With Bruce's advance preparations and my clearly documented record of achievement, I have a seamless transition into Dream McKean.

* * * * * * *

Compared to the penitentiary, McKean *is* a dream. Although a handful of prisoners on the compound serve life sentences, the tension at McKean isn't as pervasive or palpable as it was at USP Atlanta. Professional, intelligent leadership is the reason behind the tranquility. Warden Dennis Luther doesn't cling to the simplistic notion that prisons should exist solely to isolate and punish. Instead of relying on policies that crush hope, and managing by threat of further punishment, Warden Luther uses a highly effective system of positive incentives.

I no longer live in a cauldron ready to boil over. To leave my cell in Atlanta I had to wait for specific times and pass through eight separate checkpoints, metal detectors, and searches just to get to the weight pile. By contrast, the doors don't lock at McKean and our liberty to walk freely encourages a responsible independence, thus lessening the tension all the way around.

McKean has a token economy where prisoners can earn points individually and collectively. We redeem the points for privileges and rewards that ease our time. The progressive system vests the population with incentives to exercise self-control. By keeping rooms and housing units clean, prisoners earn the privilege of more access to television and the phones. Those who accumulate enough points earn the privilege of having a portable television and VCR in their rooms. By minimizing disciplinary infractions, prisoners can participate in family picnics, order food and goods from local businesses, and wear personal rather than institutional clothing.

No one wants problems that can lead to the loss of privileges or lockdowns. The system works exceptionally well, eliminating problems like gangs and violence. The rigid bureaucracy of Atlanta stands in stark opposition to McKean. Ideas for my master's thesis begin to form as I study Luther's management style. Eagerly, I write a letter explaining my intentions to him. He's not only supportive but invites me to his office and makes himself available as an interview subject.

* * * * * * *

"I'm here to see Warden Luther," I explain to the guard who eyes me suspiciously when I present myself to the control area. The guard is stationed in a locked booth, an area that is off limits to prisoners. After he makes a call and confirms that I'm authorized to visit the warden in his office, the guard–still wary–

buzzes the door open and I walk in.

Tall indoor plants with heavy green leaves fill the atrium-like lobby. I look up and see several skylights. Brightly colored fish swim in a large aquarium adjacent to the receptionist's desk. She tells me to walk up the stairs.

"The warden's office will be to the left."

When I walk into the office the warden's secretary greets me from her desk. "Have a seat Mr. Santos. Warden Luther will see you momentarily."

She smiles at me and offers to pour me a cup of coffee, as if I'm a colleague calling on a business acquaintance. I thank her but decline the coffee while picking up a magazine on the wooden table beside the chair. The trade magazine serves the prison industry and those who work in prison management. In perusing the table of contents I quickly spot an article that Warden Luther coauthored with one of my mentors, Professor John DiIulio.

The phone on the secretary's desk rings and she tells me I can walk into the warden's office. My legs shake a little as I walk on the plush carpet. Warden Dennis Luther sits in a high-backed leather chair, at a desk of cherry wood. Behind him a large window overlooks the center of McKean's compound. An American flag and another flag bearing the Department of Justice insignia hang from poles in the corner. Bookshelves line the wall and I see photographs of him with other Bureau of Prisons officials, including Director Kathy Hawk.

"Have a seat." Warden Luther gestures to a couch adjacent to his desk. It's the first couch I've sat on since my term began. "Tell me about your thesis and how I can help," he encourages me.

"I'm at a stage where I have to propose my thesis subject to the graduate committee. I'd like to write about the incentive system and the token economy you've initiated here. I could make a more persuasive case if I could learn about the influences that shaped your management philosophy."

"Okay. We can start right now. What are your questions?"

"Wow. I wasn't expecting to start today, but since you're offering, I'd like to hear about your relationship with Professor

John DiIulio."

My question surprises him, and I'm sure he wonders how I know about the Princeton professor. "John DiIulio? Why would you ask about him?"

"Well, while I was waiting in your outer office, I flipped through the magazine on the table. I didn't have time to read it, but I saw that you coauthored an article with Dr. DiIulio. For the past few years I've had an ongoing correspondence with him and I've read all of his books. From what I've learned through our correspondence and from his books, *Governing Prisons* and *No Escape*, I'm surprised that you two would collaborate as colleagues."

He chuckles. "The truth is, John and I share more in common than you might think."

* * * * * * *

After an hour with the warden I return to my room and immediately write a letter to Dr. DiIulio. I explain that I'm proposing to center my thesis on Warden Luther's management style, contrasting his token economy with the goals of isolation and punishment that Professor James Q. Wilson promotes, and even with the strict control model that DiIulio himself extols.

Dr. DiIulio surprises me with his quick response to my letter. He writes that he's glad I've settled in so well at FCI McKean and that I've had an opportunity to learn from his friend, Warden Luther. "What if I could arrange to bring a class of Princeton students on a field trip to McKean? That way they could tour the prison and perhaps spend some time listening to you and Warden Luther describe your perspectives on confinement."

It's an incredible offer for me, and I accept with enthusiasm.

* * * * * * *

On a Saturday morning, in the fall of 1994, I wake at three o'clock as a guard shines his flashlight into my single-man cell for the census count. After climbing out from under the covers and flipping on the light, I sit at my desk to read through the notes I've taken from Dr. DiIulio's books.

In a few hours I'll receive an honor that I know will have

meaning for the rest of my life. Although not quite equivalent to lecturing at Princeton, I'm looking forward to speaking with a group of Ivy League students, contributing to their education and to their understanding of America's prison system. Few prisoners will ever enjoy such an honor and I bask, momentarily, in my good fortune. I feel as if I'm charting my own course, making progress.

At nine o'clock I walk to Warden Luther's office, ready, intent on making a favorable impression while giving Dr. DiIulio and his students a different perspective on the need for prison reform. Three of us, including Warden Luther, Associate Warden Craig Apker, and I sit in a conference room.

"Care for coffee or hot chocolate?" Warden Luther points to the buffet table.

I walk over and pour hot chocolate from a thermos. While admiring the array of pastries on the oak table I suddenly realize it's the first time I've sipped from a ceramic mug since I've been incarcerated. I'm used to plastic and this heavy mug dings against my teeth. The whole experience makes me grin.

"Did you sleep well?" the warden asks.

He's dressed casually, in brown corduroys and a tan sweater over a shirt with a button-down Oxford collar. He looks preppy, which I guess is appropriate for a meeting with the undergrads.

"I've been awake since three," I admit. "This is a big day for me and I wanted to study the notes I've taken on Dr. DiIulio's books."

Through the conference room window the three of us watch the charter bus come to a stop in front of the administration building. I've seen photographs of Dr. DiIulio before and recognize him as he steps off the bus. I've read everything I could about him. I know that he earned his Ph.D. from Harvard, and also that he was one of the youngest professors at Princeton to receive tenure.

I count fourteen students, all well dressed, and I contemplate the brilliant futures that await them. These are future leaders being groomed in one of the world's finest universities. Some may be offspring of legislators and judges. I'm thinking of the influence they represent and I'm grateful for the privilege of speaking with them while I'm wearing the khaki uniform of a prisoner.

After introductions, we sit in cushioned chairs around the highly polished wooden conference table. The students take notes as Warden Luther provides the group with details on the prison. It is a medium-security Federal Correctional Institution with a population that ranges between 1,400 and 1,800 men. He describes how he governs the prison from the perspective that prisoners are sent to prison as punishment for their crimes, rejecting the notion that he has a duty to punish them further by creating an oppressive atmosphere.

"So do you think others might construe your prison as one that coddles prisoners?" one of the students asks.

"What do you think, Michael? Are you being coddled?" Warden Luther deflects the student's question to me and I'm happy to respond.

"I served the first several years of my sentence in a high-security prison, an environment that really dehumanizes everyone. Although I was able to create a routine and focus on educating myself, most of the other prisoners abandoned hope. Those perceptions and attitudes stoked their hostility. That level of anger doesn't exist here, and from that perspective, it's better, at least for me.

"Some people might believe this atmosphere coddles prisoners, but it has many advantages that should interest taxpayers. I don't sense a strong gang presence, I haven't seen any bloodshed, and the prisoners work together to sustain the availability of privileges we can work toward. We're still in prison, still living without family, without liberty. When I'm lying on a steel rack in a locked room at night, with an aching to see my mother again, or to hug my sisters, or when I'm suffering from the estrangement I feel from society, from women, I'm aware of my punishment. I've been living that way for more than 2,500 days already. To me it doesn't feel like I'm being coddled."

"What kind of changes do you think Congress could make that would serve the interests of taxpayers?" Dr. DiIulio asks Warden Luther.

"One change I'd recommend would be to close all

minimum-security prison camps. The camps don't serve a useful purpose. Fences don't confine the camp prisoners, and the men aren't a threat to society. Camp prisoners should serve their sanctions in home-confinement or under some other form of community-based sanction that would not require taxpayers to spend more than $10,000 a year to support each man we confine in a camp."

"How about you, Michael? What kind of changes would you like to see Congress make?"

"Well, as a long-term prisoner, I'd like to see citizens and members of Congress rethink the concept of justice. Instead of measuring justice by the number of calendar years a person serves in prison, I'd like to see changes that would measure justice by the efforts an offender makes to redeem his crimes and reconcile with society. Reforms should encourage offenders to work toward earning freedom through merit and redemptive acts."

"How about violent offenders?" Another student interjects. "Should offenders who violently prey on society have opportunities to earn freedom?"

"I'm a big believer in a person's capacity to change, to lead a productive and contributing life. An enlightened society such as ours ought to allow its criminal justice system to evolve. I don't know the mechanisms citizens or leaders ought to put in place, or what challenges an individual ought to overcome to earn freedom, but I think we can come up with a system that serves society better than locking a human being in a cage for decades. Perhaps some offenders won't express remorse, or work to atone, or do enough to earn freedom. But many will. And such a system, I'm sure, would serve the interests of society better than one limiting itself to isolating and punishing."

* * * * * * *

The hours we spend together in Warden Luther's conference room raise my spirit. When we leave I'm the tour guide, responding to student questions as we walk through the housing units, recreation areas, and prison compound. After our tour we return for a second conference that lasts another few hours. I'm energized as I finally walk them out to their bus, and I don't mind at all when the guard at the gate leading back into the prison orders me against the wall so he can pat me down. Indifferent to the degradation and assault on my human dignity, I smile back at the group of students who watch the search.

"Who're they?" the guard asks, curious about why I'm with the group.

"They're students from Princeton."

He's giving me a thorough search, perhaps because the group is looking on. I'm a spectacle, on display, with the guard's hands working their way along my arms as if he's squeezing meat into a sausage casing.

"So why they coming to see you? You go to Princeton?"

"No. I correspond with their professor, who has a relationship with Warden Luther. The students came on a field trip and I was invited to participate."

"Lucky you," he says as he clears me to walk through the gate and into the prison yard.

* * * * * * *

My meeting with Dr. DiIulio and his students inspires my thesis. It becomes a project that succeeds in making me feel luckier still, opening new avenues few long-term prisoners enjoy. Warden Luther authorizes me to record a video for presentation at the 1994 Annual Conference of the American Society of Criminology, and in May of 1995, Hofstra awards my Master of Arts degree. With those credentials and letters of endorsement from my growing support network, Dr. George Cole convinces his colleagues to admit me into a program at the University of Connecticut that will lead to my Ph.D. Eight years into my sentence and I'm on my way toward becoming a scholar of distinction. Or so I think.

Chapter Seven: 1995
Months 93-95

Hofstra awards my master's degree in May of 1995 and I begin working my way toward a doctorate at the University of Connecticut. The textbooks on penology could cure insomnia, but the clear path to a Ph.D. motivates me, keeping me cocooned in my room except for my early morning exercise. I think about the authors sometimes, wondering what inspired them to study and write about prisons. For them, I know, a lengthy sentence didn't provide the impetus. I don't have any idea what compels someone to build a career around the walled concrete and steel compounds that now hold more than two million people in the U.S.

I have eighteen more years to serve and at times I feel disconnected, as if I'm living behind a glass wall, where I can see but not participate in the broader society. I'm isolated, though my projects bring meaning into my life and dissipate feelings of loneliness or despair. I feel driven by goals every day, racing to finish one project so that I can begin another. Despite the length of time I have to serve, I still feel as if I can't afford to waste a single second.

When I hear news that Warden Luther plans to retire in June, I worry that his departure will lead to changes that could disrupt my progress. I seek him out and inquire about who will replace him as warden.

"You'll be fine," the warden assures me. "It doesn't matter who comes. Just keep working on your education and you'll continue to live productively in here."

Under Warden Luther's leadership, McKean enjoys a reputation of having comparatively well-behaved prisoners. Despite the long sentences that many men serve, they appreciate the privileges of "open movement," the absence of lockdowns, the ability to order food from the community, and the privilege of participating in Luther's token economy. Men who transfer from other prisons leave their tension, hostility, and gang problems at the door. Throughout the institution, he hangs copies of a framed memorandum titled: Warden Luther's Beliefs about the Treatment of Inmates. The 28 beliefs begin like this:

1. Inmates are sent to prison as punishment and not for punishment.
2. Correctional workers have a responsibility to ensure that inmates are returned to the community no more angry or hostile than when they were committed.
3. Inmates are entitled to a safe and humane environment while in prison.
4. You must believe in man's capacity to change his behavior.
5. Normalize the environment to the extent possible by providing programs, amenities, and services. The denial of such must be related to maintaining order and security rather than punishment.
6. Most inmates will respond favorably to a clean and aesthetically pleasing physical environment and will not vandalize or destroy it.

Luther's philosophy, albeit powerful and positive, exists at FCI McKean but nowhere else that I'm aware of within the Bureau of Prisons. It won't last beyond his departure and I sense trouble.

Some staff members resent the privileges Warden Luther extends to me, and I can understand why they would. After all, he treats me kindly, and it isn't unusual for me to receive a page over the loudspeaker to report to the warden's office. He openly supports my academic program, authorizing me free access to a computer lab, allowing me to use the word processors for my academic program as well as for correspondence with my growing support network. On one occasion, he introduced me to a tour group he was leading through the prison.

"This is inmate Santos. He knows more about prisons than many on my staff." He treats me more like a colleague than a prisoner, and some staff members resent it. I don't miss the frozen expression on their face, the body language that implies definite disagreement on that point.

My profile at McKean has become too high. Every staff member knows Warden Luther supports and sponsors my work and I sense that his retirement puts a target on my back. I begin contemplating the merits of requesting a transfer to someplace new, someplace where I can serve my sentence anonymously. If I were to ask for a transfer, I feel confident that my support network could help make it happen. Doing so, however, would mean the immediate loss of the privileges I enjoy here, and so I put off the decision, deciding to see what comes with the change in leadership.

* * * * * * *

Within weeks of Luther's departure Warden Meko arrives, blasting Luther's token economy out of operation and blowing the atmosphere of trust to smithereens. The new warden institutes the oppressive controls characteristic of other prisons, giving quick rise to levels of anger and hostilities that weren't around under Luther's leadership.

Warden Meko is all law and order. If you put a pair of mirrored sunglasses on him, he could pose for a highway patrol poster. He and his staff quickly assess that the prisoners at FCI McKean have been living too well, and they're determined to tone down the atmosphere, to bring us into line with their beliefs of how prisoners should live. In stripping away the incentives prisoners have grown accustomed to, he also rips away the sense of camaraderie and tolerance. McKean's atmosphere quickly changes to discontent with growing racial tensions and threats, eradicating the hope that Warden Luther worked so hard to instill. The new regime wants a standard-issue prison and welcomes the hostility its punitive system breeds. Tensions become more palpable.

Last April authorities arrested Timothy McVeigh for bombing the Murray Federal Building in Oklahoma City, killing 168 people. Judicial proceedings are all over the news. Many prisoners in FCI McKean now openly root for McVeigh, cheering every sign of civil unrest, from militia groups to incidences of civil rebellion. This atmosphere feels ripe for rebellion.

It's October and another fervor is emerging. Louis Farrakhan, minister of the influential Nation of Islam, has organized The Million Man March on Washington to protest injustice in America. He calls for black men to unite and for legislators to bring fairness to a criminal justice system that disproportionately locks up blacks and Hispanics. Media attention stokes the anger of prisoners at McKean, and there is constant chatter on the compound about a need to unite, to take a stand, to do something. Whereas Warden Luther would've led us positively through this collective desire for rebellion, Warden Meko turns up the heat to see how far the prisoners are willing to take their anger. Had Luther been in charge, I suspect he would've called a Town Hall meeting, assembling all the prisoners to remind them that he didn't have any power over the length of their sentences. He likely would've communicated a message as follows:

"Although I can't do anything to change the length of time any of you are serving, wardens set the tone for the environment in these places. I do my best to operate an efficient institution that allows every man to serve his sentence with dignity. At McKean we offer privileges and incentives conditionally to everyone who acts responsibly, but any hint of rebellion will result in changes that could include lockdowns, strict controls, and the loss of privileges that none of us want. I'm encouraging you guys to work together, to act responsibly so that we can keep things working well here."

The administration under Warden Meko's leadership, on the other hand, sees opportunity in the brewing resentment. An organized disturbance would provide the cover necessary to completely dismantle the progressive policies that Warden Luther favored. Whereas the prisoners resent the new administration, most staff members eagerly embrace changes that Meko's regime is putting in place. It's as if they're goading prisoners on to carry out threats of a rebellion. They don't have to wait long.

When I open my door at 5:20 in the morning, it's hard to believe that Luther retired only three months ago. Instead of the calm that previously reigned over McKean, I see fires blazing in front of me. Prisoners are on a rampage, wool caps pulled over their faces, smashing windows, breaking chairs, tables, and desks. Guards have deserted their stations, leaving the entire building devoid of order. I close the door and retreat into my room, knowing I've already seen more of this melee than I'd like.

Although prisoners run wild through common areas, locked steel doors prohibit them from exiting to the compound. Destruction, not escape, is the purpose of their anarchy. It isn't only our housing unit erupting in bedlam, as through the narrow window of my room, I watch orange flames reaching the ceiling in the next unit, where a pool table burns.

As I've done so many other times, I lie on my rack and pull my pillow over my eyes, a conscious effort to tune out my environment. Hearing no evil, seeing no evil, and speaking no evil is part of my deliberate strategy to survive in here. Violence and disturbance represent a part of the journey, and I've just got to roll with it. I know that we'll be on lockdown soon, and an official inquiry will follow. I'm best served now by trying to sleep through this mess.

* * * * * * *

"All inmates! Stand for count!" The guard's bullhorn demand from the common area wakes me at 10:30 in the morning.

Five hours have passed since I saw the blazes outside my door and windows. Now I see a dozen guards dressed in camouflage and wearing helmets with clear visors standing alert. They hold batons, and plastic grips for quick handcuffing along with canisters of mace hang from their heavy leather belts. I brace myself for the riot squad, seeing that they're all suited up and ready for combat. One holds a video camcorder, filming the destruction, while another snaps photos of the debris with an instant camera.

"I repeat!" the guard yells again. "Stand for count! Any inmate who refuses to stand is resisting and my officers will respond accordingly. So I repeat again! Stand for count!"

Some prisoners yell obscenities from their cells, taunting the guards. I back against my rack and stand stoically, letting everyone see that I don't have a stake in this fight. Predictably, the riot team responds aggressively to defiance, rushing into rooms, restraining any belligerent, taunting, or resisting prisoners with plastic quick ties and marching them straight out to waiting buses. Those men are gone, being transferred to penitentiaries thousands of miles away. It isn't my concern, as I don't feel any alignment with the shortsighted prisoners who set this problem in motion.

I've read of and thought about the struggle and suffering of Elie Wiesel, Viktor Frankl, and the millions of others who perished because of anti-Semitism in Hitler's camps. I've also read extensively about the persecution of blacks and injustice in our country. Those stories inspire me, as by reading them I have examples of amazing survivors who overcame those severe violations of human rights. Now, while locked in my cell, I contemplate the strategies I'll use to triumph over the dehumanizing indignities about to ensue. I have what I need, including books, space to exercise, a plan, a growing ability to express myself, and a professional audience of mentors who validate my efforts. I'll make it. I may lose access to computers and other privileges that have made my studies easier, but I'll make it through, relying on a stash of pens and the skill I've developed to write in straight rows across unlined paper.

Being locked in my closet-sized cell prohibits access to the track or weight room. So I exercise alone, ignoring the outbursts of other prisoners who kick their doors to protest the lockdown. I run in place for hours, pulling my knees up high and then dropping down to blast out several hundred pushups. With a dirty towel, I mop the sweat that rolls off me and puddles on the floor. A shower may be a few days off but I've got soap and a sink with running water to clean myself. I wash my underwear and t-shirt, hanging them to dry on a hook against the wall. I can do this for as long as it takes.

Guards bring white bread with a slice of bologna in a brown sack twice a day. As weeks pass, I draw strength from knowing that prisoners such as Nelson Mandela, Alexander Solzhenitsyn, and many, many others have endured much worse.

* * * * * * *

"Normal" operations resume at McKean in November of 1995, albeit with more restrictions and more controls. It's like other penitentiaries now, with metal detectors, locked gates, and more cell confinement. Hundreds of prisoners were shipped off to other institutions after the riot, and investigations continue. The local newspaper covers the riot and reports that damages to the prison exceed a million dollars. That's a lot of broken windows and smashed furniture, although I suspect that Warden Meko padded those costs by keeping us on lockdown, generating immense staff overtime and installing new security measures like surveillance cameras throughout the compound. He succeeds in turning Dream McKean into a nightmare.

Some prisoners face new criminal charges and others will spend years in isolation without access to visits, telephone, or other privileges they once took for granted. Losses of television, pool tables, bingo, and videos don't affect my adjustment to this new regime. Instead of pacifiers, I need permission to receive books through the mail from the University of Connecticut for my second semester, as the long lockdown has given me the time to finish my first semester from my cell. I'm eager to resume my studies, but before I can, I need that permission to receive more books. Only an associate warden can provide me with that permission.

It's Thanksgiving Day when I see Associate Warden Nuss in the chow hall. He sports a flap of dark hair styled with gel to conceal his receding hairline and stands with military bearing, hands clasped behind his back, barely moving. Even his face is frozen, as if a smile might crack it. Eyeglasses with circular lenses in a thin, almost invisible wire frame reminiscent of those worn by Teddy and Franklin Roosevelt complete the austere image he projects.

I inch forward through the line with hundreds of other prisoners toward the serving bar. I've never spoken to Nuss but I know he's part of the new Meko administration, referred to as Meko's hatchet man. He's in charge of security, the man who oversees the work of captains, lieutenants, and guards. I saw his signature on memorandums that replaced the old incentive system with threats of disciplinary action and punishment.

I need to speak with AW Nuss to obtain his written approval to receive my textbooks. From across the noisy chow hall, I try to gauge his mood, assessing whether this is a good time to approach him.

I've been creeping forward in line for 12 minutes with my eyes on him the entire time, noting that no one has dared approach him. Finally, a prisoner gripping his brown plastic tray of turkey and mashed potatoes ventures forth and initiates a conversation. Nuss looks through the prisoner with no change in his facial expression, nods slightly, and the prisoner walks on.

I estimate it'll be another 10 minutes before the line servers load my tray. I don't want to speak with Nuss, but since I need his authorization for the university to send me books for the next term, I don't have a choice. He may leave by the time I find a place to sit, so I decide to abandon my spot in the slowly moving serving line and approach him.

The prisoner who was in line behind me issues a warning. "A yo! Once you leave, dat's it dawg. I ain't savin' no spot."

I shrug my shoulders. "I didn't ask you to save my spot."

"I'm jus' sayin' yo, ain't savin' no spot." The gold grill in his mouth glitters as I walk away.

I weave my way through the crowd toward the far wall where Nuss stands. His eyes scan the room slowly, looking from one side to the other over 500 prisoners' heads. He shifts his glance toward me as he notices me walking toward him.

"Excuse me, Mr. Nuss. May I speak to you?"

His nod is nearly imperceptible but we lock eyes. While his stern demeanor suggests that he considers our relationship inherently adversarial, I know he's giving me his full attention.

"My name is Michael Santos."

"I know who you are Mr. Santos," he says, cutting me off and startling me with his sharp tone.

"I'd like to talk with you about my educational program."

He nods, and I proceed.

"I'm enrolled in a doctoral program at the University of Connecticut."

"Spare me the résumé. What's on your mind?"

"Well, I've completed my coursework for this term and I'm signing up for the next semester. I'll need a package permit to receive new books from the university."

"Not going to happen." He doesn't elaborate.

"I'm sorry?"

Nuss doesn't offer an explanation. He stands still and stares into my eyes without blinking.

"I need the books to complete my program."

"And I've got a prison to run."

My pulse quickens, as I sense he's about to disrupt my world. I can't believe he's going to block my education without even offering an explanation. "You know, sir, I've been in prison for more than eight years and my disciplinary record is as clean as the day I came in?"

He's totally motionless, just staring, as if expecting me to grovel. "So you're a candidate for sainthood. What else is new?"

"May I ask why you won't authorize me to receive books?"

"They interfere with the security of my institution."

"Books?"

"That's right."

"But they're academic texts and they'll come directly from the library of a major university."

"How would I know what's in them? I don't have the staff available to look through books."

"Mr. Nuss, this isn't radical literature. I'm studying theory, relationships, social order and allocation of public resources for prisons."

"I've made my decision, Mr. Santos. You've done just fine for yourself as an inmate at FCI McKean. But this is a new McKean, a federal prison, not a college."

Getting nowhere I muster a "thanks" for his consideration and walk away. There's no way I can enjoy a Thanksgiving meal. I return to the housing unit with thoughts of how I'm going to overcome this hurdle. The doctoral degree has an integral link to the future I'm striving to create, and to my sense of self. I can't give up, as I've got more than 17 years to go but I don't know what I'll do without the sublimation that study provides.

I call Bruce to let him know what I'm up against and he offers to do what he can, saying he'll call his contact at BOP headquarters, Sylvia McCollum, after the holiday weekend. As a high-level education administrator in the BOP, perhaps she'll have a solution. My next call is to Norval at the University of Chicago, who promises to intervene at a higher level.

"I've got a meeting with the National Institute of Corrections in December," he says. "Kathy Hawk is going to be there and I'll have a chat with her. Perhaps it's time to find another prison for you, one better able to accommodate your studies."

Dr. Kathy Hawk is the Director of the Bureau of Prisons. President Bush appointed her and President Clinton has kept her on to lead this massive, rapidly growing agency. I've read about her and I know she has a doctorate, either in education or psychology. Norval once sent me a copy of a letter she wrote to him referencing me, so I know she's aware of my efforts and she can help. With a phone call she could resolve my problems at McKean, or order my transfer to a prison where I'd be able to complete my studies.

With Bruce and Norval ready to lobby on my behalf, my tension eases. A new focus leads me to read through everything I find in the law library about potential prisons where I can transfer. It would be nice if Bruce could make another information-gathering trip to other prisons, but I doubt he has the time, and actually, neither do I. President Clinton hasn't ruled on my clemency petition yet, but it's important that I finish my doctoral studies by the time I hit my 10-year mark. I can't afford to miss an entire semester because of bureaucratic resistance and bottlenecks.

I haven't thought much about security levels of prisons since my initial incarceration. Yet as I read through the Bureau of Prisons Custody and Classification manual, I stumble upon the formula case managers use to determine them. A number of factors convince me that my security level should be low rather than medium. Specifically, I don't have a history of violence, I wasn't incarcerated before this case, I don't have a history of disciplinary infractions, and I'm within 18 years of my release date. All of those factors mean that I should be classified as low rather than medium security.

Low-security classification would open more options, but in order to pursue a transfer to one of those prisons I need to meet with my case manager and verify my status. If I can persuade him that I'm entitled to a low-security classification, perhaps I can also persuade him to recommend a transfer.

* * * * * * *

In search of the associate warden, I walk to the chow hall during the noon meal and I see Nuss standing in line, looking like the Grim Reaper. Knowing that he can influence my transfer to low-security, I approach him.

"I spent the weekend reading through the Custody and Classification manual," I tell him. "According to the formula in the policy statement, I calculate that I should be in a low-, not a medium-security prison. When my case manager comes in I'll see what he thinks. If I've got a low-security rating, would you support my transfer?"

"Don't you have 45 years?"

"Yes. But I've done eight years without any problems or disciplinary infractions."

"But you led a criminal organization." His knowledge of my case makes me wonder what he has against me.

"I don't have a history of violence or weapons, and I'm within 18 years of my release." I counter.

"When's your release date?"

"August, 2013."

He looks up, does the math in his head. "You're just barely under 18 years, by three months."

"Still, I'm under 18 years. That qualifies me for placement in a low-security prison. I'd like a transfer."

"Where do you want to transfer?"

"Wherever I can complete my schooling. I'm from Seattle, but I don't care where I serve my sentence. I just want to earn my degree and I might face fewer restrictions if I'm in a low."

"Let's see what your case manager says."

193

A bit more optimistic, I walk to the serving line and notice pizza on the menu. It's little more than tomato sauce and cheese melted over a cardboard-like crust, but I've grown to like it. The line server drops a postcard-size slice on my plastic tray. I fill a plastic cup with water from the beverage bar and weave my way through the crowd to an empty table.

A lieutenant with a lumberjack's weathered face and a wad of chewing tobacco bulging in her lower lip walks toward where I'm sitting. We've never spoken before. "When you finish your lunch, come see me," she barks, spitting tobacco juice into a foam cup she holds.

I haven't taken a bite, but I'm curious about what she wants with me and I ask her what's up.

"I'll talk with you outside," she says, as if challenging me.

"I can go now."

"Come with me."

With some apprehension over what she wants, I stand and follow her out of the chow hall, leaving my tray on the table. I can't think of any reason why a lieutenant would want to talk with me. We leave through the glass door and she turns to the left.

"Put your hands up against the wall," she orders as I step out of the chow hall.

"What?"

"You heard me," the lieutenant orders. "Put your hands up on the wall."

I can't believe this, but I know that it doesn't make any sense to resist or to ask for an explanation. I raise my arms and lean against the wall while she searches me, running her hands along my outstretched arms, my torso, and down my legs.

"Put your hands behind your back."

I comply, and she snaps steel handcuffs around my wrists.

"Let's go." She grabs the short chain between the cuffs to guide me.

I'm silent as we walk across the compound and listen while she speaks through her radio. "I've got one en route to SHU."

194

We reach the door to the Special Housing Unit, the jail within the prison, and a guard buzzes the lock. She escorts me inside, handing me to the guards stationed there. "Lock this one up. I'll send the paperwork over later."

"What's he in for?" the SHU guard inquires, looking past me. To him I'm not human.

"Investigation. Nuss's orders."

"Got it."

My mind spins. I'm not being charged with a disciplinary infraction, but I suspect this disturbance won't look good on my petition for clemency. The strict rules in SHU will prohibit access to my books, and I know that an investigation can last years. Consistent with the administration's *you've got nothin' comin'* attitude, Nuss wants to bury me in here, limiting my ability to communicate, to study, or earn a Ph.D.

After strip searching me the guard issues an orange jumpsuit with the letters SHU stamped on the back, a broken zipper on the front.

"It's too big," I tell him.

"That's all we got. Let's go."

I dress in the baggy orange suit, and he then locks me back in cuffs before he leads me through the gates into the segregation tier. I'm puzzled by water I see flowing from under cell doors and flooding the tier walkway. The icy water quickly covers my institutional-issue plastic sandals, soaking my socks. As we walk by, prisoners kick their steel doors and slap hands against the glass windows. The noise is deafening.

One calls out. "Day got Santos!"

"Yo Dawg! What up? What day be done got you fo'?" One prisoner yells out, his face against the cutout window.

"What up Homie?" Another yells, slapping the steel door.

The prison lingo annoys me and at this moment I detest every aspect of institutional living.

I look straight ahead, trying to ignore the mayhem and prisoners who've been locked up since the riot, as I'm shivering from wet feet as we slosh through the flooded tier. Since I know the guard won't issue me a dry pair of socks, I don't bother asking.

The guard uses his heavy metal lock to tap against a cell door's window. "Step to the back wall." He orders to a prisoner inside.

"Come on boss, I'm in my rack." I recognize Red's voice coming from inside the cell.

"I said get up and step to the back of the cell. Stand against the wall." Guards take the security precaution to prevent a prisoner in the SHU from attacking the incoming prisoner while he stands defenseless in handcuffs.

The guard unlocks the cell door and I step over the sheets placed to block water from flowing into the cell from the tier. The guard locks me inside and then unlocks a trap in the center of the door.

"Back up to the door so I can unlock your cuffs," he tells me.

I squat and the guard holds my wrists through the door trap with one hand, using his other to turn the key. He slams the trap door shut and I hear his boots sloshing through the water as he walks down the tier.

"Hey Homie, what's up?" Red greets me.

I express surprise at seeing him and ask how long he's been locked in the SHU.

"Four months now, two to go."

"Why? You just disappeared. I never heard why they nabbed you off the compound."

Red was once assigned to a room on my tier, but guards came for him one night. They escorted him off the compound and I didn't hear anything about what happened. Since it wasn't my business, I didn't ask. I've seen thousands of prisoners' faces, and I've heard nearly as many stories, so I didn't miss Red, just as I'm sure that no one's missing me.

"Busted me on a three-way."

"What?"

"A three-way."

"What's that?"

"I was on the phone with my ol' lady and she conferenced me into another call with my homie."

196

"A three way phone call? You've been in here four months because you made a three-way phone call?" I ask, incredulous.

"And I got two more months to go. Plus they done took my phone and visits away for a year. These sanctions ain't no joke."

"Did you appeal?"

Red shrugged. "What's the point? Ain't gonna change nothin'. I told the DHO that I got a baby girl, a family. Takin' my phone *and* my visits was jus' gonna drive 'em away."

"What'd he say to that?" The Disciplinary Hearing Officer determines guilt on institutional rule violations and imposes sanctions.

"Fuck him! Said I should'a thought about my baby girl 'fore I done made the three-way phone call. How 'bout you? What'd they get you fo'?"

"Investigation," I reply.

"You? What're they investigatin' you for? Too many books?"

"Something like that. I had a conversation with Nuss about my school last Thursday. Spoke with him again today, and here I am."

"That's all it takes. Fuckin' Nazi!"

I climb up to the top rack, pull my wet socks off and hang them over the edge to dry. I lie down. The metal plank that serves as my bed pops from my weight while an overhead fluorescent light blinds my eyes and forced air from the vent blows my hair back.

"Is it always this cold in here?"

"Part 'a the gig, Homie. I done tried to block the vent by pressin' shit paper into the screen, but the fuckin' jerk-off cop said he'd gimme a shot if I did it again."

"What's with all the water on the tier?" I ask.

"The homies keep floodin' it, stuffin' sheets in the toilet and hittin' the flusher 'til the water floods the cell, spillin' out onto the tier."

"What's the point?"

"Piss the guards off. They gotta mop it up."

"Do you have anything to read?" I ask.

197

He shuffles around on the bunk beneath me and offers up three torn, stained Maxim magazines that don't interest me.

"Anything else?" I ask.

"Got a Bible."

"I'll take it."

* * * * * * *

The continuous glare of fluorescent light in the windowless room causes me to lose sense of time. Red doesn't have any postage stamps so I won't be able to write anyone about this latest development until next week, when I'll be allowed to submit a commissary order. Reading the Book of Job lessens my anxieties and I drift into sleep.

"Santos!" A guard yells and kicks the steel door twice with his boot, waking me.

I sit up. "What?"

"Roll up!"

We converse by shouting through the locked steel door.

"Am I going back to the compound?"

"Roll up for transfer. You're outta here."

"What?" I'm groggy from sleep deprivation, but I can't believe what he's telling me. "Where'm I going?"

"Just get dressed. Wake your cellie up. Tell him to stand against the wall so I can cuff you."

My immediate thoughts concern my school responsibilities. I wonder what is going to happen to the books I left behind in my locker before I went to lunch yesterday. The university library holds me accountable for those books and I have many. Guards resent packing personal property of prisoners transferred to the SHU or off the compound. They frequently "lose" heavy items and I know it's unlikely I'll ever see those books again.

The guard doesn't give me time to worry about what I'm leaving behind. He taps his key against the window.

"Get movin'! Now! Wake your cellie up."

I jump down from the top bunk and pull on my damp socks, slipping my feet into the plastic sandals before backing up to the steel door. My roommate, Red, has moved from his bed and now stands with his nose against the far wall, hands behind his back. I squat and the guard snaps the cold metal bracelets around my wrists.

"Take care, Red."

"Be cool, Bro."

I back out of the cell with the guard's grip on my handcuffs. We walk down the tier and I'm processed out, chained up, and marched outside with 20 other prisoners. Our traveling clothes are nothing more than khaki trousers, t-shirts, and blue canvas deck shoes despite the late November cold. We trudge through the snow, flanked by guards bundled into blue winter parkas, black leather gloves, and wool caps.

The guard in front unlocks the final gate and I follow the procession onto the bus, drop into a seat, and begin to thaw, grateful for the heat pumping through the vent beside me. Even though it's dark outside I peer through the window at FCI McKean, knowing it's the last time I'll see this prison that has held me for 18 months.

The two-lane road winds through pristine, snow blanketed forests, but my mind isn't on the beautiful scenery. I'm bracing myself for the worst-case scenario, wondering why Nuss felt compelled to transfer me in this hasty manner. He seems to resent my education and that I've earned my degrees while in prison, as if somehow I'd put one over on the system. The way he had the lieutenant lock me up during lunch yesterday was a clear message that he positively didn't want me making the case for a reclassification to low security. He wants me gone, and this intentionally abrupt transfer doesn't bode well for me.

On the Interstate, I see overhead road signs with names I don't recognize. They zip past my window as the bus rolls on. It's overcast and cold, so I press against the heater vent, trying to relax and rest, deluding myself with the mantra that one prison is the same as the next and that I can make it anywhere.

After several hours pass, we pull into the Federal Correctional Complex at Allenwood, Pennsylvania, dropping some prisoners off at the low-security correctional institution. When my name's not called, my anxiety increases. The bus drives on, leaving Allenwood behind and passing through other small towns. Storefront signs advertise the businesses in downtown Lewisburg, Pennsylvania, a prison town, and giving me some insight on where we're going. The bus winds along the serpentine drive leading into USP Lewisburg. I see gun towers, razor-wire topped fences, and the high stone wall that looms in front of me. I sense that I'm about to be locked inside another high-security penitentiary.

Even though I know a hundred prisoners inside the Lewisburg walls who were once with me in Atlanta, I can't believe I'm back at a high-security USP. I breathe in slowly to steady myself for the tension that is coming, not wanting to go through this again.

The first gate rolls open and the bus inches its way inside, stopping in front of the second gate. Guards step out to check their firearms and exchange paperwork. Then the second gate rolls open and our driver pulls us inside the walls of USP Lewisburg.

The medieval buildings feature heavy blocks of red brick and gothic turrets reminiscent of a monastery. But black iron bars over all the windows make clear that this isn't a monastery. As the tires crunch over gravel leading to the prisoners' entrance, I ready and steady myself, clenching my jaw and tightening my fists, pumping blood into my arms and chest to psyche myself up for the aggravations to come.

Once the bus stops, the driver pulls a lever opening the door and we all file out. Guards in BOP uniforms gripping assault rifles stand outside. They order us into a line alongside the bus. I'm shivering, cold, and aggravated as the guards count us, matching our faces to mug shots on their files. Taunts from prisoners we can't see echo from inside the buildings.

"You's up in Lewisburg now!"

"Too late to get scared!"

"Daddy got just wha'choo need!"

"You gonna be mine tonight bitch!"

The guards march us forward to a flight of stairs and we descend into a basement that feels more like a dungeon. I'm looking for the sign from Danté's *Divine Comedy* when he descends into hell: "Abandon hope, all ye who enter here." The iron door swings open into a heated waiting room and we crowd in to stand in place while guards unchain our ankles and wrists.

I crouch near a radiator to let it warm me and I look around. I came into prison with a few pimples on my face, now, eight years later, I'm no longer the youngest man in the room but I haven't yet gotten used to this. I'll never grow used to it.

Every man in this room was with me at McKean, but I don't really know anyone. I watch their lips move with nervous chatter but recede into a space in my mind. *Okay. I've been here before. One penitentiary is the same as another. I'll find my way again. Familiar faces will tell me what I need to know about Lewisburg and I'll master it.*

A guard comes through to hand us each a brown sack lunch, snapping me out of my thoughts. I dig inside and find white bread, cheese, bologna, crackers, a red apple, and a carton of milk, all of which I inhale.

The guards begin calling us one at a time. I'm ready.

"Santos?"

I stand, tossing my crumpled bag into the corner trash, and I step toward the guard.

"Number 16377-004," I answer him with my registration number.

"Let's go."

Moving from one room to another without cuffs or shackles, I'm processed in, my heart pounding. Every prison has the same routine of fingerprinting, mug shots, and strip searches. A plain round clock hangs on the wall right beneath the side-by-side pictures of President Bill Clinton, Attorney General Janet Reno, and BOP Director Kathy Hawk. The apathetic guard orders me to strip naked so he can inspect me for contraband.

"Hands up."

"Open your mouth."

"Run your fingers through your hair."

"Let me see your ears."

"Lift 'em."

"Turn around."

"Let me see the bottoms of your feet."

"Bend over."

"Spread 'em."

I smirk, knowing that I've just mooned portraits of our president, attorney general, and the director of our prison system.

201

The guard tosses me an orange jump suit, underwear, and plastic sandals. I dress and move on to the next station, where the nurse reviews forms I hand her. Finally I step into another office where the case manager sits at a metal desk reviewing files.

"Name?" The tortoiseshell glasses sit at the bottom of his nose, and rather than lifting his head to acknowledge me, his bloodshot eyes look over the top of his frames.

"Michael Santos," I answer him.

"Number?" He inquires.

"16377-004."

"You know where you're going?"

I nod, then make a request. "If I could, I'd like to go to J-unit. I was with some guys in Atlanta who are assigned to that unit and I'd like to see them again."

"What're you talking about?" the case manager asks, finally lifting his head.

"J-unit," I say. "I'd like you to assign me to J-Unit."

"You mean here?"

I shrug, not following his question.

"You're not stayin' here. You're going to Fairton."

"The medium?" I ask about the security level at the Fairton prison.

"You're a medium, right?"

I smile as tension drains from my mind and body. Ever since the guards called me out of the cell early this morning I was convinced that Nuss had finagled some paperwork to boost my security level and place me back in a penitentiary. With the news that I'm en route to another Federal Correctional Institution, I exhale with relief, as I didn't want to endure another USP battle zone.

* * * * * * *

Other prisoners have told me that the bus ride to FCI Fairton only takes a few hours, and I'm determined not to waste this opportunity to enjoy our American landscape. Still in a state of euphoria over news of my transfer, I don't nap as we drive the two-lane highway that feels far too narrow for this bus. Other than a few days in Manhattan, I've never been in the Northeast. The road signs that announce the Delaware River, Philadelphia,

The Ben Franklin Bridge, and The George Washington Bridge remind me of American history. The irony of the moment isn't lost on me. I'm in the birthplace of our nation, close to the Liberty Bell, the places where early American leaders signed The Constitution and The Declaration of Independence, guaranteeing freedom for all, and I'm in chains.

My only essential need at Fairton is permission to receive packages of books from the university library. I'd like to have access to a word processor, but if the education department denies that, I'm confident my professors will accept handwritten term papers.

Radio station announcements I hear through the bus's speakers inform me that we're near a major metropolitan area. I like the idea of being in the most densely populated area of our country. Fairton is close to New York, Washington, Philadelphia, and even Boston. Certainly Bruce will find it easier to travel here for visits. Maybe Dr. DiIulio will bring more students from Princeton for another field trip.

When we pull into FCI Fairton, I see that like McKean and Miami, it's a modern facility, with clusters of stone buildings on manicured lawns, all enclosed by high chain-link fences and coils of shiny razor wire. I actually welcome the sight of those fences. They're so much more inviting than the high, impregnable penitentiary walls topped by gun-towers.

After the processing ritual of forms, fingerprinting, mug shots, and strip searches, I carry my bedroll to the D-right housing unit. In this population of 1,500, a few familiar faces from McKean and Atlanta welcome me. They lend shoes, sweatshirts, and toiletries until my belongings arrive from McKean.

I'm assigned to a room with Henry, a Colombian who is my age and doesn't speak English. Although I'm not fluent, I've learned enough Spanish to express myself and I understand his explanations about the routines at Fairton. Henry helps me secure a job as a unit orderly, and I assume responsibility for cleaning toilets in a common-area restroom. I'm grateful for a job that will give me sufficient time to study after I make the necessary arrangements with the education department.

The number of books in Fairton's library impresses me. I browse through rows of bookshelves and see thousands of paperbacks with titles by Hemingway, Faulkner, Fitzgerald, and other writers of classic American literature, few of which I've read. The heavy coursework I'm studying limits my reading to nonfiction, mostly from the social sciences. To round out my education, I want to read these authors, but right now leisure reading isn't a luxury I can afford. Time is a precious resource, and despite the length of my sentence, I don't have enough of it.

I began college as a way to overcome the stigma of my crime. Not being a natural scholar, I have to work hard, but as I've progressed through my confinement, I've come to love the process of learning. Now I look forward to doing the critical analysis and writing required to earn my doctorate.

Reluctantly, I leave the shelves of fiction and present myself at the office door of Ms. Howell, Fairton's supervisor of education. She wears her black hair tightly pulled back in a severe bun. Her glasses hang from a burgundy strap like a necklace. She's at her desk when I knock on her open door. As she lifts the glasses to her eyes and looks at me, my immediate impression is that she's a woman who considers herself a correctional officer first.

"May I speak with you?" I ask.

"Got a pass?" she barks back, confirming that my assessment is correct.

"Yes. It's right here." I hold up the slip of paper from my unit officer that authorizes me to be in the library.

"Let me see it."

I hand her the pass.

"This pass was issued 20 minutes ago. I could lock you up for being late. Why didn't you bring it to me at once?"

"I saw you on the telephone. I was standing right over there, by the bookshelves."

"Next time an officer gives you a pass to my library, I suggest you have me or one of my staff sign it before you start looking around. If I catch you late again, I'll lock you up for being out of bounds."

"Yes ma'am. I apologize, and I'll try to do better." I've learned that this type of response generally appeases staff members who covet power.

"Now what is it you want?" Ms. Howell signs my pass, completing my authorization to be in the library.

"I've been incarcerated for a long time, and the pursuit of my education has been essential to my adjustment."

"Good. We've got plenty to offer. GED, typing. We've got independent study on the computer with courses like Fun with Math and Spelling Wiz."

"I'm enrolled in an independent study program at the University of Connecticut. What I need is authorization to receive books from the university library."

"I'm not authorizing any packages. You want to study in college, we support courses in bookkeeping and janitorial services through a local vocational school. That's all we're set up for. You can enroll in the programs we make available here."

"Ms. Howell, please. If you'll look at my record, you'll see that I'm not any trouble. I don't need anything from the institution."

"You said you needed a package permit."

"Just to receive the books that the university would send."

She shakes her head. "Not on my watch. We offer all the books you need. Got cases of bestsellers."

"I've seen the books, it's a great library here. The best I've seen. But if you'll look at my record, you'll see that I've been enrolled in correspondence study for several years. I've already earned two degrees, and if you let me receive the books, I can finish my program without being any trouble to you or your staff."

"What are you? Stupid? You're giving me trouble right now. I told you I'm not accepting any packages from an outside university. That's final. If you don't like it, file a grievance report on me. This isn't a college. It's a prison and don't forget that."

Ms. Howell peremptorily signs my pass again, indicating our meeting is over. When the guard who controls the PA system announces "movement," I return to the housing unit, down, but not out. She has given me a setback, but it's not the first I've faced and I'm confident I can maneuver around her. When she dared me with a "file on me," I know she meant for me to file a grievance through the administrative remedy procedure, but filing the paperwork only wastes my time. She's a department head and has discretion to run the education department as she chooses. I know that studying through correspondence has been a privilege other administrators have extended to me, not a right.

Also, filing paperwork puts me on weak ground. The default response from "correctional" staff is to deny, knowing that their colleagues will support their categorical "No." When I worked for Ms. Stephens, she told me that her colleagues mocked anyone who made life easy for prisoners, labeling them as "inmate lovers," or "hug-a-thugs." Denying prisoner requests is always easier and more consistent with the culture of corrections.

Instead of going through the futile process of appealing and getting a rubber-stamp denial, I go to the chow hall where I can approach the warden directly. He'll make the ultimate decision anyway. I'll take my chances of talking to him face-to-face rather than trying to rationalize my request in writing.

Warden Morris isn't hard to spot. He wears a navy suit, a white shirt, and a gray tie, looking every bit the CEO of Fairton, an institution that employs more than 300 people. He holds court each day in the center of the chow hall during lunch. Three or four senior staff members always kowtow around him. I throw away the remains of my taco casserole, hand the plastic tray over to the guy on dishwasher duty, and I walk over to stand behind two men waiting to speak with the warden. My turn comes.

"Warden Morris, my name is Michael Santos, and I'd like to speak with you about my education program."

At six-feet-two, he's taller than I am.

"Okay," he says as he looks down and nods his head, indicating permission for me to continue. When he does, Mr. Trevor, his executive assistant, inches closer, ensuring that he'll hear every word.

"I've been incarcerated since 1987 and I have 17 more years to serve. Since I've been in prison I've used educational programs to help me prepare for release."

"How long have you been in my institution?"

"Three days."

"And you've already got a problem that needs my attention?"

"It's a problem that your discretion can fix, and I hope you'll hear me out."

"What is it?" His forehead creases as his eyebrows come together. I sense that he's already denied me as a matter of course, but I press on.

"I'm enrolled in a graduate program at The University of Connecticut."

"No you're not," Mr. Trevor interrupts. I wasn't speaking to him, but as the warden's sidekick, he interjects with his authority.

"Yes, sir, I am," I counter firmly.

"We don't have a relationship with that school." Mr. Trevor addresses the warden rather than me.

"I enrolled before I arrived here, when I was at the previous institution, and I'd like to continue my studies while I'm here."

"Where'd you come from?" Mr. Trevor demands, clearly annoyed. His blatant efforts to shut me down strike me as an effort to impress the warden, while his condescending tone reveals his mind-set about prisoners.

"I came from FCI McKean."

Mr. Trevor looks up at Warden Morris and smirks.

"That explains it," the warden chuckles as he returns Trevor's smirk. "What is it that they were doing for you at *The Dream McKean* that we're not doing for you here?"

"In order to complete my studies I need permission to receive academic books through the mail from the university library."

"Why can't you use the books we make available through our library?" The double team continues, with Mr. Trevor's interference.

"I'm in a graduate program, studying toward a doctorate. I need specific texts and reference books to complete my term papers. We don't have those kinds of books here."

"A *doctorate*? In *what*?" Mr. Trevor is incredulous.

"I'm studying the American prison system, sir. I earned my master's last year from Hofstra."

"Let me get this straight," Warden Morris pipes in. "You want to study prison, earn a doctorate, from inside my institution?" He looks at Mr. Trevor with mock incredulity as if I've just asked him to release me.

"Yes sir, with your permission." I meet the warden's eyes.

"Did you see the sign when the bus brought you in here? It said Fairton Correctional Institution, not Fairton University. We're not going to receive any books from your university, especially not books on prisons."

The discussion is over. His decision is final and I hear the two of them laugh as I walk away, deflated.

By years' end, 1995, I force myself to accept the possibility that my formal education has come to an end. Administrators in two separate prisons have now blocked my studies. This way of thinking represents the wave of the future, a commitment to tougher prisons, isolation, punishment. Last year, after legislators decided prisoners shouldn't have the privilege of earning university degrees, Congress eliminated Pell grants to fund undergraduate programs for prisoners. I know that Bruce and Norval may be able to help me sort this out, and I'm hopeful they'll succeed in persuading senior administrators in Washington to intervene on my behalf, but discouragement is seeping in.

"It's not going to happen," Bruce tells me during a visit about a conversation he had with Sylvia McCollum, his contact in Washington. "She confirmed what you told me. Wardens have discretion on these matters and she's not in a position to overrule such decisions."

Norval couldn't help either, despite his serving on the board of the National Institute of Corrections with Dr. Kathy Hawk. Since he knows her well, he spoke with her about the problems I was having, trying to persuade her to authorize my transfer to a minimum-security camp. Norval mailed me a copy of the note Dr. Hawk sent him in response. She wrote that she had looked into my case personally, but since I have more than

17 years remaining to serve, my placement in an unsecured camp wouldn't be appropriate.

This news leads me to accept that I'm not going to be earning a doctorate during my imprisonment. The punitive changes in the prison system suggest that if I hadn't already earned my other degrees, those also would've been beyond my reach.

The political climate is cold, with Newt Gingrich leading the House of Representatives in what he calls "The Contract with America." Besides calling for fewer privileges in prison, he seeks tougher legal sanctions as well. If Gingrich's proposals become law, the Continuing Criminal Enterprise crime I was convicted of committing would warrant the death penalty. I'm thankful that my legal proceedings concluded long ago, and grateful that at least I've had school to sustain me until now.

Education has been my solace, an exciting and challenging escape from the monotony of confinement. I have to think through this change, because other than studying and working for the next degree, I don't know how to distinguish myself, or how I'll show my commitment to redemption.

* * * * * * *

It's Christmas Eve, 1995, and as I'm walking through the housing unit, I turn when I hear my case manager calling me.

"I received a letter from the pardon attorney," she says.

"Yes, what about?" I ask, bracing for bad news.

"Did you submit a petition for clemency?"

"I submitted it more than two years ago, when I was in Atlanta."

"Well it's denied."

"Any reason why, or advice on what I can do to improve my chances next time?"

"Nope. I was instructed to tell you your petition was denied. That's it. Sorry."

Chapter Eight: 1996-1998
Months 103-127

As I cross through another holiday season and into January 1996, I look through a few birthday cards I received from my family. It's hard to accept that I'm turning 32 in prison, but I'm not a stranger to these milestones passing. Not anymore.

For years I've been climbing toward 1997, hoping that the end of my first decade would mean something special to me. Now I'm closing in on that milestone, but it no longer seems significant. One year feels the same as the next and I don't yet foresee any break from the monotony.

I rely upon clearly defined goals to stay the course. By studying, writing, and working to earn credentials, I've hoped to define myself as something more than a prisoner. The effort, I believed, would help reclaim my humanity from this so-called system of corrections. Now I'm not so sure. It is a system that strikes hard, like a wrecking ball, further dehumanizing me with every passing day.

The Bureau of Prisons extinguishes my aspirations of earning a doctorate degree and the pardon attorney has dismissed hopes for a sentence commutation. Accepting that I won't reach the goals I set for my first decade disorients me. I need to create a new aspiration and redirect my attention toward new goals that are in harmony with my commitment to restoring my dignity. In time I must show the world that I'm a man, something more than a prisoner, but I don't know how I'm going to create an identity that separates me from the bad decisions of my early 20s.

* * * * * * *

Without the continuous demands of an academic schedule, I accelerate my daily exercise routine, running seven miles each morning, following the run with a thousand crunches and a thousand leg lifts. In the afternoons I work out with weights, training for strength and size. I take advantage of the library, reading for enjoyment, though I'm simply passing time.

By the spring of 1996, I feel my physical strength peaking, but my spirit feels empty. When I was working toward my academic degrees I had a solid link to the real world. Similar to my correspondence and visits with mentors, every paper I submitted provided a tangible outside connection. Now, without clear objectives, my sense of meaning or relevance as a man fades away, disappearing like a ship sailing over the horizon. I don't have a woman to love. I spend my days working out, eating, reading, and sleeping, mirroring the meanderings of other prisoners around me.

My frustration increases when I see university students, legislators, attorneys, judges, and other citizens touring the grounds and buildings. FCI Fairton is within driving distance of major cities. Tour groups from Philadelphia, Baltimore, and Wilmington frequently walk through the prison. Guards flank these tour groups, ensuring that prisoners don't interact with the visitors. I'm completely alienated from society as I watch them gawking at the fences that have held me for the past 3,000 days. I imagine the inaccurate spiel guards recite to the visitors:

"This is a modern correctional institution, and our professionally trained correctional officers provide numerous opportunities for the inmates to prepare for law-abiding lives— blah, blah, blah."

I fixate on the women in the tour groups, wondering what it would be like to know them, for them to know me. To them I'm not a man but prisoner in a cage, or worse, an *inmate*, that dehumanizing term I've been hearing for far too long. I have to get out of here.

* * * * * * *

"There's a mistake in my classification," I say to Ms. Dobson, my case manager. We're alone in her brightly lit office and I'm doing my best to ignore the light floral fragrance of her perfume. "I should be classified as a low- rather than medium-security prisoner."

"Let's see what the computer says. What's your number?" She's competent and totally professional. As such, I wonder what draws her to work in a prison instead of working in a more honorable profession, as a nurse, a teacher, a journalist, or anything other than a functionary of this wretched system.

I give her my registration number. She's fast on the keyboard, clicking my number with the speed and precision of an accountant on a ten-key. When the appropriate screen appears, she studies her computer.

"Well, you don't have a history of violence, and no prior incarceration, so your security points are low enough, but your sentence is too long. It gives you an automatic management variable that keeps you as a medium-security inmate." Despite her assessment of the information on the screen, I know it's wrong.

"You know how much time I've already served, don't you?" I ask.

"You've served 104 months, but in order to transfer to a low, you need to be within 18 years of your release date. Sorry." It's disconcerting to hear how much time I have remaining to serve, but she has miscalculated.

"I *am* within 18 years of my release," I clarify.

"The computer shows that you have 247 months remaining to serve, that you won't be released until August, 2013."

"Okay, it's April, 1996. If you do the math, I'm 17 years, four months to release. That's only 208 months, not 247 months."

"Are you sure?" Ms. Dobson is looking at the monitor, wondering. She writes out the number of months on a BOP notepad, multiplies, and smiles when she confirms that my numbers match hers. She then clicks a few more keys on the keyboard. "Hey, you're a 'low'. Congratulations!"

I laugh.

"You know what that means, don't you?"

"That I'm going to a low?" I venture.

"That's right. I've got to submit you for transfer. Where would you like to go?"

* * * * * * *

The guards tell me it's a short drive from Fairton, New Jersey to Fort Dix, New Jersey and I appreciate the smooth ride in the white van as we maneuver through city traffic. From an open front window I feel the breeze and smell the fragrant, blooming cherry blossoms. Children carrying colorful lunch boxes and wearing backpacks meander on sidewalks, savoring their time until school bells ring. I hear horns blasting, dogs barking, and I take in the kaleidoscope of city life. Someday I'll return to a city, but for now I'm chained and strapped to a bench seat. Nevertheless, I'm filled with optimism that my transition to the low-security FCI in Fort Dix means new opportunities as well as respite from the inescapable pressure, stress and volatility of higher security.

In four months I'll complete my ninth year. I've walked through puddles of blood in high- and medium-security prisons. I've carefully navigated and deliberately avoided problems that complicate the lives of so many other young prisoners. Still, as eager as I am for life in a low-tension environment, I'm still wrestling with the enigma of figuring out what society expects of me. I wonder what more I can do, given the restrictions this system places on me.

Guards roll open the gates and the van drives inside. I'm untroubled by the cyclone fences, by the coils of glistening razor wire, and by the white cars slowly patrolling the perimeter. I'm desensitized to the ritualistic processing and I shrug off the forms, the fingerprinting, the mug shots, the strip searches, and the staff interviews. I grab my bedroll and walk to building 5702 on the east side of the prison.

Despite the fences surrounding Fort Dix it doesn't feel like a prison. One reason may be the friendlier temperament of the population here. In place of intimidating glares and scowls I see smiles and nods. Even the layout differs, as I walk on what once was an asphalt road, and the long, rectangular-shaped, brick buildings on either side of me have windows without bars that are large enough to pass a sofa through.

Fort Dix is part of an active army base. Military jets land on a runway only a stone's throw away, and the acrid smell of jet fuel lingers in the air. Before the Bureau of Prisons erected fences to enclose the FCI, these buildings were part of the base, serving as officers' housing and soldiers' barracks. Military personnel currently live just outside the fences in buildings of the same design.

The buildings were erected before World War II and the age shows. As I walk into my housing unit I notice that decades of foot traffic have worn the checkered-pattern ceramic tiles down to the cement on the hallway floors. Without air conditioning, or even a ventilation system, humidity turns the housing unit into a sauna. The guard tells me I'm assigned to room 217, on the second floor.

I sweat as I climb the concrete stairs. When I open the steel door on the second-floor landing, the long, narrow hallway reminds me of a low-rent apartment building with concrete-block walls and unadorned wooden doors on each side. I pause at room 217, tap the door twice as a courtesy, and then walk into the 12-bunk room.

A man sits at a table against the wall of windows on the far side of the room. He's writing, but looks up as I close the door. He's probably in his late 50s, with reading glasses resting halfway down his nose that give him the cerebral look of a professional.

"I'm Michael Santos," I introduce myself. "I've been assigned to this room, bunk two, upper."

"Paul Murray," he stands and walks over to shake my hand. I appreciate the genuine handshake rather than a fist bump. "This is your bunk," he shows me. "I'm right beneath you. This is your locker."

The metal locker is six feet tall, three feet wide, and two feet deep. He opens the double-door, revealing a spacious interior that is easily four times as large as the lockers I've used over the past several years. I'm astonished by the amount of storage I'll have.

"I can't pick up my belongings until tomorrow, but at least I'll be able to store everything in here."

"Why can't you get your property?" he asks.

"The guards who processed me said it was too late to inventory."

"I've got some things that'll hold you over until you get your belongings," he offers, and then he opens his locker to hand me a pair of sweats, a tube of toothpaste, a toothbrush, and a bar of soap.

"Thanks. This helps. I'll get it back to you when I shop."

"No problem. Where're you coming from?"

"I was at FCI Fairton for the past few months. Before that I was at FCI McKean, and USP Atlanta before then."

"Oh, so you've been down for a while."

"I'll finish my ninth year in August."

"Nine years! My God, are you almost out?"

"I wish. I've still got more than 17 to go."

"Months?"

"No, 17 more years."

"Whoa! I don't think there's anyone here with that much time. What'd they get you for?"

"I sold cocaine." It's always the same question and I always qualify my answer. "No violence or weapons. It's my first time in prison but my judge sentenced me to 45 years."

Paul shakes his head. "These drug sentences are ungodly. I never realized how bad they were until I got here. The sentences seem more severe than the crimes warrant. Murderers serve less time."

"How about you? How long have you been here?"

Paul shakes his head. "I'm embarrassed to say after listening to you. I'm serving an 18-month sentence for health-care fraud. I've been here for nine months."

"Are you a doctor?"

"No. I was a lawyer, but I resigned from the bar. The felony would've resulted in my disbarment at some point anyway."

"So why does a lawyer serve time for health-care fraud?"

"Long story. My practice represented medical clinics and testing labs. Billing problems tangled me up with the law and here I sit. I call it my sabbatical."

* * * * * * *

I settle into the Fort Dix community, grateful for the lower volatility levels. My housing unit is one of six on the compound, each holding 400 men. Most prisoners serve time for drugs, but many others like Paul serve short sentences.

Thoughts about how I'm going to spend the rest of my time continue to trouble me, especially when administrators confirm that they won't permit the university library to send me books.

"Our policy provides for you to receive hardcover books from a bookstore or a publisher, not libraries." The supervisor of education doesn't leave any room for special circumstances. "And I'm not going to make an exception. If I make an exception for you, I'm going to have to make one for everybody."

"Really? How many prisoners do you have here who are candidates for a Ph.D.?" I ask.

"That's not the point. Our policies reflect the need to preserve the security of the institution. If you wanted to pursue a Ph.D., you should've thought about that before you came to prison."

It's the same admonition I've heard repeatedly and I don't see much upside in trying to press for permission. Prison guards find it easy to hide behind the shortsighted "security of the institution" mantra. Frustrated, I search for an activity that will sustain me, something I can pursue on my own without the need for permission from authorities.

My exercise regimen continues, though it's not nearly enough to ease the sense of hopelessness I'm struggling to suppress. I exercise until I exhaust myself physically, running longer distances and lifting weights. In search of something more, I join a therapy group that Dr. Warren, a psychologist, sponsors. She calls it the Long-term Prisoners Group and I agree to attend the two-hour discussion each Wednesday afternoon.

Afro-centric art decorates Dr. Warren's office. Portraits of Malcolm X and Marcus Garvey hang on her wall. I'm curious whether she's met resistance from BOP colleagues who consider such leaders revolutionaries. Sitting in Dr. Warren's group is as close as I can come to sitting in a classroom and I admire the soothing way she manages the group. Although I want to emulate her compassion, I have a hard time tolerating the self-pity and hypocrisy expressed by other group members.

Eight people participate in our group and we all sit in chairs that form an oval circle in Dr. Warren's carpeted office. Bored, sometimes I drift into my own thoughts, trying to get a feel for Dr. Warren's interests by reading the titles on the spines of books that pack her wooden shelves. I see works by Toni Morrison, Cornel West, Henry Louis Gates. I've continued coming to the meetings because I learn from listening to her. Even though she allows the prisoner participants to rant, I admire the nonjudgmental patience I hear in her questions. Regardless of how frequently some men in the group shift blame for their actions, she kindly nods, indicating agreement or understanding.

Despite Dr. Warren's efforts to engage us, I don't connect with the other men, and I can't conceal my contempt when they whine about their circumstances.

"I'm only in prison because my best friend snitched me out," says Eric.

"Didn't you have anything to do with getting caught?" I ask.

"He's the one who got busted. All he had to do was keep his mouth shut and no one would've knowed about me." Eric doesn't like my challenging him.

"But you said you pleaded guilty." I point out.

"Only 'cause the snitch was gonna testify 'gainst me. I'm servin' 10 years even though the DEA didn't catch me with nothin'."

"Aren't you serving 10 years because you sold cocaine, and because you stood in front of the judge and admitted guilt?"

"Yeah, but if the snitch wouldn't of said nothin' I wouldn't of even been charged. Them conspiracy laws ain't right, they just ain't fair."

In an effort to advance the discussion, Dr. Warren suggests a creative exercise. "Before we meet next week," she instructs, "I want you to think about what you value most in life. I'd like each of you to come prepared to discuss what you consider your highest value. And remember, what we say in the group stays in the group."

I know exactly what values drive me, and when I return for our next meeting I'm hopeful that the discussion will advance beyond complaining about sentence lengths and unjust prosecutions.

"So why don't we begin with you, Jim," Dr. Warren begins. "Have you been able to pinpoint your highest value?"

"Yes, I have." Jim responds. He sits to the immediate right of Dr. Warren. He's 35 and has served four years of a nine-year sentence, his second time in prison for distributing methamphetamines. Jim shaves his head, but he grows long, red whiskers from his goatee and he's always twisting them when he talks. We're in a room with standard lighting, but he insists on wearing sunglasses because his eyes are sensitive, he says. The words "love" and "hate" are tattooed on the knuckles of his left and right hand. "Most important value to me is my relationship with Jesus Christ, my personal Lord and savior."

"Amen!" another group member exclaims, voicing his approval.

Dr. Warren nods, encouraging Jim to continue. "And how does your relationship with Jesus help you through each day?"

"Well I'm very spiritual," Jim twists his whiskers as he slouches in the chair. "I hardly ever miss services, and every night I say my prayers."

"What do you pray about?" I ask.

"It's personal."

"Generally, I mean," prodding him further.

"Do you want to share with the group what you pray about, Jim?" Dr. Warren turns her head from Jim to cast me a warning look. "We'll all understand if you'd prefer to keep your prayers to yourself."

"Mostly I pray that I'll get out early, and that my ol' lady don't sell my Harley 'fore I get home."

Dr. Warren nods.

"That's very spiritual," I chuckle.

"Michael, do you have something you'd like to share?" It's clear that Dr. Warren doesn't approve of my sarcasm.

"Sorry, I'll wait my turn."

Jim glances my way, but he doesn't say anything and I can't read his eyes through the dark shades.

"Bob, would you care to share your values with the group?" Dr. Warren turns to another prisoner.

"I'd like to pass." He folds his arms and stares at the floor.

Dr. Warren nods. "Is everything okay, Bob?"

Bob shrugs, "I just don't know what to say."

"Well, if you feel like talking, we'd like to listen," she tells him. The room is quiet, except for the tick of the second hand on a wooden clock carved in the shape of the African continent. "Tom, how about you, are you ready?" She encourages him, smiling. "Would you go next?"

"The most important thing in the world to me is just gettin' through this time. I hate bein' locked up." Tom is serving his fourth prison term for drugs. He wears an orange cap over greasy hair, and tattoos of three falling tears blemish his face.

"Have you thought about anything you can do to ease your way through?" Dr. Warren probes, trying to gauge how constructive he's being with his time.

"There's nothin' to do," Tom opens his hands. "I done finished my GED. Ain't no college classes. I been sleepin' a lot, readin', watching' TV."

"What do you like to read?" she asks.

"I like lookin' at the *Maxim*, *People*, car magazines, anything that lets me know what's goin' on in the world."

"Do you ever read books?" Dr. Warren queries, trying to engage him.

"Nah. I get bored too easy." He looks up at the ceiling, stretches his neck from side to side.

"And you don't have any interest in tutoring others or participating in religious services, like Jim?"

"I like sleepin' mostly. When I'm 'sleep, it's like I ain't even in prison."

"Steve, have you thought about what you value most in life?" Dr. Warren moves on.

"I'm like Jim. God's most impor'ant to me. I be readin' my Bible, goin' to services. I been in a Bible study group for like two months now and I'm learnin' a lot. Jesus is helpin' me get through this." Steve braids his hair in cornrows and wears a goatee, neatly trimmed.

I look at the floor, shaking my head.

"I think it's commendable that you've found peace, Steve. We all need to find strength to get us through tough times, and it sounds as if you've found yours through religion." Dr. Warren nods as she compliments Steve.

"Amen," Steve says.

"Praise God," Jim twists his whiskers, nodding in unison.

"Bill, how about you? What do you value most highly?" Dr. Warren smiles, inviting Bill to share.

Bill is assigned to the room across the hall from me. I see him frequently because he sleeps in the bunk above Al, a guy I sometimes tutor. Bill is in his late 20s. He's active on the compound, always sitting at a card table, playing dominos, running a gambling pool.

"I dunno. I guess I value my wife, and God too."

I slouch, massaging my forehead with one hand.

"Why you be hatin' on the Lord?" Steve challenges me as he tilts his head and scowls.

"Is something bothering you, Steve?" Dr. Warren prods, pushing Steve to express himself.

"Yes," I invite him to open up. "Speak your mind, say something, get us away from the BS in here."

"I'm just sayin', we're up in here givin' praise to Jesus, and he's all slouchin' in his chair," Steve points at me, "like he's bored or ain't wanna hear it."

"Michael, do you have anything you'd like to say?" Dr. Warren asks me.

"Everything said in the group stays in the group?" I ask, welcoming the confrontation.

"Of course. You can speak freely in here," Dr. Warren confirms, glancing at everyone in the group.

The length of time I've served has numbed my sense of empathy. I've grown less tolerant of listening to whiners week after week. I sit up in my chair. "Okay. It bothers me that Dr. Warren gave us all an opportunity to learn from each other. We're all serving time, locked inside the same fences, going through the same struggles. She asked us to think about our highest values, what's most important in our lives, but instead of speaking honestly, talking about what you really feel, you're talking about what you think she wants to hear. This isn't an application for parole. No one's getting a time cut for this. I was hoping something more substantive would come from our meeting today. Instead, it's the same as always."

"What makes you think you be knowin' so much?" Steve asks.

"I know that God isn't the highest priority in your life, I know that much."

"How you be knowin' what I feel?"

"Because if God was the highest value in your life, you wouldn't be whining in here each week about how you don't belong in prison, about how it's all a snitch's fault that you're here. If God were the highest value in your life, you would accept that you're exactly where God wants you to be. That's how I see it." I turn to Bill. "If your relationship with your wife had the highest value to you, would you really have slutty magazine pictures taped all over your locker? Come on, fellas. Why are we doing this? Who are we trying to impress?"

"That's quite a tirade," Dr. Warren says. "What the others said really bothered you."

"He ain't even said what his values is, but he be tryin' to say that we ain't bein' real," Steve directs his comment to Eric.

"My highest value is simple. What I value most is liberty, and I don't have it. All I'm thinking about is what I can do while I'm in here to make sure that once I get out, I'll never lose it again."

"Oh, and you ain't think we wanna get out?" Steve challenges me.

"If you want to get out, if that's what's most important to you, then I want to hear what you're doing to get out, and what you're doing to make sure that once you get out, you never come back."

"But there ain't nothin' we can do! Besides, what you doin' that's so diff'rent? You sayin' we be whinin', but you's in here ever' week complainin' 'bout how no one's lettin' you finish school. Shee-it, you be whinin' just like every'n else," Steve says.

"You know what? You're right. I'm changing that, starting now, as of this minute. For 10 years I've been trying to build a record so the world would consider me differently from other prisoners. Now I'm finished. Going forward, I'm doing what's necessary to ensure that when I walk out of here, I walk out as a man with dignity, ready to stand on my own. This system may hold me for 16 more years, but I'm not going to let it condition me for failure and ruin the rest of my life. I suggest you guys do the same."

"So what're you going to do? What changes are you making?" Jim leans back on the chair, twisting his whiskers.

"I'm enrolling in law school."

"Shee-it! You's in prison yo! Can't be goin' to no law school from here. Even if you could, what good it gonna do? Ain't no one gonna hire no lawyer from prison." Steve flicks his hand in the air, dismissing my comment.

"He has a good point, Michael. Have you thought about the ways your felony might influence a lawyer's career?" Dr. Warren asks.

"I didn't say I wanted to be a lawyer. I said I'm enrolling in law school. Instead of thinking about what I *can't* do, I'm going to think about what I *can* do. I know my strengths and weaknesses, and I know I'm going to serve 16 more years. I may not be able to become a member of the legal profession, but if I earn a law degree I'll be able to help other prisoners who want to file their own legal motions."

"So you want to be a jailhouse lawyer?" Jim nods his head, still twisting the whiskers.

"Not just a jailhouse lawyer. I'll study and become the *best* jailhouse lawyer in the system. It's one way I can make myself useful in here."

"That's a plan," Dr. Warren agrees, smiling.

* * * * * * *

While planning for law school I continue to build a strong network of support. To overcome the resistance and bias I expect to encounter, I put together a package that I call my portfolio. It describes my crime, expresses remorse, and articulates the steps I've taken over the past decade to atone. The portfolio includes copies of my university degrees and endorsement letters from the distinguished academics who support me. I'm certain that a wide support network will open more options upon my release and I send the portfolios to people who might sponsor my efforts.

My strategy is simple. I'll continue what I began before I was sentenced, when I wrote to Stuart Eskenazi, the journalist who covered my trial for readers of the *Tacoma News Tribune*.

In my letter to him, I expressed my intentions to live usefully in prison and redeem myself by preparing for a law-abiding life upon release.

The new portfolio I'm creating not only records my accomplishments but also shows my progress toward the clearly defined goals I set. In it, I ask readers to consider me as the man I'm becoming rather than the one who made bad decisions in his early 20s. Taking a lesson from business stories I read in *The Wall Street Journal*, I supplement the portfolio by writing quarterly reports every 90 days and I distribute the reports to those in my growing support network. My quarterly reports describe my projects, the ways that they contribute to my preparations for release, and my challenges. They are my accountability tools.

By living transparently I invite people to hold me accountable, to judge me by what I do, not by what I say. Any prisoner can say he wants to succeed upon release, but my daily commitment and the actions I take allows others to evaluate whether they should continue giving me their trust, sponsorship, and support.

With pride in my progress, and the ways I've responded to the challenges of imprisonment, my parents share the portfolio with others. My father gives a copy to his friend, Norm Zachary, and Norm passes it along to his sister, Carol Zachary. I'm thrilled when my father tells me over the phone that Carol wants to help and that I should call her. She is a married mother of two who lives in Washington, D.C., where her husband, Jon Axelrod, practices law.

"This is Michael Santos, calling from the federal prison in Fort Dix." I introduce myself. "My father suggested I should call to speak with Ms. Zachary."

"Oh, Michael! I'm so glad you called. Please call me Carol. My husband and I have read through your portfolio and we want to help. You may not remember, but Norm brought me to a party at your parents' house when you were a child. We spoke about the Hubble telescope."

"I remember. I was about seven or eight then."

She corrects me, reminding me that I was older when we met, already a teenager. Then she says that she would like to build a friendship and asks that I send her the forms necessary to visit. "I want to bring Zach and Tris, my sons. We need to talk about what we can do to get you out, and if you'll let me, I'd like to lead the effort."

This is precisely the type of support I hoped to find as a result of preparing that portfolio. As Ralph Waldo Emerson was known for having observed, shallow men believe in luck, but strong men believe in cause and effect. Ever since Bruce came into my life I've known and appreciated the value of mentors. He guided me from the beginning through our weekly correspondence and his regular visits. Because of his support, I've matured and grown in confidence, as a scholar, in mental discipline, and I'm well prepared to contribute positively to society. By taking deliberate action steps to expand my support network, I really scored, attracting Carol's attention. When I walk into the visiting room to meet her and her sons, Zach and Tristan, they greet me with an embrace, as if I'm already family.

While sitting across from each other in the hard, plastic chairs of Fort Dix's brightly lit visiting room, I learn about the Axelrod family. Carol, a former English teacher, is a Boy Scout leader who takes an active interest in her community. She volunteers for the Red Cross, substitutes in the local schools, and, along with her husband Jon, is deeply involved in her sons' sports and school. She's determined to groom them as responsible citizens.

Zach is 12 and he tells me about his baseball and hockey teams. When I ask what he wants to do when he grows up, he answers without hesitation: "I want to be the CEO of a publicly traded company," and I don't doubt for a second that he'll succeed. His intelligence impresses me, especially when he grills me about what I'm planning to do with my life once I'm released.

"I'm looking into law school right now," I answer.

"Do you think people will want to hire a lawyer who's been in prison?" Zach asks the question with a genuine eagerness to learn more about me.

"Zachary," scolds Carol.

"What, Mom? I'm just curious."

"Of course people will hire him," she tries to soften his bluntness.

"That's a good question, Zach." I'm impressed with his confidence and directness.

"See, Mom."

"But I'm not going to law school to practice law. I'm convinced that more education will open career opportunities once I'm home, and studying law will help me through whatever time I've got left to serve. Wherever I serve my sentence, prisoners will need legal assistance and if I study law, I'll be in a position to help."

"That makes sense," Tristan, Zach's younger brother, considers my response.

"What we need to do is get you out of here," Carol says, bringing us back to the central issue. "Jon and I have spoken with some acquaintances who work for the Justice Department. They can't get involved because of rules about conflicts of interest, but they did insist that we need a top-notch Washington lawyer to represent you."

"I'd love to have a lawyer. But the truth is, I don't have any financial resources."

"Well we're going to raise some."

"How?"

"You've built this wonderful support network. I'm sure the people who believe in you will help."

"But I can't ask them for money."

"Why not? They want to help you."

"I just wouldn't feel right asking anyone for money. I've already lost one effort at clemency, and I'm coming to terms with the likelihood that I'm going to serve my entire sentence. I'm trying to build my network so I'll have people who will help me overcome the challenges that I'm going to face."

"But we're not going to let you serve 16 more years, at least not without trying to get you out. You may not want to ask others for financial assistance, but as long as you don't object, I'm going to ask on your behalf."

I'm speechless, suppressing emotions that I'm not accustomed to feeling. Of course I crave my freedom. I'm 33, well educated now, and after 10 years inside, I'm as ready for release as I'll ever be. If I could return to society now, I would still have a reasonable chance to build a career and begin a family. Carol's offer to advocate for my freedom validates me, bringing a sense of liberty, of worthiness that I cherish and appreciate.

* * * * * * *

Carol coordinates a team to help me. She persuades Tony Bisceglie, a highly regarded Washington, DC lawyer, to represent me *pro bono*. She travels to meet with my mentors, Bruce, Phil McPherson (Bruce's brother), and George Cole. With assistance from Julie, my friends Nick and Nancy Karis, and other friends from Seattle and elsewhere, Carol launches a fundraiser to begin the Michael Santos Legal Defense Fund, and she solicits thousands of dollars to cover legal expenses. The money comes from anonymous donors, people who now have a vested interest in my freedom. I can't participate from prison, and I don't know what success they'll have, but their combined energy fills me with hope.

Tony orders transcripts that document my case. After reading them he determines that I have grounds to file for relief from the court. I'm ambivalent about the plan of a judicial action because I wanted to earn my freedom rather than pursue liberty through a legal technicality. More than a decade has passed since my conviction became final and we know the request for judicial relief is a long shot. Further, the judge who presided over my trial is known for meting out long sentences and never reducing them. Through his research Tony discovers that the prosecutors in my case once tried to settle. If I had pleaded guilty instead of going to trial, the prosecutors would've agreed that a 20-year sentence was appropriate. Since Raymond, my trial attorney, never told me of the government's offer, Tony insists that rather than pursuing a commutation of sentence, I need to file a petition with the court for relief.

To prepare the legal motion, Tony enlists the help and support of Tom Hillier, the Federal Public Defender for the Western District of Washington, to accept my case. Tom then recruits Jonathan Solovy, a top-notch Seattle attorney who agrees to prepare the documents and argue for my release. Coordinating

227

all these efforts requires hundreds of hours, and I'm moved that professionals who've never met me give of themselves so generously for the singular purpose of freeing me.

The legal team employs investigators to gather evidence that will bolster my petition. Jonathan works diligently to persuade both the government and the judge to reconsider my sentence.

But in the end, we lose. Judge Tanner is unmoved and he lets the sentence stand. Everyone on the team is concerned about how I'll react to the decision. Strangely, I'm at peace, grateful to have received love and support from so many strangers who've now become friends.

*   *   *   *   *   *   *

Bruce visits me at the beginning of 1998, beyond my 10-year mark. He wants to discuss my plans for law school. Through letters we've discussed possibilities for moving through the remainder of my sentence productively. He's not convinced that studying law by correspondence is my best option.

"I really liked your idea of spending the final years of your sentence becoming an artist, a painter, or a musician, or even studying a foreign language. Those pursuits would round out your education and maybe free some creativity within you," Bruce says, sitting across from me in the visiting room.

"Bruce, I'm going to serve 16 more years. I'm not even halfway through my term. I don't want to devote myself to another project that prison administrators can take away. Although I've thought about learning to paint or play the piano, if I were transferred I'd have to go through all this frustration again because of red tape, and that's only if I could continue. Some prisons don't even offer music or art programs."

Bruce nods his head as I describe my reasons, then he leans back in his chair. "But that's the essence of a liberal education. You could study painting and piano here, and if you're transferred you could study foreign languages or poetry there. The more you learn, the more you'll be able to appreciate when you come home."

"It's going home that I'm thinking about. What will I face when I walk out of here?"

"You'll have friends who will help you."

"Yes, but I want to stand on my own feet, not come out weak, with my hat in hand looking for handouts."

"Don't express yourself with clichés," he admonishes.

"You know what I mean. By then I will have served 26 years, and I need to anticipate the obstacles I'll face. I'll be nearly 50, but I won't have any savings, I won't have a home, I won't even have any clothes to wear. With my prison record, employers will resist hiring me. If I don't prepare for those obstacles, I'm going to run into tremendous resistance. How will I start my life?"

Bruce rubs his head. "The law school you're considering, though, isn't of the same caliber as your other schools. Hofstra and Mercer have impeccable credentials. Wherever you go, people will respect those degrees. If you want to study law, I think you should wait until you're home, where you could earn a degree from a nationally accredited school, not a correspondence school that the bar association doesn't recognize. What's the real value of that degree? It won't even permit you to sit for a bar exam."

I lean forward, eagerly trying to explain my decision. "That's what I couldn't be so clear about in the letters I wrote to you; I have to be careful of what the guards read. I'm not studying law because I want to practice as a lawyer. I'm studying law because I want to use what I learn to help other prisoners who want to litigate their cases. Look around this room. Nearly every prisoner here wants another shot at getting back into court. If I study law, I'll be able to help them."

"But if you're not a lawyer, how can you represent them?"

"I'm not intending to represent them. What I'll do is help them research the law and write the briefs. They'll submit their own legal documents, *pro se*. Sometimes I may help people persuade lawyers to take their cases, like Tony and Jonathan took mine. A law school education, together with my experience, will enable me to offer more and better assistance. Prisoners will pay for my services."

"That's what troubles me." Bruce says, shaking his head. "You've worked all this time to build a record as a model prisoner, to educate yourself and keep a clean disciplinary record. Now you're talking about breaking the rules by becoming some kind of jailhouse lawyer, exposing yourself to disciplinary infractions and possible problems with the system. It doesn't make sense to me."

"Yes, I've worked hard to live as a model prisoner. What has it gotten me? Instead of support, I meet resistance. Administrators transfer me to frustrate my efforts and to block me from completing my studies. I don't have any interest in being a model prisoner. My interest, my only interest, is succeeding upon release. And I think the best way I can do that is by preparing myself financially."

"So how are the prisoners going to pay you?" Bruce smirks at my plan. "Are they going to fill your locker with candy bars and sodas? How will that help when you get out?"

"They won't pay me directly. If a guy asks for my help, we'll agree on a price. Then he'll have his family send the funds to my family."

"But is that legal?"

"Although we have too many laws in this country, as far as I know, it's still legal for one citizen to send money to another citizen. My sister will pay taxes on any money she receives and she'll hold it for me until I come home. Prison administrators may not like it, but it's not against the law for Julie to receive money from another prisoner's family. My helping another prisoner with legal motions isn't against the law either."

"It just seems kind of sneaky, totally different from the open-book, transparent approach that you've followed." Bruce remains skeptical.

"I don't see it that way. The plan is totally consistent with the open-book approach, and I intend to do it openly."

"How so? You won't even receive payment directly."

I shrug my shoulders. "That's only because I'm living within the rules imposed on me. But I'll be honest about what I'm doing, and truthfully, I'll take pride in beating a system that perpetuates failure."

Bruce shakes his head again. "You might be living within the letter of the rules by not receiving money directly, but you won't be living within the spirit of the rules."

"Prison rules don't concern me. Living as a model inmate isn't going to help me when I walk out of here. No one is going to care that I didn't receive any disciplinary infractions. People may not even look beyond the fact that I served 26 years in prison. I need enough money in the bank to meet all of my expenses during my first year of freedom, whether I receive a paycheck or not. I'll have to buy a car, pay rent, buy clothes, and pay for everything else I'll need to start my life. Meeting those responsibilities has much more value to me than observing the 'spirit' of prison rules."

"You've really thought this through," Bruce begins to relent. "Have you considered the possible consequences? What if they transfer you back to high security?"

"I don't care where they send me. From now on, my sole focus is to prepare for a successful, contributing life. That's not going to happen by accident."

"What prompted this new resolve? The court decision that denied you an early release?" Bruce's support for me is evident in his caring tone and genuine interest, and I appreciate his willingness to listen as I share my thoughts.

"I know that you limit your reading to classical literature, but it was a book I read by Stephen Covey, *The Seven Habits of Highly Effective People*. Have you ever heard of him?"

"No," Bruce says ruefully, laughing. "I enjoy an occasional good detective story, but I don't read much from the self-help or inspiration genres."

"Well I find it helpful and I think you might identify with Covey."

"What makes you think so?"

"He's a former professor who taught at Brigham Young University, and his focus of study was leadership. Covey's book validates my choices, the way I've lived for the past 10 years, and it's helped me set the strategy I'll use going forward."

"How so?" Bruce asks, curious.

I'm eager to explain.

"In his study of leadership, Dr. Covey found that successful people share seven habits in common." I hold up my hand and use my fingers to tick them off. "One, they're proactive. Two, they begin with the end in mind. Three, they put first things first. Four, they seek first to understand, then to be understood. Five, they think win-win. Six, they synergize. And seven, they constantly work to sharpen their approach."

"What? Are you telling me that's a revelation for you? You still haven't answered my question."

"What question?"

"Why the shift in your strategy?" Bruce asks again, clarifying.

"I'm pragmatic. Truthfully, it's more of an *evolution* than a shift. I've been following Covey's seven habits of leadership ever since I was in the county jail, when I read of Socrates. By continuing to educate myself, I'm taking proactive steps to overcome my adversity. By knowing the challenges that await my release, I'm beginning with the end in mind. By enrolling in law school, I'm putting first things first. I understand my environment, my limitations, and the ways I can make myself most useful. By pursuing this goal I'll be able to generate the resources necessary to stand on my own when I leave prison. *That's* win-win. It's a way to use my education and to lead a more meaningful life in here."

"Have you figured out your rates yet, Counselor?" Bruce teases.

"Whatever the market will bear. Isn't that the American way?" I grin, 100 percent committed to the strategy driving my plans.

"I'm serious. What do you expect to gain from all of this?"

"The law school program is self-paced, independent study. I expect to finish in 2001. If I charge $500 for research or writing legal motions, I think I can earn an average of $1,000 a month over the 12 years I'll still have to serve. After taxes, that would leave me close to $100,000 in the bank when I walk out of prison."

Bruce nods, smiling. "I only have one more question. If the warden won't let you receive books from U. Conn., what makes you think he's going to let you receive books from the law school in California?"

"That's the nice thing about law school. I won't need to access an outside library. Every federal prison has its own law library. I'll just purchase the other books I need. As long as the bookstore sends the books directly, I won't need special permission from the prison."

"So you're all set then?"

"I'm ready."

* * * * * * *

Julie and Tim agree to finance my tuition and book expenses with the understanding that I'll reimburse them from my earnings. When the mailroom delivers my coursework for first-year law, the stack of textbooks reaches halfway up my thigh. As I fan through thousands of fine-print pages optimism surges through me. I'm making progress, feeling a renewed energy, convinced that these books will change my life.

I create a new daily schedule, committing myself to wake and to begin studying after the guards complete the 3:00 a.m. census, allowing myself three hours of reading and note-taking before I exercise. Then I can study again from 9:00 a.m. until 8:00 p.m. By the end of 1998, I'll finish my first-year courses. The self-imposed structure brings the illusion that I'm back in control of my life.

A scandalous affair between President Clinton and a young White House intern dominates the news, but I barely notice. I have tunnel vision again, devoting all of my energies toward mastering a new vocabulary, learning how to research the law, and writing lengthy papers.

After sending in my first batch of assignments, I move on to the next course. It's early morning, still dark outside, and I'm studying in bed. My tiny book light is clipped on the metal chair beside my rack, illuminating the thick textbook propped upon my thighs. Eleven other men sleep nearby, but my earplugs muffle the sound of their snores. I'm invigorated by the work. Instead of wasting time, I'm developing skills that can never be taken away.

Later in the week, when I open the envelope containing my first graded assignments, I'm deeply disappointed. Because of my experience at Hofstra and Mercer, I expected these law professors to challenge me, to expose flaws in my reasoning, to show an interest in my work. I invested more than 100 hours reading and writing nearly 50 pages of carefully researched reasoning and arguments. Despite the efforts I made, the professor only drew a red circle around the "A" in the top right corner of the first page, and that letter grade represented the extent of his commentary. I toss the envelope to the bottom of my locker in disgust, doubtful that anyone read what I wrote.

Now I understand what Bruce meant when he said this law degree would cheapen my other degrees. The costly tuition appears to cover the expense of a diploma, not for an education in the law. But I didn't enroll to receive another piece of paper to frame and hang. I could've simply purchased the books and studied on my own. Although I wouldn't earn a degree, I would gain the same knowledge through a completely independent study. Nevertheless, I've paid the non-refundable fee for the first year so I continue.

* * * * * * *

It's 4:00 a.m., and I've found a quiet room where I'm finishing my final assignment for the term. My legal dictionary, a book on case law, and two supplementary texts lay open on the table. When the door behind me opens I turn around, surprised that anyone else is awake at this hour. It's Gary, one of the 400 prisoners assigned to my unit. Wearing gray sweats, slip-on shoes, and carrying a plastic mug with steaming coffee, he makes his way through the room with quiet footsteps and stands in front me.

We've never spoken before. Although I recognize faces, I prefer to remain cloistered in my own space, absorbed with my books and studies. I cherish the early morning solitude and Gary's intrusion annoys me.

"I heard you study law," he says in a strong Russian accent, looking down at me.

I lean back in my chair, lock my hands behind my head and yawn as I stretch. "That's right," I answer, finally making eye contact with him.

"I need some help with my case."

"Can't help you. I'm wrapped up with school. You should check out the law library. A few guys do legal work there."

Gary moves around the table and stands beside me, sipping his coffee, looking at my books. "I've watched you. Very serious. You study all the time. Don't talk much. Are you almost finished?"

"I'm finishing first year. I'll need two more years to complete the program."

"Read my case," Gary proposes, taking another sip from his coffee mug. "I want your opinion. My lawyer sent boxes of paper from my appeal. I don't understand. You could help."

"No. I can't. I've got too much to read."

Gary nods his head. "Help me. I'll pay you well."

His offer to pay is a novel concept to me and I inquire further. "What is it that you want me to read?"

"I lost my appeal. Now my attorneys want to file a new motion in court. Why? I want to know."

"I can't answer that question without reading all of your transcripts, your appeal, and researching the court's rulings. That would take weeks and I can't afford to take that time away from my studies."

"I don't want those guys in the law library. I want you. Money's no object. Name your price."

I stretch again, thinking of a number that will send him away, or, if he accepts, make the effort worth my while. "Two thousand dollars."

"Okay. Give me instructions on where to wire the funds."

"No wire. I'll give you an address. Think about it, because all I'm going to do is read everything, then tell you my opinion. I'm not filing any motions or writing any briefs. If the check arrives, I'll come by, pick up the boxes and start reading. If not, I'll know you changed your mind."

"Give me the address."

* * * * * * *

"Do you know someone from New York?" Julie asks during our phone call.

"Why?"

"Because I received a check in the mail from a New York address. A note says it's for Gary's case. We don't know anyone

235

from New York who would send us $2,000. I figured it must be someone you know."

A week has passed since Gary visited me in the quiet room. Expecting him to be as full of hot air as most other prisoners, I didn't forewarn my sister that she might receive a check. News of the money's arrival makes me smile. For the first time since I've been in prison, I've got money of my own.

"Yes, I know Gary. Sorry I didn't write you about it before. I'll send you a letter this week explaining everything."

"Well what am I supposed to do with the check?"

"Do you need it?"

"We don't need it. Do you want me to save it for you?"

"If you don't need it, I want you to open an online brokerage account. Make it a margin account. We're going to use it to buy stock. I want to start building a stock portfolio that can grow during the rest of the time I have to serve."

"What should I buy?"

"When the account's open, buy Yahoo!."

"How many shares?"

"Buy as much as you can. If you open a margin account, the broker will let you borrow against the stock to double up, enabling you to purchase $3,000 worth of the stock. We'll add to the account over time."

"Are you sure you know what you're doing?" My sister doesn't have any experience investing in stocks and she's worried about exposure.

"Just call the broker and open the account. He'll confirm that you can do this." I know that Julie will help.

I don't have access to computers, but I've been reading about the Internet in the Wall Street Journal for several years. I've seen the phenomenon of such companies as Netscape, America Online, and Amazon.com. I'm certain the Internet will change the world, influencing people's lives more than the telephone, television, and radio combined. Although I may not be able to use it until I'm free, I want a stock portfolio that will allow me to own a slice of the companies I expect will dominate the Web, and I intend to start with Yahoo!.

* * * * * * *

I walk into Gary's room to invite him for a walk. He's sitting on his bunk, leaning back against the wall, reading *The Deptford Trilogy* by the Canadian novelist Robertson Davies. He reads novels to improve his English, which he speaks well. He's also fluent in Spanish, French, and Russian. I've read every page of the transcripts from Gary's trial, as well as all accompanying documents that he gave me. Court papers have a tendency to portray defendants in an unflattering light. Gary's papers, on the other hand, expose a remarkable history of a self-made man.

After earning tens of millions as a mining entrepreneur in Russia, Gary relocated to the United States where he began accumulating blocks of commercial real estate. Criminal charges led to his trial, and although a jury convicted Gary of one count related to complexities with his businesses' accounting, the jury acquitted him of several others. He has served two years since his conviction and faces one more.

"You've read through everything?"

He hops down from the rack and laces up his sneakers.

"I've read everything. But let's talk outside."

The summer of 1998 brings high humidity to the East Coast. It's against prison rules to take off our shirts, so within seconds of stepping outside my tank top is damp with sweat and stuck to my back. Both of us carry plastic water bottles and wear sunglasses. Under his white baseball cap Gary looks much younger than 36, too young to have built and operated all the businesses his court papers describe.

"My lawyers want another hundred grand to file the last motion," he says.

"I'll bet you never thought justice cost so much."

Gary waves his hand. "I'm tired of all this, with the trial and the appeal going on and on. This mess has already cost me more than a million. I just want it over."

"You've already served two years. No one can take that away."

"But I've served every day thinking it would be my last, that I'd win something and be released."

"There comes a time, Gary, when it's easier to let go, to accept the sentence and focus on the future you can control, rather than hanging on to the past you can't change."

237

I explain to Gary my interpretation of his case. The only mechanism available for him to seek relief is a habeas corpus petition. Statistics show that courts refuse to grant relief through those petitions nine out of ten times, and at least nine months would pass before he received a hearing.

"With less than 12 months before release," I explain, "I don't think it makes sense to put yourself on that emotional roller coaster, not to mention the cost of another legal motion."

"I don't care about the money."

"Your lawyers must know that."

"Why do you say that?"

"They represented you through trial and on your appeal. It's not like they'll have to read all the papers again. The price they're asking to prepare the motion seems about ten times too high."

"Could you write the motion from here?"

"I wouldn't want to try."

"Why not? I'd rather pay you than them."

I'm silent, thinking, as gravel crunches beneath our steps. Gary's offer isn't lost on me. I know he's in the prisoner mindset of desperation, clinging to hope that something will free him and he's willing to pay for that delusion.

"Gary, you don't have any upside to filing this motion. You'll be out by the time a judge hears it, and even if he does hear the motion, you'll probably lose. I'd rather show you strategies that will help ease the last 12 months you're going to serve. Regardless of what you pay, the reality is that you're going to serve your time. I'll serve it with you."

Gary takes his ball cap off and scratches his head. We walk alongside bleachers where several hundred prisoners cheer for the teams playing softball.

"So there's nothing we can do?"

"I wouldn't say that. With the right frame of mind we can figure out a plan to make your last year pass easier than the first two. It *will* pass. If you keep waiting for something to change through the courts, on the other hand, this last year will hang over your head like a dark cloud, making you miserable."

"I can't believe you've done 11 years. How can you put up with this for so long without going crazy?"

238

"I've got a deliberate plan. Every day I work hard to prepare myself for the time when I'll go home."

"But 45 years? How do you prepare for that?"

"I won't serve that long. The only way I'd serve that long would be if I lost good time from disciplinary actions, and I haven't lost any yet. I know what I'm doing. I completely understand prisons and the way to avoid problems. Since I'm always working toward the next goal, time passes quickly."

"How much time do you have left?" he asks.

"I'm supposed to get out in 2013. Fifteen more years."

"Fifteen years! You say it like it's nothing, like you're asking for a glass of water. I'd rather hang myself."

"No you wouldn't. You'd find your way. Anyone can serve time in prison. The challenge is to serve it in a way that will make you emerge stronger than when you started."

"How can you stay strong through 15 more years of this?"

"By owning it. I know where I am and I know the problems that await me. I spend every day working to prepare for what's ahead. That strategy makes me feel like I'm the captain of my own ship. It's the reason I'm studying law. To prepare."

"To prepare for what? To be a lawyer?"

"I'm never going to be a lawyer. But by studying law I can make myself useful in here. I'll earn money by helping other prisoners who want to fight their cases. You were the first person to pay me. When I walk out of here, I intend to have enough money saved to build a life for myself."

"Two thousand dollars?" Gary scoffs. "You've been in here too long, my friend. That isn't enough for one dinner bill."

"For you, maybe. Remember, I'm starting from zero, and I've got 15 years for the money to grow. You paid me seed money. I intend to keep adding to it through my work. It's already tripled. By the time I'm released, I'll have enough to buy more than dinner. I'll be able to start my life."

"What do you mean it tripled?"

"I used it to buy stock."

"In the stock market?"

"That's right."

"How do you do that from here?"

As we round the soccer field, I explain. "I spoke with the prison's head of security, the captain, and he confirmed that I was within my rights to advise my sister on stock purchases. By using the $2,000 from you, and borrowing another $1,000 from the brokerage house on margin, Julie purchased 50 shares of Yahoo! at $60 per share. Then the stock split two-for-one, giving us 100 shares. Those shares now trade at $70, giving our portfolio $7,000 in value. With the $1,000 we owe in margin debt, the account now has $6,000 in equity. That's triple the $2,000 you paid me."

"I've been involved in every kind of business, but I've never understood the stock market. If you would have had $2 million and you made the same purchase, are you telling me you would've had $6 million now?" Leveraged trading intrigues Gary.

I laugh. "Theoretically. But if I had $2 million, I wouldn't have made the same purchase."

"Why not?"

"Like you said, $2,000 isn't much money. My brother-in-law suggested I sock it away in a Certificate of Deposit. It would've been safer, but I was willing to take more risk. The company I bought stock in is new, and most investors say it's overpriced because the Internet is all hype. If the Internet grows, on the other hand, then this company will grow with it, causing the stock price to surge. I could take the risk with $2,000, but if I had $2 million, I'd choose safer investments."

"You're too young to be making safe investments. That's the problem with this country. Too many people are afraid of risk. Remember one lesson from a man who knows: the timid never make fortunes."

"I'm not trying to build a fortune. All I want is enough in the bank so that I'm not desperate for an immediate paycheck when I get out."

"So write my motion. I'll pay you a hundred grand if you can get me out of prison."

"I can't get myself out of prison, and writing a motion isn't going to get you out either, I'm sorry to say. Instead of thinking about getting out, why don't we figure out what you can do while you're here to pass the time more easily?"

Gary shakes his head. "I can't serve 12 more months."

"Yes you can," I laugh. "I'll serve it with you, and when you go, I'll be another year closer to home."

"How about you teach me about the stock market?"

"I can tell you what to read and how I learned over the years, but I don't have time to teach."

"I'll make you a deal. I'll send you the hundred thousand I was going to spend on this motion. You won't owe me anything. Just show me what you're going to buy, how much, and explain the reason why. The only condition is that you *don't* play it safe. I want you to take the same risk that you took with the $2,000. Try to triple the money I send, turn it into $300,000. If we lose, we lose. If we win, we split the profits."

"What about the taxes?"

"You pay the taxes. We'll split the profit after the taxes."

"Gary, I read how much you earn. To you, $100,000 is pocket change, but to me, where I am at this stage in my life, that may as well be all the money in the world. I couldn't speculate with it the same way I'd speculate with $2,000. In order to turn the $2,000 into $6,000, I had to borrow against the equity by using margin. The leverage I used is what made the investment triple."

"So use leverage."

"I could do that, but if the market goes the other way, and it could, I'd either have to dump the stock in a down market to raise cash, or you would have to put up more money for the margin call in order to hold the position."

"Too many details. I believe in people, and you're my guy. I'm betting on you to play it smart enough for both of us. Yes?" he nods his head. "Be aggressive. If you lose everything, not to worry. You won't owe me a dime, and I'll send you $50,000 more that you can use to start your life. How does that sound?" He puts out his hand. "Deal?"

"Okay." We shake hands.

...I Conquered

Chapter Nine: 1998-2002
Months 127-180

The summer of 1998 advances me into my 11th continuous year of imprisonment, and I'm coming to the conclusion that it's not so bad. Human beings can adapt to any environment. As crazy as it may sound, I'm now used to imprisonment. It has become the only life that I know, and I really know Fort Dix, the low-security prison where I'm serving this portion of my sentence.

Fort Dix is a big prison, with three separate compounds. About 2,400 other prisoners share space with me inside this low-security facility, and an adjacent facility of the same size is on the other side of these fences. A few hundred men serve their sentences in a minimum-security facility outside of the gated perimeter. My studies and preparations for the future keep my thoughts focused on where I'm going, not where I am.

Law school was an important step toward my pursuit of financial stability, as the population of prisoners on this compound could have provided me with sufficient business opportunities to reach my goal of earning $10,000 a year as a jailhouse lawyer. But Gary's offer to fund stock investments tempts me. With his offer to provide capital, possibilities open for me to become financially independent much sooner. The stock market is an engine that is driving economic growth in America, and with what Gary describes as "pocket change," I can seize a life-changing opportunity. I'm not going to let it pass.

Another benefit of shifting my focus to the stock market is that it can help divert unwanted attention I've begun receiving from Lieutenant Nesbitt. I think that I knew of Nesbitt several years ago when he was a lieutenant at Fairton, before he transferred to Fort Dix. I would've avoided him then at Fairton and I avoid him now in Fort Dix.

Rumor has it that Nesbitt cultivates snitches that dial him into the flow of the prison underground. Apparently someone gave him my number, because I feel the intense stare from his icy blue eyes while I walk toward the chow hall's dish room with my plastic green tray. As usual, he's standing in the center of the noisy dining room with both hands clutching the stem of his long, black flashlight that he positions across his crotch. His barrel-shaped body is stuffed into his rumpled BOP uniform and he's alert, turning his head from side to side, scanning every face in the crowd until he finds what he's looking for. We've never spoken before or had any interaction, but Nesbitt reminds me of a schoolyard bully, and today he's after me. I feign indifference as I pass by, but my efforts to avoid him fail.

"Santos!" He jerks his head to motion me over.

I step toward him and stand, suspicious of what he wants.

"How's the law business?" He smirks as he begins his interrogation.

"What do you mean?"

He glares into my eyes. "You know exactly what I mean, *Counselor*."

"I've finished the first year of law school, if that's what you mean."

Nesbitt grips his flashlight harder, with both hands.

"Understand one thing, inmate. This is my institution. Got it?"

I nod.

"I know everything that goes on here, and I know what you're up to. You're running a law clinic and I'm gonna nail you. When I do, I'm gonna write you up, send you back to a higher security institution." A cold smile tightens his lips as he waits for me to grovel.

I chuckle because he's a funny little round ball of a man. "Lieutenant Nesbitt, with all due respect," I tell him, "I've been in prison for 11 years and I've got 15 more to go. I'm sleeping on the top bunk in a 12-man room. I'm not doing anything that I'm not within my rights to do. But know this, I'm more than 2,000 miles away from Seattle, and wherever you send me, I'll be closer to home. So if you can arrange a transfer," I shrug nonchalantly, "do me the favor. Higher security doesn't mean anything to me. I can study law anywhere."

"Watch your step."

"Is that it? Can I go?"

"Get outta my face!"

If it were a different time, I suspect he would've used his flashlight to club me. But I walk away from him without incident, dropping my tray at the dish room and returning to my housing unit. I walked into this phase of my journey knowing that a quasi-career as a jailhouse lawyer could invite scrutiny from staff, though I'm surprised that Nesbitt harassed me today. Other than reading Gary's case, I haven't done any legal work.

Someone tipped off Nesbitt, and I'm wondering whether Gary told anyone about paying me to read his legal papers. Predictably, I find him sitting alone playing solitary chess at a picnic table beneath a maple tree. Hundreds of prisoners cluster in groups at other tables on the dry, prickly grass.

"I've heard that game's more challenging when you play against someone else," I tell him.

He looks up at me.

"Do you play?" he inquires indifferently.

"I can play at the intermediate level," I answer him.

"By whose standards?"

I laugh. "Not the International Chess Federation's."

"Sit." He invites me to join him, gesturing toward the empty seat.

"I haven't played in a while," I say, giving the disclaimer I may need later as Gary sets up the pieces on the board. He will play with the white pieces and I'm going to play with the black.

"Not to worry," he says with his Russian accent. "To make things fair, I'll give you my queen and one other piece."

"Come on. You can't give me the most powerful piece on the board. I'm not *that* bad."

"My queen, and any other piece of your choice," he insists, waiting for my selection. "I'm not a...how you say, an intermediate player."

"Okay, I'll take the castle."

He hands me the two pieces. "It's not a 'castle'," he corrects me. "In chess, we call the piece a rook." Gary advances the king's pawn and our game begins.

I meet his pawn to battle for the board's center.

"You've forfeited two major pieces. To win, all I need to do is force you into exchanges," I say, declaring my strategy.

Gary nods his head. "Good. You've figured it all out early." He brings out his knight, not particularly concerned with my game plan.

"Nesbitt stopped me as I was leaving the chow hall this morning," I tell him while pushing a pawn.

"Oh? What did that pathetic excuse for a human being want?" Gary brings out his bishop.

I'm staring at the chessboard, deliberating possible moves. "He asked me about my legal business." I push another pawn.

Gary advances his other knight, on the attack. "Is he bothering you?"

"Not bothering me," I'm slow to move, trying to figure out how best to exchange a piece. "He's fishing for something. Did you tell anyone about the $2,000 you sent to my sister?"

He advances a knight again. "Who I am going to tell, the rap stars?" He jerks his head toward the men singing and grooving to the beat of urban music on our right. "Maybe the Mafia?" He indicates the group of men chomping on cigars around the bocce court on our left, rolling red and green balls.

Gary's pieces encroach but I improve my position by bringing out a knight. "I guess the mailroom must've alerted him to all the legal books I've had sent in."

"Check," Gary captures a pawn with his knight and forces me to move my king. "Did you call your sister?"

I'm on defense now, moving the king out of position. "No," I answer him.

"Check," he says, pinning my king with his second knight. "Call her. My partner sent a cashier's check for $50,000. She should have it by now. The second half is coming from Hong Kong next month. When my partner receives it, he'll send that, too."

I move my king, trying to keep him from a checkmate, but I'm distracted by this revelation that Gary's for real. I'll soon have the money to buy more stock in Yahoo!, the leading Internet search engine.

"You'd better pick stocks better than you play chess.

Checkmate," he declares.

Our game ends after 16 moves, not enough time for me to capture more than the two pieces he forfeited. He challenges me to a second match, this time keeping all of his pieces on the board at the game's start, but handicapping himself by insisting that the only possibility for him to win is to checkmate me on a specific square with a specific piece that he identifies before we start. When I say "impossible," he shrugs, and then goes about proving me wrong. It turns out he was a chess Grand Master at 16.

* * * * * * *

When I call my sister, Julie tells me that she's received the first $50,000 installment. Even though it doesn't belong to me, the money validates my sense of self. Gary, a man who earned tens of millions by judging character and competence in others, handed me $50,000 and promised more. It's a sign of trust, more tangible than any I've ever received. It isn't lost on me that I cultivated this trust while living inside of prison fences.

"Buy 300 shares of America Online and 400 shares of Yahoo!"

Julie calculates the total cost of the purchase. "But that's more than $80,000," she sounds alarmed.

"That's why you opened a margin account," I remind her. "You're borrowing $30,000 against the equity. It's going to increase in value and when it does you'll borrow against it to buy more stock. We'll keep buying until the account grows to 1,000 shares of AOL and 1,000 shares of Yahoo!"

"How do you know the stock is going to increase? What if the value goes down instead? Then what?"

"Just place the order. Let me worry about that. I'll call you every morning before the market opens and advise you on what to do."

Julie promises to make the daily stock orders for me, then asks about law school and whether she should send the tuition payment for a second year.

"I'm done with law school," I tell her. "I'm not going to let this opportunity pass. Order me subscriptions for *Investor's Business Daily, Forbes,* and *Fortune.* I'm going to learn everything I can about the money game."

My routine changes. Instead of studying legal procedures and contracts, I'm now as loyal to CNBC as any Wall Street fanatic. The ticker streams news that ignites my adrenaline. When the guards clear the morning census count at 5:00, I'm out of my room, down the stairs, and first in the television room to watch Joe Kernan, David Faber, Tom Costello, Mark Haines, and the other anchors as they report the morning's business news. I have a calculator and I consult it repeatedly as I observe and record market indicators, futures, trading patterns in London, Frankfurt, Paris, Tokyo, and Hong Kong in my journal.

* * * * * * *

It's 4:30 a.m. on August 18, 1998, and I haven't slept at all. My neck aches from the tension gripping my shoulders as I pace my room, waiting for the guards to clear count. I've been on my rack listening through my Sony headphones to Bloomberg radio broadcasts. The news reports that Russia is devaluing its currency, devastating financial markets around the world. My account stands to lose tens of thousands in equity when the opening bell rings on Wall Street at 9:30, and I know a margin call will come. With my outstanding debt, I'll either have to raise more cash or sell into weakness, taking huge losses.

I'm in a two-man room now, and my roommate, Toro, a Dominican man I hardly know, sleeps soundly. He snores, wearing a watch cap to cover his eyes from the early morning light. I'd like to relax so easily, but I have real money on the line and I'm anxious to watch the CNBC ticker even though I know I'll see red arrows pointing down across the board.

Finally, the count clears and I rush to the TV room. When I turn on the news I see exactly what I expect. The market is set for the worst point drop in history. The prices of AOL and Yahoo! rise like rockets with good news, but I'm certain they'll drop like bricks today. Gary doesn't usually wake until 9:00 and when he does, I'll have to give him the news. According to my calculations, the drop in equity that I anticipate will require that I deposit $10,000 to reduce my debt from $30,000 to $20,000. We began the Internet stocks venture less than a month ago. Obviously I didn't foresee an event such as Russia's currency devaluation causing such a disaster.

Gary strolls into the TV room carrying his white coffee mug advertising "Nescafé" in bold red letters on the front. I'm at the table in front of the TV with my eyes fixed on the ticker scrolling across the bottom of the screen.

"Why the sad face? Somebody die?" he jokes.

"Not yet. But when the market opens we're going to get slaughtered."

He sips from his mug, looks at the monitor, and nods his head. "What happened?"

"The Russian government made a change with its currency valuation last night, causing a global financial panic. I was going to wake you but I knew you'd come down before the market opened."

"Never wake me for money problems."

"We've got problems. If I don't deposit $10,000 this morning, I'm going to have to sell at much lower prices than I paid to buy."

Gary takes another sip. "Has your opinion on the companies or business changed?"

"Yahoo! and AOL are still the strongest Internet companies. That hasn't changed, but the market has changed. Until it recovers, the account can't sustain so much debt."

"So what's the big deal? Call your sister and get me her bank's routing number. I'll have a friend wire transfer $10,000 to her before lunch."

"That simple?"

Gary laughs. "One phone call. That's all it takes. Come, let's go to the gym."

"Not today. I need to watch the market."

He shrugs. "Don't let this go to your head. Get me that routing number and I'll take care of it."

* * * * * * *

Gary's deposit solves my first problem of the day, but within hours, a crisis of a different sort erupts. I'm staring at the ticker, watching the Dow drop more than 500 points, worrying that the sell-off will accelerate as the trading day proceeds. I'm frozen to the TV when Al, another prisoner, delivers a message that snaps me out of my zone.

"They've been pagin' you to R&D all mornin'."

At first I think he's joking, but we're not close friends so I doubt he'd play a practical joke on me. I don't understand why the Receive and Discharge department would be paging me. I look at the red arrows on the TV one last time before leaving the television room.

Outside, the warm temperature heats my skin as I make the quarter-mile walk across the compound to R&D. Fumes from the adjacent military base pollute the air, and I plug my ears to block the sound of screeching engines as the jets and giant cargo planes repeatedly land and take off. The market weighs on my mind, but I'm also institutionalized, accustomed to my fixed routine, and wondering why anyone from R&D would want to talk to me. I'm troubled by the unexpected summons.

I knock on the steel door, and wait for the guard.

"What's your name and number?"

I give the guard my red ID card.

"Where've you been? I've been paging you for two hours." The guard scowls at me.

"I didn't hear any of the pages. I was watching TV."

"Roll up," the guard commands, passing me three large duffle bags and then flicking my ID card back at me

"Roll up?" I catch the ID card in mid air. "What do you mean, 'roll up'? Where am I going?"

"Can't tell you that. Get your shit. I've got to pack you out now."

"I need to know what's going on. I'm not supposed to be leaving. There's a mistake." I counter, my pulse racing from the adrenaline surging through my body with this news.

"No mistake. Either pack your bags and bring 'em up here, or I'll have the officer pack you out. I need all your property here before 1:00 this afternoon. Either way, you're going."

"I'm leaving today?"

"Get your belongings here before 1:00," he orders, slamming the door in my face without answering.

With limited time to gather information, I rush back to my housing unit and hurry from one staff member to another, trying to find out what's happening. I can't find anyone who has information or who cares enough to answer my questions. Finally, I locate Mr. Boatwright, a case manager who spoke with me on occasion about the market. I tell him my problem and he invites me back to his office.

"Give me your number."

I hear him clicking the information onto his keyboard as he stares at the monitor. My heart races and my legs twitch with anxiety, making it hard to stand still.

"You're on your way to Miami."

"*Miami*? That doesn't make sense. The only prison in Miami is a medium. Did someone raise my security level?"

"Not the FCI," Mr. Boatwright answers, still looking at his screen. "You're going to the detention center."

"What? There's a mistake. I've been in for more than 11 years. Why would I be going to a detention center?" Detention centers hold prisoners who face unresolved criminal charges, but those kinds of problems are behind me.

"Let's see what I can find." I hear him clicking keys again and see that he's reading information. He looks up. "You're going to a state prison. The detention center's only a stop."

My stomach lurches. "Who can fix this mess? It's a mistake. I don't have criminal charges in the state of Florida."

"No one here can fix this. The transfer order came from Washington."

I steady myself with this news. "Okay. Thanks for checking. I've got to use the phone."

I walk out to call my sister and explain all that I've learned. It's already noon, and since the R&D guard only gave me an hour to pack all of my belongings, I ask Julie to call everyone in my support network. This inexplicable transfer to state prison threatens to disrupt my life and I want help from anyone who can undo this mess. I'm intimately familiar with the federal prison system. I know it like I know my own face in the mirror. The rules, the people, the absurdity of it don't faze me at all anymore. But if I transfer to a state prison in Florida, I'll be starting from scratch, facing ridiculous "tests" and challenges from prisoners I don't know and who don't know me. I don't have any doubt that I can master any prison, but I detest the thought of upsetting my routine at Fort Dix.

When I hang up with Julie, I see Gary waiting for me outside the phone room.

"They've been paging you all morning to R&D. Did you hear?"

"I heard. I've got bad news. They're transferring me to a state prison in Florida."

"Florida? Why?"

"No one will tell me. My sister's on the phone now, trying to get in touch with my friends to rally support to fix this mess." This unwelcome news feels like I've just been diagnosed with a terminal illness. We walk to my room and Gary helps me pack my sweats, sneakers, toiletries and books.

"What do you want me to do with the stocks? Should I sell them?" I ask while pulling and tying the draw strings of my three full duffle bags; everything I own fits inside of them.

"Why?"

"If I'm in Florida I won't be able to talk with you."

"That doesn't change anything. Don't worry about talking with me. When you have a chance, write me, tell me what stocks you bought or sold. By the end of the year I'll send the rest of the money to your sister. The transfer doesn't change anything between us."

I'll miss Gary. As we say goodbye it's another reminder that I'm a pawn in this game. I don't know where I'll be tomorrow because someone else moves the pieces that control the external circumstances of my life. All I can do is respond.

It's early on Wednesday morning, my last at Fort Dix. I breathe deeply as I lie on my bed, listening to the whir of the generator outside my window, Toro's light snoring, and the occasional footsteps of other prisoners who walk to the bathroom down the hall. I know that I only have a few more minutes of peace before the guard arrives.

I'll miss my two-man room in Fort Dix. These are the best living conditions I've had since I've been in prison. I arrived here in April of 1996 and I had to wait 28 months for enough seniority before I could transfer from a 12-man room to "preferred housing." I'll miss the standard twin mattress that rests on springs, I'll miss the two sliding windows that aren't blocked with bars, and I'll miss being able to look up at the moon. It shines through now, lighting the white, bare, concrete-block walls of the room.

Mostly, I'll miss the windowless wooden entry door with its yellow doorknob that turns. The door isn't any different from the type found in a typical home, but it's fundamentally different from the industrial strength steel doors used in most prisons. Once I leave here, I won't be able to close the door to separate myself from the chaos of prison and escape into the privacy of my room, or at least the illusion of privacy.

I hear keys clinking and heavy boots on the tile floor outside my room and I know it's time. I've been trying to enjoy the solitude of this final night but my heart pounds, as I know that I'll soon be locked in chains again.

"Santos," the guard barks as he opens the door, oblivious to the disruption this transfer is about to bring to my life. "Report to R&D."

I'm the only prisoner walking on the compound. I see stars in the clear sky and the moon illuminates rustling leaves of maple trees. The cold morning wind chills my face. Shivering, I take one last look at the red brick buildings and knock on the steel door of R&D, bracing myself for the indignities of another BOP transfer.

The guard locks me in a holding cell with other prisoners I recognize. I stretch, sit on the concrete floor, and rest my back against the wall. Through the door I can hear chains clanking against the concrete floor, signaling that my unexpected transfer is imminent. Guards are untangling and preparing the requisite heavy metal shackles they'll secure around my waist, wrists, and ankles. I hate this.

We're processed out and marched onto the bus, bound for Stewart Air Force Base. I look through the bars on the tinted windows at the people driving in their cars only a few yards away–families, businessmen, and couples.

I strain my head to watch a woman in the passenger seat of a white sports car. She's rubbing the back of a man's neck. He's about my age, probably her husband, wearing a crisp white shirt, pale blue tie. This glimpse of the outside world leaves me feeling deeply alienated. It's been so long since I've felt the touch of a woman and I miss it. Observing the couple's simple act of affection causes me to shake my head and withdraw into my seat. I close my eyes but I can't block out the sight of that woman's hand.

For hours the bus rolls along the interstate before pulling onto the military base. It stops on the tarmac and guards pass us sack lunches while we wait for the marshal's plane to land. With my wrists cuffed to the chain around my waist, it's a challenge to free the cheese sandwich from the clear plastic baggie. It's only white bread and cheese. The bread is moist and spongy in my mouth–bland, but easy to swallow. I bend over to eat the whole sandwich, but since I'm dreading the airsickness that's sure to come, I leave the crackers and juice in the bag.

The unmarked white plane lands and guards carrying assault rifles position themselves around it. Men and women in chains step off and guards order them into columns for searches. I've seen this predictable routine time and again, and it never fails to disgust me. I prefer the routines of prison to the dehumanizing rituals of transit. When my turn comes I climb the stairs into the belly of the plane, drop into my seat, buckle my belt, and I close my eyes. I don't want to talk.

When the plane lands in Oklahoma City, we exit directly into the terminal reserved for the FTC, or Federal Transit Center. It's a new "holdover destination" for prisoners transferring to prisons across state lines. This FTC is a model of efficiency, processing prisoners like FedEx handles packages. After four hours in holding cells crammed with hundreds of prisoners, I reach my housing unit just in time to be ordered into my cell for the evening lockdown. I won't be able to call my sister to find out whether she's made any progress in trying to resolve this fiasco, and the disconnect bums me out.

My cellmate arrives and I ask his name after the guard locks us in.

"I'm Paul." He says, shaking my hand. I sense that he's young and afraid, and the encounter temporarily throws me back to 1987, when my own term began.

"I'm Michael. Where're you headed?"

"Yazoo, Mississippi." He sets his bedroll on the top rack.

"Have you been anywhere else?" I ask, trying to ease his apparent anxiety.

"I was in the Houston detention center and I got sentenced two weeks ago."

"How much time did you get?"

"Ten years."

"Don't worry. It's going to pass easier than you think." I know what he's going through.

"How long have you been in?"

"Eleven years. I was about your age when I started. How old are you?"

"Twenty-five."

I tie my sheets around the vinyl mat on the lower rack and describe for Paul what he can expect. Although I've never been to Yazoo, I know that it's a low-security prison and the prisoners will behave similarly to the men I was with at Fort Dix. Paul asks questions for hours. By talking with him about steps he can take to improve his life, I ease my own tensions.

The guards unlock the cell doors well before dawn and my heart sinks when they call Paul instead of me. Wanting to get on with the transfer and settle into a routine, I tighten the green wool blanket around my body and pull it over my head as a shield against the forced air shooting through the ceiling vent above my head. I sleep off and on, accepting that this is going to be another miserable day of waiting

The sound of wheels from the breakfast cart rolling across the concrete floor signals me that it's time to get up. Guards traverse the long aisles of cells, thrusting keys into locks that click loudly as the heavy deadbolts are released. Clatter soon fills the unit as prisoners emerge from their cells, looking for familiar faces. Impromptu conversations begin with discussions about where prisoners are going, where they're coming from, common acquaintances, and what's going on in prisons across the country.

I'm guessing that 200 of us share the two-tiered, triangular shaped pod. As I wait in line for my breakfast tray I scan the room, looking for familiar faces, or anyone I might have known previously. This FTC houses prisoners of every security level. Some serve multiple life sentences for murder convictions, others serve sentences of only a few months for mail fraud convictions. I recognize tattoos from various prison gangs that rival each other. Although most prisoners in transit want to reach their next stop without problems, I'm hyper alert for the tension that can explode into unexpected violence.

At the food cart an orderly passes me a green plastic tray with corn flakes and two cartons of milk. I walk to a table with four plastic swivel chairs and sit down. Another prisoner sits across from me. He wears his black hair long and ties it in several places down his back, making a tight ponytail.

"Where're you headed?" I ask, stirring my cereal.

"Miami."

"Really? Me too. I'm going to the detention center." He looks up and I notice a crooked scar beneath his right eye.

"Are you going to a state prison?" he asks.

"That's what I've been told. You?"

He nods, confirming that he received the same information.

"Where'd you come from?" I ask.

"Petersburg, Virginia."

"The medium or the low?" I want to know his security level.

"I was in the low."

"I was in the low at Fort Dix. My name's Michael."

"Ty." We shake hands.

"What did you hear about this transfer?"

"I didn't hear anything except that the order for the transfer came from DC. Another guy sitting next to me on the plane said he was going on the same program. His case manager told him the feds were processing some state prisoners into the federal system and exchanging federal prisoners with the Florida state system."

"Where was he coming from?"

"Big Springs."

"That's a low-security prison," I say.

"Are you from Florida?"

"Miami," he nods.

"How 'bout you?"

"I was living there when I got arrested, but I'm from

Seattle."

"You probably got rounded up because the computer thinks you're from Florida."

"Maybe so. I guess we'll find out what's up when we get there."

When the phones become available, I call Julie to update her on where I am and what I've learned from Ty. She's already spoken with Carol Zachary and Bruce McPherson, and they're all working the phones to get the transfer reversed. Bruce spoke with Sylvia McCollum at BOP headquarters. Through discreet inquiries Sylvia learned that administrators assigned me as part of a prisoner exchange program with the state of Florida because my registration number identified me as being a Florida resident. I'm relieved to learn that my friends and family are using their influence to show that although I was arrested in Florida, I'm not a resident of that state.

* * * * * * *

The plane lands at the marshals' airstrip adjacent to the Miami International Airport. As I leave the plane with the screeching sound of jet engines in my ears, the Miami humidity blasts me like a furnace. For a moment, I look around to admire the beds of tropical flowers and palm trees that I've missed.

Two buses, three white vans, and four cars await us. I'm tired of seeing guards carrying assault rifles, but they're a part of every landscape where prisoner transport takes place. After inspecting my chains, then searching and identifying me, BOP guards direct me to a bus. I notice the familiar street signs of Flagler, Biscayne Boulevard, I-95, and Palmetto Expressway as we drive.

The bus approaches a high-rise building in a downtown district that I don't recognize. We pause in a driveway while a corrugated steel gate rolls open. The bus pushes through, drives down a ramp, and stops inside the dark basement of the Miami Federal Detention Center.

After I complete the requisite forms, fingerprints, mug shots, strip searches, interviews, and hours of waiting in holding cages, I carry my bedroll to join nine other men for an elevator ride to the eleventh floor. We exit into a foyer and the guard unlocks a steel door that opens to a brightly lit, two-tiered housing unit. I see Ty waiting by the guard's station. The deafening noise, steel tubular railings, stationary tables and stools remind me of the first housing unit I was in after my arrest.

I see a familiar face in the crowd, though I don't recall his name or where I saw him last. He recognizes me and walks over.

"Yo, wasn't youse up in Atlanta back in da day?" He's my height but carries an extra 100 pounds.

"That's right. I was in B-cellblock. Michael Santos," I extend my hand.

"Ace, Homie." He bumps fists, gives me a hug, even though I don't remember speaking to him before. "What'cha doin' up in here dog? Catch a new case?"

"I'm in transit, on my way to a state prison."

"State joint? What up wit' dat?" he looks at me suspiciously.

"I don't know. They packed me out. A few others are transferring with me. None of us know where we're going or why."

"Ain't none a youse got no state charges?"

I shake my head. "We've all been down for awhile. How about you? What're you doing here?"

The detention center holds people facing new criminal charges and prisoners in transit. It's not a place where prisoners ordinarily serve their sentences.

"New case, Dawg," he shrugs. "I got out in '93. Been on the streets for fi' years fo' I caught dis new joint."

"What're you looking at now?"

"It's all she wrote, Homie. Life. Know what I'm sayin'? I'm headin' back to the A-T-L."

"Sorry."

"Ain't nothin' Dawg. You know how we do."

I shake my head, not knowing what to say. "Let me get over into this line, see about getting a cell. We'll talk more once I settle in."

"You got it Dawg. Yo, I got ev'thin' you need. Dis my house up in here." He pounds his chest.

"Thanks, Ace."

"Ain't nothing." He puts his fist out, we bump knuckles again, and I walk away wondering when I will leave this madness behind.

At the guard's station I stand in line behind Ty, hoping the guard will assign us to the same cell.

"I don't have any empty cells," the guard says. He sends me to the second tier. I give the cell door a courtesy tap before I pull it open. A man wearing an orange jumpsuit identical to mine lies on the lower rack reading an issue of *Maxim*.

"What's up? You new?" he asks, leaning up on his right elbow.

I nod. "I'm Michael Santos," I set my bedroll on the top rack. "In transit," I say.

"Where to?"

I give the man my story. Then I get his. His name is Rico and he's deliberating on whether to accept the government's plea offer of 10 years. As we talk, I advise him to take the offer, not needing to know anything more than he's charged with a drug crime.

"But I've got a baby girl. I don't think I can do 10 years."

"No one does when they start. If you don't take this deal, chances are you'll serve a lot longer and you'll serve it in tougher prisons. With 10 years you'll only serve about eight, and you might get a year off that if you go through the drug treatment program.

"I don't think I can do it."

* * * * * * *

It's September 11, 1998. I've been in Miami for a week and since my counselor hasn't yet given me a PIN code, I haven't been able to use the telephone. The staff isn't giving me any information about my transfer and I don't know if Bruce and Carol have made progress toward getting me out of here. Ty and I are resigned to the likelihood that we're both on our way to state prison, knowing that we'll leave whenever officials from the Florida Department of Corrections arrive to pick us up. We exercise together, doing pushups, deep knee bends, and stomach crunches.

After our early morning workout, I glance at the dorm's television screen, appalled to see President Clinton and his media machine. He organized a nationally televised prayer breakfast, assembling Billy Graham, Jesse Jackson, and other distinguished clergymen. They pray for forgiveness of Clinton's indiscretion with Monica Lewinsky.

The irony is not lost on me. President Clinton scandalized the country. He told lie after lie to the American people and to Congress about "not having sexual relations with that woman."

Anyone else would serve prison time for telling such lies to Congress. Although I was young and uneducated, my own sentence was extended by two years because I lied during my trial. It angers me, because the president should be held to a higher standard. After all, President Clinton is a graduate of Yale law school, a Rhodes scholar, and a former attorney general. Yet he gets a pass for *his* offense by saying he's sorry.

I've been working to atone for 11 years, not with televised speeches but with measurable actions. It infuriates me to see the inequality as I sit in an orange jumpsuit, knowing that my acts of atonement mean nothing while the president can exonerate himself with a simple prayer meeting.

"Santos!" The guard yells into the housing unit as he steps out from his station, interrupting my mental rant. "Roll up!"

"What about Moreno?" Ty asks.

"I said Santos."

"Can you tell me where I'm going?" I feel queasy, my legs weakening. "FTD."

I recognize those initials as the BOP designation for Fort Dix. My face immediately broadens into a smile.

"Fort Dix?" I ask to confirm.

"All's it says here is FTD. Pack yer shit."

"How'd you' pull that off?" Ty looks at me, disappointment in his eyes.

"I don't know. My family must've gotten through to the right person." I say carefully, suddenly aware of the impact this news has on Ty. We've only known each other for a few days, but through exercise, chess games, and talk, we've bonded and had hoped to see it through as a team. Now I'm deserting him.

Although the news elates me, I don't compound his loss by gloating over being spared a tour through a Florida state prison.

* * * * * * *

My support network really came through for me, and I'm thrilled when guards lock me in a holding cage on the main floor of FDC Miami to process me out. I'm grateful, optimistic, and eager to begin the return trip to Ford Dix. My spirits are dampened, however, when I notice a woman sitting alone in another holding cell directly across from me. She's crying. I step to the front of my cage, wrap my fingers around the bars, and she looks at me. The guards who patrol the corridor prohibit us from talking, so instead we communicate with our eyes. In hers, I see such sadness that it pains me. She tilts her head as she opens her hands in a gesture of helplessness, as if to say "I want to talk to you, too, but we can't." Her smile is modest, but I see a dimple in her cheek. She has long brown hair, and even in the green, oversized jumpsuit I can see her slender figure. Her eyes are blue, or maybe green. It doesn't matter. We'll never meet. I hope she'll find the strength to sustain herself through the loneliness. I look away as guards come to fasten her in chains.

My return to Fort Dix takes me on a 30-day detour through USP Atlanta. It surprises me to feel some nostalgia at my first sight of the high walls. While locked in a holdover unit I see several staff members I used to know. One of them sends a message to Lynn Stephens, my former work supervisor. After receiving news from her colleague that I'm in the holdover unit, Lynn walks over to see me. More than four years have passed since my departure from USP Atlanta and seeing her feels almost like a reunion. She had such an essential role in my early adjustment, allowing me to study in the office we shared, providing sanctuary from the penitentiary madness that destroys the lives of so many young prisoners. She's barely aged but tells me she'll be retiring in another few years, and she updates me on her family while asking about mine. Since she knew me in my 20s, naive to prison life, Lynn is amazed that I'm now nearly 35 and comfortable in my surroundings. Our unexpected reunion helps me measure how much I've matured since beginning my term.

I talk with prisoners I knew when I served my sentence in Atlanta, but after a month, I'm glad to leave the penitentiary behind. Ironically, Fort Dix feels like home and I look forward to my return.

After several hours our plane lands briefly for a prisoner exchange in Manchester, New Hampshire. From my window seat I look at a dense growth of trees with leaves that flutter in the wind and appear to change colors before my eyes. It's a spectacular natural display of orange, yellow, red, and green, and I realize that during the two months I've been locked inside Oklahoma, Miami, and Atlanta prisons, summer has turned to fall. The plane takes off again, and a few hours later, on Thursday, October 15, 1998, I'm processed in and admitted back inside the gated community of FCI Fort Dix.

My friend Carol Zachary is responsible for my return. She met with a high-ranking decision-maker in Washington, and that meeting resulted in the reversal of my transfer order, immediately blocking my move to a Florida state prison.

I walk back onto the Fort Dix compound, and my friend Gary welcomes me with a white mesh laundry bag full of commissary items.

"Welcome back," he laughs, embracing me.

"I can't tell you how good it feels to be back."

"Did you hear the news?" Gary asks.

"What news?"

Gary smiles, knowing that financial news interests me. "The Fed lowered the interest rate and the market's on fire. I hope you didn't sell."

"Sell? Are you kidding? I'm a buyer, not a seller."

"The prices for Yahoo! and AOL are almost back to where they were before you left."

"Don't tell me you're hooked on the stock market now, too."

Gary laughs, telling me that he needed something to pass the time.

* * * * * * *

As we approach the transition from the 20th to the 21st century, fears spread throughout the business community that many of the world's computer programs will fail. Every day, pundits on CNBC discuss the upcoming "Y2K" problem, hyping up the calamity that would befall the world if computers crash. As a market speculator, I'm paying attention to these stories.

To ease worries about how the markets will react at midnight on the last day of 1999, central bankers from around the world take action by lowering key interest rates in the fall of 1998. Their objective is to provide more liquidity for business, thereby averting panic. An offshoot of their strategy is rampant speculation, and I'm one of the euphoric participants.

I follow the flow of easy credit and hot money by subscribing to a dozen financial publications and studying them daily. I'm fascinated with the technology sector, as I perceive companies with an effective Internet strategy as having the most upside. Understanding the risk, I concentrate all of my stock holdings in speculative Internet stocks. That approach proves a winner, and I revel in watching my equity increase, sometimes by tens of thousands each day. I tap that equity by using it as collateral to leverage my holdings. I've got 100 percent of my holdings in Internet stocks, and by using margin I've got double exposure to the market swings.

"You know, I really think it's time you diversify," Jon, another prisoner, advises me. "This market bubble can't last forever. Perhaps you should sell now, put your money in fixed income."

"I can't sell. All my gains have been short-term. I need to hold on to my positions for at least one year, otherwise I'll owe too much tax."

Jon shakes his head. "All wise men diversify."

I'm reluctant to sell any holdings for two reasons. On the one hand, I don't want Julie to incur short-term capital gains taxes, and on the other I'm convinced the market euphoria will last longer than a year. Each evening, after the market's close, I chart my day's progress, read my industry news, and then I walk outside to tell Gary how we did.

"How was the casino today?"

"I bought Cisco, Real Networks, and At Home Communications."

Besides being a Grand Master at chess, Gary has

tremendous musical talents. We sit under a maple tree in early March 1999, bundled in our green jackets and orange knit caps. Spring is in the air but it's still chilly. Gary strums an acoustic guitar and practices while we talk. As a child, he played for weddings and parties in Russia. I test his talents by asking him to play music from China, Spain, Japan, Italy, or Greece and in an instant his songs transport me to those countries.

"So, what's in the account now?"

"We're holding $600,000 worth of stocks, and we've got $300,000 out in margin loans. Equity's at $300,000."

"You're a winner," he says, strumming his guitar.

The value of Internet stocks surge through the spring, and I continue using margin to leverage a bigger position with all of my holdings. On April 12, 1999, when the bell rings closed on Wall Street, the 4,000 shares of AOL, 2,000 shares of At Home and a scattering of other high flyers have a value that exceeds $2 million. With $1 million out in margin loans, the account's equity surpasses $1 million. I'm tempted to tell Julie to sell, but if I do, the short-term capital gains will incur a tax obligation of nearly $400,000. One year ago I didn't have commissary money, but now greed rather than a principled position prevents me from feeling satisfied with what I have. I'm determined to hold on until my equity reaches $1.6 million. That will generate a million dollars after taxes, and if I sell at that level, I'll be able to put that cash in the bank. I'm shooting for a two-comma cash balance. Until I hit it, I'm determined to continue swinging for the fences.

The value of my account doesn't change my status in prison, of course. I still stand for census counts and strip naked for searches whenever a guard commands. I'm scheduled to serve 14 more years, yet the time now is just something I tolerate. I don't need school or library books as I'm living vicariously through the market, a phenomenon the BOP is powerless to stop.

* * * * * * *

Two brutal trading days in April wipe out more than $400,000 from my account's equity, causing me to change strategy. Rather than holding on, I pull the trigger, calling my sister with instructions to sell. That move eliminates my margin debt, allows me to return the money Gary advanced, provides the resources to pay off the IRS, and leaves me with a cash-balance measured in six figures. It's far lower than the peak value, but far higher than where I began with my trading career.

"Remember one thing," Gary says, trying to cheer me up as we walk around the yard on one of his last days before authorities deport him to Russia. "Money doesn't make the man; the man makes the money."

"I know, but I can't stop thinking about what we could've had if I would've sold sooner."

"What's the big deal? You started out wanting to finish law school, to work for 15 years to earn a lousy hundred grand. Now you've got that in the bank and you didn't have to hustle with any of these schmucks. No one else in here earned what you did."

He advises me to forget about the market and to use the rest of my time in prison to do something else with my life, assuring me that I need to prepare for the endless opportunities that will await my release.

* * * * * * *

When we move into the new century, I know that I need something new to occupy my time, some project I can work on independently, without interference from the prison system. In August I'll finish my 13th year, meaning I'm halfway through, with only 13 more years until release. I must find a way to make them productive.

Carol Zachary and Jon Axelrod bring Zachary and Tristan to visit for Thanksgiving and as we sit, side-by-side in the brightly lit and crowded Fort Dix visiting room. Carol inquires whether I'd like to renew my petition for clemency.

"I can't bring myself to go through all that again," I tell her. "It's too much of an emotional roller coaster. I need stability, something I can work toward. Instead of waiting for someone else to make a decision that will determine my future, I need to find something that will allow me to chart my own course."

"Have you spoken with Tony? What does he have to say?" She asks about Tony Bisceglie, the prominent lawyer she persuaded to spearhead the legal effort to free me in 1997.

"Tony is honest. He said that my chances of the president commuting my sentence are less than one in a million. Besides that, I'm no longer indigent. If I were to move forward with the petition, Tony's fee would start at $50,000. I'm not willing to part with the resources to pay that fee."

"Michael, you've got to do it," Carol urges me.

"Don't you think you could earn that money again once you were released?" Zach, a sophomore in high school now, asks. He's a student athlete who looks forward to studying business and economics.

I lean forward, resting my elbows on my knees. "The thing is, I've been living inside prison walls and fences for my entire adult life." Although I feel their love and concern for me, I want them to understand why I perceive my situation differently from others who haven't lived in confinement. "When people leave prison, they have a hard time finding employment, and financial pressures block them from making a new start. I see it every week when prisoners return after failing in society. If I thought we had a better chance at commutation, I'd take it. But when one of the top lawyers in Washington spells out the odds, I have to weigh the costs. The truth is, I'm more afraid of going home broke, into a tornado of financial uncertainty, than I am of serving another 13 years."

Carol folds her arms across her chest and nods her head sympathetically. Jon observes silently, and then says, "You're going to have options when you come home, Michael. People love you and will stand by to help you."

I shake my head. "I need to build more support. If I could persuade 1,000 people to support my petition, then I'd feel better about moving forward with it."

"Too bad you can't use the Internet," Tristan states. He's in eighth grade and an aspiring musician. We have an ongoing chess game that we play by sending our respective moves through the mail. "You'd be able to find 1,000 supporters on the Web easily."

"I've got some friends from school who're pretty good on the Web," Zach suggests. "Maybe I could help."

"I'd like to invest my time and money into an idea like

that. Why don't we start a Web business? I'll write and type the content, then you guys coordinate putting it online," I suggest.

Jon looks at Carol. "We could buy a scanner to convert the typewritten pages into digital files. It might be a good project to give the boys some business experience."

"I could be the CEO," Zach lights up.

"What about hockey, baseball? You can't fall behind with school," Carol admonishes, taking in the scope of this possible business with more caution.

"Mom, I can do it," Zach asserts.

"The business could earn revenues by charging a fee for prisoners to publish their information, giving them a platform to build support," I say.

"And once we build enough traffic, we could charge for advertising space," Zach is on the edge of his seat, already chapters ahead in a business plan.

"Hold on a minute," Carol barks, throwing up her hands in a "time out" move, speaking as the voice of reason. "We're talking about a project to generate support for Michael, to get him out of here. Let's not distract ourselves with how much money we can make."

"I could really use a project like this, one that would take my mind away from here. I could work on it every day. If I build support, then we can explore the possibilities for clemency."

Carol nods her head. "Okay it's a deal. We're after a thousand people. Then we'll move forward with a new clemency petition."

* * * * * * *

"I've been following your writing on the Web," my friend George tells me during our visit. "It's very good."

Dr. George Cole is the author of *American Corrections*, the leading textbook used in universities to teach students about America's prison system. He's been my mentor for nearly a decade and he led the push for my acceptance into the doctoral program at the University of Connecticut. "Why don't you write a book about your prison experience? I'll present it to my publishers as a supplemental text to sell alongside my textbook."

It's the most exciting proposition I've had since I began

in the stock market and I ask George to advise me on how I can start."

He tells me to write a proposal for Wadsworth-Thompson Publishers to consider. The suggestion presents me with a new opportunity to turn the page, inspiring me with the confidence to launch the next chapter of my life. With my responsibilities to write for the Internet project that Zach coordinates, and the hours I invest to write the new book proposal, the outline, and the sample chapters, I have new reasons to wake before dawn and work 12-hour days.

Unlike studying toward advanced degrees, writing doesn't require me to seek permission from small-minded administrators. The activity is like a respite, freeing me from spending time with inmates who whine about the injustice of 12-month prison sentences. Further, it doesn't require me to read a dozen financial publications, it cuts my CNBC ticker addiction, and it provides a new challenge of learning how to express myself more fluently.

To write, all I need is a pen, blank pages of paper, and a dictionary. Still, I know where I am, and I ask for written clarification from the BOP legal department on the rules that govern prisoners who write for publication. That inquiry brings confirmation from a BOP staff attorney who says that as long as I'm not inciting others or being compensated for my writing, I'm within my rights to continue.

Working to write for publication becomes a goal I can pursue with gusto, and I welcome the challenge of persuading publishers to work with me. To succeed, I must work to become a better writer, and by doing so, I'll transcend prison boundaries, connect with readers everywhere, and build support. I go to the library in search of more information.

"Do you have any books on the shelves about the publishing business?" I'm hopeful that the librarian can steer me in the right direction.

"All we've got is an old-edition of *The Writer's Market*."

"I'll take it," I say.

The reference book shows the difficult odds that beginning writers face. Fewer than one in 1,000 authors sign publishing agreements. Those who succeed frequently toil for years, writing many manuscripts before they see one of their books in print. I perceive an edge because of the mentor relationships I've nurtured over the years, and because I'm writing about a unique subject matter.

After I write my proposal for *About Prison*, George advises me to send it to Sabra Horne, a senior acquisition editor at Wadsworth-Thompson. She responds with a publishing agreement, and I write the manuscript that described my first decade as a prisoner. The academic publisher will package the book as a supplementary text for university professors who teach courses in criminal justice.

With that project behind me, I write to Dr. Marilyn McShane, another mentor who, in addition to teaching criminal justice and authoring books, is a senior editor for Greenwood-Praeger Publishing. She offers to publish *Profiles From Prison*, my second book, which describes backgrounds, adjustment patterns, and future expectations of 20 prisoners.

The thousands of hours I spend writing, typing, and editing the manuscripts gives me the feeling that I'm doing something more than simply serving time. It's as if I'm making a societal contribution, living a life of meaning and relevance. If readers find value in the books once they're published, perhaps more people will see the need to think *smarter* rather than *tougher* about America's dysfunctional prison system.

As the final months of Clinton's presidency approach, I'm at ease with my decision to focus on writing. The book projects, together with weekly contributions I'm making for the Web site, provide readers with a prisoner's perspective of confinement, and the work connects me in ways that make me feel almost whole. I'm leading a useful life, feeling legitimized as a citizen. After more than 13 years I no longer feel the "punishment." Writing counteracts the "isolation," neutralizing the stated goals of imprisonment.

* * * * * * *

I'm alone in the visiting room on my work assignment, buffing the tile floor and thinking about what I'll write the next day when my friend Tom walks in and taps my shoulder.

I release the lever that powers the machine. "Hey, Bud, I

didn't hear you come in."

Tom shakes his head. "Did you hear the news?"

"What news?"

"Clinton commuted the sentences of about 20 people, two from Fort Dix."

"Who'd he let out?"

"It doesn't matter. Sorry, Pal. It should've been you."

I made my choice of not pursuing the clemency application, so I'll live with it and move on, even though I'm disappointed to accept the reality that I missed a genuine opportunity for liberty.

Tony had a clear plan for pursuing my commutation. He intended to use endorsements from my network of mentors and supporters to persuade my former prosecutors and judge that I had earned freedom. If he succeeded in getting that support, he was going to lobby his Washington contacts to bring my petition to the attention of the White House. In light of the president granting clemency to so many, I sense that Tony's strategy might have succeeded. I may have been freed. Thirteen years of imprisonment have institutionalized me, blinding me to the possibility of liberty. With the controversial election of George W. Bush, I've missed my opportunity.

* * * * * * *

On late February of 2002, I'm standing shoulder-to-shoulder with two hundred prisoners in the television room, listening as the guard shouts out names to distribute mail. My mentor, Bruce, and I still exchange weekly letters. As I work to improve my craft, he's my first reader, one of several who challenge me "to show rather than tell" through my writing. It's a lesson I struggle to learn.

"Santos!" The guard shouts my name.

"Back here, by the microwave," I yell over the noise of the crowd. I'm waiting for an envelope that I expect will include Bruce's comments on one of my manuscript drafts.

The guard continues hollering names, but I tune him out and watch the envelope that works its way back toward me, passing from one man's hand to the next. The envelope looks too small to contain my manuscript, and when I take it from the prisoner who stands in front of me, I look at the return address. It's written in a woman's graceful penmanship, though her name isn't one I recognize.

I open the envelope while still standing amidst all the other prisoners, and I pull out an artistic postcard. It features a print by Henri Lautrec that I admire. Bruce works at infusing my life with art and artists and I smile, knowing he would be proud of my new cultural awareness. When I open the card, curious to know who wrote it, I see that the sender is Carole Goodwin, a former classmate of mine from Shorecrest High School, class of 1982.

Carole and I grew up in Lake Forest Park, Washington, attending school together from the time we were in fifth grade. We spent our summers at the same beach club on Lake Washington. Carole and I were not close but I have a clear memory of walking with her, holding hands, and kissing her once during the celebration following our high school graduation.

Ten years earlier in my sentence, I corresponded with Susan, Carole's younger sister. From Susan I learned that Carole married someone after high school and that she had two children, Michael and Nichole. But my correspondence with Susan came to an end many years ago and I didn't know anything more about the Goodwin sisters. I'm surprised to receive this letter from Carole.

I'm even more surprised by what I read in the card and in her accompanying letter. She's scolding me, telling me how she knows people who became substance abusers, and how as a mother of two children, she abhors drugs, saying that she thinks it's awful that I sold cocaine.

I read Carole's letter again. Apparently, while she was coordinating our 20-year high school reunion, she received an unsolicited e-mail from an anonymous writer asking whether the reunion was for the same graduating class as mine. When Carole requested more information from the sender, he simply wrote that he'd come across my website and was curious. Carole searched the Internet for my site. Reading about my crime and sentencing prompted her to send me her thoughts.

"Hey, Marcello," I say, nudging a friend who was

standing next to me as I read Carole's card and letter. "Check this letter out and tell me what you think."

I pass Marcello the letter.

"She sounds angry," he states flatly, handing it back.

"That's what I thought." I fold the letter from Carole back into its envelope along with the card. "I don't get it. If it were someone I didn't know, maybe a law-and-order fanatic, or a prison guard, I'd get it. But this is a woman I grew up with. I kissed her in high school." I shrug my shoulders. "I've been in prison for more than 15 years. Why do you think she'd write to scold me now, after all this time?"

"She's probably a Republican."

"Maybe," I laugh, "but I'm going to write her back. I'll bet I can change her mind."

The first time I see Bob Brennan he's carefully selecting items from the salad bar. He expertly manipulates the stainless-steel tongs, piling the freshest tomatoes, radishes, chopped iceberg lettuce, and spinach leaves on his plastic tray. He's oblivious to the growing line of angry men standing in line and the other 500 prisoners in the noisy chow hall.

Bob stands taller than six feet, with glacial blue eyes and a full head of blond hair that he combs neatly. I know he's new to Fort Dix, and I suspect he's in his late-fifties. He's trim and clean-cut. As I watch him from a nearby table, I can't help but wonder why he's here. I've read of professionals and businessmen who've run afoul of the law, but those offenders don't generally serve time with us inside double fences laced with coils of razor wire. Bob looks like the type of man who sends people *to* prison, not one who serves time *in* prison.

Other white-collar types approach him, smiling, offering to help him settle in. Bob, however, remains tight-lipped, responding only with curt nods. When he clenches his jaw he projects defiance rather than the fear I'm used to seeing in newcomers.

A few days have passed since I saw him in the chow hall, and I see him again while I'm running around the track. He's sitting on the railroad ties that serve as steps separating the court from the track, eating a green apple and watching Ironhead, a more typical prisoner, shoot baskets alone on the asphalt court inside the track.

Ironhead is a guy who looks like he's been in prison all his life. His shaved head glistens with sweat and he distinguishes himself with a mouthful of gold-capped teeth. He's tall and muscular. Arching over his shoulder blades is a tattoo with bold capital letters that spell out "destroyer." On his stomach is another that reads "thug for life."

I'm used to seeing Ironhead shoot baskets while I run. We don't share much in common and we never talk. He exercises alone, and I exercise alone. Today Bob sits between our workouts, eating his apple and watching.

While running, I drift into thoughts about my writing projects and about the relationship Carole and I are building through our letters. As my steps crunch along the gravel track today, I tune into Bob, wondering whether he's going to make the mistake of interrupting Ironhead's workout.

"You'd make more shots if you'd set your stance before shooting," Bob instructs.

Ironhead ignores him, takes another shot, and misses.

"See what I mean? You're losing your balance."

Ironhead grabs the rebound. Then he presses his left fist into his hip, and with his right hand, palms the basketball as he addresses Bob.

"A-yo Gee! Who you be talkin' to?" Ironhead snarls, strutting toward Bob.

Bob takes the last bite of his apple and then sets the core on the step, standing to meet Ironhead.

"I'll show you what I mean," Bob says with a combination of innocence and coaching authority that actually disarms the unlikely student. Then he opens his hands, gesturing for Ironhead to pass him the ball. Ironhead scowls, bounces the ball twice, then hurls the ball at Bob. He dribbles to the top of the key, plants and sinks the ball, then proceeds to coach Ironhead on shooting skills. Before I finish my run, I'm surprised to see the two are on the court together playing one on one.

Later in the afternoon I see Bob sitting alone at a picnic table beneath one of the maple trees. He's writing a letter on a yellow legal pad, gold-frame reading glasses perched on his nose. I approach and interrupt him.

"Can I have a minute?"

He looks up, quickly evaluating me like an employer deliberating whether I'm worthy of an interview. Then he answers with a half-dismissive "I'll be with you in a minute." He finishes writing his paragraph, leaving me waiting.

"Now," he sets his pen down, "how can I help you?"

"My name's Michael Santos," I say, introducing myself.

276

"I'm a long-term prisoner and aspiring writer. I've just finished a manuscript describing some of my experiences that I'm about ready to send to my publisher. If you've got time to read it, I'd appreciate any advice you might offer on what I can do to strengthen my manuscript."

Bob removes his glasses and rubs his eyes. "Why ask me?"

"You're new to prison, I'm guessing, and you're as close as I'm going to get in here to the demographic I'm trying to reach."

"What's that, old white guys?"

"No, college-educated people who don't have experience with confinement."

"Let me see it."

I pass him the envelope containing my manuscript. He pulls the document out and glances through the 400 pages.

"Did you type this here?"

"My girlfriend typed it for me."

"She did a nice job." He places it back in the envelope. "I've got a full plate right now, but if you leave it with me, I'll read it over the next few days."

"Sounds good. I'm not in a rush. What's your name?"

"I'm Bob Brennan," he says, as if I should recognize the name, and extends his hand.

* * * * * * *

In the weeks to come Bob and I develop a friendship. We walk the track together and I listen to his story. From his demeanor, I correctly surmised that he was a man accustomed to pulling strings at the top levels of American business. Bob was the founder and CEO of numerous businesses, both public and private. For many years he was his company's spokesman on national television commercials that invited investors to grow with him at First Jersey Securities, his most well known company. Bob owned personal jets, helicopters, and palatial homes, and thoroughbred racehorses. Over the course of his distinguished career, he earned hundreds of millions and nurtured friendships with distinguished people such as President Ronald Reagan, President George H.W. Bush, and President

George W. Bush. A jury convicted Bob for a crime that he described to me as "lying on a government form." Now he's beginning a sentence that threatens to confine him for a decade.

We sit on a steel bench beneath a cherry tree on this late summer evening in 2002. Hundreds of prisoners walk along the wide path circling the compound. Bob knows all about my story because he read the manuscript I prepared. I listen to his story with a sense of loss at what my imprisonment has cost me when he describes his career, his experiences at creating jobs for tens of thousands of well-paid people that his companies employed.

"You know what a Democrat is, don't you?" I tease Bob.

"What's that?"

"It's a Republican who's been arrested." Bob laughs, but his smile fades as he scans the Fort Dix compound. "This isn't the place to spend your life."

"I'm used to it," I say.

"That's a shame," he says knowingly.

"What do you miss most from all that you've lost?" I probe. Bob is a man who has lost much.

Bob looks up at the sky, thinking. "My Gulfstream jet and the freedom to fly away."

"That's what you miss most?" I can hardly believe him.

"There's nothing like being able to fly wherever you want, whenever you want." He affirms his answer with a nod.

"I guess traveling isn't an aspiration I can relate to anymore."

"So how's your romance going with Carole? Did you get a letter from her today?" Bob asks, deliberately changing the subject.

"Yes, we write every day, although she might not like what I wrote back today."

"What's that?"

"It's nothing serious, but something she wrote bothered me, and I let her know."

"What bothered you?"

"She wrote about lottery tickets."

"So?"

"Come on, a lottery ticket? It doesn't sit well with me. When I think of people who buy lottery tickets, I think of a poverty state of mind, of people who don't work hard enough to make things happen on their own. Instead, they're waiting for something to happen for them."

"You've got to lighten up, Michael. Not everyone in the world is like you."

"Do you buy lottery tickets?"

Bob doesn't dignify the question with an answer. "It's not about what *I* do. I'm talking about understanding other people. People like to dream. Las Vegas is built on that concept."

"I want her to have stability and independence in her life so she's not worried about whether child support checks come on time, or anything else."

"Give her a break. Why're you trying to control her life?"

"I'm not trying to control anything."

"The hell you aren't. When you judge someone for buying a lottery ticket, you're trying to control them."

"We're growing closer and I want her to know how I think."

"You haven't been with a woman in 15 years, and you haven't even seen Carole since high school. How're you going to build a relationship from here, when she's living on the West Coast, and you're locked inside a Jersey prison?"

"The circumstances might not be ideal, I'll give you that. But the distance between us doesn't mean we can't fall in love, build a life together."

Bob laughs. "Love? A life together? Listen to yourself! You've been locked up since 1987. This is a divorced mother of two. You're both desperate. If you string this woman along, all you're going to do is make both of your lives miserable."

"I'm not stringing her along, and I'm not desperate. Neither is she. We're two people in our mid-thirties falling in love. We're not teenagers."

"Michael, you're a smart guy. Think about what you're doing. You've got 11 more years to serve in prison. When you go home you'll be heading into a world that you haven't seen for 26 years. You don't know anything about women, about love, about what it means to build a life with someone else."

"You're right about one thing, Bob. I've been doing this a long time. But you're wrong when you say I don't know anything about love. Living in prison has been like watching earth from a different planet. My separation from society has given me a chance to observe, to learn from the lives of others. I've read that 50 percent of marriages end in divorce. You've been a rich man since your early 30s, yet two of your marriages ended in divorce, and you're breaking off a relationship now. I may be separated from the rest of the world, but I've studied people from a different perspective, and I've learned from them."

"Oh really? What've you learned?" He scoffs.

"One thing for sure, in order to create lasting love, I'll need to appreciate Carole more than I'd appreciate a jet."

Bob grunts. "You've never had a Gulfstream."

* * * * * * *

As other prisoners count the days until release, I'm counting down the days until my first visit with Carole. It's evening on October 16, 2002. I lie on my bunk using a small, battery-powered light to read Carole's long letters. I have my favorites, the ones I devour repeatedly. We've been writing daily for eight months, and when I wake tomorrow, we'll begin five glorious days of visiting together. I'm going to hold her, to kiss her for as long as guards will permit. I stare at her photograph and fall asleep, the book light still burning.

When I wake, my smile stretches across my face. It's a good day. Visiting doesn't begin until 1:00, so I have time to make my bed, wash my face, brush my teeth, and then sit at my desk to write her a love letter. I want her to know how grateful I am that she flew from Oregon to hold my hand under the harsh lights of a New Jersey prison visiting room.

I stack the paper and books from my desk in my locker. While sitting on my mattress I lace my sneakers, rise, straighten the wrinkles on my bed, and look around to ensure everything is in its proper place in case the guards come in for a surprise cell inspection. I can't leave anything visible without risking the loss of my 2-man room; a failed inspection would put me back in a 12-man room. With a final glance to make sure I'm leaving the room in perfect condition, I close the door and walk outside for an early exercise session.

I jog eight miles, watching as the wind tosses leaves in

waves from the maple trees. They flutter to the grass in different shades of yellow and orange. These same trees were in their early spring bloom when Carole began typing my manuscript, *About Prison.* In June she was typing my second manuscript, *Profiles From Prison,* and our romance began. By summer's end we were pledging our love. But it's been all correspondence and phone calls until today.

I check my watch and expect that her plane has landed by now. She's renting a car and is only hours away from the jolting reality of my world. She'll see the fences with the coils of razor wire, the checkpoints with armed, uniformed guards. I wonder how she'll respond to the metal detectors, the bureaucratic condemnation, the numerous rules, and the forms required of visitors to federal prisons.

I follow my run with pushups. As I'm finishing Bob comes out for his walk. "So today's your day!" He smiles in good spirits, happy for me.

"She'll be here at one." I stand and brush the dirt from my hands.

"Will you be there until visiting ends?"

"That's the plan."

"Okay then. I'll be waiting for you when you come out. We'll walk a few laps and you can tell me how things went."

"I'll see you then," I promise.

I return to my housing unit, shower, shave closely with a new, double-blade razor, and dress in clean sweats. Pancho, my friend down the hall, ironed my khakis and shined my shoes in exchange for a three-can pack of tuna. The clothes hang against my wall. With a few hours to pass before our visit, I pick up Nelson Mandela's *A Long Walk to Freedom,* the biography that describes his wretched and unjust multi-decade stretch in an African prison.

I set the book on my chest and I let my mind wander. Carole's love has given me hope for a life most men take for granted. When it's almost one o'clock, I stand to change.

My heart beats faster when I hear my name being paged, and I walk across the compound, through the gates, toward the visiting room. The guard takes a long time answering the door after I push the button, frustrating me as I lose minutes I could be sharing with Carole.

After months of waiting, she's finally here, on the other side of this wall. It's been 28 years since I first played kickball with her in fifth grade and 20 years since our high school graduation.

The guard unlocks the door. "Name and number?"

"Santos, 16377-004," I state, handing him my red ID card.

"We paged you 15 minutes ago. Where've you been?"

"Right here. I pushed the button," I respond, suppressing my impatience and irritation.

"Come on. You know the drill."

I step into the room and undress for the guard to search me. "Do you know the rules about physical contact?"

"I know the rules."

"One kiss when you come in, one kiss when you leave."

"Can I hold her hand?"

He nods. "Just don't get too frisky. I don't wanna be sendin' anyone to the SHU today."

"Of course you don't."

Prison guards exhibit an attitude of indifference when it comes to their callous dehumanization of prisoners.

"What was that?" He challenges me with his glare.

"Never mind." Not even a surly prison guard can dampen my enthusiasm today.

"Can I go in now?"

"Have a nice visit." His flat expression and monotone contradict his good wishes. Anticipation for a blind date with a woman I already love sends adrenaline racing through me as I open the door and enter. I scan the faces and spot Carole, far away, sitting beneath a window screened with black iron mesh. Our eyes lock and she stands, smiling radiantly. Holding her gaze, I zigzag through a maze of maroon plastic chairs, remembering just in time to drop my ID card with the guard who operates the computer surveillance system.

Carole looks lovely in fitted denim jeans, black heels, and beige knit sweater. Her long blonde hair falls past her shoulders. Seconds later she's in my arms, welcoming my embrace. I can't believe I'm holding her.

"Let me look at you," I breathe her in.

She's smiling, and in her sparkling hazel eyes I see her love for me.

"We can only kiss once, the guards are watching," I whisper, wanting to remember this moment with her body pressing against mine.

I tilt my head to the right and bend to meet her lips as she leans into me. With my hands on her back I feel the warmth of her flesh through her clothing. Her heart's beating fast, and I welcome her tongue, the unfamiliar sensation of her breasts pressed against my chest, and the feminine arch of her slender hips. It awakens the man in me, as if I'm feeling a woman for the first time. I don't care about the other 50 visitors in the room and I kiss her as long as I can, though I'm conscious of the guards, knowing they'll humiliate me by yelling my name and issuing a warning if I don't release her.

"Let's sit," I tell her.

"Hold me for a second longer." She presses her cheek against mine. "I love you."

I'm so grateful that she's in my life and I assure her of my love. We sit beside each other, holding hands, locking our fingers together, and I stare into her eyes. After so many years of living in prison, I feel incredibly fortunate to have her with me. When she averts her eyes, glancing down, I tilt her chin up with my index finger. "I want to look at your face."

"Why?" she asks nervously, with her cheek twitching.

"Because you're beautiful and I need to memorize every curve of your face. Why are you so nervous?"

"I can't help it," she admits, squeezing my hands. "I'm just happy to be here."

"The fences and razor wire didn't bother you?" I know how foreboding they can seem at first.

"The only thing that bothers me is that I can't take you home with me. If this is where you are, this is where I want to be," she promises, and I see the sincerity in her eyes.

"I want to kiss you again," I tell her. Concerns that the realities of prison could overwhelm her begin to dissipate after Carole's affirmation.

"So kiss me." She says softly, smiling

"We can't. Those guards sitting on the platform will give me a disciplinary infraction if I kiss you again."

"They're not watching us."

"Yes, they are. Those black bubbles in the ceiling are cameras, and the guards have several monitors at their desk. They sit there with a joystick, moving the cameras around the room. If they catch me kissing you again, they'll end our visit."

Carole looks around, taking in the severity of the room. A guard in the standard BOP uniform walks through the aisles, his eyes scanning the room. "I don't understand," she says. "Why would they care if you kissed me?"

"Those manuscripts you've been typing for me aren't fiction. In prison the priority is security, and they view kissing as a threat to institutional security. This is my life for 11 more years."

"You won't serve 11 more years."

"Yes I will, Honey." I brush a strand of hair from her face. "I've already served 15 and I'll serve 11 more."

"Then I'll serve them with you."

"You don't know what you're saying."

"I *do* know what I'm saying. My love for you is a woman's love, Michael, not a little girl's crush. I'll serve this sentence with you, whatever it takes."

"Let's see how you feel on Monday, after our last visit."

"It won't be our last visit. I'm coming back." In those first hours together, I tell Carole how I spend each day, describing when I wake, how I exercise, and where I shower. By using my finger as a pointer on her knee, I draw a diagram, showing her the layout of my room, where I store my belongings, even how far down the hall I am from the community bathroom. I tell her about my friends, Bob and Geoff. I answer her questions about how I plan to earn a living after my release, explaining that I'll write about my prison experience, consult with people who face challenges with the criminal justice system, and speak on how others can employ effective strategies to overcome challenges they may face.

Carole's eyes never leave me as I talk, and she listens closely, asking insightful questions, such as whether the prison system will give me any trouble when the books I've written

284

reach the market.

I explain the reasons why I don't anticipate any disciplinary problems as a consequence of my writing books while I serve the remainder of my sentence. "One policy says I can't run a business, so I don't. A different policy states that the BOP encourages prisoners to write manuscripts, and authorizes them to mail the manuscripts without staff interference. Once I send out my manuscripts, they're not mine. I assign the publishing royalties to Julie, or my mom."

"But your name's on the book?"

"I'm the author, but I don't receive any money for my work."

"Your family's getting the money though, saving it for you when you get out. Isn't that a problem?"

"Although others may receive royalty payments, I would argue that since I don't have a right to the money, I'm within the rules. After all, if my mom or my sister choose to keep the payments they receive, I wouldn't have any grounds to challenge them. They pay taxes on it, not me. But even if the prison did charge me with a disciplinary infraction, I wouldn't care. It's my responsibility to prepare for the future and I'm proud of my work. I'm determined to leave here stable and independent."

"I want to help you."

"You *are* helping me. Without you, I couldn't have converted my manuscripts to digital files. You help me by inspiring me to work harder. Ever since my term began, I've been preparing for you. I willed you into my life."

"No. I mean I want to help you more. I want my life with you. I want to grow with you. I want to get you out of here." She squeezes my hand to emphasize her promise.

"Baby, let's not waste time on things beyond our control, like my being released early. Let's focus on how we can best prepare for the challenges we'll face when I'm released."

"Then I want to help you with that. What can we do, together?"

* * * * * * *

Five extraordinary days with Carole lead to the preliminary plans for the rest of our lives. We pledge to build our relationship, growing together through the challenges I'm certain will come because of my imprisonment. Carole wants to marry me now, but I explain the reasons why she should understand more about the prison system's stranglehold on my life before rushing into marriage. Although I want to marry her, it's necessary, I think, that she prepare herself for the unrelenting controls of the prison system and the strain it places on families. Her love comforts me, inspires me, and gives me a sense of belonging. Whether we marry now or not, I'm no longer alone. I stare at the walls, trying to contemplate ways that I'll be able to provide for her. I aspire to live as a worthy partner for her while I climb through the remainder of my sentence.

Carole returns to Oregon, leaving me with an ache in my heart. I want to hold and kiss her. Our physical separation leaves me bereft and longing. Writing her each day isn't enough, but words on a page are all that I have while she's gone.

Despite my wanting her with me, I have major concerns about finances and my ability to support her. Although I still own stock that I could liquidate to raise cash, I've been counting on that capital to help launch my life when I leave prison.

I love her, but I'm under no delusions about the challenges I'll face with another decade of imprisonment ahead. Carole doesn't have the resources to relocate to New Jersey, and I don't know how I'll earn them from inside of these boundaries. Like me, she's 38 and divorced, but it wouldn't be just the two of us. She has two children: Michael is 13 and Nichole is 11. Although Michael lives with his father, moving Carole to New Jersey would mean bringing Nichole, too. I don't know how I would be able to take on this responsibility.

I stretch back in my chair, run my fingers through my hair, and think of her while staring at photographs of us together in the visiting room. Although I'm confident that I can navigate the challenges of serving another decade in prison, devoting my life to Carole means I'll be complicating the rest of my journey– albeit in magnificent ways. When I'm released we'll both be 49, but I want to begin my life with her now. I've got to figure out how to generate enough resources to support her.

The only way I know how to earn money is through writing, so I invite Carole to join me in launching an effort to use the knowledge I've gained in prison. She agrees enthusiastically and asks how we'll do it. I explain that she can start a publishing company; it will produce and distribute books I write that describe the criminal justice system from the perspective of a man going through it. From our efforts, we hope to build a sustainable income that will support her and Nichole while simultaneously providing guidance to people who need it.

* * * * * * *

After two guards open my door for the 3:00 a.m. census count and pass by, I throw back the covers and get out of bed. It's time to work. Emmanuel, my roommate, still sleeps soundly, so I'm quiet. I've cut holes into tennis balls and slid them onto the legs of my metal folding chair so it doesn't make noise when I sit at the desk. I'm in my sweats and socks, with only my two book lights illuminating the page as I work quietly in the dark.

Since beginning this publishing project, my goal has been to write 15 pages of content each day. It's work, requiring a disciplined strategy. I mail the pages I write to Carole each evening. Upon receiving the handwritten pages, Carole types them and returns them to me double-spaced, ready for editing. We're a cross-country team, partners in the effort to raise money for her move to New Jersey. At the pace we're going, we're ahead of schedule. The manuscript should be finished within a month.

This evening, as I'm using a blue pen to edit the pages Carole returned, my friend Geoff lies supine on the floor of my room. Geoff is an urbane cardiologist serving a 36-month sentence for the crime of treating poor people in his clinic and billing Medicaid for medicine and lab tests that weren't covered. For 30 years he's owned his Upper East Side medical clinic and the building where it's located. We've become good friends. Geoff's in his mid-60s, but his daily discipline over diet and exercise enable him to retain a high degree of fitness. In fact, fitness is a top priority for Geoff, and because I enjoy his company, I offer him the use of my floor. He devotes an hour each evening to working his abdominal muscles, with a combination of leg lifts and extensions that he does methodically and effortlessly. Usually, he simultaneously reads his beloved

New York Times, or classic literature, devouring books by Tolstoy, Hugo, and Joyce. But tonight Geoff is upset and wants to talk. I set my pen down to listen.

While lying on his back, he holds his extended legs steady, six inches off the floor, and tells me about business troubles at his clinic. Before surrendering to serve his sentence at Fort Dix, Geoff gave his business manager, Ted, authority to preside over his clinic. Through Ted's mismanagement, or possible fraud, Geoff tells me that he's losing $20,000 a month.

"Why don't you close the clinic down?" I suggest.

"I can't just close it. I employ three other cardiologists, an internist, and several nurses. The clinic sees more than 50 patients a day," he explains while raising his legs higher, a foot off the ground, and holding them steady.

"Then why not sell the practice to the doctors? You've worked long enough. You could rent *them* space, and leave *them* the headaches. By the time you finish this sentence, you'll be almost 70 anyway. You could retire."

"I've thought about selling. The trouble is I don't have any way of communicating from here. I'm totally in the dark while I serve this sentence. All I get are messages that Ted needs more money to meet payroll."

"Was the clinic losing money when you came in?"

"No. Rather than costing me money, it should be earning 20 to 30 thousand each month. Ted is screwing up the billing, or something."

"You know what you need?" I have an idea.

"What's that?"

"An office informant, someone who can tell you what's going on."

"You've got that right."

"Why don't you hire Carole?"

"Who, your Carole?"

"She could work at your office, then come visit us here and let you know what's going on."

"Is she a lawyer?"

"No, why?"

"Well, I could use a lawyer to sort through the billing mess." He lifts his legs higher, 18 inches off the floor. "Besides, how would she come visit us both if she's not a lawyer?"

"She can visit me, and you bring someone else to visit you. We'll sit beside each other in the visiting room and she can tell you what she sees going on in your office. At least you would know."

"Do you think she'd be willing to come to New York?"

"I can ask."

"How much would she want to earn?"

"She'd have to earn enough to live."

"Living on the Upper East Side of New York City isn't the same as living in Oregon."

"What's it cost to rent an apartment near your office?"

"Too much. But I've got a vacant apartment in the city, and I've got a car she can drive. She can use the apartment and the car, and I'll pay her $2,000 a month. Does that sound fair?"

"I'll call and ask."

While Geoff continues with his leg lifts on the floor, I rush out of my room to secure a spot in line for a telephone. When she answers, the question spills out before I can ask about her day.

"Would you move to New York if I could arrange an apartment, a car, and a job that would pay you $2,000 a month?"

She doesn't hesitate, saying she would. "What kind of job?"

"Remember I told you about my friend who's a doctor?"

"Yes."

"He needs an office person, someone who can keep an eye on things and report back to him."

"I can do that. How often could we see each other?"

"Every week. We're only an hour apart. When could you be here?"

"I'm ready to go whenever the job's open."

"What about Nichole?"

"She'll come with me."

* * * * * * *

Geoff's desperation to resolve his crisis at the office precipitates his decision to hire Carole on the spot. He needs information. People he trusts are stealing from him and mismanaging a business he spent a lifetime building. As a prisoner, he doesn't have access to information he needs about daily activities in his clinic. The prison system limits each prisoner to 300 minutes of telephone use each month, and that isn't sufficient for a man like Geoff, who has existing business interests. In an effort to get a handle on things, he pays Carole's expenses to move to New York.

We make the arrangements quickly, as Geoff wants Carole to begin at once. I coordinate the deal for Carole, but I saddle her with the challenge of coordinating the complicated cross-country move on her own.

I don't have any responsibilities outside these prison boundaries, and I have enough money in the bank to cover my startup expenses when I'm released. After 15 years, I've mastered the challenges that mire other prisoners in failure. In moving Carole to New York, however, I'm knowingly making myself responsible for her and Nichole, her 11-year-old daughter. My credibility with family and mentors who believe in my judgment will be on the line, and maybe, too, the stability I've worked hard to create. Still, I'm confident that we can make it together.

"Honey," I warn her over the phone, "you should prepare yourself for other people's response to our plans. People are going to think you're nuts."

"They already do, but I don't care what anyone else thinks or says about me. I love you, Michael. I'm not staying in Oregon while the man I love is in New Jersey. I need to be close so we can visit as frequently as rules will allow."

"Baby, I need to be sure you fully understand my situation. I love you, and I'm the most fortunate man alive to have your love. But I've got 11 more years to serve, and I don't have any certainty about earning an income. I can't do more than arrange this job with Geoff. You have to make this move work on your own, without my help."

"Do you want me to come?"

"Yes, more than anything. But I'm used to prison life. I worry whether you'll be able to handle it. Are you sure you've thought through what 11 more years of prison means?"

"If you had a life sentence, I'd still choose you. You're

the only man I want to share my life with." Her firm, unwavering dedication convinces me we can triumph together.

"What about your family, your parents?"

"I choose you, Michael. Whatever it takes to make this relationship work, I'm all in."

Our conversations and letters deepen my commitment. I want to give her all that I have and share all that I am and all that I will become. Carole's certainty and radiance warm me like sunlight, bringing out my humanity. I embrace the joy and sense of fulfillment that comes with loving her.

Friends and family worry that I'm blinded by love, that I've lost focus, and that I'm setting myself up for a fall.

"What about when you come home, Michael?" My sister Julie presses, worrying that I haven't thought everything through. "How can you be sure she's the woman you want to spend your life with?"

"Because I love her."

"But how are you going to take care of her?"

"We'll create our life together. I can help her, just as she's helping me."

"What about your future? Are you selling the rest of your stock portfolio? Have you thought about what it will mean if you come home broke? Tim and I want to help you, but we can't support another family."

"I'm not selling the stock. Carole has a job waiting for her in New York, and I'm writing a new book for her to sell. You trust me, don't you?"

"Of course."

"Julie, I'm not going into this blindly. Carole makes everything in my life better and I want to build my life around her. With her I'm not a prisoner, I'm a man, and together we can make this work."

"You're a man, but you're still a prisoner. Just don't hurt her, Michael. She doesn't know anything about what she's getting into."

"I'll never hurt her."

My closest mentors, Bruce McPherson and Carol Zachary, also express concern about this change I'm introducing to my life, and to Carole's and Nichole's as well. I understand.

The pernicious, toxic environment of prison beats families down, tramples relationships to dust. But I know that we can make it. Whatever it takes, I'm determined, regardless of what odds conspire against us. I want her love and I'm willing to endure whatever struggles come with it. I hope that Carole can too.

* * * * * * *

Those struggles begin to manifest themselves in late December, one week before Carole's scheduled arrival. Geoff comes to my room to share some unexpected news.

"I'm being transferred," he tells me.

"What? Where to?"

"They're sending me to the drug program on the West side."

Geoff will still be at Fort Dix, but his transfer to the other compound will completely sever our ability to communicate.

"Carole's already sent her stuff with the moving company. I can't reverse her move."

"I know, and I still want her to work in the office."

"But we won't be able to visit together."

"Can't she visit me over there?"

I shrug, not knowing what guards will allow. "You can try putting her on your visiting list, but they might not let her in."

"Then she can write. Look, this is a mess, and there's nothing we can do about it. I've got to be out of here in an hour. When she gets here, have her go to the office. Ted will give her the keys to the apartment and the car. We'll work out the arrangements once she settles in."

When I call Carole to tell her about Geoff's transfer, she doesn't hesitate. "We'll make it work. I'll still fill him in on what's happening in his office, and I'll look after whatever he needs."

I admire her optimism, her commitment, and her courage. My determination equals hers. But hers is weighted with a high degree of risk. We talk about the logistics of her move and about coordinating delivery of her belongings to Geoff's empty apartment. Such mundane tasks energize me. For the first time I'm part of a family, cherishing the feeling of belonging. We save two phone minutes from my monthly allotment, as I want to call her after her flight lands. We're scheduled to visit on the morning after New Year's, 2003, when I'll meet Nichole for the first time.

* * * * * * *

It's after six on New Year's Eve, and I'm at my desk, trying to ease my anxieties by writing. I burned through the final two phone minutes from my December allotment after Carole's plane landed and I won't receive my next allocation of phone or visiting time until tomorrow, when the new month begins. Prison restrictions prevent all contact with Carole, which leaves me completely in the dark about her move. I stand, nervously pacing the floor. My old friend Windward comes to mind–he used to drive me nuts with his pacing. That was longer than a decade ago, in USP Atlanta.

This anxiety is new to me. I can't help her with this cross-country transition into a new city. At least I'll have new phone minutes tomorrow. We'll be able to talk, but we still won't be able to visit for two more days. Prisons are not family friendly.

While working through my silent worries, I hear an unexpected page.

"Michael Santos. Report to the visiting room."

It's my name being paged, but since I've expired my visiting privileges for the month, I'm confused as I walk to the visiting room.

I see the guard at the visiting room door and I ask him for confirmation that he paged me.

"You heard your name, didn't you?"

"Yes."

"Well, haven't you been in long enough to know what that means? Strip!"

I take off my clothes for the search ritual. The guard authorizes me to enter the visiting room and I see that it's packed. I walk through the crowds of people to the guard's platform, and as I hand him my ID card, I see Carole. She's bundled in a blue, floor-length wool coat, and a pale pink cashmere scarf circles her neck. She's obviously distraught. As I approach her, she walks to me quickly and wraps her arms

293

around me, crying. She buries her face into my neck and I hold her.

"Baby, what's wrong? Why are you crying?" She holds me tighter.

"What is it? Talk to me," I repeat urgently, quietly. I put my hands on her cheeks, tipping her head up to kiss her tears. "What's wrong?"

She sniffles, but between them I hear her say "No car, no apartment, no job." She's still crying and I pull her tight.

"Tell me what happened." I want to help her, and I suddenly feel the weight of what it means to accept this responsibility of love.

She takes a deep breath to steady her voice before speaking. "It's Ted, Geoff's business manager. He says *he's* in control of Geoff's practice. He refuses to give me access to the office, and he's refusing to give me keys to the apartment and the car I'm supposed to use. I'm here with Nichole, everything I own is in a moving truck on its way here, and I don't know what to do."

I breathe in deeply, needing to soothe her before asking questions. I pull her close, wrap my arm around her shoulders, and walk toward a pair of plastic purple chairs in the back of the visiting room. We sit and hold hands. It's the only comfort I can offer under the watchful eyes of cameras and guards. She sighs, exhaling with a long breath as she lays her head on my shoulder, and I feel her relax against me.

"Don't worry, Baby, I'll take care of you." I kiss her cheeks, taking a chance that in the crowded room, the guards won't notice. "I've got enough money to help you settle."

"You said you'd never sell the stocks," she says, lifting her head from my shoulder to look at me.

"I know what I said, but you're more important to me than any stocks. Of course I'll sell them. I love you, Carole. I'll do anything for you." Her head drops back onto my shoulder and I savor the feeling of her weight resting on me.

"I'll pay you back," she promises.

I chuckle at her promise, and then I ask where she is staying. "Did you get a hotel room in New York?"

"We left New York when Ted refused to give me the

apartment keys. I've still got my rental car, so I drove down and checked us into a hotel that's closer. Nichole's there now. She's watching a movie until I get back."

I'm relieved that Carole came to New Jersey. It's much less expensive here and we'll need to be careful with our money. I caress her hands and appreciate how soft and feminine they feel inside mine.

"Do you want to stay in New Jersey, or would you rather go back to Oregon?"

"I'm staying with you." Her voice so recently quivering is suddenly steady.

"Okay, Honey. That's what I want, too. We'll make a plan and together we'll make it work. I love you."

"I love you so much." She kisses me gently.

"Honey, we can't kiss anymore," I warn, conscious of the guards. "Tell me how you got in here. I didn't have any visiting points left for the month."

"I know. I called here all day and I told your unit manger it was an emergency, but he wouldn't let me talk to you. I decided to drive over and try to talk my way in. Thank goodness Officer Cruz was on duty. He must've believed me when I told him I had to see you. He changed something on the computer and here I am. I think he was worried I was going to burst into tears in front of him."

"See, I told you that God's been protecting me through this journey. Now he's protecting you. And although many people who work for the prison system make things difficult, some are nice."

"Yes, he was very nice. I'm grateful, because I really needed to see you, and I want to come back tomorrow, too."

"Tomorrow's New Year's Day, Honey. Holiday visiting privileges cost us double against my allotment for the month. Let's wait until the day after tomorrow to visit. The rules limit me to a maximum of 30 hours in the visiting room for the month and we can't squander them." She's going to get an immersion course in the complications of my imprisonment.

"Michael, I need to see you! We need to make a plan."

"Okay," I relent. "You can come for one hour, but it's going to cost us two hours against my monthly allotment of 30 points."

"I'll bring Nichole."

* * * * * * *

It's cold. My green jacket and orange knit cap aren't enough to keep me from shivering when I leave the visiting room. Maybe I shiver more from worry than the frigid December temperatures. I can handle the cold, but as I cross the nameless road that leads to my housing unit, I realize for the first time in 38 years that the local economy is relevant to my life.

As the president tries to push us into a second war in Iraq, the newspapers have been reporting on high unemployment rates. These didn't concern me until an hour ago. But I've brought Carole here, thousands of miles away from her friends and family, on a promise. The promise went south. Now two lives hang on my ability to bring her stability, and suddenly the 11 years of prison that await me feel heavier.

"Hey, I heard them call you for a visit." Bob catches up to me, his tone revealing curiosity. "I thought you said you were out of points."

"I was. Carole talked her way in."

"Huh, I'm impressed. It'd be easier to talk your way out. She must've charmed them, but that's like charming a rattlesnake. How's her move coming along?"

"Totally derailed. Geoff's business manager is refusing to give Carole the job, the apartment, or the car. She's stranded, and all her things are packed in a moving truck that's supposed to arrive in New York next week."

"Wow." We take a few steps with only the sound of crunching gravel and howling wind between us. "How can I help?"

"I'll take care of it. My sister is in Hawaii for the holidays, but when she returns, I'll have her sell enough stock to send Carole the money she needs to settle."

"I could get her a few thousand to tide her over if it would help."

"Thanks. I appreciate the offer, but I put her in this mess. I'll get her out."

"Well let me know if you need anything." Bob is a good

friend, willing to lend me money even though we're both in prison. I'm grateful for the gesture.

I walk into the housing unit and search for Richard, a young offender I interviewed recently for a story I wrote. While talking with him, I remember Richard telling me that his wife lived only a few miles from the prison. She was struggling financially, like many prison families, because of her husband's imprisonment. He's sitting on the stairs, slumped, his elbows resting on his knees.

"What's troubling you?" I ask.

He looks up at me and takes off his glasses, rubbing his eyes. "Holidays. I miss my wife and son."

"That's what I came to ask you about. Do you think your wife would want a housemate?"

"Whadda ya mean?"

"I'm in a bind. My fiancée and her daughter just moved here from Oregon. They thought they had an apartment, but the arrangements didn't work out. I need to help her find a new place and I thought of you. Your wife could probably use the money, and they could support each other."

He puts his glasses back on. "That could really help. How old is your fiancée's daughter?"

"Eleven."

"I'm in line for the phone now. I'll come by your room after I talk with my wife."

* * * * * * *

When I enter the visiting room on New Year's morning, the large room feels empty. I appreciate the relative silence. Other than the whir of the vending machine, there's nothing else to distract us. Carole and her daughter sit beside each other in the maroon plastic chairs.

Carole looks lovely in her heavy wool coat, long blonde hair contrasting beautifully against the navy blue. She stands to greet me as I walk toward her.

Nichole sits calmly, showing none of the distress I see in her mother. At 11 she resembles Carole, but with dark hair curling in natural waves around her heart-shaped face. A light sprinkle of freckles dot the bridge of her nose. Her hazel-blue eyes look directly into mine as I kneel in front of her chair and greet her. "You must be Nichole. I'm Michael, and I'm very happy to meet you."

"Hi Michael. This place is huge."

"Yes, and we're lucky that it's not filled with people already," I say with a smile.

"Nichole, honey," Carole says "we're only going to be here for an hour. Why don't you get a hot chocolate from the vending machine and then walk over and see what's in the kids' area. I need to talk with Michael."

"But I want to talk with him too."

"We're going to visit again in a couple of days," I tell her. "And if you want, you can sit with your mom and me the whole time. Is that okay?"

Nichole nods her head. Carole hands her several quarters from the clear plastic coin purse she brings for buying the vending machine food. As Nichole walks toward the kids' area, sipping hot chocolate, I hold Carole's hands in mine and squeeze them to reassure her. "Did you sleep okay?"

She breathes in deeply and slowly, exhales, and then says she slept fine.

"Honey, I should be comforting you, but we don't have much time. Because it's a holiday, every hour we spend in here today is costing us double against our monthly allotment of 30 hours. We have to act fast, and we need a plan, okay?"

"If we run out of time, I think Office Cruz will let me in."

"Carole," I caution her, "this is prison. He may have let you in last night because he was alone and he felt sorry for you. We can't live on the edge like that. We have to budget our visits. The system controls everything and we have to succeed in spite of it."

"What do you want me to do?" she asks, eyes filling with tears.

"Last night you said you wanted to stay here. Are you sure?"

"I'm absolutely sure."

"Good, because I want you to stay with me. Every decision we make has to be consistent with our goal of bringing you stability, and it's not going to be easy. But we have to make a 100 percent commitment to making it work, no matter how painful the decisions."

"I've already got the newspaper and I'm looking for apartments."

"Honey, think about that. You don't know this area, the schools, the neighborhood, or where you're going to work. How much do you think it will cost to rent an apartment?"

"I'm guessing about $1,000 a month, more or less," she answers.

"To move in, then, you'll need first, last, and security. Then you'll need money for utilities and necessities. You're going to drop $5,000 minimum to set yourself up. That doesn't seem like a good plan to me, especially since you don't know where you'll work or how much you'll earn. We need stability."

"What do you think I should do?"

"Remember the story I wrote about Richard, a guy who arrived here a few months ago? You typed it for me and posted it on the Web."

Carole pauses, trying to recall. "Vaguely. You've sent me so many stories."

"Richard's wife lives a few miles from here, in Mount Holly. She has a little boy and a four-bedroom house. I asked Richard last night if his wife would rent you a couple of rooms. You could move in today, and the two of you could support each other. Nichole would have another child to keep her company, and you could catch your breath, get your bearings."

"Michael, I can't move in with a stranger." Carole doesn't see the merit in my suggestion.

"Carole, this isn't going to be easy. I'm sending you $10,000. That money has to cover all of your expenses until you start earning a paycheck. You need to get settled. You need a car. Nichole needs to start school again next week. This lady can help you."

"But I don't know her, Michael. You're asking me to live with a stranger. I'm not concerned about me, Honey. I have to consider Nichole's well-being."

I put my arm around her and pull her close. "Do you trust me?"

"Of course I trust you."

299

"And do you want to build your life with me, grow old with me?"

"Yes."

"Then you have to work with me. I can steer us through this crisis, but we both have to understand that the decisions we make today, from this minute, will determine where we are tomorrow." I extend my arm and open my hand. "Do you see that?"

"See what?"

"My fingers. Each of those represents a year. That's five years. Can you make it through five years with me?"

"I'm going to make it through forever with you."

"Okay. Well let's focus on five years. In five years, your life will be totally different from what it is now if we work together. You'll be stable, with your own money in the bank, money you've earned. We won't succeed by accident. We need to make tough decisions now, to commit and recommit 100 percent with every decision, reaching toward that five-year mark. When we make it to five, then we'll work toward the next five. By then I'll almost be ready for release. And you'll be independent. Do you want that?"

"Yes."

"Then you have to make hard choices now. Thank God we have this money from my stock account. But we can't squander it with bad decisions. We have to focus on stabilizing you as quickly as possible. If you meet Richard's wife with that goal in mind, understanding that she's an answer to a prayer for us to be together, then you'll see the move as a step that leads us closer to our five-year goal."

"What if we don't get along?"

"That's up to you and the way that you approach her. She needs you and you need her. You can make it work."

* * * * * * *

Carole settles in with her new housemate, Catherine, and she enrolls Nichole in school. It's early spring, 2003, and the job market is terrible. Through sheer resourcefulness, Carole learns that she can earn an income by providing notary services to the mortgage industry. She secures the necessary credentials and becomes self-employed, earning an income sufficient to support her and Nichole.

I'm walking along the road inside the Fort Dix fences, admiring the warm sunbeams that cut through the wire mesh and razor wire, reflecting off the shiny metal. Fragrant cherry blossoms and blooming flowerbeds fill the air with the scent of spring. I'm filled with appreciation for the blessings in my life. Through the fence I watch Carole's tan Toyota Corolla pull into the visitor's parking lot.

She can't see me, as I'm only one prisoner among thousands wearing khakis inside the compound. I watch her walk briskly, wearing her red skirt and jacket, heels clicking on the asphalt, hair blowing behind her, rushing to pass through the checkpoints to visit me. She thinks she's surprising me, but my only surprise is her remarkable consistency and devotion to serving this time with me. Carole wants us to marry, but I put her off. Marriage is easy for me, I tell her. I'm a prisoner and she's a beautiful woman. I'm giving her all that I am as it is, and I freely commit to her, but there's no rush. I want her to understand all the complications of prison before we marry.

"I watched you as you parked, as you rushed across the parking lot. You didn't surprise me," I tell her after our kiss.

"I drove fast to get here in time for the last two hours of visiting."

"I'm always expecting you."

The visiting room has become our living room. We sometimes walk through the rows and aisles of chairs, holding hands, chatting with other prison families. She buys dinner for me from the vending machines. It's always the same menu choice of frozen pizza, burritos, or hamburgers that she cooks in the microwave.

"I like preparing your food," she says, and watches me eat.

"This is what it's going to be like when we're old and living together in a nursing home," I tease. "We'll have familiar faces around us, strangers we recognize, but we'll have our own life. You can push my wheelchair."

"Wherever you are, that's where I want to be," she wipes a napkin against my mouth. "Why do you eat so fast?"

"I got used to it over the years. The guards rush us out of the chow hall. You'll have to teach me manners once they release me."

"You don't even taste your food. You just inhale." She tilts her head in amazement. "And how can you eat so much?"

"Believe me, I taste it. Besides, this is how I test if you really love me. If you can stand to watch me eat, I know you'll stay with me."

"I'll stay with you," she says, and then adds, "but you better stay with *me* at the dinner table until I'm finished!"

We walk around the room and stop by the television as President Bush grabs hold of the lectern to address the nation.

"I can't stand all this talk about going into Iraq. For what?" I say, shaking my head in disgust at the image of Bush in his familiar blue suit with his open arms and ridiculous gestures. "How many soldiers have to lose their lives for his ambitions?"

"I just wish he'd let you out," Carole squeezes my hand.

"Forget about that happening under his rule."

* * * * * * *

When I return to the housing unit after our visit I see scores of prisoners gathered in front of the bulletin board. They're cursing and complaining.

"What's up?" I ask.

"Fuckin' warden," one prisoner says. "More fuckin' bullshit, fuckin' with my peoples. I ain't gonna be able to see my babies' mammas."

I push my way through the crowd to read the memo. It cites the nation's elevated security-threat level and the imminent war in Iraq as a reason behind the warden's new rule that limits visiting to immediate family members only. That means he will only authorize parents, children, siblings, and wives to visit until further notice. My heart sinks.

Carole has only been living in New Jersey for three months, but our lives are now linked. She is overseeing the development of my new website, MichaelSantos.net, and helping to establish my "brand." She is the link between my publishers and me, and she has complete responsibility for the publishing company she formed to market and distribute books I'm writing.

We've begun our lives as a family, planning and preparing for my life upon release in 2013. Despite Carole's cross-country move to living just minutes away, this new rule will not permit us to see each other. I call to tell her about the new mandate.

"Well, are they going to increase the phone-minute allotment so we can at least talk more?"

"We'll still have to make do with 300 phone minutes a month."

"How can they say they promote community ties if they make rules that are so hard on families?"

"Honey, this is my life. It's what I've been telling you. They can do whatever they choose and for any reason. I don't have any control."

"Then we have to get married, Michael. We can't wait. We're a family."

"Baby, we shouldn't get married just to visit. Marriage is for the rest of our lives, and you have to be absolutely sure you can handle the rest of my sentence."

"I know exactly what I'm doing. Whatever the system does to you, it does to me, too. We're in this together."

Carole is an amazing woman and I feel so grateful to have her love.

* * * * * * *

I initiate the necessary paperwork to marry. My case manager, Mr. Lawson, is sitting behind his messy metal desk when I hand him the official request.

"What's this, a marriage request?"

"That's right. I'm getting married."

"Thought you was smarter den dat. After all dese years, you ain't learnt? Prison's a place to get divorced, not married." He laughs.

"When I start looking for advice on building happiness from prison guards, I'll look you up," I respond. There's too much venom in my retort.

Mr. Lawson puts the forms on his desk and glares at me. "I's a case manager. Ain't no prison guards here. Dey's 'correctional officers'. Get it straight."

Mr. Lawson reviews the form. "Goin' hafta run dis by da unit team, den send it on up to da warden. I'll let you know. Now git."

"This isn't a discretionary issue," I tell him. "The Supreme Court says I have a constitutional right to marry. You can't block the request."

"Boy, don't be spittin' no law at me. We gots a war goin' on. Security 'a da insta-tution. We goin' review yo request, an' like I says, I'll let you know. Wha's up? You gotta problem wit dat?"

While I brace myself for a bureaucratic struggle to receive permission to marry, I urge Carole to use this time when we can't visit to enroll in a real estate class. The wife of another prisoner is a broker for Prudential. She's offered to bring Carole on as an agent and teach her the trade.

Instead of a bureaucratic struggle, a staff shakeup results in a new case manager who is much nicer, and a new unit manager, Mr. Jones, who recently transferred to Fort Dix from USP Leavenworth. Mr. Jones, or TJ, as I've heard staff members cordially refer to him, is in his early 30s, black, well dressed, and built like an NFL linebacker. He is respectful and totally professional. When I approach him about my marriage request he congratulates me, assuring me that he'll push the approval through in time for a June wedding.

* * * * * * *

I wake early on my wedding day, June 24, 2003, smiling. I'll celebrate this day with Carole for the rest of my life. I step outside to run, feeling the humidity of an East Coast summer, but the breeze I generate by running cools my skin. I've paid a heavy price with this prison term, surrendering most of my life as a consequence, but now I have Carole. Although prison rules require two witnesses at our wedding, Nichole isn't allowed to participate because she's still younger than 18. I would've liked Julie to come, but she just gave birth to her second child, Sophia. My father is in an Alzheimer's home, unable even to talk with me over the phone, much less travel. But I'm happy that both my mom and my younger sister, Christina, are flying in from Miami for the ceremony. My mother calls Carole my 'angel' and the description suits her perfectly.

Two hours in the visiting room is all that we're going to have, but it's a fitting place for the ceremony because it's where we spend all of our time together. I'll wear a wedding ring when I walk out. Julie sent us the matching silver bands as a wedding gift. The rings will symbolize our commitment and once Carole slides mine onto my finger, I intend to keep it on forever. We'll make this work.

I finish running eight miles and slow my pace to a walk when I see Bob. He extends his hand. "Congratulations, Buddy. I'm glad we've met, and I wish you and Carole happiness, good health, and prosperity. You're going to make her an excellent husband."

"Thanks, Bob. Your friendship means a great deal to me, and I appreciate your good wishes. I'm sorry you can't be there for the ceremony."

"We'll have a party when you're out, when we're both home."

"I'm looking forward to it."

"Are your mom and sister here?"

"I hope so. They're supposed to be with Carole now. I'd better go shower."

"Good luck, and God bless."

Wearing crisply ironed khakis and polished black leather shoes, I look as sharp as a prisoner can when I present my ID card to Lieutenant Marks.

"This has got to be the stupidest thing you've ever done," the lieutenant says sarcastically, shaking his head. "You ought to tattoo the word 'fool' right across your forehead." He points to his head then loudly slurps coffee from his foam cup.

I strain to hold my sarcasm in check. He'd like nothing better than to unsnap one of the leather compartments on his heavy black leather belt, pull out a set of shiny metal handcuffs, and slap them on my wrist, canceling this special day for Carole and me.

"If you're going through with it, let's go. I got a prison to run." He leads me into the visiting room, without a preliminary strip search. Four other prisoners come along, as they'll be marrying today as well. I don't know them. I'm too consumed with the excitement coursing through me to concern myself with anyone else.

I sit in a chair and watch for Carole. When the door opens I stand, smiling as this beautiful lady walks toward me. More than a year has passed since my mother or Christina have visited and I'm grateful they made the special trip for my wedding ceremony, but I can't take my eyes off of Carole. Her cream-colored suit compliments her slender figure, and I like the graceful way she walks. She opens her arms and we embrace, sharing a kiss while my mom and sister stand by watching.

"Thanks for coming, Mom," I turn to hug her. She's always emotional when she sees me, and this morning isn't any different. My imprisonment has been incredibly difficult for my mom.

"I'm so happy you have such a beautiful bride, so happy for both of you."

I hug my sister next. Christina is four years younger than I am, petite and pretty, with long brown hair and a glowing face that resists aging. She's been married for 15 years and is the mother of two girls, Isabella and Camilla, but she still can't buy a bottle of wine without showing her ID.

"You've got to be the luckiest man in the world, convincing this beautiful woman to marry you in here," my sister says, smiling.

"You've got that right!" I keep my arm around Carole and kiss her cheek.

"Honey, did you talk to Bob?" Carole asks.

"I saw him this morning. He sent his good wishes, why?"

"Did he tell you what he did?"

"No, what?"

"He sent a personal messenger to my house last night to deliver a wedding card, and inside there were two cashiers' checks, each for five thousand dollars."

"Wow! What a thoughtful, generous friend."

"Can you believe it? I thought he didn't want you to get married."

"That was before he knew how extraordinary you were."

"I sent him a thank you letter last night. Please tell him I'm grateful. What should I do with the money?"

"Put it in the bank," I tell her.

"Geez, they should've at least done some decorating in here for the wedding," Christina remarks. She's looking around at the sterile setting of the visiting room as we all sit, side by side, in a single row of the plastic chairs placed in straight lines throughout the room. The polished floor shines. Six vending machines buzz under the bright, fluorescent lights.

"It's too bad they couldn't hold the wedding outside," my mom says. "It's such a beautiful summer day, perfect for a garden wedding."

"We're just happy that the day is finally here," Carole says.

"I'll marry you again when I come home," I promise Carole while looking into her eyes.

"Honey, that must be the man who's going to marry us," Carole gestures to an older man in a black robe who walks in with Mr. Jones, my unit manager. The white-haired man carries a black leather portfolio, and he's shaking hands with the two guards who supervise us from the platform.

"Is he a chaplain?" my mom asks.

"I think he's a justice of the peace," I answer.

"No," Carole corrects me. "He's the deputy mayor of New Hanover Township. That's where I sent the check for our marriage license."

The deputy mayor comes over to introduce himself, presents us with papers to sign, and instructs Carole about how to get an official copy of our marriage certificate. We're the first couple to be married. He stands in front of us and begins the ceremony. Mom and Christina flank us, smiling. I hold Carole's hand, grinning as I listen to him recite the marital vows, asking us in turn whether we take each other, in sickness and in health, for better or worse, until death parts us. Carole fills my heart with her "I do," and I say the same. We're married. Finally I get to kiss my bride, the lovely Carole Santos.

"I can't believe they won't give you any time alone," Christina says. "That's so cruel."

"The honeymoon's going to have to wait," I say.

"We have the rest of our lives for our honeymoon," Carole answers, kissing my cheek.

My mom and sister sit with us for a while, and then graciously leave to give Carole and me the last hour together. We're not alone. Four other couples also being married today sit with their families in the chairs around us waiting for their turn.

"You've honored me today, Carole, making me as happy as I can possibly be."

"I love you, Michael."

"Someday I'll buy you a house," I promise.

"Someday I'll make you a home," she adds. "In the meantime, 'home' will be wherever we are. We're in this together."

"This is forever," I twist my silver wedding band.

"There's no place I'd rather be than with you."

Lieutenant Marks brings an end to our time together. Ms. Davis, an attractive young woman who looks out of place in a prison guard's uniform, smiles as she escorts Carole and the other brides out. Mr. Rodriguez, a guard who sports a tattoo of an American flag on his forearm, strip searches the five grooms, side by side. The other prisoners and I dress and return to the compound, each with a new wedding ring on his finger.

* * * * * * *

On August 9, 2003, Justice Anthony Kennedy of the U.S. Supreme Court delivers an extraordinary keynote speech at the American Bar Association's annual convention in San Francisco. Carole sends me a copy of the text and highlights the parts she wants me to pay close attention to. I can't believe what the Justice says to the nation's lawyers. Justice Kennedy calls for prison reform, saying that America incarcerates too many people, that American prisoners often serve draconian sentences, and that a nation confident in its laws should not be afraid of compassion and mercy.

"Michael," Carole urges during our evening visit, "don't you think you should at least try for clemency again, especially after what Justice Kennedy said in his speech?"

"Baby, we can't afford it. I'm not going to spend our money on an attorney when the odds are so far against us. President Bush isn't going to commute my sentence."

"But you've done so much. No other prisoner has earned

308

university degrees, served 16 years, and published books that universities from across the country use. You don't have any history of violence and now you're married. I'll bet if the president knew about you, he'd commute your sentence."

"That's the problem, he doesn't know who I am. And unless I have a top legal team representing me, he'll never know who I am. That's one of the reasons we're building the website. We need to attract lawyers who want to represent me because I've earned freedom, because they believe in me. Right now we don't have the money to hire lawyers."

"But you could at least file a clemency petition on your own. We don't need lawyers to fill out the petition and send it in. At least that way we'd have a chance."

"Okay," I concede. "Print a blank petition and mail it to me. I'll fill it out and we'll collect some new supporting letters to file with it. But don't get your hopes up on this. We need to keep preparing for 2013. That means I need to write, and you need to earn and save."

"I'm doing my part."

"Yes you are," I squeeze her hand. "You're wonderful."

* * * * * * *

It's Monday, November 17, 2003. Carole and I have been married for nearly five months when she comes to share her good news. When I walk toward her, she's standing, wearing a glowing smile. The bright room is filled with other visitors, as noisy as a full auditorium.

"I passed my real estate test."

"Congratulations!" I grab her in my arms, pull her close, and kiss her. "I told you all of your studying would pay off. How did you find out?"

"I called the real estate board this morning. I got a 97 on my exam."

"Baby, you deserve to feel proud of yourself."

She's smiling. "I'm so happy honey, because I did it for you."

When hundreds of people pack the visiting room, like today, some couples succeed in stealing a few extra kisses through the visit. I only kissed Carole when our visit began, as rules permit. That's why I'm startled when the guard yells my name.

"Santos!" he hollers. An immediate hush quiets the entire room with his outburst.

I point my finger at my chest, making sure he's yelling at me.

"Come to the desk," he orders.

"But you didn't do anything," Carole objects as I stand and let go of her hands.

"Let me see what he wants."

I walk through the columns and rows of visitors to approach the guard's platform.

"Lieutenant wants to see you," he tells me.

"Can't it wait until after my visit?"

"Now. Officer Ruiz will take you through the back." I don't look back at Carole, but follow Officer Ruiz to the dressing room. My heart starts beating faster, as I've never known anything good to come from a talk with a lieutenant.

"Where's the lieutenant?" I inquire, looking around the empty room.

"Not here," Officer Ruiz says. "He wants to see you in his office."

"For what? What's this about?"

"I don't know," Officer Ruiz admits. "He called us and told us to escort you over."

"What about my visit?"

"He terminated your visit. Put your hands behind your back. I've got to cuff you up."

Officer Ruiz grips the handcuffs that secure my wrists behind my back as we walk across the lawn. He's a rookie in his early 20s, slight, and wearing a uniform that looks two sizes too big for him.

The lieutenant's office at Fort Dix is a single story, red brick building, only 20 yards away from the visiting room. Ruiz pulls open the heavy steel door and steers me inside the narrow corridor. We walk past an open office on the left and I see Lieutenant Nesbitt. He's the embodiment of BOP cruelty, with his faded blue eyes and crooked nose, intoxicated by power.

"Lieutenant, I've got Inmate Santos," Officer Ruiz's polite voice cracks as he announces our arrival.

"I'll get to him when I'm ready." I hear the lieutenant call from the office. "Have him face the wall."

"Yes sir."

Ruiz leaves me with my toes touching the wall. While closing my eyes and resting my forehead against the cold concrete, I worry about Carole in the visiting room, knowing she must be frantic. Jingling keys that hang from the heavy black leather belts of the guards who cross the hallway a few feet away grate on my nerves. To the guards, a man facing the wall in restraints for hours at a time is no different from the red fire extinguisher beside me; they're used to inanimate objects. I had hoped I'd never wear cuffs and chains again, but with nearly 10 years still to serve, that's not realistic. I wonder if I'm here because of the books I wrote.

"Bring Inmate Santos in here," the lieutenant finally calls out.

I feel a tug when the guard's hand grips the chain on my cuffs to pull me back from the wall. As if I'm a four-legged animal on a leash, he steers me down the hall to the lieutenant's office where Nesbitt is leaning back in his swivel chair behind a cluttered wooden desk.

"Well, Counselor. It seems we meet again." His eyes drill into me. "Tell me what's going on in my institution."

I return his stare with a neutral expression and shrug my shoulders. "I don't have anything to tell you, but I'd like to know why I'm here and why you terminated my visit."

He scowls. "Have it your way," he spins his chair away from me. "Lock him up."

The guard turns me around and leads me through the front door, across a courtyard, and into the parking lot outside the prison gates where he unlocks the sliding door of a white van. I step in and sit on the black vinyl bench seat, pressing my knees against the steel mesh that separates the driver from his passengers. He drives across the parking lot and down the road to the entrance of Fort Dix West, the adjacent compound. I'm going to the Special Housing Unit (SHU), "the hole."

Associate Warden Nuss, at McKean, was the last petty bureaucrat who ordered me locked in SHU, but that was only for one night, and it was for administrative reasons, when he was transferring me out seven years ago. I don't know what put me in Lieutenant Nesbitt's crosshairs, and the guards who process me refuse to give any information as they strip search and lock me in a single cell. I start to pace, coming up blank as I try to think of any possible reason that could justify this change.

I don't have contraband in my cell, and I don't have a single enemy. I wonder why Nesbitt would bother me, even though I know I may as well be wondering why a rattlesnake strikes. It's his nature. Still, I don't have any idea why I'm here.

My worries about Carole escalate, as I wonder how she's handling this disruption. Guards took me away before her eyes and I know that she's frightened for me. Being married to a prisoner means never taking tomorrow for granted. I hope she's called Julie and Carol Zachary by now. They'll help her get through this.

The light in my cell is always on. I lie on my stomach, crossing my arms to use as a pillow beneath my head on the gray vinyl mat. I try to sleep but a wicked anxiety prevents me from being able to relax. Several hours after midnight I give up on sleep and start exercising, doing pushups on the concrete floor.

When my body heats up, I step out of my orange jumpsuit and continue in my boxers.

Sometime after dawn the square trap in my cell door opens and an orderly slides in breakfast on a plastic brown tray. It's a bowl of unappealing hot cereal and a red apple. I push the button on the aluminum sink and rinse the apple in cold water that arcs from the faucet, then bite into the crispy red skin of the fruit. It's fresh and I savor it as sweet juice shoots through my mouth. I eat the entire apple to its core and wish I had another, but this is it until lunch.

When the guard returns for the tray, he looks through the square window of the cell and sees me in my boxers doing pushups on the floor.

"What're *you* doing in the hole?" It's Officer Flores asking. I know him from when he worked in the Fort Dix housing units. He's a friendly man in his 40s, with kind brown eyes and compassion.

"No one's told me anything." I step to speak through the crack of the door, brushing away beads of sweat that ooze from my forehead.

Officer Flores points to his ears and shakes his head, then steps closer to the door. "Speak into the door frame. I can't hear you," he tells me.

"I said no one has told me anything. Lieutenant Nesbitt terminated my visit yesterday and locked me in here."

"After I collect the breakfast trays, I'll see what I can find out. You didn't get a shot did you?"

I shrug. "I wouldn't know. No one has passed me any paperwork."

Officer Flores nods, and then comes into the doorframe again. "We're not allowed to read your website anymore."

"Why not?"

"I don't know," he says. "I used to read it every day at work, but now the BOP server blocks it."

"Do you think that's why I'm here?"

"Let me check. I'll be back. Do you need anything?"

"Thanks. I'd appreciate a pencil and some paper, and a Bible if you've got one." I resume my pushups, grateful for Officer Flores's kindness. If he can tell me what's going on, I'll figure out how to respond.

I squeeze two more sets of pushups in before I hear Officer Flores tapping the window of my cell door with his knuckle. I stand and walk closer. "You're on the transfer list. I've got to take you out."

"What? Transferred? Where am I going?"

"I don't have access to that information. I've got orders to take you out."

"When?"

"Right now. Roll up your stuff."

I shake my head, bothered that the complications of my life will disrupt Carole and Nichole's life yet again. Disheartened, I pull the sheets and blankets from the mat and bundle them into a ball. Then I step into the orange jumpsuit and back up against the door. Officer Flores unlocks the trap and I push my hands through the slot. I hear the metal click, as he cuffs my wrists, gently, leaving room for them to swivel. I appreciate this small act of kindness. With both hands I grab the bedding bundle while he unlocks and opens the steel door.

"You didn't know anything about a transfer?" he asks.

I shrug and shake my head. "I got married last June. My wife has just settled into this community. This transfer will devastate her."

Stepping out of the cell, I walk with him to the desk where he hands me off to a large guard I don't recognize. In front of both officers I dress out, exchanging my orange jumpsuit for traveling khakis. I nod to Officer Flores as his colleague steers me down a maze of corridors, then to another holding cell where I'm locked in with 17 boisterous prisoners. We're all "on the chain," scheduled for movement to some other prison.

The sound of waist chains, leg irons, and handcuffs dropping on the concrete floor nauseates me. I've heard it so many times over the years and I never get used to it.

My mood turns dark with sadness. I've adjusted to the institutionalized schedule at Fort Dix through my writing, my exercise, and my friendships. I married Carole here, and since last January I've spent 30 hours each month holding her soft hands in the visiting room. With those comforts gone, I sit against the wall and question what the next phase of this journey will bring.

A guard unlocks the door and calls me out first, bringing incontrovertible proof that I'm starting over, off to another prison.

"So you're the one who's causing all the trouble here." I've never seen this guard in my life, though he looks like a copy of all the others. I don't know why he's talking to me, but I try to ignore his unsettling comment, staring ahead, ignoring the queasiness in my stomach as he tugs on my restraints to ensure that I'm fully locked in.

"Nothing to say?" He's much taller than I am, and much wider. His size, coupled with a dark complexion and five o'clock shadow, give him a menacing look. I'd like him to shut his mouth and move on to belittle the next prisoner, but instead he spits a stream of brown tobacco juice into his white foam cup and glares at me.

When each prisoner is chained and secured, the guards lead us outside in a line. The sun is rising, but it's a cold November morning, and without a jacket I shiver in line, waiting for the guard with the files to call my name.

"Santos!" I step forward when he yells for me. I recite my registration number and submit to yet another yank on my restraints as guards make their final check. The leg irons are heavy. Only a few links hang between my ankles so I have to carefully climb the stairs onto the bus. I drop into an empty bench seat, taking a final look through the metal mesh at Fort Dix.

My chest tightens as sadness washes over me. It hasn't even been a day and I already miss Carole.

As we cross a bridge into Philadelphia my stomach lurches when I see the federal courthouse. It bothers me as I contemplate the possibility of going back to court, wondering whether some unknown entity is setting me up. I've been in prison too long to have any business with the court, and I'm overcome with anxiety that some guard might be framing me for new criminal charges, wanting to discredit what I write about prisons.

The bus parks in a garage beneath the courthouse, and I hear that a federal detention center exists above the courthouse. I follow the procession into a new holding cell and, after guards remove my chains, I sit on the floor. The concrete makes my butt sore, so I sit on my hands and lean my back against the wall.

A guard tosses brown sack lunches through the bars. I catch mine and look inside. Uncertainty about what's going on robs my appetite, but since I don't know when the next meal might come, I pull out the sandwich and remove the clear plastic wrap. I savor the food, still hungry after I swallow the last bite.

Prisoners are called out, one after another, until I'm left with one other man to wait. Dinner is a repeat of lunch, with the stale white bread tasting even better the second time. I wonder how much longer I'll have to wait, and when I'm the last man in the cell, I start to pace.

"Santos," an obese guard calls my name as she unlocks the gate. She leads me through a bright corridor and directs me into an office. A sandy-haired man in his mid-fifties greets me with a smile from his swivel chair behind the desk. I can't place him, but he's familiar, and I know that he must've worked in some prison where I've been held before.

"I saw 'Santos' on the file and I was wondering whether it was you," he tells me as he spins around in his chair. "How've you been?"

The black nametag pinned above the pocket of his shirt reads "Carter." I remember him as a guard from McKean.

"Fine, until yesterday," I answer.

"No one told you about this transfer?"

"I didn't know anything when the lieutenant locked me in the hole, and I still don't," I repeat for what feels like the umpteenth time. My head aches.

"Let's see where you're going. Give me your number."

I recite my registration number and listen as he types it into his computer, staring at the screen.

"You're going to FLF SCP," he reads the abbreviated designation. "It's a camp."

"*What*? Are you sure?" My anxiety turns to elation and I exhale with relief, smiling. "I'm going to a camp?"

"Yes, in Florence, Colorado. I'm surprised no one told you. It's good news, isn't it?"

"Are you kidding me? It's so good I can't believe it. I've

been in turmoil for the past 24 hours. This is incredible news. I can't wait to tell my wife, I'm sure she's going crazy with worry."

"The airlift usually leaves on Mondays, so you'll stay here through the rest of the week and the weekend," he tells me. "But you'll be flying west soon."

* * * * * * *

It's Sunday morning and I'm exercising in the housing unit at the Philadelphia Detention Center when a guard approaches me. "Are you Santos?"

"Yes."

"Come with me."

I follow him as he walks into the guards' station where he sits in the chair behind the metal desk.

"Close the door," he tells me, and when I do, the noise from the housing unit is silenced. "Are you married?" He glares and judges me.

"Yes."

"What's your wife's name?"

"Carole Santos."

He scratches his chin and stares at me. "What's she doing at my institution?"

"What are you talking about?"

"There's a woman outside claiming to be your wife, trying to talk her way into visiting."

I shrug. "So what's the problem?"

"What's the problem? You haven't been here long enough to have a visiting list approved."

"I've been here for six days. I gave the counselor my wife's name the night I was processed in."

"Visitors aren't authorized on the premises until staff approves them. She's not getting in."

"Then don't let her in," I shrug, "but deal with the consequences that will follow."

"What consequences," he asks.

"With all due respect, you're not in a position to deny her. BOP policy permits immediate family to visit. She was on my visiting list at Fort Dix, and unless you want to respond to an administrative remedy complaint about why you're disregarding BOP policy, I suggest you let me talk to the decision maker."

"What're you, a lawyer, somebody important or something?"

"I've been in prison since 1987, and if you read my file you'll find that I know my way around this system. I'm not new at this."

"Step outside," he commands. "We'll see how sharp you are when the lieutenant comes."

Through the office window I watch as he picks up the telephone receiver, pushes three buttons, and has a brief conversation before setting the phone down. He writes on a pad, then walks out of the office and locks the door behind him.

"Got your ID?" he asks, sounding annoyed.

"Yes."

"Let's go," he snaps.

He leads me from the housing unit into a lobby area, and then onto the elevator.

"Step to the back and face the wall," he directs me, pushing the ground floor button.

As the elevator starts to drop, my heart beats faster. I'm eager to hold my wife again, eager to share the news that I'm being transferred to camp.

After submitting to a quick strip search in the holding room I'm back in my green jumpsuit and hurrying through the door to the visiting room. Families sit across from each other, talking in hushed tones. It resembles any other visiting room, but it's much quieter than Fort Dix.

The guard at the desk recites the rules to me. I give him my ID card then search the room for Carole. I see her standing in her long navy wool coat, smiling and waiting for me.

"I've missed you so much." She walks forward to embrace me. Her kiss rejuvenates me, like succulent fruit after a 10-mile run on a sunny day.

"We only have an hour to visit because there's a line of people around the block and they're all waiting to get in. You have to sit across from me. We can't hold hands, and you have to raise your hand for permission to use the bathroom." Carole rattles off the rules as we sit facing each other.

"Wow!" I'm impressed with her command of the situation. "Okay, Honey. Let's make the most of the time we have." I'm laughing, happy to see her and relieved that she sounds strong and confident. "How did you know to come here and how did you talk your way in?"

"I've been following you on the BOP website. Once I knew you were in Philadelphia, I started calling and found out your housing unit is allowed to visit on Sundays. I brought the policy statement and a notarized copy of our marriage certificate with my identification. At first the guard wasn't going to let me in, but I showed him the policy statement and asked to see the officer in charge. He verified my date of birth, then let me in."

"You're incredible. Will you love me this much when my sentence ends?"

"Forever."

"That's good to hear. I thought you might just want to be a prison wife."

"Ha, ha," she smirks.

"Did you receive my letter explaining everything that happened?"

"I already knew. What do you think I've been doing since you vanished from our visit?"

"Tell me everything," I say.

"I was crazy with worry when you didn't come back. And then Officer Ruiz told me I had to leave, that our visit had been terminated. I drove home and started calling the prison right away, leaving messages with everyone I could think of. Your former unit manager, Mr. Jones, finally called me the next morning and said that he submitted you for transfer to a camp. I was instantly relieved and thrilled at the same time. We're moving to Colorado!"

"Slow down, Honey," I caution her. "You just passed your exam to sell real estate here. Don't you think you should get your license and sell a few houses, replenish our savings?"

"Honey, I'm not staying in New Jersey if you're living in Colorado."

"Let's think this through, honey. I love you and of course I want you with me. But let me get there and see how things look. We shouldn't make snap decisions, that's all I'm saying."

"I've already checked. I know exactly where you're going. Apartments cost about the same out there as they cost here."

"What about a job? You spent all this time and money to get your New Jersey real estate license. Don't you think you should at least try to make some money before we take on the cost of another cross-country move?"

"Hey, we always said our marriage would come first. I need to be where you are, and we need to visit whenever we're able to. That's what we promised each other."

"Okay, okay," I acquiesce. I'm pleased with her devotion, but worried about our finances. "We'll discuss it more when I'm there. But do some more research and see what you can learn about the local job market. We'll work something out."

* * * * * * *

On my way to Colorado my plane lands at the Federal Transit Center in Oklahoma. Five years have passed since I was here last, but the process is familiar. I even recognize faces of staff members, like the Native American guard with the long braided ponytail.

Our procession of prisoners marches single file through an efficient processing system. We stand on milk crates in groups of seven. Guards sit behind us unfastening our leg irons while another row of guards stand in front of us unlocking our handcuffs, pulling them from the metal chain around our waists to free our bodies. Guards talk among themselves, ignoring the noise of banging metal as they unlock and drop our chains into boxes. When mine come off, I note that my hands are filthy with metallic grease from the chains I've gripped for the past 12 hours.

With the news of where I'm going, I don't mind the annoyances. I'm on my way to camp, and for a long-term prisoner, that's like going to Disneyland. Inmates in higher security prisons talk about going to lower-security prisons as much as they talk about release. Placement in a camp, we hear, is as easy as it gets for a prisoner. I'm still not convinced that the BOP hasn't made some mistake, but since the mistake would be in my favor, I'm cool with it.

With a quick head count, I estimate that 200 prisoners flew into Oklahoma with me. As we sit in adjacent holding cells, I ignore the clamor and look around. I'm in the midst of convicted murderers, rapists, gang leaders, Mafia soldiers, and child molesters. Many serve life sentences, but with more than 16 years inside, and nearly 10 to go, my credentials in the society of felons is equivalent to a degree from Stanford or Harvard in the real world. I don't want to talk with anyone. I don't want to hear about what's going on at other prisons, about rivalries between prison groups, about legislation pending in Congress to reform good-time allowances, or about restoration of parole. I want to make it through this final stop, to leave behind, once and for all, the hate-filled, intolerant prison populations to finish the last decade of my sentence among white collar offenders in a minimum-security camp.

"Name and number?" A friendly face in a prison guard's uniform asks as I hand him the pile of forms I've completed. He's got red hair, freckles, and Elvis style sideburns.

"Michael Santos. Number 16377-004."

"Let's see. Santos," he looks down his list. "You're going to Florence Camp. Think you can handle that?"

He smiles and I nod. My nerves settle as I hear a second source confirm where I'm going.

I join six other prisoners, catching the bedroll and dinner sack the guard tosses after calling my name. We follow another guard through steel gates, onto an elevator, and up to the floor of our housing unit. I listen as the guard recites the rules before giving us our assigned cell numbers.

"Lockdown is at nine, so it's too late for you guys to shower or use the phone. Each cell has a panic button. Don't push it except for a genuine emergency; otherwise you'll get a shot. Listen for your name and cell number. Stand by your door. I'll walk around the tier to let you in. Any questions?"

I carry my bedroll into the familiar, triangle-shaped, two-tiered shell, then climb the concrete-and-steel staircase and walk toward cell 624. My feet hurt in the navy canvas deck shoes.

I send up a silent prayer for God to stay with me, to get me through this last transition before I make it to the camp.

When I reach my assigned cell door I look through the narrow window and swear under my breath. The prisoner inside looks as big as a Sasquatch. I can't see his face, but he sits at the desk in boxers without a shirt. His back is huge, and his arms, covered in tribal tattoos, are as big as my thighs. He's writing, gripping the pencil like it's a spear in his clenched fist. His full head of hair is an unruly black mop. I pray with renewed earnestness for God to get me through this.

The guard comes to unlock the door, and I want to protest that I'm going to camp, that he should house me with some friendly tax evader. Instead, I remain silent. I pulled a 45-year sentence and I'm expected to handle this kind of situation.

Once the guard locks me inside the cell, the rancid body odor hits me, but I shake it off. My new cellmate turns, revealing an expressionless face from the islands. I greet him while spreading the thin sheets across the top mat then tying the corners in knots beneath the mat to hold the sheets in place.

"Where you goin'?" The giant man breaks his silence.

"Florence," I say, deliberately leaving out the camp part. "I've been in for 16 years, finally making it out West," I offer, unsolicited, to let him know that I'm not new to prison.

"Where'd you come from?"

"I've been all over. Did about seven years in USP Atlanta. Spent time in McKean, Fairton, now I'm coming from Fort Dix."

He spins around and looks at me with a broad smile on his face. "Dude, I know you! You're Michael Santos."

He stands to shake my hand, nearly jerking my arm out of its socket with his enthusiasm. "I'm going to Fort Dix. I was on your website every day Bro, reading all your articles on prison before I surrendered."

I exhale and immediately relax. This man's a friend, not someone I have to fear. He's from Tonga, serving five years on an immigration violation. I stretch out on the top rack and answer his questions about life at Fort Dix.

* * * * * * *

When the guards begin clicking the locks open at 6:00, I hop down from the rack. Tonga, my cellmate, is still sleeping.

He's so tall that his ankles and feet extend beyond the edge of the rack. I tap his shoulder to wake him and tell him that we have to go downstairs for breakfast trays. He grunts, his sour breath nearly knocking me over.

I eat my oatmeal, and then walk to the phones. When the call connects to Carole, I hear her crying as she accepts the charges.

"What's wrong, Honey?"

"I have terrible news."

"What is it, what's wrong?"

"Carolyn called me. Bruce had a heart attack last night. He died, Michael."

I'm standing at a phone bank, with prisoners all around me, and it takes a second for the news to settle with me. Bruce has been a part of my life since the earliest days of this sentence, when I was beginning my university studies inside the penitentiary's walls in Atlanta. He visited me at least three times each year wherever I was held, and we spoke regularly over the phone, at least once each week for many years. I can't believe he's gone, that I'll never see him again. But more than his death, I'm surprised at why the news is hitting Carole so hard.

"Honey, why are you so emotional? You barely knew him."

"I'm sad because you loved him, and he meant so much to you."

"Yes, he was a great friend to me, but I'll be okay. It's more important that I stay strong. That's what he would've wanted. Instead of being sad at his passing, I'll celebrate his life and all he's done to make the world better. Please call Carolyn for me. Tell her how sorry I am and that I'll write today."

"That's something she asked me on the phone. She wanted to know if you could send a remembrance before the funeral."

"I'll write it today and then I'll read it over the phone the next time I call. Now don't cry anymore. Bruce would say 'keep on keepin' on,' and in his honor, that's what we're going to do."

As I walk back to my cell, I realize that Bruce has been with me for 14 years, embracing me as part of his family, working to educate me, to guide me. He defended me when necessary and smoothed the way wherever and whenever possible. With his death I've lost my first mentor, my dearest friend. I'll do my best to express appreciation for him in a eulogy.

Bruce is the second significant person in my life who has died during my imprisonment. My grandfather, Pat, having first forsaken me, forgave my behavior and spoke with me on the phone before his death in 1999. My father is confined to an Alzheimer's home. I haven't seen him since 1995, more than eight years ago, and I don't think I'm in his memory anymore. He can't travel, or even talk with me over the telephone. People I love are growing old and may die before my release. This reality starts to settle within, causing new heartache.

*   *   *   *   *   *   *

We land in Colorado. As I hobble down the stairs from the belly of the plane, with leg irons digging into my ankles, I'm surprised by the climate. It's seven in the morning on December 4, 2003, and I hear the pilot say the temperature is 40 degrees. I'm only wearing a t-shirt, khaki pants, and navy canvas deck shoes without socks, but I'm not cold. The dry air is still and the low sun shines through a cloudless blue sky.

Four silver prison buses idle on the tarmac. I count 12 vigilant guards standing in navy windbreakers wearing mirrored sunglasses, gripping assault rifles. The guard who waits at the bottom of the stairs wears plastic earmuffs over his head to block the noise from the screeching jet engines. He yells for my name and number, then checks his clipboard and directs me to join the line beside the last bus.

While standing in line, wrists cuffed to the chain around my waist, I study the faces of other prisoners as they walk down the stairs. I see Renegade, a prisoner who walked the yard with me in USP Atlanta. He's bald, with a long goatee, and I notice that he's added a few new tattoos to his neck and face. The guard directs him to the bus in front. I wonder where he's going.

After all the remaining prisoners re-board the aircraft, the guards count those of us standing in lines beside the buses headed to Florence. Apparently, we're all accounted for, as the guards start ordering us to step on board. Once we're loaded the bus convoy begins rolling down the road toward the Florence Federal Correctional Complex.

As we reach the left turn lane on Highway 33, the buses zip by the guard's shack to climb the winding and rolling hill that leads into the complex made up of four separate prisons. When our bus turns right into the long driveway of the medium-security FCI, the other buses continue up the road toward the higher-security prisons, including a high-security USP and the federal prison's ADX unit, also known as the Supermax, a cage for human beings. On the left, close to the highway and not enclosed by a fence, I see what must be the camp. Men in green uniforms mingle in the center of the compound.

Our bus stops beneath a canopy and the double doors squeak open. The lead guard stands at the head of the bus holding a stack of yellow files. He's a big man with a wad of chewing tobacco that makes his lower lip bulge. He spits brown tobacco juice into a clear plastic Coke bottle with rhythmic precision. When I hear him yell "Santos!" I shuffle forward so he can match my face to the mug shot on the file he holds. He spits into his bottle and then asks me to recite my registration number followed by my date of birth.

With his nod, I have permission to pass. When I step off the bus, I follow the other prisoners and we hobble through rows of armed guards in BOP uniforms. We continue into the foyer of the FCI. Our chains drag on the brown marble passageway making a scraping sound that disturbs the cathedral-like quiet.

We move outside, across a concrete walkway that cuts through reddish-orange gravel raked in neat rows. Another guard meets us, opening the steel door that leads into the Receiving and Discharge area. Before unlocking our chains and leg irons, a guard calls for quiet.

"Listen for your name. If you hear it, step to the front of the line," the guard calls out.

"Roberts."

"Thomas."

"Williams."

"And Santos."

I join the others at the front.

"Okay," the guard yells. "The rest of you, step into the

holding tanks so my officers can unlock your chains. I want the four of you to follow me."

We shuffle into a smaller cell and I reason that he must be separating those of us who've been assigned to the camp.

"Are you the same Santos who writes about prisons on the Web?" Williams asks me.

"That's right." I've never even seen the Internet but questions about my work give me a lift. "Did you find the information helpful?"

"More than helpful! I was worried to death about coming to prison. My lawyer didn't know anything about what it was going to be like. Once I found your site and read about all that you've done in prison, I had more hope. My wife, too."

"How do you write for the Internet from prison? Will we have computer access?" Roberts asks

"Prisoners can't access the Internet or use any kind of technology. I write in longhand and then I mail my work home. My wife types it and posts it to the website she operates for me," I explain.

"Your wife must be something special, staying with you all these years," Thomas says. "I've only got 18 months, and my wife has already filed for divorce."

"Prison is much harder on the family than it is on us," I say to the men. "We can find activities to fill our time, even work toward goals that will improve our lives. Our families have to struggle with financial problems, loneliness, and the shame of our imprisonment."

As we wait, we learn a bit more about each other. Thad Roberts interests me. He's in his mid-20s, beginning a nine-year sentence for stealing moon rocks. His wavy brown hair frames a constantly curious expression on his face. The roots of crime began with his employment as a NASA intern. In a romantic gesture, he promised to give his girlfriend the moon, and he wasn't speaking metaphorically. Thad's employment gave him access to moon rocks that astronauts brought back, and he broke federal laws by taking a few. Although he delivered on his promise to give his girlfriend the moon, he made himself vulnerable to federal law enforcement authorities when he tried to profit by selling the moon rocks on eBay.

The guards bring us our intake forms. They snap our mug shots and take our fingerprints. We answer questions from the nurse, the psychologist, and a case manager. I'm still waiting for a shoe to drop, for someone to say there's been a mistake, to tell me that I don't qualify for camp placement.

A guard opens the door and issues red ID cards to Roberts, Williams, and Thomas.

"Santos," he calls out as he looks my way.

"Yes?"

"Come with me." This could be the shoe.

I follow him through a hallway to a counter where a tall man in a dark blue suit and light blue tie stands beside a well-dressed woman with black hair and glasses. She holds a file with my picture on the cover.

"How much time are you serving?" she asks me.

"45 years."

"And you're going to the camp?" The uniformed guard interrupts while the man in the suit observes.

"I'm an old-law prisoner," I explain. "With my sentence, I earn more good time than the new-law prisoners. I only serve 26 years total, and I've already served more than 16 years. I have fewer than 10 years to go until release and I don't have any disciplinary problems or a history of violence."

The woman looks up at the man in the suit, hands him my file, and he flips through the pages.

"You're not going to run if I put you in the camp, right?" the man in the suit asks.

"No sir." He nods his head and shrugs. "Everything's in order."

The guard gives me my red ID card and tells me to wait. He calls the other three camp prisoners, and then he leads us out of the building, instructing us to grab a bedroll.

I can't believe this is really happening. Without chains or restraints of any kind, I walk through the lobby and open the glass doors. For the first time since 1987, neither walls nor barbed wire confine me. I see the highway to my left. The guard points to the camp, across the FCC road, about a half-mile away, and he tells us to walk over. I'm gripped with apprehension that someone will call me back, but I keep walking, not looking back.

* * * * * * *

The camp holds 500 prisoners, none with documented histories of violence and all with release dates within 10 years. I'm assigned to a housing unit wing with 31 other men and we sleep in two-man cubicles.

"Did you just get here?" I ask a clean-cut man who stands beside me near the unit's laundry room.

"How can you tell?" he responds.

I point to his feet. "The blue canvas shoes, they're standard issue for all new prisoners. You'll be able to buy a decent pair of tennis shoes or boots as soon as the staff activates your commissary account."

He nods his head. "I'm Eric. I got here two days ago."

"Michael. I got here this morning."

Eric is a businessman from Vail who's serving a five-month sentence for a tax dispute.

"Some of the guys are going to be here for years." I chuckle and we become friends.

Counselor Butler assigns Eric and me to work in the laundry at the Supermax. We wake early to board a bus that drives us over the hill, past the walls that enclose the USP complex, to the back gate of the Supermax. I count eight towers where guards stand post with machine guns. It's a concrete structure, partially underground, where prisoners live in near total isolation.

As one of five prisoners assigned to the laundry, I work at the sewing machine, mending clothes for prisoners in the Supermax, including the Unabomber, the man who attempted to blow up the World Trade Center in the early 1990s, and Terry Nichols, an accomplice in the Oklahoma City bombing with Timothy McVeigh. On the roster, I also see names of gang members I once knew at USP Atlanta. I wonder if Renegade, the prisoner I saw stepping off the plane when I arrived in Colorado, is here.

* * * * * * *

Carole and Nichole move from New Jersey to Colorado in mid-January. They arrive for our first family visit at Florence on Friday, January 23, 2004.

Carole and Nichole have made three moves during the past 18 months, which demonstrates her commitment to nurturing our marriage. She is determined to live near the prison that confines me, and with that principle in mind, we contemplate a new career for her, something that will allow her to earn a livable wage regardless of where prison administrators place me.

"I've been looking at different options," she tells me. "The only career I've found where I can work anywhere and earn a decent living is nursing. I'd have to return to school full-time, taking all the prerequisites in math, science, and English, followed by two years of nursing school. But with a nursing license, I could always find a job, regardless of where they moved you."

"Let's do it. We'll use our savings and income from my writing to get you through nursing school. And I'll write another book to generate more resources. We'll use all the money that comes into our household to support you."

Nichole is 12, finishing sixth grade, but we include her in the decisions we're making. It's our way of working to educate her from inside prison visiting rooms.

"Tell me about your new school," I ask her.

"It's like New Jersey. I've made a few friends and everyone's excited about starting junior high next year."

"When we were in junior high, your mom and I already knew each other."

"That's totally weird," Nichole says.

"Maybe you're going to school with your future husband," Carole teases.

"No way."

"You never know," Carole smiles.

"Keep up your good work, Nichole. Your mom and I are proud of you. If you study hard through school, you'll prepare for many opportunities that will open for you as you grow older."

* * * * * * *

It's the spring of 2004, and even at our 5,000-foot elevation, the snow has stopped falling. The Rocky Mountains are right outside the window, close enough that it looks as if I could reach out and touch them. I have a wonderful view from this prison cubicle in Florence.

Carole studies full time at Pueblo Community College and her schedule helps me mark off the weeks. We visit three hours every Friday evening, six hours on Saturdays, Sundays, and federal holidays. The more time I spend in Carole's company, with my fingers locked around hers, the more I feel as if I'm a part of something more than a prison population.

While we sit beside each other in the burgundy plastic chairs of Florence's visiting room, she tells me that we need to generate more support for my clemency petition. It's been almost a year, and we haven't heard anything.

I squeeze her hand. "I told you, President Bush isn't going to commute my sentence. Let's not divert our attention from what's really important. We're doing well and we need time to prepare for my release. You focus on finishing chemistry and biology, and I'll work on getting a publishing deal."

"It's too bad Bruce isn't alive. He could help."

"We've got to do this on our own. You get your degree, and I'll find a literary agent who will represent my work. It looks like we're going to be saddled with four more years of Bush. But if I get a book deal, we might get enough support for a reasonable chance at clemency after he's gone. And by then you'll be a nurse."

"First I need to pass algebra. These word problems were tough when I was in high school, but they're brutal now that I'm 40."

"You're smarter than I am, and I know you can do it." I pull out the algebra book she brought with her. "Let's work through some problems together."

* * * * * * *

Other than work in the Supermax laundry, exercise, and visiting with Carole, I devote all my energy to writing a book proposal and three sample chapters for a new manuscript. I'm titling it *Inside: Life Behind Bars in America*. It's my first attempt to reach a general, non-fiction audience, and I invest more than three months with a Bic pen and a dictionary to put the book proposal together. Carole types the document and sends copies to 90 literary agents I culled from an annotated list published in *Writers Market.* I'm hopeful they'll have an interest in my work.

Our effort to find a literary agent makes me a hit at mail call. The guard has been calling my name over and over, passing me no fewer than 73 rejections from literary agents who've declined to represent me. But I've also received letters from four agents who express an interest. I hold one in my hand now from James Schiavone, a Florida agent who has a doctorate in education.

Educators guided me through my first 17 years of confinement and they served as role models for me. I admire their devotion to improving society through teaching and I respect them for the energy they invest in helping others reach their potential.

I respond to Dr. Schiavone's letter, letting him know that I'd welcome an opportunity to work with him. That response leads to more correspondence. I amend my proposal according to his suggestions and sign a contract giving Schiavone Literary Agency authorization to present my manuscript to mainstream publishing houses. It thrills me to have a valid contract with a literary agent Carole and I found through our own work.

The executive staff at Florence Camp, however, doesn't share my elation. This becomes clear when the Camp Administrator, Mr. Jimenez, calls me into his office for an admonishment. My Unit Manager, Ms. Otero, is also present. Anticipating the reason for the meeting, I carry copies of *About Prison, Profiles From Prison,* and a file with letters I've received from numerous professors who use my writings as a resource to teach university students in their criminal justice and corrections courses.

Mr. Jimenez is confident and ambitious, clearly headed for higher offices with the growing Bureau of Prisons system. As the camp administrator, he's like a mini warden, and all staff members answer to him. As unit manager of the camp, Ms. Otero is his direct subordinate. She reminds me of a miniature bulldog, tough and mean.

Mr. Jimenez authorizes me to come in. He's sitting in a high-backed chair behind his large oak desk. Ms. Otero stands in front of Mr. Jimenez's desk, glaring at me like I'm a problem child she's reporting to the principal, her hands clasped behind her back. Her dark polyester suit fails to hide the roll of fat she tries to camouflage.

"Have a seat, Mr. Santos," Mr. Jimenez gestures to the green vinyl couch beside his desk.

"I'm placing you on mail-monitoring status," he says as I sit down.

"What does that mean?" I ask.

"It means that the Special Investigative Services lieutenant will review all correspondence addressed to you. From now on, the SIS will have to approve all mail before it's distributed to you."

"Why?" I ask.

"Security of the institution," Ms. Otero says.

"How long will he hold my mail?"

"We'll try to keep it reasonable," Mr. Jiminez says. "Depending on the volume of mail you receive, you can expect it in two to three weeks, assuming SIS approves it."

"What have I done to warrant this sanction?"

"You're not being sanctioned," he corrects me. "I have a responsibility to preserve the security of the institution, and this is a precautionary measure I'm taking."

"A precautionary measure against what? I'm not threatening security. My record is clear, and I'm an open book. All I'm trying to do is prepare for my successful re-entry into society."

"You've still got nine years to serve, and we don't care anything about your life after release," Ms. Otero hisses. "All we care about is the security of the institution. We don't like prisoners writing books and complaining about the system."

"Have you seen the books I write? I'm not complaining about anything."

"I don't need to see your books," she says. "I don't want any inmates under my watch writing about prison operations. It threatens security."

I'm puzzled by her hostility, and I turn to Mr. Jimenez. I sense he's uncomfortable with her self-righteous invective.

"Can I show you my books?"

He extends his hand and I give him the books and the file of letters.

"I write about the importance of accepting responsibility, about preparing for re-entry. My books don't threaten security. They offer suggestions for improvements to lower recidivism rates. Universities from coast to coast use them as teaching resources. I'm proud of my work and I'd like to have your support."

Mr. Jimenez flips through the pages.

Ms. Otero watches the exchange and, sensing that Mr. Jimenez might reconsider, she verbally challenges me again. "What are you in for? Aren't you a drug dealer?"

"I made the bad decision to sell cocaine in my early 20s. I'm 40 now, hoping you'll judge me for the record I've built over the past 17 years rather than the crime that put me here."

"I bet you would. You're serving 45 years, right? Why don't you just serve your time like everyone else? Write your books when you get out," she snarls.

I'm immune to her verbal hammer, knowing it's for Jimenez's benefit.

"Like everyone else? Ms. Otero, 70 percent of the people who leave prison return to prison. Serving my time like everyone else would only lead to my failure after 26 years. I'm determined not to let that happen. Why would you oppose me? You've got gang members running around here who thrive on crime, and you want to spend energy blocking me? Why?"

"The thing is, Mr. Santos, we've got an institution to run," Mr. Jimenez explains, returning my books. "How do you think taxpayers would respond if they heard we were allowing inmates to write books?"

"The BOP policy expressly encourages inmates to write manuscripts, and it says we don't need staff authorization."

"It doesn't say you can publish them," Ms. Otero barks, unwilling to back down.

"I'm not publishing them, someone else is. I give the manuscripts away. Wouldn't you rather have prisoners using their time productively in activities that will help them overcome the stigma of imprisonment? Isn't that better than wasting time on television and table games?"

"I told you. We don't care what happens to inmates after they leave. We're running a prison here," she snaps, angrily.

Mr. Jimenez shakes his head. "We've made our decision, Mr. Santos. As of today, you're on mail-monitoring status. You may appeal the decision, but I've consulted with the warden and he agrees that security of the institution comes first."

I walk out of his office sensing that Mr. Jimenez respects me, maybe even admires what I've done. But he's a career bureaucrat representing a system whose policies have the unintended consequences of perpetuating failure; prison management rejects the workplace practices of innovation and 'thinking outside the box.' It's so much easier to isolate and punish.

I owe no allegiance to Mr. Jimenez, Ms. Otero, or the prison system. By writing about prisons from the inside, I hope to influence support for reforms to our costly prison system that perpetuates so much failure. I feel a duty to write about America's most flawed institutions, especially a federal prison system hidden from public view and squandering billions in taxpayer resources each year.

* * * * * * *

From the window of my cubicle, I see Carole's blue Saturn two-door waiting in a line of vehicles on the side of the road. Every day brings more reason for me to appreciate the blessings of my life. With her love, I feel fortunate, strong enough to overcome whatever this prison system dishes out. When the guard at the main gate raises the barrier for cars to drive into the FCC for visiting, I leave my cubicle and walk toward the visiting room.

When Officer Zimmer pages me, I step into the room for a search. He's friendly to Carole and me, allowing Carole to bring her textbooks so I can help her study. She was excited on the phone when I spoke to her earlier, and I'm eager to hear her news.

As I enter the visiting room she stands, smiling, her arms waiting for my embrace. She serves this sentence with me. For us, these few hours together are our dates.

"What happened? Did you get an A on your chemistry

exam?" I ask.

She smiles at me. "I'm so proud of you," she says.

"Tell me why."

"Jim called. He got you a publishing deal for your book."

"With who?" I ask.

"St. Martin's Press. They're giving us an advance. You'll have distribution all over the world."

The news thrills me. It's only been a couple weeks since I signed the agreement with Jim Schiavone and in his letter he urged patience. Although my mentors, George Cole and Marilyn McShane, helped me place my first two books with academic publishers, I'm a novice author to mainstream publishers. I expected my imprisonment would present a real obstacle, but Jim is a solid professional agent. His representation brought credibility with the large New York publishing house, and once again, an educator changes my life. I'm proud that the pens and paper I buy from the prison commissary lead to work that contributes to Carole and Nichole's well-being. A sense of validation comes with this tangible proof that others see me something as more than a prisoner.

"Do I need to talk with anyone, with Jim or someone from St. Martin's?"

"Everyone understands your situation. You can send everything through me, like always. I'll type it and forward the manuscript through email. The only question is edits. How will you meet the timeline if the staff keeps holding your mail?"

"Let's send the manuscript pages to Rick," I suggest, referring to my roommate. "No one's checking his mail."

"I can't do that. They probably have some rule about my writing to another inmate."

"Honey, you're free. You can send mail to anyone you want. We can't let these mini-minds in prison block us from success."

"No way," Carole is adamant. "I'm not going to do anything that might create a problem with our visits. I'll forward the manuscript pages I type to Jennifer. She can send them to her husband, and when he gets them, he can give them to you."

"I'll meet the timeline."

"No one has any doubt about that," Carole assures me.

* * * * * * *

The BOP rule that limits prisoners to 300 telephone minutes each month stifles family ties. With an average of fewer than 10 minutes of daily telephone access, I can't afford to talk with anyone but Carole. But it's June 11, 2004, Christina's 37th birthday. I haven't spoken with my younger sister since she flew to New Jersey last year to witness my marriage to Carole, so I dial her number in Miami to surprise her.

"Happy birthday," I say when she answers.

"Hi, thanks." Christina responds softly, sadly. Then silence.

"What's wrong? You don't sound like you're celebrating," I push for an answer.

"You haven't talked to Carole?"

"She's still in school. I'll see her tonight when we visit, why?"

"Dad died today, Michael."

I knew that my father's health had been declining for the past decade. His illness prevented him from traveling to visit me after I left USP Atlanta. The news from Christina, while not unexpected, hurts. The challenges of this lengthy prison journey keep coming, but I've dealt with them repeatedly over the years and I take the news of my father's passing with stoic acceptance. I exhale, and urge my sister to be strong.

"Can you come to the funeral?" she asks, her voice sounds far away.

"No." I'm a prisoner and I know my limitations.

"We can postpone the service a few days if you need time for the request." she pleads with me.

"Christina, they won't even give me more access to the telephone. They're not going to let me travel to Seattle for a funeral.

You and Julie arrange the service without me. I'll pray here and write a eulogy."

Now the three men closest to me have died. I say prayers for my grandfather, Bruce, and my dad. My imprisonment stretches too long for them to have been able to welcome me home. Not being allowed to pay final respects and show gratitude, I silently hope my father's death is the last loss of family that I'll know as a prisoner.

* * * * * * *

Carole and I eagerly await the celebration of our second wedding anniversary in June of 2005. Just as we did on our wedding day and on our first anniversary, we'll savor a romantic dinner, whatever snacks the four vending machines offer. We both feel good about being ahead of the schedule we set. Carole is completing the final prerequisites before beginning her bachelors of science in nursing at Colorado State University, and Ben Sevier, my editor at St. Martin's Press, has accepted my manuscript for *Inside: Life Behind Bars in America.*

After the 5:00 a.m. census count clears on Wednesday, June 1, 2005, I seal the envelope that holds the prologue for *Inside* and carry it to the outgoing mailbox. Except for the final editing, I'm finished with that project and I look forward to its publication. It's time to begin something new.

I return to my cubicle and sit at the tiny metal surface mounted against the green concrete wall. The all-in-one table and stool "desk" is large enough to hold my paper and dictionary, but nothing else. I drape a folded towel over the edge to keep it from cutting into my forearm while I write in longhand. The hard metal stool mounted to a swinging arm beneath the desk is directly beside the window to my right, which frames the million-dollar view of Pike's Peak and the Rocky Mountains. After 18 months we're settled, Carole and Nichole in town and I at Florence Camp.

After two hours of writing, I hear the page. "Santos! Report to the Bubble."

The Bubble is at the camp's entrance where guards congregate. I begin my walk up with apprehension, as I know that nothing good can come from this summons.

When I get to the Bubble I see the SIS lieutenant who is in charge of security for the FCC. He's sipping coffee with the other guards in the glass enclosure and he reminds me of someone who aspires to a career as an FBI agent. The same lieutenant questioned me a few weeks ago after a newspaper reporter wrote a story about the ADX and cited my work as a source. When I told the lieutenant that I hadn't had any contact with the media, my response seemed to end his inquiry. Now I'm not so sure, as he rarely bothers with the camp. I present my red ID card to the guard at the window.

"Sit in there," he commands, pointing across the hall to the visiting room. "Someone will be here to see you." The guard keeps my ID card, and the SIS agent, who stands behind him, stares at me while sipping his coffee.

I sit alone in the visiting room and look around. Carole and I spend all of our time together here, but intuition tells me that change is about to bury the visiting schedule we value and appreciate so much. My heart beats faster when a guard I don't recognize walks in and confirms my suspicions.

"Are you Santos?"

"Yes."

"Cuff up."

Chapter Twelve: 2005-2007
Months 209-231

"What's this scumbag here for?"

The guard on duty barks as we enter the closed corridor inside the Special Housing Unit. Since he doesn't know me I surmise that his obvious contempt extends to all prisoners.

I stand silently, both hands still locked behind my back.

"One for SHU. Captain's orders." The transporting guard uncuffs me and walks away.

"Strip!" The SHU guard commands.

I unbutton and remove my green shirt, then I pull my t-shirt over my head and drop it on the floor. The guard stands close, too close, staring as I take off my sneakers, my pants, my underwear, and my socks.

"Take *everything* off."

I stand in front of him, naked, and I unfasten the rubber wristband of my Timex wristwatch, dropping the watch into his outstretched hand.

"Give me the ring."

"I don't have to give you my ring."

"What did you say, Inmate?" He takes a step closer and his breath hits my face.

I hold up my left hand. "This is a silver wedding band, without stones. BOP policy says I can wear it at all times."

The guard takes off his glasses, closes them and slides them into his shirt pocket. He inches closer to me. "You tellin' me how to run my institution, scumbag?"

"I'm not resisting you. Call the lieutenant. He'll know the policy."

"I'm in charge here." The guard balls his fists, wanting to fight. "Either take the ring off, or I'm gonna take it off. It's not coming into my unit."

Standing naked, I'm not in a position to argue for my rights. This guard thirsts for a violent confrontation, and if it comes to that, I lose. With the length of time I've served, I'm conditioned to accept that guards routinely cite their mantra about preserving security of the institution while they violate both human rights and civil rights. Despite the promise I made to Carole about never taking it off, I slide the band off my finger and I hand it to the guard. He steps back, puts his glasses back on, and then he continues the search.

The guard issues me a green jumpsuit and a bedroll. We walk down the cellblock. When he unlocks the metal door I see three prisoners inside. Rollo, a young prisoner, is on the top rack. He caused a stir at the camp several months ago when he decided that he'd had enough of confinement and walked away. Pueblo is on the lower rack, locked in SHU two months ago for fighting. Jerome sits on the floor in SHU because the guard in food services caught him going through the food line twice on hamburger day. I drop my bedroll on the floor for a cushion, and I lean my back against the wall, bending my knees to prop my feet against the steel toilet.

"What'd they get you for?" Rollo asks from his rack.

"Embezzlement. They say I transferred a million dollars from the prison's bank account to my wife's account."

"No way! Really?" Rollo would believe me if I'd told him I was locked in the SHU for not putting my napkin in my lap. He's totally gullible.

"I don't know why I'm here. They just locked me up," I admit and shrug.

"Ay Rollo you so stupid, you believe anything." Pueblo whacks him with his pillow from the lower rack.

"It could happen!" Rollo defends himself. "Ain't you never seen *The Shawshank Redemption*, Homie?"

"Dat shit was a bad-ass flick," Jerome says.

"Rollo," I ask. "Why did you walk away from the camp?"

"I missed my ol' lady."

"When he done showed up at her door, da bitch done called da FBI on his stupid ass," Jerome says, finishing Rollo's explanation.

"Is that what happened?" I ask Rollo.

He nods his head and laughs. "I'm facing five more years for escape."

340

"What were you serving before?" I ask him.

"Twenty-two months for credit card fraud."

"You'll probably get another year. You can use the time for school," I say.

"That fool ain't goin' to no school." Pueblo says. "He can't even play no cards."

I spend the entire day on the floor of the crowded cell, which won't allow for Pueblo or Rollo to step off their bunks. When someone has to use the toilet or sink, I stand in the corner. Exercise isn't an option here, and with the back and forth chatter, reading or writing will have to wait.

In the evening, a guard unlocks the door and tosses me a sleeping mat. I slide it under the steel rack, then carefully crawl under the bed, head first, and I lie still. Pueblo's steel rack is only inches above me, too close for me to turn on my side. I sleep lying on my stomach, using my crossed arms as a pillow.

"Santos! Roll up!" I haven't been asleep for long when I hear the guard kicking the metal door. He unlocks the door and opens it.

I crawl out from under the bed, careful not to step on Jerome. The guard cuffs my hands behind my back and leads me out. I don't ask questions and he doesn't offer explanations. I strip, toss my jumpsuit into a bin and I stand for the search, eager to move out.

"What size?" The guard asks.

"Two-X," I say.

He tosses a roll of traveling khakis. After I'm cuffed and chained, I join a group of other prisoners and we climb into an idling bus. The sky is still dark. We drive through the gates and join a convoy of three other buses, two carrying prisoners from the Florence penitentiary and one from the ADX.

As the buses turn right, leaving the Florence Correctional Complex behind, I look through the tinted windows and wonder where Carole lives. The house she rents is only two miles from the prison, she told me, but I don't know where. The bus moves past the dark cross streets too fast for me to see her car parked in a driveway. No matter. It's before dawn and she's asleep, oblivious to a new uprooting of our lives.

* * * * * * *

I have a window seat as the plane takes off. I expect to sleep in the Oklahoma Transit Center again tonight and wonder whether I'll see the Native American guard. I count how many times I've been on prison transport planes, and come up with 12, explaining why some of the U.S. marshals look familiar. I notice graying hair and new wrinkles in weathered faces; over the past 18 years I've flown with them throughout their careers.

We've been in the air a few hours when my ears pop and my stomach lurches. While we're descending, I glance out from the tiny window. As our plane approaches the landing strip, I see evergreen trees that surround a lake I recognize. We're approaching Seattle, the city where Carole and I grew up, where Julie and her family still live. Carole and I may have grown up here, but it's no longer home. We're nomads, a prison family.

The plane lands at Boeing Field, right beside Interstate 5. I look outside and spot guards and marshals surrounding the plane for the prisoner exchange. I wish they would call my name, as I'd like to walk on Seattle ground again. I may be in chains, but I'm breathing the same air my sister breathes, though she doesn't know I'm here. Even my wife doesn't know where I am.

After an hour we're airborne again and I take a last look out the window. It's 2005, probably eight more years before I'll see the Seattle skyline again. The Emerald City fades away as the plane banks and climbs higher. In eight years I don't know where Carole and I will make our home. We may want to make a start in a new city, or even a new country.

I see Oklahoma City again as the plane taxis. It's my fifth time here and I know the routine. Hobbling in my chains, I'm eager to fill out the forms and turn them in. The sooner processing begins, the sooner I'll find out where I'm going.

"Do you know where you're going?" the woman in uniform asks.

I shake my head "no," and pass her my intake forms.

"Santos, Michael," she says and moves her forefinger down the list of names on her computer printout. "Big Spring, Texas," she says, and my heart sinks. "No, wait, you've been re-designated. You're going to Lompoc Camp."

342

* * * * * * *

Among prisoners, Lompoc Camp on the Central Coast of California has a reputation of being the crown jewel of the federal prison system. For years I've heard that administrators reserved Lompoc Camp for politicians who've run afoul of the law and for powerful white-collar offenders.

Traveling by bus up the Pacific Coast Highway, with the salty smell of the ocean filling my lungs, invokes pleasurable childhood memories of visiting my grandparents in Los Angeles while on summer vacations. I remember swimming with my sisters at different California beaches, jumping into the waves that roll endlessly onto the shoreline. As I look at the ocean, I try to remember the sensation of floating in water. I contemplate what it might feel like to submerge my body. For 18 years the only water I've felt has sprayed from a spigot. I can't remember the sensation of buoyancy. In eight years Carole and I will bathe together and we'll swim in that ocean.

Klein Boulevard, the long thoroughfare leading into the Lompoc Federal Correctional Complex, is a crumbling asphalt road riddled with potholes. On my right is the fenced boundary of the medium-security prison, and on my left is the low-security prison. As the bus lurches along the dilapidated road toward the camp, prisoners in green uniforms walk freely on scenic trails winding between tall eucalyptus trees that fragrantly scent the air. I appreciate the natural beauty.

After six hours of processing, guards hand us our ID cards and bedrolls. I join four other prisoners walking outside the gates from the Receiving and Discharge building in the higher-security prison. Walking ahead of the crowd, I pass the field where a group of prisoners play soccer. Further down the road several men pump iron at the camp's weight pile. Pinecones that fall from the trees litter the path I'm on.

The housing unit resembles a steel, prefabricated warehouse, and the laid back guard inside looks more like a member of ZZ Top, with his long beard, black sunglasses, heavy silver rings with Gothic designs. Tattoos of double lightning bolts, flames, skulls, and cross bones cover his forearms. He's in a messy office, holding a *Maxim* magazine with a young woman in panties, sucking a lollipop, on the cover. He's leaning back in his chair, with crossed legs and heavy black leather boots resting casually on a gray metal desk.

I stand in front of him with my bedroll and the other new prisoners begin to crowd into the office, lining up behind me. The guard ignores us while flipping the pages of his magazine. Green canvas duffle bags are scattered on the scuffed and dingy tile floors. A desk fan blows and a radio broadcasts hardcore rap music by Tupac.

"Wazzup?" The guard finally lowers his magazine.

I give him my ID card and the other prisoners follow my lead.

"You guys the fresh meat?" he asks, turning down the volume of the radio.

We stand still, waiting as the guard sorts through index cards. He then pulls his feet from the desk and stands.

"Follow me," he says.

We follow him out of the office and down the narrow hall to the right. It empties into an open space as large as a private airplane hangar. For the crown jewel of the BOP, it's mighty tarnished. Six columns of gray metal bunks, 30 rows deep, fill the immense room. The noisy, crowded accommodations have a putrid stench. I follow the guard as he leads us down the center aisle and taps the fourth bed in column four.

"Santos. This is you."

He keeps walking with the others. I put down my belongings and prepare to settle in.

* * * * * * *

"Santos!" I hear the loudspeaker. "Inmate Michael Santos. Number 16377-004. Report to the administration building. Immediately!"

Not again, I groan inwardly. I've only been at Lompoc Camp for a day and I'm already being paged. I walk the short distance for yet another confrontation with BOP administrators. As I pass by a sparkling white Dodge Intrepid sedan with darkly tinted windows and three small antennae sticking out of the car's rear end, I assume it's from the fleet of the Federal Correctional Complex security force. A closer look at the elaborate communication system inside the car confirms my suspicions. Someone is here to interrogate me.

Through the smoked glass of the building's front door sits a receptionist. I knock, waiting for her to acknowledge me before opening the door. I've heard other prisoners refer to her as "the dragon lady," so I don't open the door until she indicates it's okay. It's a standoff, but I'm prepared to wait all day. I prefer the wait to being scolded and bullied.

After several minutes, she grasps that I'm not going to open the door, and I'm not going to knock again. She looks up, annoyed, and motions me in.

"I'm Michael Santos." I present my ID card. "I heard a page to the administration building."

Before she can answer, a stocky man with a chiseled face and a military-style crew cut steps into the doorway of the conference room. He's wearing a heavily starched BOP uniform.

"I paged you, come in." He directs me to a chair at the side of the table.

"Sit down. Do you know who I am?"

"No." I shake my head.

"I'm Lieutenant Merkle. Special Investigative Services." He opens a burgundy leather portfolio on the table. "It's generally not a good sign when I call an inmate for a meeting."

"I'm familiar with the role of the SIS." These guards can't intimidate me.

"I'm sure you are."

The room is quiet as he flips through his papers.

"So you're the writer. Do you know why you're here?"

"Yes, I do." I nod my head.

"And what's your interpretation?"

"When I was in my early 20s, I sold cocaine. I've been a prisoner since then, and as a prisoner I'm susceptible to these kinds of summons."

The lieutenant glances up at me. "So you're a wise guy?"

"Not at all. That's why I'm here. If I hadn't sold cocaine, we wouldn't be talking right now."

He stares at me. "But you did sell cocaine. Now you're an inmate in my institution."

He pulls out a page from his portfolio. "I received a letter from Lieutenant Knowles, SIS at Florence."

"Okay."

"You were transferred here administratively because your writing presented a threat to the security of that institution."

"How so?"

"It doesn't matter. Point is, you're in my institution now and I'm here to give you notice. If you write anything that threatens the security of my institution, I'm not going to transfer you. Instead, I'll bury you so deep in the SHU that no one will ever find you. Do you understand that?"

"What do you consider a threat to the security of the institution?"

"You're a wise guy, you figure it out. But if I lock you up for an investigation, you won't have access to telephone, mail, or visits. Do you understand?"

"For what, though?" I gesture with open hands. "I've never written a sentence that threatened security. All my work urges people to act responsibly and to lead law-abiding lives. I live by that rule. Why would you consider my writing a threat?"

"I ask the questions. I don't answer them," the lieutenant snaps, closing his file.

"Can I ask if you're placing me on mail-monitoring status?"

"Inmate Santos, you're starting here with a clean slate, no mail monitoring, no restrictions. Don't threaten security in my institution and you won't have any problems. If you see me again, it won't be good for you."

"One more thing, Lieutenant. While I was in Florence I wrote a book about what I've observed in prison. St. Martin's Press has the manuscript and intends to publish it in 2006. Is that book going to be a problem?"

He rubs his chin. "We'll visit that issue when the book comes out."

* * * * * * *

The SIS interview alerts me to my high-profile status at Lompoc and I walk out of the meeting expecting resistance from the staff. I can deal with that. *Inside* is in publication and St. Martin's Press is launching an international release that will put my work before tens of thousands. I'm willing to pay whatever price the system exacts so long as I leave prison with more skills and resources that will contribute to my family's stability.

But I also need to coast for a while, to lower my visibility and to consolidate my gains in preparation for my next project, whatever that is.

In the meantime I pay attention to two factors that influence peace in prison, a bunk assignment and a job assignment. In Lompoc's warehouse-style living, we're packed in. When I sit up on my top rack, all I see is a grid of metal bunks, with more than 160 prisoners stuffed inside the room. If I stretch out my hands, I touch the top of another man's head. If I stand on the two-feet of floor space between my bunk and metal locker, I can't open my arms without invading the space of another prisoner.

My housing unit, one of two at Lompoc Camp, is so tight its only function is to provide a place for prisoners to sleep, not to offer extra space for desks, televisions, or table games. Our inadequate community bathroom has three urinals, five toilets in stalls so small my knees touch the door when I sit, seven sinks, and four usable showers for 160 men. Prisoners clean their plastic food bowls in the same sinks where they brush their teeth. Oatmeal or last night's dinner always clogs the drain. Despite the work of the orderlies, the bathrooms remain in various stages of filth.

The living conditions in Lompoc Camp, the "crown jewel" of the federal prison system, rate as the worst I've experienced. It doesn't make a difference where I sleep, as one bunk is the same as the next. Still, despite the wretched housing, Lompoc has advantages that warrant its positive reputation. The scenic surroundings, marginal levels of staff supervision, and a high level of personal freedom combine to offset the tight quarters.

Since I can't find privacy where I sleep, I try for a job assignment that will give me some space. I want an orderly job in the housing unit, cleaning floors, toilets, or hallways. That job requires two hours of work at most each day, which would leave sufficient time to write. Mr. Castro is the counselor at Lompoc who assigns jobs to prisoners and I wait in line to see him with hopes of influencing his decision.

Mr. Castro's office is in the front of the dorm, directly across the narrow hallway from the unit officer's station where I saw the ZZ Top guard. Before I approach him, I ask Rick, a prisoner who's been in for seven years, how Castro responds to inmate requests for jobs.

"Bring him candy," Rick suggests.

"What do you mean?"

"Dude likes candy. Seriously. Bring him a Hershey's bar and you might have a chance."

"That might work for someone else. If I did it, he'd charge me with attempted bribery."

"Tell him you found two Hershey bars on top of your locker," Rick advises. "Since they're not yours, and you don't know who the candy belongs to, tell him you're turning them in. Then ask him for the job you want."

I laugh and thank Rick for the heads up. But I knock on Castro's door empty-handed.

"Come in," I hear him say, and I open the door. He sits behind his desk, looking like a beach ball, round and short.

"Mr. Castro, I'm Michael Santos, and I just arrived here. I'd like to speak with you about my job assignment."

The counselor folds his pudgy hands across his corpulent belly and grins. "I know who you are, Mr. Santos. Where do you want to work?"

"I've been in a long time. I'm hoping for a job that will give me time to write. I'd like to work as an orderly."

"Watch the callout. I've got a job in mind for you and it's not as an orderly." He keeps grinning but doesn't offer any hints.

The "callout" is the daily printout the staff posts for inmate scheduling. It lists appointments with medical staff, program assignments, unit team meetings, bed changes, and inmate jobs. When I see my name assigned to the farm, I understand Trent's grin. He prefers me shoveling cow manure to wielding a pen.

Lompoc Camp operates a working farm, several thousand acres in size, with herds of cattle, horses, and dairy cows. The dairy requires a large crew of prisoners to milk and tend to more than 300 cows daily. Prison "cowboys" perform all the ranch labor raising cattle for beef; yet another prison crew maintains the acres of corn and soybeans grown to feed the cattle. One small crew of prisoners drives 18-wheelers between Lompoc and Arizona to deliver milk produced at the camp. Those prisoners sleep in motels and eat in restaurants four days a week without staff supervision.

Besides the ranching operation, the 350 camp prisoners provide manpower to sustain the adjacent low-security and medium-security prisons. Prisoners fill positions as electricians, plumbers, painters, carpenters, landscapers, mechanics, wastewater treatment operators, and clerical workers for a community of 5,000 inmates and staff.

Some camp inmates experience an unusually high degree of freedom in their jobs, even being assigned government vehicles. While working on the farm or away from the camp, those prisoners can manipulate time for themselves. As such, Lompoc is a haven for every kind of contraband and unauthorized trysts with wives and girlfriends.

Neither the work nor the extra freedom serves my purposes. Unlike the recently convicted politicians and white collar professionals who serve short sentences at Lompoc Camp, my old-law sentence comes with an advantage that makes taking liberty with the rules dangerous. Under old-law I earn more good time. A disciplinary infraction can reduce the 19 years of good-time credit I earn against my 45-year sentence. To earn freedom, I focus exclusively on preparations that will contribute to my success upon release while avoiding behavior and interactions that could extend my imprisonment.

* * * * * * *

Carole finishes her summer courses in Colorado and she and Nichole sell most of their belongings in a yard sale. I haven't seen my wife for 73 days since they locked me in the Florence SHU. A thousand miles separated us on our second wedding anniversary on June 24, 2005, while I was in transit to Lompoc. We burn through our monthly allotment of 300 telephone minutes with endearments. It isn't enough. My mother, my grandmother, Julie, and Christina, make the long trip to Lompoc while I wait for Carole. Guards returned my wedding ring to me when they processed me in, but it still isn't enough. I ache for my wife, for the softness of her kiss.

I stand outside behind the dorm, under a row of eucalyptus trees that line the road, and I watch as Carole follows seven other cars driving slowly around the potholes to enter the FCC. My heart beats for her. When I see her turquoise Saturn approach, I smile. She drove across Colorado, New Mexico, Arizona, and California to join me, and I feel as if I'm the luckiest man alive, despite the fact that I'm beginning my 19th year in prison.

I see her turn into the camp. We wave as she drives just a few feet from me. While she parks and stands in line for processing, I walk around to the back, sit on a bench under a pine tree and wait for the visiting room guard to page me.

"Santos! Visit!" I hear the page over loudspeakers that blast through the camp.

Eager to see her, touch her, hold her again, I hand my ID card to the guard at the desk. Then I search for my wife in the crowded visiting room. She's at the vending machines waiting to purchase a cup of coffee, wearing pressed blue jeans, a white cotton blouse, and black heels that bring the top of her head to my eye level. We hold each other tightly and kiss.

"I missed you, Baby," she whispers into my ear.

"You're beautiful, prettier than ever. I'm so glad you're here," I tell her.

"We'll never stay apart this long again."

"I missed you terribly. Come on, let's sit outside." Although the living conditions at Lompoc Camp disappoint me, the camp visiting area surpasses any we've experienced. A front yard has 20 wooden picnic tables, some with two seats, others with four. They're set on a closely cut, lush green lawn still wet with morning dew on this August morning. A two-rail fence of rough timber outlines the perimeter of the visiting area. Toward the end of the yard there's a concrete bench next to a wooden carving of a friendly-looking California black bear. I lead Carole to the bench where we can sit in the shade of a tall eucalyptus tree. Through the thin forest of pines outside the visiting area, we catch glimpses of prisoners inside the gates of the adjacent low-security prison playing tennis and soccer.

"Wow! It's so beautiful here. It doesn't look like a prison," Carole muses. "Who takes such good care of the roses?"

"You'll meet him later. We call him Dave the Flower Man. He's one of the guys I've met."

"Why's he here?"

"He's a land developer from the Tahoe area, serving about a year for a business deal that went bad."

I tell Carole about the camp, about how it differs from everywhere else I've been, and that I'd like to stay here until I go home. But Carole isn't so pleased with it. She suggests that I put in for a transfer.

"Why?" I ask.

"Honey, it's going to cost me twice as much to live here as it did in Florence. I've been looking all week. Everything's more expensive, including rent, gas, and food. I'm worried about being able to afford it."

"What about school? Can you start in September?"

Carole tells me about the waiting list. In Colorado, she was scheduled to begin nursing school in September and to graduate in 2008 with a bachelor of nursing degree.

"The soonest I'm going to get into a nursing program here is in January of 2007. I won't even earn my vocational nursing degree until May of 2008, and the RN's another year after that. I don't think we'll have enough money to live here. I think you should try to transfer to Oregon, or someplace less expensive."

"Honey, it's not that easy. I've only been here for two months. No one is going to listen if I ask for a transfer, not until I've been here for at least 18 months."

"Why not? Even the SIS doesn't want you here. What's going to happen if I settle here and they transfer you again?"

I squeeze Carole's hands to reassure her. "Then we'll have to deal with it. I can ask for a transfer in the spring of 2007, but then you'll be in the nursing program. Let's make it work here."

"You've said yourself that you can't control what they're going to do to you, and the SIS has already warned you. They can take you away in the middle of the night, just like they did at

Fort Dix and at Florence." Carole's voice reveals her concern.

"I promise you, I won't do anything that causes trouble," I say, putting my arm around her.

"But you never cause trouble."

"I mean I won't write anything about prison. I'm not going to do anything that they would consider a threat to the security of their precious institution. I'll work at the dairy and I'll live like a prisoner until you finish nursing school. St. Martin's Press will release *Inside* next year and you'll receive more money when it does. We can generate more revenues through our website to help. That, along with other royalty checks will get you through nursing school. We have to make our lives work here. We'll need that security for when I come home."

* * * * * * *

Mr. Griggs, the unit manager at Lompoc Camp, loves to smoke. While standing beneath the blue and white striped awning outside the administration building, he admires rings of nicotine clouds that hang over his head. Today he watches me walk across the parking lot toward him.

"May I talk to you?" I stop outside the yellow line under the awning so as not to penetrate his space.

"Open house is at three." He shuts me down.

"I'll have to be at work then. It's only a question," I persist.

Mr. Griggs blows a cloud of smoke above his head, and he looks up to admire his work. "What is it?"

"I'd like you to authorize a job change for me."

"Why?"

"I've been working at the dairy for six months. I need to spend more time preparing for the career I want to build upon release."

"Release? Don't you have like five more years to go?"

"I get out in 2013, in seven more years."

"It's too soon for you to be thinking about release. The needs of the institution come first. You can stay at the dairy."

"The clerk in the powerhouse is leaving. I've been waiting to switch to that job." He blows another cloud of smoke, watching as it rises.

"Let me think about it."

* * * * * * *

In the spring of 2006, I finally prevail upon Mr. Griggs to authorize my job change from the dairy to the powerhouse. The powerhouse operates three massive boilers that generate steam to heat the adjacent medium-security penitentiary. It requires around-the-clock staffing. As the powerhouse clerk, I become friendly with Mr. Brown, the manager, and with his many subordinates who alternate shifts as foreman. I have an office with a large desk and credenza and bookshelves, an electric typewriter with memory, file cabinets, and a cushioned office chair. When I close the door, I'm alone.

My job requires a few duties. I keep records of all energy expenditures for the Federal Correctional Complex; I complete regulatory "safety" forms; and I tally timesheets for the 100 prisoners assigned as laborers. It's tedious administrative work, but I develop a system that allows me to stay current with my responsibilities while setting aside a few hours each day for my correspondence and independent writing projects.

I've made a new friend and mentor, Dr. Sam Torres. After retiring as a senior United States Parole Officer, he became a professor of Criminal Justice at the California State University in Long Beach. He uses my first book, *About Prison*, as required reading for courses he teaches in corrections, and that leads to a correspondence between us. Dr. Torres tried to visit when I was in Florence, and again when I moved to Lompoc. Mr. Griggs and senior BOP administrators refuse him permission on the grounds of preserving security in the institution.

They cite policy that prohibits prisoners from visiting with people they did not know prior to confinement. Ironically, as writing puts me in contact with more people, BOP administrators become more vigilant in their efforts to isolate me from society. Dr. Torres extends me the privilege of interacting with his class, and I respond to written questions from future parole officers and prison administrators whom he teaches.

My work in the powerhouse becomes much easier when Mr. Brown, one of the shop foremen, gives me a sleek new Dell computer with a speedy laser printer. It's loaded with software for word processing and spreadsheets that improve the accuracy of my work. By using the computer, I can complete in an hour what used to take five. It's a wonderful tool. I appreciate the time it saves as well as the opportunity to learn new technology.

As the powerhouse clerk, I work for all the foremen and for Mr. Johnson, the managing department head, but Mr. Brown is the foreman who hired me. He's my primary supervisor and he looks out for me. He is in his late 40s, a family man who expresses pride when he talks with me about his children. His wife lives nearby and she sometimes drops food by the powerhouse that he shares. Mr. Brown treats me like a man, an employee, rather than a prisoner. When he or any of the other staff members ask for help with personal writing, I don't hesitate.

"Mr. Brown, is it okay with you if I use the computer to work on some of my writing projects?"

"What're you writing? Another book?"

"Maybe. I don't know, I'm thinking about it. I'm here all day, and when I'm finished with my work I'd like to write, as long as it's okay with you."

"As far as I'm concerned, the computer's no different than a typewriter." He shrugs his shoulders. "It's not connected to the Internet. I can't see how anyone would have a problem with you writin' on it."

* * * * * * *

I'm about to complete my nineteenth year in prison, and I only have seven more years in front of me. Carole lives only a few miles away, close enough to visit every Saturday, Sunday, and federal holiday. Nichole is an honor student. She'll graduate from high school in June of 2008, a full year ahead of schedule. My job at the powerhouse is a breeze, leaving me with only one concern: finances. I'm responsible for providing the money to cover Carole's living expenses and I don't want her to have any financial concerns while she studies through nursing school.

"Honey, I think I should try to write another book," I suggest at the start of our visit.

She shakes her head. "Please, no more problems. We've got enough to worry about with *Inside* coming out in August. We don't know what the SIS is going to do with you once the BOP reads it, but at least you wrote it before you transferred here. He already warned you what would happen if you wrote a new book, and I'm scheduled to start the nursing program in January. Please, I'm begging you, don't do anything that could disrupt our lives again."

I hold her hand. "It's your school I'm thinking about. I've got to make sure you have enough money. What good is starting school if you don't have enough money to finish?"

"What good is it if I start school and the SIS locks you up and transfers you across country? And what if they take away our visiting?"

"I can write from SHU, I can exercise in a cell. And if they take away our visiting, we'll deal with it. What's important is that you're a nurse when I come home, because no matter how much I prepare, I might face some real challenges earning an income after 26 years in prison. We'll need your earning stability."

"What do you want to write?" Carole asks.

"I've met so many businessmen here. I could start interviewing guys who serve time for fraud, securities violations, or tax problems. I'm thinking of writing their stories for a book we could call *White Collar*. Instead of writing about prison, I'd write to describe how educated people unknowingly make decisions that lead them to prison. I think there's a market for it and I don't see how anyone could accuse me of threatening security. But I promised you I wouldn't do anything that might bring problems unless you agreed. What do you think?"

"I'm afraid they'll take you away."

"Do you trust me?"

"Of course."

"Would you still love me, stay married to me if they took me away and if we couldn't visit?"

"I'll always love you, and I'll always stay married to you, but please don't talk about being taken away."

"We both know that could happen at any time. We need to base our decisions on our future, not our visiting. Writing is the only way I can earn money for us, but I want your agreement, I need you to buy in to this plan."

Carole shakes her head, but acquiesces. "Whatever you

think is best."

* * * * * * *

Mr. Smith is the camp guard on the evening shift. He likes war books, particularly those about World War II and the Third Reich. Generally, I avoid guards, as instinct tells me they're out to score points with their superiors by writing disciplinary infractions. But someone told Mr. Smith that I'm a writer. He likes to talk to me about my work and his career, especially about his time as a soldier in Iraq. Smith once told me that he likes violence, and that he's "good at it." He's also disappointed that a reprimand for using excessive force on an inmate blemishes his employment record; that record, together with low scores on aptitude tests, hinders his chances for a job with the Highway Patrol. He dresses the part, riding into the camp each afternoon on his Harley, wearing a black, chrome-studded bomber jacket, a white helmet reminiscent of a Prussian soldier, and mirrored sunglasses in thin metal frames.

I see Mr. Smith when I return to the camp after finishing an evening shift at the powerhouse. When I ask him for my mail, he hands it over and initiates a conversation.

"Read your book," he nods his head and squirts tobacco into his disposable cup. "Good stuff. Only objection I got is that you write prison guard 'stead of correctional officer."

"I'm describing prison from a prisoner's perspective," I explain. "It's what I see. Why would that bother you?"

"Because we're not just prison guards. We've got training, policies we follow to maintain order."

"I don't write 'guard' to demean anyone, but I'm trying to show the reader accurately what prison is about. In 19 years, I've never felt the system was trying to correct me, or anyone else. Although it's called 'corrections,' and 'correctional officers' supposedly staff the system, the primary emphasis is on protecting the security of the institution. That's guarding the prison, not corrections."

"Thing is, ain't nothin' much we can do to 'correct' half the knuckleheads we got runnin' 'round the joint. Only thing they understand is a swift kick in the ass."

"That's where we disagree," I counter. "The use of force

356

instead of incentives is the main reason the prison system has such a high rate of failure, wasting billions of dollars in taxpayer resources."

"How's it not workin'?" Mr. Smith smirks. "Ain't no one escapin'."

"That's because you're guarding the prison, but you're not correcting anyone. Incentives that would include mechanisms for prisoners to work toward earning freedom would change that. They would motivate more people to grow and prepare for success."

"Sounds like a bunch of liberal bullshit." He spits into his cup.

"Fancy yourself a conservative, do you?"

"Damn straight." He walks around the desk and drops into his chair.

"Small government and all that?"

"You got it, brother. Stars and stripes all the way."

"Then how do you explain your government paycheck and guaranteed pension? You've got what, a high school diploma, but you're pulling down enough to buy a Harley, a boat, an RV, and you get more vacation than anyone in the private sector. For what?"

"Maintain' order. That's what."

"I guess that's your take. From my perspective, prisons cause more harm than good. I write what I see."

"You and I ain't so diff'rent. I could see us on the outside, bringin' the little ladies out for a bite while we chug brewskies and disagree over how the world ought to be run."

"That's going to have to wait. I've got seven more years to be corrected."

* * * * * * *

Lee Nobmann surrenders to Lompoc Camp in early July of 2006. He's in his early 50s, clean cut with snow-white hair, clear blue eyes, and a stocky build. He's alone, sitting at a picnic table that overlooks a lush valley on his first day. I'm at the next table and notice him as a new face, one that looks more like a businessman than a prisoner. I'm always fishing for prisoners from whom I can learn, especially businessmen whose stories I can write about in *White Collar*.

While I'm stealing a glance at the title of the book he reads, trying to gather clues of his interests, our eyes connect. "Are you a fan of John Grisham?" I ask him.

"What's that?" he smiles.

"John Grisham, the author of your book. Have you read much of his other work?" I walk toward his table.

He flips the book over to look at the cover. "I just picked it off the shelf in the library. I was looking for something to kill time."

I put out my hand. "I'm Michael Santos. Welcome."

"Lee Nobmann," we shake hands.

"Have you settled in okay?" I ask.

"I'm getting the hang of it," he nods his head. "It's a little slow."

"Believe me, it gets easier. How long are you going to be with us?"

"About a year. How about you?"

"I've got seven more to go, but they pass quickly, I know."

"Ouch. It hurts to hear you say it."

I smile. "It's not so bad. I've been in for a long time."

"Really? How long? I've met some guys who've been in for several years?"

"I've been in since 1987. I'm finishing my 19th year."

"*My God*! And you've got seven more to go? That's an entire life. How old are you?" He asks.

"I'm 42."

"What did you do? If you don't mind my asking?"

"No, I don't mind. I didn't pay my taxes."

"You're kidding."

"Well, I sold cocaine, too, but that's beside the point."

He laughs. "Are you serious? You've been in prison for 19 years? How come you look so normal? I thought you just came in too."

I nod my head. "What can I say? I've earned a gold medal for serving time."

"That's the craziest sentence I've ever heard. Sorry to hear it."

_ "I've been blessed in many ways. I've got a great wife, and through writing I've found a way to connect with the world."

"What do you write about?"

"Prison," I laugh. "It's the only world I know. I try to give readers a look inside."

"What do you write? Articles or something?"

"I write books."

"No kidding. You can do that from here?"

"I do."

"Are any of them published?"

"A few. I'm writing a new one now for white-collar offenders, a book that can help businessmen and other professionals understand more about the system."

"I could've used something like that. I didn't know squat about what I was getting myself into."

"What kind of work do you do?"

"I'm in retail."

"What do you sell?"

"Lumber."

"Is that against the law?"

He laughs. "I've got a tax case."

"You mind talking about it? I like learning from guys like you."

"No, I don't mind. It's not that interesting though. I took some business deductions I shouldn't have."

"It might not be that interesting to you, but I'm sure businessmen from across the country would like to know how taking deductions can lead to a prison term."

"When you put it that way, I guess you're right," Lee acknowledges.

"Are you still in business?"

"Oh yeah."

"Good size company?"

"It's fair," he nods his head.

"How many employees?" I look for a sign that will tell me who I'm talking to.

"We've got close to 500."

"Five hundred employees," I laugh. "You call that a fair size company?"

He smiles, his eyes sparkling as he bounces his hand in the air. "Keep it down. I shouldn't have said that."

"Why not?"

"It's probably not a good thing to have going around in a place like this."

"What kind of revenue does a company like that take in?"

"We should do about 450 million this year."

"Four hundred and fifty million dollars? That's a monster of a company. Is it public?"

"No," he shakes his head. "It's a family business."

Lee and I talk at the picnic table until we have to go in for the 10:00 pm census. After the count clears, we return to the picnic table and talk until midnight, enjoying the warmth of summer and each other's company. He's down to earth, really at ease. I prod him with questions about how he built his business and I respond to his questions about what it's been like to live as a prisoner. I'm glad to have a new friend, someone I can admire and learn from. For someone in prison, a friend is the greatest thing in the world.

* * * * * * *

It's Monday, August 6, 2006, the day that *Inside: Life Behind Bars in America* hits bookstores across America. I wrote the proposal and sample chapter more than two years ago, and I've worked on the project in one way or another every day since. As I walk from my rack down the center hall of the housing unit to the bathroom, I check my watch. It's only six in California, but nine on the East Coast and bookstores have opened in New York, Washington, Boston, and other big cities. I stand in line waiting to use the sink, wondering whether anyone's reading my book. In only seven more years I'll walk into a bookstore or library and see books on a shelf with my name on the spine. But now, I need to remove the rice, beans, and hair someone left in the drain filter of the sink so I can brush my teeth before work.

My job in the powerhouse gives me a great escape from the crowded feeling of the housing unit. I like to spend time in what I've come to call 'my office.' It's small, only enough room for one, and I've personalized it. A picture of Carole and me rests on a black metal file cabinet in a frame that I bought from a guy who devotes hours to craft projects; he wove the frame out of discarded potato chip bags, shiny side out. On the shelf above my desk, I have dictionaries, reference books, quotation books, and an almanac. When I close the door I'm alone, productive. The guards on duty leave me to my work, except when they need help with their own projects.

"Did you see this?" Mr. Lime asks me. He works in the office next to mine as the shop supervisor, and he hands me an Internet printout from *The Los Angeles Times Sunday Book Review.* Ed Humes, a Pulitzer Prize-winning author wrote about my book, *Inside,* and the full-page review has my photograph.

"Thanks," I say. I feel validated, because although I'm a long-term prisoner, my work is now published in open society and this review will forever bolster my résumé. I strive to prove worthy of Carole's love and of the support I receive from so many people. It thrills me to have the review that exposes my work to millions.

"You got a copy of the book?" Mr. Lime asks.

"I'll have some this week, assuming the mailroom passes them through."

"Let me check it out."

"You bet, boss."

Two hours pass and I'm using a plastic spoon to dig tuna from its pack when Mr. Johnson opens the door behind me. I set the pack down on the credenza and spin my chair around to face him. His smoker's rasp, out of the left side of his mouth since his cigarette is on the right side, adds to his East Texas hillbilly twang. I like him.

"Caught that piece 'bout ya in the paper," he said.

"Thanks," I reply.

He stands in the doorframe, papers in his hand, with the unlit cigarette dangling from his lips. His tie is loosened, the top button of his blue shirt undone. Through brown reading glasses he studies the papers he holds.

"Can I help you with something?" I ask, gathering that he wants something.

"If ya please, I'd like ya ta take a look at some papers."

"Anything, of course."

"Job's comin' up, project manager for the city of Santa Maria. I done filled out a résumé, cover letter, and what have ya. Seein' as yer a writer and all, think ya could look it over for me?"

"Absolutely."

Mr. Johnson passes me his papers and then stands watching over me as I read through them. I've been working as the powerhouse clerk for six months and we have an easy relationship. He uses profanity when he tells me stories about his weekends. He says that he watches a standup comedian by the name of Larry the Cable Guy. Despite the familiarity, I'm intuitively uncomfortable evaluating his shoddy writing and don't know what I should say.

"Would it be okay if I made some suggestions?"

"You betcha. I was hopin' ya'd fix it up."

"It would probably be easier if I retyped it."

"Fix whatever it needs. I know I got some weaknesses, seein' as I didn't finish college and they're asking' for a college diploma, but I'll be retirin' with 30 years in the Bureau, runnin' facilities of ev'ry size. That oughta count for somethin'. Doctor it up as best ya can."

"I'm going to need a few hours."

"Take as long as you like. I'll pick'r up tomorra." He walks out, leaving me alone.

* * * * * * *

Jeff, a recent Lompoc arrival from Seattle, is in the beginning months of a 10-year sentence for selling cocaine. I'm standing in the narrow space between my bunk and my locker when he taps me on the shoulder.

"Have you seen this article?" Jeff passes me the magazine section from *The Seattle Times,* Sunday, September 24, 2006. My picture is on the cover, showcasing a story by Stewart Eskenazi, the same guy who covered my trial for the newspaper. My letter to him in 1988 led to an interview and a front-page story where I expressed regret for selling cocaine and committed to using my time in prison to reform and contribute to society. The reporter's follow-up story, two decades later, describes my progress. Jeff's parents had sent him the magazine to encourage him as he began serving his sentence.

I open the magazine and I flip through the pages. "I've read the text of the article. But this is the first time I've seen the magazine. My sister sent me a copy but I haven't gotten it yet."

"Dude, I can't believe you've done all that from prison." Jeff nods in admiration.

"It's been a long time. Can I hold onto the magazine? I want to show it to a friend."

"Sure. My mom ordered your book for me."

"Cool, thanks for the support. I'll give you back the magazine when I get mine."

"Keep it." He says.

"Thanks, I appreciate it."

"No problem."

I walk through the narrow passage between bunks and turn down the crowded walkway to Lee's bunk. He's sitting on the metal chair in front of his open locker, wearing gray sweats and black reading glasses. He's placing his crisply folded clothes on the locker shelves.

"Can't you pay someone to do that for you? CEOs don't do the grunt work."

Lee laughs, brings his finger to his lips. "Some things a guy's gotta do for himself. What's up?"

"Check this out." I hand him the magazine. "Whoa! Cover story," he smiles. "That's cool."

"I'll leave it with you. Let's meet out on the picnic tables after count."

"You bet. Thanks."

The guards don't take long to count the 340 camp prisoners at Lompoc, and by 4:20, Lee and I walk with the crowd shoulder to shoulder down the dorm's narrow hall as if we're all part of a cattle herd. Some prisoners even moo. Once we pass through the door and we're in the clear, he tells me how impressed he was with the article. The sun is still warm as we move into California's Indian summer.

"Why aren't more of these guys doing what you did?" Lee asks. "Seems all anyone wants to do around here is play cards and waste time."

"It's not really their fault. Prison has a rigid structure, and

363

it doesn't offer any hope for these guys. A prisoner can do any number of things that'll bring him more problems, but there's no mechanism that encourages him to better his life or shorten his sentence. Trying to get an education is almost impossible with all of the staff resistance. He can't work toward improving himself, and since the system doesn't see him for more than the crime that put him in here, the default response is to just give up and accept that prison is for serving time."

"You didn't."

"It was different for me. I had so much time to serve that I knew prison was going to eat up a big chunk of my life. I didn't want it to define me. I knew that I didn't want to be prisonized, and I knew that if I didn't educate myself I'd never be able to function outside."

"This system is messed up. We've got to do something to change it."

"That's what my work is about. One advantage of having served this much time is that I have credibility with other prisoners. I hope to show them by example that with discipline they can develop skills that will prepare them to reenter society and have meaningful lives. Few want to live as criminals, but when they don't believe in themselves, they give up. That failure pattern starts when they're young. Without understanding the consequences, kids drop out of school, join gangs, sell drugs, and when they come to prison, they fall further into failure. Through example, I hope to show how they can climb out."

"But how? The people who need the message most don't buy books. Many don't even read."

"They only read about what interests them, and you're right, they don't buy books. But if I write about people they identify with, experiences and lifestyles they identify with, I can help. What I need is sponsorship. I need to find businesses and organizations with a social conscience that will buy and distribute the books to those who need them. When I'm out, I'll find those sponsors. I hope you'll help."

"Why wait until you get out?" Lee asks. "I'll sponsor you right now. What would you like to do?"

As we sit at the picnic table, Lee listens as I pitch two book ideas. I propose interviewing prisoners who will talk about their criminal histories. Specifically, I want to write about people who quit school, joined gangs, and became involved with drugs or crime. I suggest a book that would profile prisoners and be followed by a series of open-ended discussion questions for the readers to consider. With Lee's sponsorship, I could produce and distribute the books free to schools with large groups of at-risk kids. Teachers and counselors could use the books to show actual stories of the consequences that follow criminal decisions.

The second book would be for adults who are beginning their terms in prison. That book would also tell prisoners' stories, but the stories would highlight steps they took to turn their lives around and to live responsibly. This book would show how anyone could use discipline and readily available prison resources to prepare for a successful life upon release.

"What would you call that one?" Lee asks.

"I haven't thought it through yet, but I'd base it on what I've learned."

"I'll sponsor those projects right now. Count on me for $75,000. That should give you enough to write and print both books, distribute them at no charge, and take the pressure off Carole while she finishes school."

"Are you serious?"

"Believe me, my family's been blessed in many ways," he says. "I'm completely serious. One lesson I've learned is that supporting worthwhile projects for society comes back a hundred-fold. Besides, after all the work you've done in here, you deserve it."

Chapter Thirteen: 2007
Months 232-233

It's Wednesday, April 18, 2007 and our family is making excellent progress. While Carole studies for the final exams to complete her first semester of nursing school, I'm finishing the writing projects that I began with Lee Nobmann's sponsorship. Despite the six years of prison that I have ahead, I'm making progress, living a productive life, and that makes all of the difference in the world.

Mr. Dorkin, a guard who joyfully equates harassing men in minimum-security camps with protecting the homeland, opens the door to the office at 2:00 in the afternoon while I'm typing. Dorkin's a guard I avoid. He's constantly annoying prisoners and his sudden appearance in my office alarms me.

"Yes?" I say as I look up and see Mr. Brown, my supervisor, standing behind him.

Dorkin's grinning. "Santos," he commands. "Stand up, take your hands off the keyboard, and put them behind your head."

Not a stranger to these orders, I comply. Dorkin puts his big hands on me. He pats my chest, my waist, and then runs his fingers along the inside of my belt. He pats each of my legs, swiveling his two-handed grip down each leg to my sneakers, then he inserts his finger between my shoe and ankle.

"Would you prefer that I take my shoes off?" I ask.

"There'll be plenty of time for that. Just keep lookin' straight ahead." Mr. Dorkin orders. "Okay, drop your hands. Put 'em behind your back."

He unsnaps one of the leather pouches of his black belt and removes the cuffs. The familiar sound of clicking metal teeth follows cold steel closing around my wrists. I wonder when such intrusions into my life will end, if ever.

"What kind 'a contraband am I gonna find in here?" he asks.

"I don't have any contraband," I state unequivocally, wondering what this moron wants with me.

"Gee. I've never heard that before," he says sarcastically. Then he spins me to the door, grabbing the chain between my handcuffs to steer me toward it. "Let's go. Move it."

Dorkin marches me down the hallway and out into the sunshine where I see a white Dodge Intrepid waiting. He opens the car's rear door and, with his palm on my head, he pushes me into the back seat. He straps the seatbelt over my waist and then slams the door shut. I look through the tinted window at Mr. Brown, relatively certain that this will be the last time I see him.

Through the black metal mesh separating his seat from mine, Dorkin taunts me. "Got anything to say, Santos?"

I continue staring out the window, immune to his heckling. "Take me wherever you're taking me and do what you've got to do."

"That's the way you wanna play it?" Dorkin uses his authority like a weapon and he's accustomed to having an effect on prisoners. When I don't respond, he scowls because I've spoiled his game.

Silently, I watch as we pass through the eucalyptus and pine trees. Although I don't know why I'm being harassed this time, I'm pretty sure I won't be seeing Lompoc Camp again. At the double gates that lead to the Special Housing Unit, Dorkin pulls the radio from his belt, brings it to his mouth says: "Got one for SHU."

The gates open and he drives inside, parks in front of a second gate, and turns off the car. Another guard walks toward the car and opens the back door.

"What we got here?" the new guard asks. "Another genius from the camp?"

"Ten-four," Dorkin says. "Lock 'im up. Captain's order."

The guard orders me out of the car, gripping the handcuffs behind my back as I scoot off the backseat and exit the vehicle. He steers me through the gates and into the building, then deeper inside the windowless, concrete maze. Surveillance cameras are mounted in every corner. Someone is always watching, as shadowy guards sit in a distant control center. They monitor our movements and control heavy deadbolts with electronic locks. I hear the click, and the doors open automatically. We pass through, and the doors lock behind us. This stark area of the prison reeks like a jail, like a law enforcement cavern that feels very, very sinister.

The holding cell isn't any bigger than a broom closet, and once I'm secured inside, I back up to the bars. The guard inserts his key to unlock my handcuffs. I open my arms to stretch and it's so narrow I can press against the opposing concrete walls at the same time. Another guard wheels a laundry bin to the gate.

"What size?" he asks me.

"Two X." I strip naked, not waiting for an order from the guard who returns with faded boxers, white tube socks with worn elastic, the requisite orange jumpsuit with chrome snaps, a towel, and a bedroll. He searches my body and after he peers into my rectum I pass inspection.

"Get dressed," he says.

In less than a minute I'm clothed in the bright orange SHU uniform and blue canvas deck shoes. A thousand prisoners have worn these same clothes before me, and a thousand more will wear them after I'm gone. I roll my shoulders in an attempt to shrug off my growing stress, then squat to the floor and hold my knees to my chest while resting my back against the concrete wall, waiting.

I can only see the gray concrete walls of my cell, the bars, the narrow hallway and concrete wall outside the cell. I don't have a sense of time but, in the distance, I hear the crackle of a radio and the electronic click of deadbolts locking or unlocking steel doors. I roll my head from side to side, trying to dissipate or ease off the tension.

Footsteps approach my cell and a guard appears. It's Velez, a guard from the camp.

"What're you doing here?" he stops in front of the gate.

"I don't know," I respond, looking up from the floor.

"Did you get a shot?"

"If I did, I wouldn't know it."

"Let me see what I can find out."

Velez walks away and I massage my forehead. Carole is going to take this hard. Yesterday she celebrated her 42nd birthday and now she's going to have to confront this new drama in our life. I don't know when I'll be able to call her. I hope my friend Lee has heard about my misfortune and that he'll relay a message to Carole soon. She needs to know that a guard took me away, even though she'll worry. This disruption might be much harder on her than it is on me. She has semester finals in May and doesn't need this stress.

Footsteps accompanied by the sound of jingling keys announce Velez's return.

"You're here under investigation," he states, completely devoid of emotion.

"For what?"

"Captain's order. Stand up. I've got to cuff you. I'll take you to your cell."

I back against the bars and feel the metal bracelets click locked around my wrists. He unlocks the gates and leads me down the hall, past the raised control center. Inside the hub, I see blinking lights and movements of two guards through darkly tinted glass. Velez waits for one of them to release the electronic lock on the first gate. We walk through and it closes behind us. With his large key he unlocks the second gate and then locks it behind us. We're in a tunnel, with cell doors on each side. I don't recognize any of the prisoners who peer through the windows in their doors. These men probably come from the adjacent low- or medium-security prisons at Lompoc.

We stop in front of a cell and Velez taps with his key on the small window within the door.

"Move to the back of the cell," he instructs as the prisoner inside begins to move. "Face the wall. Don't turn around."

Velez unlocks the steel door and nudges me inside. The door closes behind me and I hear the deadbolt lock. I back up and push my hands to the open trap. He unlocks and removes my cuffs then slams the trap shut. The sound of his footsteps and jingling keys fade as he walks down the tier toward the gates.

"How you doing, Bud?" I say to the large man who is still facing the far wall of the cell. He's tall, with unruly brown hair.

"Hi." He greets me as he turns around.

I extend my hand. "My name's Michael Santos."

370

"I'm Marty Frankl." We shake hands.

"Where're you coming from?"

"I was at Terminal Island," he names a low-security prison in Los Angeles. "I'm on my way to the camp. A paperwork mix-up has me stuck in here."

"That happens. How long have you been in the SHU?

"Since Monday."

"They'll probably have it straightened out by Friday. You'll like the camp once you get there."

"Are you from the camp?" He asks as he sits on the lower bunk.

I throw my bedroll on the top rack and start tying my sheets around the mat. "I've been there for two years. It's been the easiest time I ever served."

"Are you the writer?"

"That's me."

"My girlfriend's been sending printouts from your website ever since I was charged. Part of the reason I pled guilty was because of what you wrote."

"What kind of case do you have?"

"Money laundering. I'm serving eight years."

"It passes faster than you think. You'll like the camp better than Terminal Island."

"Are you going back?"

"I don't even know why they locked me up, but it's not a good sign. I've never served time in SHU for a shot, only for transfer to another prison."

"That sucks. I know you've been in a long time. How many years do you have left?"

"Six, maybe a little more. I'm scheduled for release in August of 2013."

I describe the camp for Marty and answer his many questions. He gives me some paper, an envelope, and stamps. I fold the end of the mat on my rack to prop up my chest and I use the steel bunk as a surface to write Carole a long letter, explaining what I know. It's the beginning of a journal she'll post on my website at MichaelSantos.net describing my experience.

In the evening, a guard slides a form under the cell door

that officially informs me that I'm being investigated for running a business.

* * * * * * *

Marty's paperwork clears the following morning and he transfers to the camp. I appreciate the single cell and I strip to my boxers to begin my solitary exercise routine: pushups, deep knee bends, running in place. I exercise until sweat puddles beneath me. Then I wash my boxers in the sink and hang them to dry from the top rack, ignoring the staff and administrators who periodically walk by and peer through the window in my door.

On Saturday morning a guard I don't recognize startles me by tapping his key on the small window, scowling.

"Santos! What're you here for?" I step toward the doorframe and speak to him through the crack. "Investigation for running a business."

He shakes his head. "Cuff up. You've got a visit."

Knowing that Carole is here, I tolerate the dehumanizing handcuffs and strip search when I leave the cell. I'll go through anything to see my wife. After the guard from the visiting room unlocks my cuffs, strip searches me again, and advises me of the rules, I walk into the tightly controlled visiting area with surveillance cameras in the ceiling and uniformed guards patrolling the aisles. Prisoners are required to sit at tables across from their visitors, neither touching nor holding hands. I walk to Carole. Her smile warms me, but tears glisten in her eyes. We hold each other briefly, not saying anything.

"We'd better sit, Honey. I don't know how long we have," I tell her.

Carole takes in my orange jumpsuit and blue canvas shoes, my unshaven face, knowing what it means.

"Don't cry, Honey. It's okay. It's okay. I'm okay."

She wipes her eyes. "I hate to see you like this. Are they transferring us again?"

"I don't know, but I'm fine. Come on. Don't cry. You'll make me sad."

"What do you want me to do?" she asks.

"Regardless of what happens to me, you have to stay in school and finish the nursing program. It's only two more semesters and we can't let my problems interfere."

"Why are they doing this to you?"

"All I know is that I'm being investigated for running a business. I don't know whether it's for *Inside,* our website, or the books that Lee sponsored."

"Melodee told me that Lee heard that the guards took the computer from your office."

I'm glad to hear that Lee told his wife what he knows, and that Melodee called Carole. "She said they would help with whatever we need, even hire you a lawyer."

I tell Carole that we don't need a lawyer and that she should bring attention to my situation by calling some of the influential people in our network. I can't use the telephone while I'm in the SHU and guards monitor everything I write. So I suggest that she ask our friends to write reference letters to the warden at Lompoc and to ask professors who use my books to write letters describing the contributions my work makes to their students. She should contact journalists and other media representatives who have interviewed me or shown interest in my work, asking if they would make official inquiries. Also, she should ask Jon Axelrod, our lawyer friend in Washington D.C., to write a formal letter protesting my segregation and demanding an explanation. We have our support network in place and I urge Carole to mobilize it, including making calls to administrators in the BOP's Western Regional Office to complain.

"Someone is trying to bury me in the system, and from in here, all I can do is write about what's going on," I tell her. "The BOP operates behind closed doors and covers its actions with that 'security-of-the-institution' catchall. In order to force their hand to end the investigation, we have to expose their efforts to frame me. Let's use all of our resources to spotlight what's going on."

"What about the sponsorship funds that Lee gave? Can you get in trouble for that?"

"I didn't receive any funds. A private foundation sent checks to the publishing company that you own, not me. *You* paid taxes on the money. I wrote the manuscripts, but I wasn't compensated. I'm completely within the letter of the law. And if they want to give me a shot for what I did, I don't care. I'm proud of our work and I'm not hiding anything."

* * * * * * *

Confinement in SHU, "the hole," is intended as further punishment to imprisonment. It is constant deprivation, without phone calls, commissary, or access to recreation yards. The forced segregation can last for days, weeks, months, or years. Sometimes it causes men to flip out, kicking on the doors, banging fists or heads against the walls, or becoming delusional. But I'll be okay, regardless of what this system does.

Although I've never been locked in SHU for a disciplinary infraction, I've been in enough during transfers and holdovers that the close quarters don't bother me. I block out the noise from other cells. Carole sends me subscriptions to four news magazines. She also sends three books a week. I finish reading two extensive biographies by Ron Chernow, one on J.D. Rockefeller and another on J.P. Morgan. I read the Bible and exercise daily on my tiny patch of cement floor. I didn't expect the abrupt change, but it doesn't paralyze me. The solitude allows me time to stare at the concrete walls and think. Only the taunting from petty bureaucrats like Erwin Meinberg disturbs my serenity.

Mr. Meinberg is the Camp Administrator at Lompoc, essentially the CEO of the camp. I met him during my first week here, back in July of 2005. After my hasty transfer from the Florence Camp, I needed some assurance that my published writings wouldn't cause problems. If Carole was going through the expense of moving to California, we had to be reasonably certain staff wouldn't transfer me again. After his gatekeeper, the dragon lady, let me in, Meinberg agreed to talk to me in his conference room.

Meinberg presents an imposing figure. He stands six-five, wears cowboy boots, has a powerful build with an alabaster round head, fleshy cheeks, and blue eyes that remain half-closed whenever he addresses a prisoner. When I stood in front of his desk the first time we met, he leaned back in his chair to applaud me, a corner of his mouth rising in a sarcastic sneer.

"Well, Mr. San-tos, you must be very proud of yourself." He derisively hyphenates my last name with his affected drawl.

374

"Why's that?" I was not surprised that he knew my name.

"You're the first person I've met who comes up first when I Google his name."

"I wouldn't know. I've never used the Internet."

"Let's not kid each other, Mr. San-tos. You know exactly what you're doing."

"Do you have a problem with my writing? That's what I wanted to talk to you about. My wife is planning on moving here, and before she does I want to make sure I'm not going to be transferred."

He shrugged. "That's entirely up to you"

"I don't do anything that violates the rules. But I have a new book coming out," I told him. "Will that cause me any problems here?"

He shook his head. "We'll just have to wait and see. I don't have a crystal ball, can't make no guarantees."

When I went to see Mr. Meinberg for that face-to-face conversation two years ago, I was making the record clear about my work. I purposely avoided him after that meeting. Now that I'm locked in SHU, he appears at my cell, leans against the doorframe, and peers through the window cut into the door. I ignore him, though his big, clean shaven head fills the window and I can sense his contempt.

He taps the window with his ring and I look over. "Got any questions for me, Mr. San-tos?"

I shake my head.

He jerks his head, gesturing that I should walk toward the door. "Your wife's causing all kinds of ruckus out here, making extra work for me."

"I've got a few problems of my own," I say into the doorframe.

He nods his head, irritation evident in his tight-lipped expression.

"I need you to sign these releases." He slides a file with papers under the door along with a pen.

"What are they for?" I ask.

"They authorize me to communicate information to the people bothering me about your case."

"I'm an open book. I've got nothing to hide. You can

communicate with anyone who asks about me."

"Sign the forms," he gestures with his index finger. After signing, I slide the file back under the door.

"I'll need that pen back, Mr. San-tos." I slide him the pen.

"You know you'll never return to a camp, don't you?" he grins, appearing quite pleased.

"Do those 20 years that I've already served still count?" My question diminishes some of the pleasure he derives from taunting prisoners.

"What's that?" he asks.

"The past 20 years I've served, do they still count?"

Meinberg doesn't respond but nods his big, shiny head and walks down the hall gripping his file folder full of signed forms.

* * * * * * *

A week passes and a guard finally comes, ordering me to cuff up. I grab an envelope that contains a statement I wrote to detail my version of events. Then I back up to the trap for handcuffing. The guard grips the chain and leads me from my cell down the corridor, through the gates, past the control bubble, and into an office with walls covered in dark acoustic padding for soundproofing. Behind a desk a lieutenant sits with his back to me as he types. He has a pale, bald head, and three rolls of fat droop at the base of his thick neck.

"I've got Inmate Santos," the guard announces.

"That'll be all, Officer," the lieutenant says. The guard releases his grip on my handcuffs and walks out, leaving me standing in front of the desk with my hands cuffed behind my back.

After he finishes typing, the lieutenant spins his cushioned chair around to face me.

"Do you know who I am?"

"I know you're a lieutenant."

He nods his head. "That's right. I'm Lieutenant Tremble and I understand you're some kind of celebrity around here."

"I'm a long-term prisoner. That's it."

"Good, I'm glad to hear we understand each other,

376

because no matter how many people you have calling this prison, or how many letters people write, I'm not treatin' you any diff'rent than I treat anyone else."

Firm but fair. That's the BOP motto. But I know that if it weren't for my wife's success in mobilizing my friends and those in my support network, this lieutenant would've kept me stewing for a month "under investigation" before he called me in.

"I'm investigatin' the two disciplinary infractions you're bein' charged with," Lieutenant Tremble says.

"What are the charges?"

"Conducting a business and unauthorized use of government equipment. Specifically, you used a computer. Now Whadda ya have to tell me?"

"I'm not running a business, and I had staff authorization for my work on the computer. I prepared a written statement that I want you to make part of the record."

"Let me have the statement."

I turn my back to him and he grabs the envelope from my cuffed hands. "It's all in there," I say, turning to face him again.

The lieutenant opens the envelope and pulls out the three yellow pages. "You want me to include all of this?"

"I want a full written record. This isn't my first problem with the BOP and I've learned that documenting everything serves my interests well."

The lieutenant shakes his head. "Do you realize I've got to type all this?"

"I take disciplinary charges seriously and I intend to prove I wasn't doing anything that could be considered against the rules."

"Fine. I'll read your statement later. Give me the quick version now."

I shrug my shoulders. "I don't run a business. I write and type manuscripts for books. The books describe prison and encourage readers to lead responsible lives. BOP policy allows me to do this without staff permission and my Central File includes a letter from a BOP attorney specifically authorizing my work. I send the manuscripts home. My wife converts them into books. I assign away the rights to all royalties so I don't have any financial or business interest in the work. I don't have anything to hide."

"What about the computer?" Lieutenant Tremble asks.

"Mr. Brown authorized me to use it after I completed my required duties. No one in the powerhouse is going to complain about my work."

"Well why don't you think anyone from the powerhouse is steppin' up to bail you out?"

"I don't know what they're doing or why."

"Mr. Brown doesn't have the authority to grant you permission to use the computer for personal work. Staff members don't even have permission to use computers for personal work. These computers are for government work only. Besides that, I already spoke with Mr. Brown. He says that he never gave you permission to use the computer for anything but government work."

I shake my head, not surprised to learn that my supervisor takes the cowardly route of self-preservation, denying the truth.

"You know what that means?" The lieutenant smiles derisively.

"I don't. What does that mean?"

"I'm going to have to amend the disciplinary report. I'll be adding a third charge of lying to a staff member. You lied when you told me that you had permission to use the computer for personal work."

"Did it ever occur to you that the staff may be lying?"

"Be careful, Inmate Santos. You don't wanna dig yourself in deeper, do you?"

"Check the files in the computer. You'll see that I typed plenty of documents for staff members."

"What kind of documents?" The lieutenant shifts, smelling a bigger fish.

"Documents that don't have anything to do with government work."

"You're telling me that BOP staff members had an inmate typin' their personal information? I don't buy it."

"Check it out. When staff asked for my help, I complied. Those computer files will show that I typed letters pertaining to their personal real estate holdings, résumés, and applications for jobs with other agencies."

He's incredulous. "Are you telling me that my staff members asked you to type their résumés? They gave you personal information?"

"Well I don't know whether they'd consider themselves your staff members, but I certainly typed up their personal work at their request?"

"Then it looks like I've got more investigatin' to do."

"Then you better go about your investigating.   It shouldn't be hard. The files are all over the computer."

* * * * * * *

I've been locked in the hole for a month and I'm keeping my family and friends apprised of my situation by writing a daily journal describing the routine I've created. Carole posts the articles on MichaelSantos.net, connecting me to the world even if I am locked in a box. When the guard escorts me out to visit Carole on Saturday morning, she delivers wonderful news.

"I've been talking with a high-level contact in the regional office," Carole's eyes sparkle. "I don't even want to say her name in here."

"Okay, I get it. What's up?"

"I've sent her all of your books. She's reviewed your entire file and she's totally impressed with your record. She saw all the efforts you made to let the staff know about your writing and she reviewed the documents you typed for your supervisors at the powerhouse."

"And? I'm still being charged with running a business, using the computer, and lying to staff."

"Not anymore. You've been totally cleared of those charges and you're being transferred to another camp. Honey, this mess is finally *over*."

That news from Carole elevates my spirit. Any day I expect guards will pull me out for transfer. Instead, on Tuesday evening, May 22nd, Lieutenant Marx taps his steel key against my window, smiling with his nod for me to approach the doorframe.

"Got a new disciplinary infraction for ya," he grins wickedly, "hun'red series."

"What are you talking about?" My stomach drops like a

brick. A 100-series disciplinary infraction characterizes it as being one of the greatest in severity, exposing a prisoner to potential new criminal prosecution.

"We found your weapon." He nods gleefully.

"Weapon? I've been locked in SHU for 31 days. You're telling me you found a weapon *today*? That's ridiculous," I yell into the doorframe.

He slides the disciplinary report under the door. "Prove it." He shrugs, grins, and vanishes from sight down the tier.

When Dorkin locked me in segregation in April he separated me from access to my personal property. He and Mr. Smith packed all of my belongings into green duffle bags. They filled out property forms that detailed every item they packed in the bags, down to the number of Bic pens. I have copies of those property forms and they don't mention my having anything that could be construed as a weapon. Yet this new disciplinary infraction Lieutenant Marx just delivered accuses me of possessing a "sharpened metal weapon."

I've been locked in high security penitentiaries and I've thrived through 20 years of imprisonment without problems. Now I have to argue against a charge that I packed a weapon in camp cupcake? I'm being framed. Regardless of the guards' motivation, a 100-series disciplinary infraction exposes me to the possibility of criminal charges. I spend the evening writing a lengthy protest on my yellow legal pad.

On Saturday morning, Carole comes to visit and I tell her about this latest disruption.

"They're retaliating against you because the regional director expunged the other charges," Carole understands the gravity of this new problem as I tell her of the weapons charge. She worries that this isn't ever going to end.

"Whatever it takes, we're going to fight this. If there was a weapon in my property, one of these crooked guards planted it. I haven't had access to my property for more than a month."

"Michael, I hate this place and everything about it. I'm calling my contact at the region as soon as I leave here. Even an idiot can see that you're being framed. We'll get you out of this."

Despite Carole's confidence, I feel like I'm in a viper pit.

* * * * * * *

I'm on the toilet when I hear tapping on the window. I don't even have to look up to know Meinberg has returned. He gestures with his shaved head for me to step to the doorframe. While I finish using the toilet, his big head stays in the window. I take my time washing my hands, then step closer while drying my hands on the threadbare towel.

"Got calls from National Geographic Television and BBC radio requesting interviews with you. Looks like your wife's been busy."

"Is that what you came to tell me?" I speak into the frame.

"Do you want to participate in the interviews?"

"Yes."

"Sign these release forms."

He slides the folder under the door with a pen. I sign both and slide them back.

Meinberg picks up the folder, and then he opens it to make sure I signed on the right spot.

"The requests are denied," he states with a sneer and walks away.

* * * * * * *

On Thursday a guard comes for me. He cuffs and marches me out from my cell, down the tunnel and through the gates to the soundproof lieutenant's office.

"That will be all, Officer." It's Merkle, the SIS. He walks out from behind his desk and unlocks my handcuffs.

"Remember me?" he asks.

"Yes," I say, even though two years have passed since I last saw the SIS lieutenant.

"Sit down." A stack of papers sits neatly on his desk. "I've prepared an affidavit. I'd like you to read it over. If it's accurate, I'd like you to sign it. If anything is inaccurate, I'd like you to tell me so I can correct it. Okay?"

"Fine. Give me the affidavit."

The document describes my use of the computer in the powerhouse, emphasizing the résumés, job applications, and rental agreements I typed for staff members at their direction.

"The affidavit doesn't mention anything about the weapon planted in my property after I was exonerated from charges of lying to staff, running a business, and using the computer for personal work," I point out.

"That's a separate investigation," he says.

"Can I use your pen?"

He pulls a gold pen from the inside pocket of his blazer and passes it to me. When I sign, I appreciate the smooth precision of the roller ball.

"What are you in here for?" he asks.

"When I was in my early 20s, I sold cocaine. It was a bad decision." I return his pen. "Nice pen."

"Didn't the president's brother sell cocaine?" He puts the pen back in his inside pocket.

"That was Roger Clinton. The president pardoned him before leaving office."

"And 'justice' for all," the SIS officer smirks.

* * * * * * *

I've been locked in SHU for 60 days on the Saturday morning when I walk into the visiting room and see Carole's radiant smile. "You look like you have good news," I ask after we kiss and sit across from each other.

"Can't I just be happy to see my husband?"

"Oh, so you like seeing me in my orange jumpsuit, unshaven?"

"I talked to my contact at the region yesterday. The regional director knows you didn't have a weapon. Every charge against you is already expunged and your record is totally clear again. You're being transferred to another camp."

"Which camp?"

"I'll know on Monday. It doesn't matter. I want you out of Lompoc."

Returning to my cell after our visit, relief floods through me and I thank God for the many blessings in my life. Some may consider Lompoc Camp as a "crown jewel" in the BOP system, but it's tarnished and toxic, top to bottom. Maybe something bigger will come from my being thrown in SHU on trumped up charges. Maybe this crown jewel will get a much-needed cleaning.

I hear Meinberg's voice. He's talking to a prisoner in a cell down the tier. He doesn't stick his big round head in my window to watch me today. As he walks back toward the gates, I knock for him to approach.

"What is it, Mr. San-tos?" He leans into the door from the hallway.

"Did you hear that your superiors at the region have completely exonerated me of all those charges?"

He looks at me with his signature sneer. "I did hear something about that."

"I guess I'll be going to another camp after all," I smile.

After more than two months in SHU I can't contain the mockery in my tone.

"Looks that way," he responds with studied neutrality.

"I'm requesting a furlough transfer."

With a furlough transfer, Carole would be able to transport me to the new camp where I would surrender, sparing me the indignity of chains and guards.

He shakes his head. "Don't count on it, Mr. San-tos. You'll be traveling in chains."

Chapter Fourteen: 2007-2009
Months 233-266

Early on the morning of June 21, I learn that I'm no longer designated to FCC Lompoc. Two guards from the Taft Correctional Institution arrive. They lock six of us in chains, and then they load us into a white van. We're on our way to the Central Valley of California, leaving Lompoc behind for good.

Lompoc Camp was already a memory after 65 days locked in SHU, but I'm a little sad when the van exits the main gate and turns left toward the highway. I'll miss running long distances in the shade of Lompoc's majestic eucalyptus trees, enjoying the fragrances of the pines mixed with breezes from the nearby Pacific Ocean. I'll miss my friend Lee and the nearly private space I enjoyed in the powerhouse office.

The two-lane road climbs east through low mountains, drops into the San Joaquin Valley, and it finally whips through high desert. It's a landscape of blowing dust, sagebrush, and unsightly steel pumps sucking oil from the arid soil. I lean involuntarily as the van turns right onto the long entry road leading to the prison, bouncing over yellow speed bumps.

At the parking lot of the double-fenced, low-security prison, manicured lawns and palm trees welcome us. Blooming gardens create the illusion of a lush oasis in this desert.

After the requisite intake processing, three of us designated to minimum-security take our bedrolls and board the white van, unrestrained, for a short ride to Taft Camp's low, gray, concrete administration building. Located behind the low-security prison, the modern, single-story design features tinted windows and round pillars supporting an extended roof shading spacious walkways. The building looks more like the headquarters for a software engineering firm than a prison. Taft Camp appears to be well maintained.

In the administration building, the round schoolhouse clock in the glass-enclosed guard's station reads just past five. I cross the tile floor and push open the glass door to the camp's compound. After more than two months in Lompoc's SHU I revel in this less-stressful environment.

Wide, clean, concrete walkways cut across pristine lawns in the center of the camp compound. Decorative, knee-high light posts illuminate the walks leading to the glass-enclosed chow hall and across the lawn to the two-storied housing unit with its horizontal rows of tall, unbarred, wide windows of tinted glass. In the distance, an oval track surrounds softball and soccer fields. Men in khakis, white t-shirts, and sneakers visit outside the housing units. They appear friendly, smiling and nodding as I climb the stairs to A4D, my assigned housing unit.

The air conditioning feels good, cooling me as I step inside the high-ceilinged dorm, one of four identical housing units. Six telephones hang across from each other on the two walls immediately inside the foyer, and I don't see any guards.

Unlike the open dormitories at Lompoc, two and three-man cubicles divide the housing unit, creating a grid that provides a semblance of privacy for the 140 men in my unit. The bathroom facilities are much larger than Lompoc's. They include 16 shower areas with doors and plenty of toilet stalls, urinals, and sinks. The unit reserves a room for four microwaves and an ice machine, rooms with six televisions and game tables, and a small study room that overlooks the lawns.

In cubicle 36, a three-man room, I meet my two roommates. "I'm Rick," one man offers, extending his hand. Dan, a slender, blond man in his early 50s, introduces himself as well. I set my bedroll on the top rack. "Let me show you how to make up your bed," Dan offers. "It can be a little tricky to keep your sheets in place. What you want to do is...."

"Thanks for the tip," I raise my hand to stop his instruction. "I'd like to say I'm new, but I've been at this awhile."

"Oh, I thought you were fresh off the streets. Did you come in from the county jail?"

I chuckle as I tie the corners of my sheets around the mat. "Not jail. I was at Lompoc Camp."

"Really? Lompoc Camp! I've heard that's the best place in the system." Dan turns to Rick. "My lawyer tried to get me sent to Lompoc, but the schmuck got me sent to this dump filled with drug dealers and criminals."

"Yeah," Rick agrees. "I've heard about Lompoc. *Forbes* runs an article each year that ranks the best prisons for white-collar offenders and Lompoc Camp always comes out on top. Is it true that they've got a golf course?" Rick simulates a golf swing.

"I didn't see a golf course," I laugh. "But Lompoc does have its bright spots."

"You're not going to like the change," Dan warns. "This place is a real prison."

"No kidding? What's not to like?" I ask.

Rick and Dan exchange a knowing glance. "You'll find out soon enough," Dan says.

"The food is awful, the staff is incompetent, and 95 percent of the men here are dim bulbs, borderline imbeciles," Rick tells me.

"Well, I guess I lucked out then, being assigned to this cubicle. What do you guys do for a living?"

"I'm an accountant," Rick says.

"And what brings you to Taft Camp?" I stuff my pillow into the pillowcase.

"Overzealous prosecutors," he answers. "Saddled me with three years for advising clients on offshore accounts. It was totally above board. I shouldn't even be here."

"Did you take the case to trial?"

"Oh no. If I'd lost at trial I would've been facing ten years. Better to plead guilty, take the three years and move on with my life."

"What about you?" I ask Dan.

"I'm in investments."

"Oh? What kind?"

"All kinds," he says. "My company purchases real estate, financial instruments, businesses. Private equity."

"And how long are you with us?" I ask.

"Serving 46 months," Dan says. "It doesn't make any sense at all. We've got drug dealers and other real criminals running around here serving half the sentence I'm serving."

"What did they charge you with?" I ask.

"You're not going to believe it," he says.

"Try me," I smile.

"Fraud. Said I was running a Ponzi. I offered investors a legitimate 10 percent annual return on their money. I got a little behind the eight ball when markets started going sideways on me, and before you know it, boom, I got the FBI breathing down my neck."

"How much was the amount of loss?"

"A lousy four million. If the investors would've just been patient, the deals would've worked out. Totally legit. Now it's all gone." He waves his hand dismissively.

"What're you, a lawyer?" Rick asks as he sits on his lower rack.

"No. I'm serving a 45 year sentence for selling cocaine."

Silence. Don and Rick look at each other. Then Rick explodes with laughter.

"No way! You wouldn't be in camp with a sentence like that."

"I'm totally serious. Of course, I've been in a long time."

"But you said you came from Lompoc Camp. That's a spot for white-collar offenders."

"Not only white-collar offenders, and I did come from Lompoc Camp. But I was in several prisons before Lompoc Camp."

"Like where?" Rick asks, still skeptical, unable to hide his curiosity and incredulity.

"I started in USP Atlanta," I toss out, humoring myself with my new roommates.

Rick scoots to the edge of his rack, leans in. "No way. You were in a *penitentiary?*"

"I spent six Christmases inside those walls. Then I transferred to McKean, in Pennsylvania. From there I transferred to Fairton, in New Jersey. I spent almost eight years at Fort Dix. Then I was in Florence Camp, Lompoc Camp, and now I'm here."

They stare at me for a moment in silence.

"How long have you been in prison?" Rick finally blurts out.

"Twenty years."

"Twenty years?" Don whistles. "I've never met anyone who's been in longer than five. Listen, I hope I didn't offend you with anything I said. I didn't know."

"After 20 years in prison, do you really think I could be offended by something you'd say?"

"So no hard feelings then?" Dan puts out his hand.

"Think nothing of it." We shake hands again.

* * * * * * *

I meet my counselor and my case manager. Both women speak to me kindly, taken aback that I've been in prison for so long.

"Where are all your tattoos?" My counselor teases. She grants my request for a phone call to Carole and immediately approves a visiting list authorizing Carole to visit over the weekend.

"You could put a different set of clothes on and I wouldn't know you've been in prison at all." My case manager says.

"Does that surprise you?" I ask with a laugh.

"Totally. I was a little girl when you came to prison. I would've expected you to be angry and bitter. But you're all smiles, normal, like you haven't ever served time in prison."

"Isn't that ironic?" I ask.

"What's that?"

"That I'm unscathed after 20 years of imprisonment, with all my teeth and no tattoos, yet you wonder what went wrong. You expect two decades in prison should turn me angry and bitter. When you see that it hasn't, you wonder why."

"Oh! I didn't think of that."

* * * * * * *

When Carole and I were in Fort Dix we were able to visit five days a week. Those ample visits allowed us to deepen our relationship and allowed me to play an influential role in Nichole's life. In Florence Camp, rules allowed us to visit every Friday, Saturday, Sunday, and federal holiday. At Lompoc, restrictions were tighter. Authorized visits were only Saturdays, Sundays, and holidays. Still, we appreciated the time together.

In Taft Camp, I learn, a point structure penalizes families who visit on weekends or holidays. Because Carole is in school on Fridays, we'll only be able to visit on weekends, limiting us to a maximum of two or three visits each month, depending on whether we visit on Saturdays or Sundays. The visiting restrictions will complicate our life, but we'll make it through. Carole arrives early on Sunday for our first visit at Taft.

"Tell me all about it. How do you like it here?" Carole smiles, eager to hear about this newest transition.

"Without a doubt, this is the easiest prison in the world."

"How are the people?"

"Do you mean the other prisoners or the staff?"

"Both."

"The prisoners are the same as in every other camp, but the guards are different. It's only been a few days, but the staff I've spoken to seem a much friendlier group than the standard-issue BOP brand."

"What do you mean?"

"Rather than the BOP, a private company manages this place. I don't know why, but it's different from other prisons. The guards don't give the impression that they're out to harass me, and the unit team members, meaning the counselors and case managers, treat me like a person, not a prisoner."

"My contact at the Regional Office said Taft was the best spot for you. That's why I want you to make me a promise."

"What's that?" I ask warily. "What kind of promise do you want me to make?"

"Just listen. Thanks to Lee, we have enough in the bank to pay for everything we need until I finish nursing school. Nichole's going to graduate next June, and by then I'll have my nursing license. I don't want you to do anything that might send you to the hole or get you transferred. Don't write anything about prison, and don't tell me to make any stock trades. Nothing. I don't want any problems that might waken the beast."

"I don't want problems either," I say, wanting to reassure her.

"You know what I mean. No more writing until I graduate. After that, I can get a job anywhere if they decide to transfer you for publishing or for some other ridiculous reason."

"I have to prepare for my release and the only way I know how to do that is by writing. We can't allow the system to keep me from working."

"The system isn't stopping you," Carole says. *"I'm* asking you to stop. It's just for one year, until I graduate."

"You want me to give up a year of work?"

"Please, Michael. No writing about prison or prisoners."

I shake my head. "Nothing?"

"Nothing." I pause. Writing enables me to transcend the boundaries, allowing me to connect with the society I long to join. By writing about what I've learned from others, observed, and experienced, I take meaningful steps to reform this system, showing taxpayers what those within the prison industrial complex don't want citizens to see. As a writer, I'm relevant, more than a prisoner, part of something bigger than me. But I won't deny Carole and so I agree to suspend my work until she graduates. I don't want to give prison administrators cause to uproot our lives again.

"Okay. I promise."

* * * * * * *

Tavo may not have much of an education, but he maneuvers his way around Taft Camp just fine, providing for himself with a hustle here and a hustle there. He's five foot-six and doesn't weigh more than130 pounds. He wears his straight black hair parted down the middle and feathered back. His eyes are a startling green and, despite his 40 years, there's not a whisker on his face. Tavo has a trace of an accent even though he was born and reared in Los Angeles. He keeps up with who's being released from the camp, negotiating a price for each departing prisoner's sneakers, sweats, radios, and other belongings. He tacks on a markup and sells the goods to newcomers, even providing a payment plan when necessary. He has a commissary squeeze where he charges a fee for providing candy, soda, chips, or other items on days when the prisoners aren't authorized to shop. For his most lucrative gig, Tavo provides the service of doubling mattresses.

Bed frames at Taft Camp consist of metal slabs welded to four metal posts. The narrow slabs have lips that rise an inch around the edges to hold the sleeping mats in place. Tavo understands that some prisoners in camp are sensitive to the harshness of institutional living. He charges $40 to cut through the seam, stuff a second mat into the casing and sew it shut, thus converting the mat to a mattress.

"You've got to meet Tavo," Rick, my roommate nudges. "For 40 bucks he'll hook up the mattress in a way that makes sleeping almost bearable."

"Appreciate the tip. I'm good," I say.

"Can't pay enough for a good night's sleep," Dan seconds the suggestion. "Sit on mine."

"I'm sure it's comfortable," I shrug. "But I've known hundreds of Tavos. The double mattress is great until guards come through on a shakedown and issue shots for destruction of government property. I don't need the headache."

"They can't do that," Rick says. "I'd just say the mattress was issued to me this way. Check it out. You can't even tell."

"I'll be okay. Thanks."

Rick and Dan serve their time as a team. They eat meals together, walk the track together, and they partner in card tournaments. But in the afternoon, when rules require us all to stand in the cube for the daily census count, we sometimes discuss our lives and thoughts. They question me about other prisons and what it's been like to serve so many years.

"I'll tell you one thing. Serving time in other prisons has made it easy for me to appreciate Taft."

"You see, that's not normal," Dan tells me. "You've been in too long, so long that prison doesn't bother you anymore. Truth is, this is inhumane. The lengths of the sentences don't make any sense at all."

"What he's saying," Rick jumps in, "is that some people might belong in prison. But guys like us shouldn't be in here at all."

"What do you mean, 'like us'? I'm in here for selling cocaine. The first day I came into the cube you were saying that people who sold drugs were the real criminals who belong in prison."

"Not for 20 years," Dan amends. "Besides, you're different now. You've educated yourself and you've got things going on in the world. Prison should be for the criminal types, the guys who keep selling drugs or committing crimes."

"You mean guys like Tavo?" I ask.

Rick shifts uncomfortably. "Well, Tavo's a nice enough guy, but what's he going to do in the world? No one's going to hire him. He's not doing anything to change his ways. Chances are, he's probably going to leave here and hustle drugs again."

"Chances are," I say, "that he came from a poor family, quit school before tenth grade, can't read well, and had to hustle for survival. How about you? Where did you go to school?"

"Cal State Northridge," Rick says.

"You went to USC right?" I nod at Dan.

"Go Trojans," Dan waves two fingers in the air.

"Should society hold people who come from poverty to the same standard as people who come from privilege?"

"You break the law, you break the law," Dan explains smugly.

"We all make our choices."

"But you guys whine in here every day about your discomfort and the living conditions. Guys like Tavo are getting by the only way they know how. This might be as good as he's ever had it." I argue.

"He's a criminal. He sold drugs," Dan counters.

"I don't know what Tavo did, but he probably sold drugs to consenting adults and he probably serves at least twice as long as you. Who would the investors in your scam think is the worse criminal, Tavo or you?" I ask.

"You don't know anything about my case," Dan hisses. "I didn't set out to lose anyone's money. Markets just went against me. I couldn't control it. It's not my fault."

"That may be," I shrug. "But you pled guilty. That means you had to stand in court, and while under oath, admit to committing fraud."

"I only pled guilty because I would've gotten a longer sentence if I went to trial."

"Either way, you're not in a position to be judging anyone else in here."

That argument serves me well, as neither Rick nor Dan speak to me again. We pass each other silently for three months before a staff member grants my request to move into a two-man cube further back in the housing unit with David Muniz, a married father of two. Since I'm keeping my promise to Carole that I won't write, I devote my time to exercising and spending several hours each week tutoring and coaching David on steps he can take to prepare for release.

We laugh as guards wheel a cart through the unit one day, confiscating all double mattresses. When one of the guards threatens Dan with a shot, Dan doesn't hesitate to snitch on Tavo.

Rick, however, argues with the guard "You can't take my mattress! I've got a bad back."

"This mattress isn't standard issue, it's been altered. It's contraband." The guard doesn't have any concern about the condition of Rick's back.

"If you don't provide me with a double mattress, my lawyer will slap a lawsuit on this prison so fast it'll make the warden's head spin."

"Really," the guard says in a voice dripping with sarcasm. "Let's see you launch that lawsuit from the SHU."

* * * * * * *

Carole and I celebrate Christmas day sitting beside each other in the visiting room. Wreathes, blinking lights, a Christmas tree, and a full-sized red, wooden sleigh decorate the room. A prisoner in a Santa outfit walks around the crowded room handing out candy canes, but my gift is sitting beside me.

"This is your 21st Christmas in prison," Carole says. "Our sixth together since we've been married."

"We only have six more to go."

"Five," she corrects me.

"No, 2013."

"But you'll be home in August. We'll spend Christmas together that year."

The years blend together for me now, but Carole helps me visualize our life ahead. It's not easy to imagine being free. Strange. "Time will move so much faster starting in 2008," I say.

"How so?"

"We've got all these events to mark the time. They'll

come like milestones, passing quickly, giving us real markers to look toward."

"Like what?"

"What do you mean 'like what'?" I hold up my fingers to count. "In January the political season kicks off with the primaries. We'll follow all the races, starting in Iowa. After the primaries roll around, we'll have a better idea who our next president is going to be."

Carole squeezes my hand. "I'm so sick of politics. It doesn't matter who wins, nothing changes."

"Then in March the $500,000 fine that my judge imposed expires. We can open a joint bank account as husband and wife. In May, you graduate from nursing school. In June, Nichole graduates from high school. Sometime during the summer the political conventions will name the candidates. The fall will make politics really exciting. Then it will be Christmas again."

"The years take much longer to pass than you make it sound," Carole says.

"Remember what we were doing five years ago?" I ask her.

"I had just moved to Fort Dix."

"Remember what I told you on New Year's Day, when you and Nichole came to visit?"

"Tell me again."

"I put up my hand and opened five fingers like this," I repeat the action. "I said that in five years, if you stayed with me, your life would be completely different. And look at you now, five years later."

She smiles and brushes her cheek against mine. "Do you think I'm so different?"

"You're a magnificent wife. No matter what happens in my life, nothing will bring me more happiness than my marriage to you."

* * * * * * *

On June 11, 2008, I stand in front of 30 prisoners who sit under dim lights on cushioned chairs in the corner of an industrial warehouse, one of the few buildings at Taft Camp without air conditioning. The summer heat, together with swarms of flies, keeps us pulling at our shirts and swatting air, but it's the only available room large enough for me to facilitate a series of self-help classes that I enjoy leading.

The warehouse has high ceilings with exposed pipes, wiring, and metal walls supported by thick steel beams. If it had a grass floor, the space would be sufficient for indoor football. But the floor is concrete, and except for the niche carved out for our class area, wheelchairs in various stages of repair are stacked ten-feet high in rows from the front of the warehouse to the back. My roommate, David, leads a crew of prisoners from Taft who spend their days refurbishing the wheelchairs for donation to Wheels of the World, a prison-sponsored program providing rebuilt wheelchairs to needy communities.

Prisoners, even those in camp, struggle with their separation from society. Motivating men who worry about the challenges that await them, who wonder daily about their wives, about their children, about how they will find employment upon release, or about how to muster the strength to pass through years of imprisonment, requires preparation. By the summer of 2008 I've had 21 years of preparation. I love to teach about concepts I know work, like the proven strategies for values-based, goal-driven life plans that helped me.

"Define for me a successful prisoner," I ask the class. "What is the best possible outcome for a man who serves a prison sentence?" Hands shoot up, and I call on Sam. "It's someone who doesn't receive any disciplinary reports."

"Okay," I use a blue felt pen to write his answer on the whiteboard. "How about you, Jim? How do you define a successful prisoner?"

"Someone who can hold onto his family while in prison." I write Jim's answer on the board, and then I call on Pablo.

"A person who educates himself."

"Bob, how about you?" I ask while writing Pablo's answer. "What's a successful prisoner to you?"

"A successful prisoner is a guy who manages to hang on to at least some resources in the world so that when he gets out, he has a shot at making a new start," Bob says.

After writing Bob's answer on the board, I walk into the center of the crowd and face the board. "These are the types of answers prison administrators love to hear. Isn't that right Mr. Moreland?" The staff member sits in the back of the class, observing.

"They sound like good answers to me," he acknowledges.

"Good answers, Mr. Moreland says," I repeat loud enough so everyone will hear. "But I'd give each answer a C-minus at best, and I'm being generous," I say.

Men shift silently in their chairs and the supervising staff member puts down his candy bar. I have their attention.

"Those answers reflect the common response of all prisoners across the nation. But they're not enough. To be a successful prisoner requires you to do more."

I walk toward the board and check off the class responses as I work through each.

—"Instead of focusing on avoiding disciplinary infractions, he selects positive activities that will contribute to success upon release.

—"He doesn't only hold on to his family, he works daily to strengthen family bonds and to contribute in meaningful ways to his family.

—"He not only educates himself, but he uses what he learns to enrich himself and society.

—"He not only hangs on to resources, but creates new resources that will assure he leaves prison strong, with absolute certainty that he will succeed upon release.

"The key to a successful prison experience is to envision clearly how you want to emerge. Don't limit yourself to the minimum, but envision the best possible outcome, and use that vision as a beacon to make certain that every step leads you closer to the outcome you choose."

"But prison blocks us from doing things like that," Tim objects. "How are we supposed to contribute to our families when we're not allowed to earn an income?"

Over the next ten weeks I engage the class, drawing on my experiences to inspire them to create their own successful life plans.

"Success does not materialize by accident," I emphasize, "but through deliberate actions."

In each session I challenge the men to accept full responsibility for their lives and to focus on what they can accomplish rather than the obstacles that limit them.

Justin Paperny, a white-collar offender who reported to Taft Camp in the late spring of 2008, becomes the most enthusiastic participant in my class. Justin graduated from the University of Southern California, and then he went on to earn a six-figure income as a young stockbroker. Indiscretion with his oversight of a hedge fund led to Justin's 18-month sentence for securities law violations.

"The thing is," Justin comments from his seat in the center of the class, "some of us might have to start over completely when we leave here. Our convictions mean that we can't return to the same professions. With this dismal economy, it's tough to stay motivated when we know what we're facing outside."

"That's a good start," I respond. "It shows that you understand what's ahead. Since you've thought about those issues, may I ask you a few questions?"

He shrugs. "Go ahead."

"You've been here for a month now," I observe. "Please tell the class how your life differs today from the day you surrendered."

"What do you mean?"

"How is your life different?" I press. "That's not such a tough question."

He laughs. "Well, it's obvious. I'm a prisoner."

"Well, we're all in prison. But what have you been doing with your time since you surrendered a month ago?"

"Oh, I've got you," he says. "Mostly I've been exercising. I've dropped 10 pounds and I'm getting stronger with pull-ups. While I'm here I intend to exercise regularly, to get back into great physical shape."

"Who in here is exercising?" I ask the class. Most hands shoot up. "Excellent. I exercise every day. However, exercise for me is only a small part of my day. It's only one part, like brushing my teeth. I exercise to maintain a high fitness level, but one certainty I can count on is that no one is going to pay me for how many pushups I can do, or how many miles I can run when I get out of here. Unless you're planning for a career as a fitness model or a personal trainer, I suggest you devote more time to preparing to conquer the obstacles that you know await you."

"But what else can I do?" Justin asks.

"That's the question each man here must answer for himself every day, and the answer for one person isn't going to be the same as for another. If employment prospects await, if family relationships are important, or if you need an education, then you should ask yourself, 'what else can I do to prepare?' When you live that way, you never stumble when someone asks a question such as 'How is your life different?' You don't stumble because you're on the course you charted for success as you define it."

"What if we don't know what we want to do?" Charles asks. He's a middle-aged, disbarred lawyer from Newport Beach serving a two-year sentence for misappropriating funds from his client's trust account.

"Are any of you familiar with Viktor Frankl?" I ask the class. No one raises a hand.

"Viktor Frankl was a medical doctor in Germany," I tell the class. "The Nazis threw him and his family into concentration camps. They murdered his family, but he survived. Dr. Frankl later wrote that as long as man could find meaning in life, he could overcome anything. He spent three years as a Nazi prisoner, never knowing from one day to the next whether he would be alive the following day. He found, however, that he drew strength by helping others. If any of you don't know what you want to do, then I suggest you start by helping others. In doing so, be open to acknowledging what brings meaning, happiness, positive challenges, and stimulation to your life. By helping others you open possibilities for finding your particular path."

I give examples describing how other prisoners I've known used their time inside to effectively launch new careers. I tell of one prisoner who studied science during his term, and left prison to launch a company that converts discarded cooking oil into fuel for heavy equipment. I talk about another prisoner who secured several offers of employment simply by writing unsolicited letters to prospective employers from his community, describing his work ethic, and asking for a chance. The point I try to make, and the example I try to set, is that we cannot wait until release. We have a responsibility *now* to anticipate the problems we'll face after prison, and we *must* prepare every day to overcome them.

* * * * * * *

"Why do you write so much?" Justin asks as he sits across from me at the round table where I work.

"Because I can't sell stocks," I answer him.

He laughs. "I'm serious."

"I am too. I write every day because I want to become a better communicator. I plan to build a career around the experiences I've had in prison. The strategies that pulled me through can be applied to any kind of adversity. Since my prison record will make it difficult to support myself any other way, and since I need to support my family, I invest between 10 and 12 hours every day writing, reading, or preparing presentations."

"I wish I had that kind of clarity about my future."

"When do you get out?" I ask Justin.

"I finish my sentence in August of 2009."

"Why don't you do the same thing?" I ask.

"What do you mean? Write? Speak?"

"Sure. Why not? You've got a degree from USC. You were a registered investment advisor caught up in an ethics scandal. Don't you think others have made the same bad decisions?"

"Probably."

"Of course they did. If you watch the news, or look at our prison system, you'll see that millions of people lose their way. Figure out how you can help them, and you've got a new career. You can spend your time in Taft like I do, preparing for a career upon release."

Justin locks his fingers behind his head and leans back. He pauses in thought while I write. "Do you think there's a market for that?" he asks.

"Only if you prepare. You've got to create the market, and if that's what you want to pursue, you've got to work as many hours as I do."

* * * * * * *

The schedule I keep doesn't lend itself to building friendships. Also, I search for privacy wherever I can find it, nurturing my need for solace by writing, reading, and exercising. When I spend time with others it's usually related to my work. I interview for a story I want to write, or I practice my speaking skills by teaching a class. Sometimes I'll work one-on-one with another prisoner, like David, helping him prepare for the GED exam. "Write short sentences using words that you're certain you can spell correctly" is the advice I drill into him during our lessons. He passes the essay portion of his exam and continues to study as a college student.

Justin, however, isn't studying for a GED. He has a degree from a great university and a history of earning major money. As an investment professional for one of the most prestigious brokerage houses on Wall Street, Justin earned a significant income for his financial judgment, for his skill at assessing opportunity, and for managing investors' money. It is from men like Justin that I learn and advance. When others mistake me for a man who recently surrendered, or when their jaws drop as they learn I've been a prisoner since 1987, they unknowingly pay me the highest compliment. I want others to see me as a citizen with something to contribute. That validation comes when men like Justin seek my counsel.

Justin takes my advice and begins working closely with me. He gives up television and table games and devotes himself wholeheartedly to exercise and preparation for life after prison. We become close friends. I suggest steps he can take to position himself for a new career as a speaker and consultant upon his release.

I show him how I reach beyond prison boundaries to connect with the world by writing for MichaelSantos.net, and he launches his own website at JustinPaperny.com. I urge him to write a manuscript, so he outlines chapters for his book, *Lessons From Prison*. Our friendship grows when he introduces Carole and me to his family and friends who visit each week.

"I've told Brad about your work ethic, about all you've done in here and your plans for when you get out," Justin tells me after Carole and I meet some of his friends in the visiting room. His friend, Brad Fullmer, had a superstar career in professional baseball. Brad turned down a full scholarship to play baseball at Stanford when the Montreal Expos drafted him in the first round after Brad graduated from Montclair Prep. Brad is one of the few players to hit a homerun in his first Major League at bat, and he capped his long career in professional baseball by stealing home during the World Series for the California Angels. "What do you think about letting Brad and me make an investment in your career?" Justin asks.

"Have you told him that I'm scheduled to serve five more years?"

"He knows," Justin tells me, "and I know. Some investments take years to pay off. We think you're a winner and we'd like to participate."

"Let me think about it."

In weighing the possibility of selling a piece of my future earnings, I sit alone in my cubicle. I'm on a plastic chair, leaning back against a concrete wall, propping my feet against the steel post that supports the rack I call my bed. My steel locker has two shelves on the left that hold my folded gray sweats and underwear; it's above the shelf where I store my dictionary, papers, and dusty running shoes.

Over the past 21 years I've had to store my possessions inside these types of lockers. But from these lockers with only pens, discipline, and work, I've created a life for myself. I look at the pictures of Carole that I've taped to the inside of my locker's doors. She's the most beautiful woman in the world to me, not only because of her sparkling eyes and smile, but because of the way she has believed in me, given herself so completely to me, strengthening me in ways that no one else could as she served this sentence with me. I look forward to making her life better, just as she has made my life better.

I pull Carole's picture down and hold it in my hands. The image is a poor substitute for holding my wife, but on non-visiting days, I sometimes need this tangible feeling of her in my hands.

During the five years we've been married my writing has generated more than $200,000 in after-tax earnings for Carole. That's not much by the standards of society, but I'm immensely proud to have earned it from prison, with only pens, paper, and perseverance. Those funds supported her and Nichole, allowing them to move from state to state following my "prison trail." They allowed Carole to return to college. Despite tremendous hardships and obstacles, she graduated first in her nursing class and now earns her own income. I don't need to sell a piece of what I've worked so hard to create, yet I want to give my wife the security that savings in the bank can provide.

I stare at the concrete walls and block out the buzz from the fluorescent light to calculate a fair, present-day value for earnings that will not begin to flow until my release from prison, in five years. What a ridiculous concept. I'm a prisoner, and after more than a quarter century inside, conventional wisdom would question whether I could earn minimum wage, if I could find employment at all. Whatever earnings come, I'll have to create them. And who can judge the market or anticipate earnings for a man with five years remaining to serve?

My experience as a speculator in the stock market convinced me that an investment is only worth what the next investor is willing to pay for it. I'm flattered that Brad and Justin want to invest in my potential, but I'm also aware that I don't have a line of investors waiting to hand me a check for the right to a percentage of my future earnings, if I ever have any earnings.

I negotiate a number. It's enough to ensure that I can live a full year upon release without earning a single dime, enough to provide Carole with security while I finish serving this sentence. In exchange for money in the bank today, I sell the right to ten cents of every dollar parts of the Michael Santos brand will earn. Time will tell whether I sold too cheaply, but the agreement is fair to me today. When I tell my wife about the check Brad is going to hand her in the prison's parking lot after our visit concludes, her smile makes the deal worthwhile. I'm easing Carole's life during the worst economic recession of our lifetime, and I'm coordinating the deal from prison. That's priceless.

* * * * * * *

My counselor has more than 150 prisoners on her caseload. Among her responsibilities is the approval of visiting lists. Although administrators at Florence Camp and Lompoc Camp have denied my request to visit with Dr. Sam Torres, I'm willing to try again here in Taft. I knock on my counselor's office door.

"Sit down," she invites me when I ask for a moment of her time.

"Do you remember when you asked me why I changed and worked so hard to reform during my imprisonment?"

She takes her hands off the keyboard and rotates her chair from the computer to face me directly. "Yes."

"One of the primary reasons was that I wanted to prove worthy of the trust my mentors give in investing so much of their time in me."

She nods while looking at me.

"Most of my mentors come from universities. One of them retired from law enforcement before he became a professor. His name is Dr. Sam Torres and because he retired from an earlier career as a federal probation officer, I consider it a real honor that he has taken the time to develop a friendship with me. We've corresponded for years. He uses two of my texts in the college courses he teaches. By talking with him, I can learn more about what to expect while I'm on supervised release. He can help me prepare, but rules don't allow him to visit. I'm asking you to make an exception and put him on my visiting list."

"You didn't know him before prison?"

"Of course not," I say. "I met him through my work during my confinement. But he's the type of mentor I need in order to understand more about the obstacles awaiting me."

The counselor turns back to her computer, nodding. "I'm going to trust you," she says. "Have him send me a visiting form and I'll authorize him to visit."

Small victories such as this are as good as it gets in a system designed to extinguish hope.

* * * * * * *

I sit beside Justin, watching as election results declare

Barack Obama America's 44th President. I began serving my term under Ronald Reagan. When the first George Bush spoke about a kinder, gentler America, I thought change might come. Bill Clinton encouraged me to hope. With George W. Bush, I shook my head and accepted that his call for second chances and compassion would never extend to those in prison. President-elect Obama calls for a bottom-up government that values all American citizens. I'm filled with hope because it seems America has elected a compassionate leader who understands the needs of our society, *all* of our society, maybe even those in prison.

* * * * * * *

Carole and I enjoy a wonderful visit on Friday, March 27, 2009. I call her in the late afternoon to ensure that she arrived home safely, and when she answers, I learn that Joan Petersilia, a distinguished professor from the Stanford law school, sent a message through our website. Early in my term I began sending out unsolicited letters to academics I admired, and I remember writing to Joan on two separate occasions. I feel like a fisherman at sea, casting lines, hoping to make a connection, but knowing that sometimes those connections take years to materialize. Sometimes people respond, other times they don't. For every 100 letters I send out, I expect to receive a single reply. I consider that ratio a wonderful success, even when the reply doesn't come for years, as it has with this message from Joan.

Dr. Petersilia wrote that she's been using my work for years as a resource for teaching her classes, which is wonderful news. She astounds me with an invitation to contribute a chapter for *The Oxford Handbook on Sentencing and Corrections*, a new book she is co-authoring with Kevin Reitz, a law professor from the University of Minnesota. Professor Petersilia is one of the nation's most distinguished penologists, serving as an advisor to the governor on matters concerning the state of California's prison system. Legislators and other government leaders from across the nation seek her counsel. As one of one out of 2.3 million prisoners in the United States, I feel honored that even knows who I am. Her invitation to publish alongside her leaves me amazed and deeply honored. I set to work at once, eager to finish the chapter long before the due date.

I consider these types of writing projects as enormous opportunities. For decades I've worked hard to earn credentials and develop skills that would allow me to make meaningful contributions to society, but I'm in a different phase of the journey now. Every day it becomes more apparent to me that I must make a shift in strategy. I'm in the final months of my imprisonment now, and I have to think about deliberate steps I can take that will help ease my transition into society upon release. It's coming.

Writing for Professor Petersilia is a wonderful opportunity, as it will introduce my work to thousands of scholars who have an interest in improving our nation's prison system. When I emerge from prison, I'll need to earn a living, and doing so will require that I surmount some enormous hurdles. Since I intend to build a career around all that I learned as a long-term prisoner, I'll need the types of professional relationships that distinguished scholars like Joan Petersilia can open. She is the type of role model I need, and as I've done with all of my mentors, I intend to prove worthy of her support.

Besides building contacts, however, I also need to focus on steps I can take to build an income stream. It's going to cost me an enormous amount of financial resources to settle in society. I don't know where Carole and I will make our home, but wherever we go, I'll need to have a substantial savings account in place to cover the costs of my reentry. During my initial months of liberty, I will need to purchase items that most people accumulate over decades. With the cost of clothes, computers, and housing, those expenses likely will set me back at least $40,000, and it's money I intend to have in a savings account that is separate from the account I've been building to fund me through my first year of liberty. I'm determined to succeed, and I won't permit external influences like economic challenges to block me. I must leave prison ready, with values, skills, and resources in place to make it.

Epilogue: 2009-2012
Months 260-300

It's May 20, 2009 and my friend Justin Paperny is being released from prison today. We work well together and I'll miss his companionship. For the past several months Justin has been joining me in a quiet room where I write each morning. One early morning session began with an idea for launching a nonprofit organization. Undertaking such a task would assist us in raising financial resources that we could rely upon to create products for the purpose of reducing recidivism.

Our reasoning is simple, just an assessment of the facts. High-recidivism rates challenge our society in numerous ways, influencing the lives of citizens who don't grasp how America's commitment to mass incarceration influences their everyday lives. Whereas taxpayers want safer communities, better schools, and better health care, those who represent the prison machine want bigger budgets. That mindset of locking people up and throwing away the key leads to more overtime, more jobs for prison guards, and more expenditures on barbed wire fences, but it doesn't lead to safer communities. Rather, it diverts resources that society could use to build better schools, better hospitals, and offer more social services.

People who serve time struggle to emerge with the types of values, skills, and resources that translate into success upon release. Statistics illustrate the problem. More than one out of every two people who serve time face continuing challenges from the criminal justice system after their release. That rate of failure leads to enormous costs for taxpayers, depleting public resources that would be better spent on education, health care, or other social services. I'm convinced that by working together, Justin and I can help reduce costs of recidivism and contribute to safer communities. Doing so will require financial teamwork and money for obvious reasons: neither Justin nor I can work for free. We have to earn a living, and the nonprofit could raise resources for the purposes of paying us for services we can offer.

While Justin served time with me here in Taft it wasn't possible to advance the idea of launching a nonprofit. After all, forming a nonprofit organization isn't easy, especially when the principals are incarcerated.

One lesson I learned over the decades is that all worthwhile goals begin with vision, but achieving them requires persistence and commitment. With Justin's release, we can work together to advance this idea of launching a nonprofit. He will do his part from outside fences, and I'll do my part from in here. Although I understand that we may face many challenges along the way, I'm confident that we have a unified vision with regard to what we're trying to create, and we both will drive forward with persistence and commitment. This work will further my goal of living a life of relevance while I serve what I expect to be my final three years.

Research we've done to inquire on what it takes to form a nonprofit organization has given us an understanding of how to proceed. First of all, we must persuade the Internal Revenue Service that we can provide a benefit to people in society. If we succeed in that endeavor, the IRS will authorize the organization to raise money from philanthropic organizations, corporations, and individuals who support charitable giving. Raising financial resources in this dismal economic climate will prove challenging, especially when the people striving to raise the money have felony convictions. But without valid credentials from the IRS, we may not be able to raise money at all.

I understand that some may question why we need to raise financial resources. We need money because we're working to build a sustainable operation, one that can help transform troubled lives. Our target market will include at-risk youth and incarcerated individuals, people who cannot pay for the products we'll create and distribute. I will undertake the responsibility of showing taxpayers the reasons why it's in their best interest to support our cause.

If we receive authorization from the IRS, we'll work together to transform at-risk lives, empowering them to live as contributing citizens. I'm glad Justin joined me in formulating this plan of action. Now we must execute the plan.

* * * * * * *

The fall of 2009 passes easily for me here in the Taft federal prison camp. I've now served more than 22 years of my sentence. Although I don't know precisely when I'll walk out, I'm feeling strong, expecting that release will come within the next three years. I'm truly in the end game, and I'm fully aware of my responsibilities to have a plan in place for my return to society.

Carole is working as a licensed vocational nurse in Los Angeles and studying microbiology in preparation to resume nursing school in January. Nichole, her daughter, is beginning studies at Washington State University, on her way to beginning a career in nursing as well. As far as I'm concerned, our family has triumphed over prison. Whereas the design of this system seems uniquely structured to lead individuals and families into perpetuating cycles of failure, the strategic, disciplined plan by which we've lived has brought us many blessings and strengthened us. Continuous progress keeps my spirit strong.

Justin's attorney has assured him that the nonprofit paperwork is in order, and we expect to receive authorization from the IRS to operate The Michael G. Santos Foundation by the end of this year. Three people have accepted Justin's invitation to serve as board members of the nonprofit, and although I don't know those board members, their oversight provides me with a real job: working to write proposals in search of funding.

Although Justin has identified many potential philanthropic organizations, and I'm writing grant requests to each of them, The California Wellness Foundation impresses me as being the most promising. It has a multi-billion dollar endowment that is reserved for programs that enhance public safety.

Julio Marcial serves as Justin's contact at The California Wellness Foundation. We've learned that Julio has a real passion for helping at-risk youth. He knows that many of them grow up without resources or support systems in place, and few understand what steps they must take to leave the gangs and negative influences behind.

As executive director of the Michael G. Santos Foundation, Justin told Julio about my journey. He made a strong case that we could create a program to show others how to embrace the same types of strategic, deliberate paths that empowered me to tune out the noise of external influences and prepare for success. Julio wants to see more.

Despite the boldness of the request, I'm writing a proposal that shows why The California Wellness Foundation should fund The Michael G. Santos Foundation with a $150,000 grant. In this economic environment, resources are scarce and we face a huge challenge because many established nonprofit organizations will compete for the same limited funds. Still, despite my imprisonment and Justin's recent release from imprisonment, I'm confident we can craft a winning plan.

As someone who has spent more than half of his life in prison, I have strong opinions on why so many people struggle to adjust upon release. From my perspective, although the system is very good at warehousing human beings, the system fails in preparing offenders for law-abiding, contributing lives. Instead of encouraging offenders to work toward developing values, skills, and resources that will assist them upon release, it extinguishes hope and strives to suppress the human spirit. I'm asking the California Wellness Foundation to provide funding so that Justin's foundation can craft a self-directed program that shows others how to transform their lives regardless of external influences or the noise of imprisonment. We can make a difference, but doing so will require us to confront headwinds from a system with a strong self-interest in perpetuating failure.

* * * * * * *

I pass through Christmas of 2009, my 23rd holiday season in prison, and into January of 2010, another new year. I'm still counting, not quite sure how many days of prison I have ahead of me, but I know that I have 8,180 days of imprisonment behind me. At this stage, prison doesn't bother me in the least. I feel focused and driven, eager to seize every opportunity that comes my way.

Carole has begun studies that will last throughout the year and conclude with her board-certified credentials as a registered nurse. It's a big step for our family, but one that will provide Carole with a more fulfilling career, one that brings her more respect from her peers, colleagues, and community. I'm so happy for her, so proud of her, and so grateful that I've had income opportunities to support her through the journey. She is my center and I look forward to encouraging her through this year.

It isn't easy to live as the wife of a prisoner. For Carole, the challenge was particularly difficult because she came into my life when I had more than 15 years of prison behind me and more than a decade to go. Despite others always questioning her judgment, over the past seven years we've worked alongside each other, confronting repeated transfers and interferences from prison administrators to build a life of our own. Things are much better now, and they promise to improve as we cross through year 2010.

Julio Marcial has told Justin that he intends to recommend a $150,000 grant for The Michael G. Santos Foundation. The premise is quite simple. Through the proposal I wrote, we argued that the system does not invest resources in preparing individuals for success upon release. It's stated focus is to preserve security of the institution, and it doesn't offer reentry programs until it's too late, frequently only weeks or months before the scheduled release date. By that time, the prisoner is lost, without resources or a support network to assist his reentry.

With funding, I suggested that I could write a program that would encourage prisoners and at-risk youth to pursue a self-directed path. I would do so by writing a series of books and workbooks that would show the precise steps I took to educate myself, contribute to society, and build a support network that would assist my transition upon release. It was what I said I would do very early on in my term, during that uncomfortable transition between my conviction and sentencing, during that time that I fell under the tutelage of Socrates.

Recipients of the literature and coursework that I intend to write will see that they have the power within to change their lives. My job is to inspire hope, and together with Justin's work, we've persuaded Julio to recommend that The California Wellness Foundation fund the vision. That funding provides resources to pay for my work, enough to ensure that I'll have an easier transition upon my release. If all goes well, I'll have $40,000 in savings to meet all of my financial expenses associated with my reentry, and another $40,000 in savings that I can draw upon to carry me through my first year of liberty. Through my work, I'll show other prisoners how to empower themselves in the same measurable ways.

* * * * * * *

It's Saturday morning, September 11, 2010, and as I'm returning from an early morning run, I approach a new face as I return to the housing unit from the track. More than 500 people serve time inside these boundaries, and although I don't communicate or interact with many on a personal level, I recognize the men around me. This new guy and I don't exchange words, but the way he nods at me in acknowledgement communicates volumes. That simple gesture is enough to let me know that he leads, that he's capable of whatever he sets his mind to do, and that he is someone from whom I can learn.

We're assigned to the same housing unit. I look forward to introducing myself and I seize the opportunity a few hours later when I see him outside on the track. He's taller than I am, with silver hair and olive skin. I guess that we're about the same age, but I suspect we've had very different experiences. I know this world and I can help him understand it, but I sense that he's from a different world that I'd like to learn more about.

"Good morning," I walk towards him. "Care to join me for a few laps around the track?"

He agrees and we begin circling the dirt oval that surrounds ball fields and tennis courts.

"Believe me," I tell him, "it gets easier than it feels right now."

He looks at me, as if trying to figure out what I'm after.

412

"My name is Michael Santos. I've been here for a while and can help you understand what you're up against if you're interested in a guide."

"Thanks," he says. "I know a little about you because my family has been reading your website."

"That's good to hear. I've been writing for the web for more than a decade but I've never actually seen a real webpage. I look forward to using the Internet for the first time, but that will have to wait for a couple more years at least."

"How do you publish your stuff online from in here?"

"I write everything by hand and send it to my wife. She coordinates everything for me, typing it and then posting the content on my website. The work gets me through the time and helps build awareness about this wretched system we're in. How long are you going to be with us?"

"I've got 18 months."

"Well take a breath. You won't serve that long. You'll receive some good-time credits that will reduce the term by about three months, taking it down to about 15 months. Depending on your personal circumstances, you may serve the final months of your term in a halfway house or home confinement."

"How do I arrange that?"

"You'll go through some administrative processing over the next couple of weeks. Don't push these people, the staff I mean. Just let it evolve. There isn't much of anything you can do to influence events in here. But if you let things take their course, and you don't bother the staff with too many requests, you'll probably be living in a halfway house a year from now. The secret to serving that time is to make progress every day that you're here, to work toward something that will improve your life some."

He snarls. "Like what? What can a guy do from inside this hellhole?"

I laugh. "It's not that bad. Where're you from?"

"Silicon Valley."

"What're you, a banker or a broker?" From his diction and mannerisms, I know that he's in here for a white-collar crime, but I don't know what type of work he did. He doesn't strike me as engineer.

"I was the CEO of a technology company."

"Which one?"

"Brocade Communications."

I stop on the track and look at him. "You're Greg Reyes."

He stares back at me and I see his brow wrinkle, a cross between curiosity and ferocity, guarded, as if he doesn't know what to make of my intentions.

"I don't mean to be intrusive, dude," I say, "but I've admired your courage and strength for many years. I read the *Wall Street Journal's* coverage of your case. When it reported on your conviction, I told my wife about you and that I hoped to meet you, to learn from you. In fact, in some twisted way, I feel as if I willed you here. As the years passed and you didn't show up, I assumed that you must've won on appeal."

Greg relaxes with my explanation of why I'm familiar with his background. Not only did I read the *Forbes* profile of him being one of America's youngest billionaires, but I also watched his stewardship of Brocade, taking it public and steering it to a peak market valuation that once exceeded $20 billion.

"I did win on appeal," he tells me. "The appeals court reversed my conviction because the prosecution lied repeatedly through my first trial. But the government tried me a second time. Prosecutors told new lies that brought a second conviction. I'm on appeal for that case as well. Rather than wait it out, I turned myself in because I didn't want to live with the horror of this prison sentence hanging over my head."

The national business news reports on Greg's case frequently. Although more than 200 CEOs in Silicon Valley authorized the practice of backdating stock options for rank-and-file employees, no one authorized those practices with any criminal intent or with a goal of self-enrichment. There isn't another CEO in America who serves time for the offense, and Greg expresses considerable anger at having his name dragged through the mud because of these accusations.

"Why don't you use this time to write your story," I suggest. "Set the record straight, explaining in your own words exactly what happened. If you don't do it, the only record out there is going to be the government allegations."

"Writing isn't my strong suit."

"I'll help you," I urge him on. "This is an important project. You have to tell your story. If you can talk about it, I can help you write it in your own words. It would be a great project, carrying both of us through the next year."

I see him churning over the idea. "How would you see the project unfolding?"

"It's simple. I'll ask you questions. Some of the questions may seem foolish and irrelevant, but I'll ask because I want to understand as much as you'll share. We'll talk each day for several hours. Early each morning, I'll write out notes of what I learned. After you've told me everything, I'll outline the story, try to put some structure around it. If I can tell it back to you, then we'll move forward with a more formal, chapter-by-chapter interview. I'll write a chapter, then read it to you. If you approve it, we'll move on to the next one and repeat the sequence until we've told the entire story."

He reaches over and shakes my hand. "Let's do it."

* * * * * * *

It's Christmas, 2010, my 24th Christmas morning as a federal prisoner. I've now served eight thousand, five hundred, and thirty-nine days, but today is a very special day and I'm excited to call my wife. For the first time that I can remember, I'll be giving her a magnificent surprise.

I've been awake since 2:17, writing her a letter while I wait for the phones to turn on. Now it's nearly six and I expect to hear a dial tone soon. She received the envelope that I sent her, but we agreed that she would not open it until I called her this morning. While waiting for the phone to turn on, I've been writing a letter to her, describing the joy that I feel at crossing into 2011. We will begin making final plans for my release from prison, my return to society, and I am ready.

"Merry Christmas honey," she answers my call at precisely 6:01 am."

"Merry Christmas. Are you ready to leave?" Carole's driving up to Taft for a visit this morning and I want to make

415

sure that leaves on time so that she arrives as soon as the visiting room opens at 8:00 am.

"I'm ready. Can I open the envelope now?"

"Do you promise you haven't opened it yet honey?"

"I told you I wouldn't."

"Okay precious. Merry Christmas. You can open it now." I wait, listening to her slice open the envelope. "Be careful, my love, you won't want to slice what's inside."

"What is it?" I hear her giggle. "Oh my God! It's a check for $45,000."

"That's for us honey, to help start our life when I come home to you. I want you to set that aside so that we don't have any financial stress when I walk out of here to you."

"But we've already saved enough money. How did you do that?"

"I work hard for you, my love. You're my inspiration and nothing fulfills me more than to think that I'm providing for you, making your life better. It's the only way that I can feel like a man rather than a prisoner."

Whenever I earn financial resources from prison, whether it's through a writing fee or a stock trade, I derive an enormous sense of gratification. This environment is designed to crush the human spirit. Prisoners are supposed to go home broken, without financial resources, without a support network, destitute. Yet despite the quarter century that I'm serving, I'm going to walk out of here strong, stable. My wife has earned her credentials as a registered nurse. She has secured a job at Cottage Hospital in Santa Barbara and expects to earn $80,000 per year. Besides that income, men who know the value of work have paid me well, sufficiently to have supported my wife through what others would construe as incomprehensible struggle. After all of those expense, we've managed to build an after-tax savings account that now exceeds $100,000. Having achieved these goals from within prison boundaries magnifies the delight I feel.

* * * * * * *

It's April 12 of 2011 and I have to make a decision. My release date is scheduled for August 12, 2013. I have 284 months behind me and a maximum of only 28 more months of prison ahead of me.

But I know that I won't serve a full 28 months. Some complications surround my release date because I have that sliver of parole eligibility. It's strange. My case is so old that I'm one of the few prisoners remaining in the federal system that qualifies for an initial parole hearing. By my calculations, members of the U.S. Parole Commission have the discretion to release me as soon as February of 2013, in only 22 more months.

That doesn't tell the whole story. Besides the parole date, I qualify for up to 12 months of halfway house time. If I were to receive the February 2013 parole date, I could transfer to a halfway house as soon as February of 2012, in only 10 more months. But even in the unlikely event that the U.S. Parole Commission declined to grant me parole, I'm eligible to transfer to a halfway house 12 months before my scheduled release date, which would be in August of 2012. That means release should come for me somewhere between 10 and 16 months from today.

I need to decide where Carole and I are going to make our home. We don't have roots anywhere. It feels as if we're going to be hatched in society. Carole's children, Michael and Nichole are grown and building lives of their own in Washington state. She has agreed to let me choose where we should start our life together. I'm thinking about what city would be best.

My sister Julie lives in Seattle, and that's an obvious possibility. Both Carole and I grew up in Seattle, but after 25 years, we don't have a home anywhere. My younger sister, Christina, lives in Miami, which is another possibility we've discussed as a potential starting point. My mother lives in Los Angeles with my grandmother, and in light of the foundation that my friend Justin established, we're thinking about LA as well.

"The reality, honey," I tell my wife during a visit, "is that we're both going to be 48 years old when I walk out of here in the next 10 to 16 months. We'll only have 12 years before we're 60. Just as the decisions that I made early in my prison term played a pivotal, influential role in my journey, these decisions I make going forward are going to have an enormous influence on where we're going to be when we're 60."

"That's why I want you to choose, where we go." Carole holds my hand during our visit. It's the only physical contact we've ever had during our entire marriage, but that life of celibacy is coming to an end. "As long as I'm with you, I don't care where we go."

"What's most important to me is that I go to the city where I have the best opportunity to earn an income and bring stability to our life."

"As a registered nurse, I can get a job anywhere. And we have enough savings to give you that stability. You should arrange your release to wherever you want to go. How about Santa Barbara?"

"The market is too small, honey. As I see it, we have three choices. We can choose Los Angeles, we can choose San Francisco, or we can choose New York. I need to be in a big city."

"But how will you start in New York or San Francisco? We don't know anyone there."

"Geoff is in New York and Lee is in San Francisco. Both of them would help us if I asked." I remind her of my friend Geoff Richstone, the cardiologist from New York and my friend Lee Nobmann, the lumber baron of Northern California.

"You choose, honey. Wherever you want to go, I'm with you."

* * * * * * *

I'm waiting on the track at Taft camp on Friday morning, April 22, 2011. My friend Lee Nobmann is flying in for a visit today and his pilot will land the private jet, a Cessna Citation, at Taft's airport. I see the blinding spotlight as it approaches and then I hear the roar of the engines. It's a magnificent airplane, a sign of Lee's business brilliance and the successful company he built in Golden State Lumber. Carole is picking him up at the airport.

"It's good to see," I say when I walk into the visiting room. He is a great man and a great friend.

I tell Lee about the dilemma I'm facing with regard to which city I should choose to launch my life. While we dine on vending machine hamburgers, he listens to the different options I present and to the plans I have for building a career around all that I've learned as a federal prisoner.

"Do you really want to be talking about your experiences in federal prison for the rest of your life? I've got to tell you," he says, "no one in the real world is really going to care anything about prison. Why don't you come work with me? I could always use a man with your intensity and I've got the perfect spot for you in a real estate development company that my kids are running."

I have enormous respect for Lee. He isn't only an extraordinarily successful businessman, employing several hundred people, but he's also genuinely happy, with a loving marriage that has spanned four decades and great relationships with his children. When he extends an offer for me to work with him, it's an offer that I have to consider.

"If that's what you think would be best for me," I tell him, "then that's what I'm going to do. But I'm passionate about this idea I have of building a business around all that I've learned. There aren't many people who've sustained a high level of discipline and focus through a quarter century of adversity. I'm confident that I can find a market for products and services I intend to create around that journey."

Lee leans back and looks at me. He has blue, penetrating eyes, white hair, and looks every bit the self-made man that he is. I admire him immensely and I aspire to earn his respect. It's as if I'm always auditioning for him, trying to prove worthy of the trust he places in me with his friendship.

"Here's what we're going to do," he settles it. "Tell your case manager here that you're going to relocate to the Bay area. I've got a fully furnished guesthouse on my property. You won't need anything at all. It has everything, including towels, silverware, even a coffee pot. Use that as your release address. You and Carole can stay there for a year without any cost. One of my companies will employ you for a year so that you can earn an income while you build your business. If it doesn't work out, then you come work with me."

With Lee's generosity, my decision becomes easy. As he would say, it's a no brainer. Our home is going to be in the city by the Bay, a city I've never visited before.

* * * * * * *

It's Wednesday, April 27th, 2011 and I'm sitting on a bench with my friend Greg Reyes. We're reviewing edits I've been making to the manuscript that describes his life and he turns to me with a peculiar question. "Do you think you could run a marathon?"

I've run every day without a single day of rest since Saturday, December 13, 2008. During the 866 days that have passed since then, I've run 7,795 miles. The strict accountability logs that I keep give me a clear indication of where I am. I've averaged more than nine miles every day, but I've never been inclined to run a marathon distance of 26.2 miles. The longest distance I've ever run has been 20 miles, and I've done that about a half dozen times. I'm not a natural athlete, but running is an exercise of will, and these 8,661 days of imprisonment have given me a strong determination.

"Anyone can run a marathon, I tell Greg. But what's the point?"

"I'd like to run one before I get out."

Like my friend Lee, Greg is the type of man who clearly defines goals, and then he puts a deliberate course of action in place to achieve them. As I do with Lee, I feel as if I'm always auditioning for Greg's respect. Since prison consumed more of my life than I lived outside, I need these tests to feel as I can carry my own around guys who've truly succeeded.

"Then let's run one this weekend," I say.

Greg laughs. "You're too much. We've got to train for running a marathon. Every book I've read talks about a strict training regimen, increasing distances in incremental levels."

Greg walked into prison weighing 252 pounds. Besides working together on writing his life story, we set a disciplined exercise regimen in place. He wasn't a runner before, but he has run alongside me on several occasions and he's lost more than 60 pounds during the eight months that he's served. He now has a chiseled physique.

"That's ridiculous, Greg. We can do it. Those books aren't for people like you. Running is all in your mind. Let's just do it."

"You're nuts." He laughs. "I've got four months left to serve. Let's just set a training plan in place and get to one marathon distance before I go."

"Look we can do this," I tell him. "But let's start by running 20 miles on Saturday."

"I've never run longer than 10 miles in my life," he says. "I'm not running 20 miles on Saturday."

"You may not have run more than 10 miles," I tell him. "But you can run that routinely now and you run much faster than I do. Without a doubt, you can run 15 miles. Let's set our mind to that. You'll see. It's no big deal. Then we'll run 20 miles on the next Saturday."

He agrees and on Saturday, April 30th, we run through 15 miles as if it isn't anything. On Saturday May 7th, we meet on the track with a joint commitment of running 20 miles.

Greg may not have run before he surrendered to serve his sentence but he has developed into a strong runner. We run around a dusty dirt track, and since he goes at faster pace, he laps me numerous times. He paces alongside me at the 18-mile mark and asks how I'm feeling.

"I feel great. How 'bout you?"

"I'm okay."

"You know," I remind him, "we're in May now. Every day going forward will bring hotter temperatures here in Taft. If you feel up to it, I think we should just knock out the full marathon distance today and be done with it. What do you think?"

"Let's get through the 20 and see how we feel."

At 20 miles he is still lapping me. He finishes his first marathon distance in four hours and 14 minutes; it takes me 15 minutes longer to complete the 26.2-mile distance.

We celebrate with a good meal that my roommate prepares for us. He's elated at the accomplishment, as he should be.

"I've got to tell you, what you've done today is really impressive," I tell him.

"We both did it," he says.

"Well, it's not quite the same," I say.

"What do you mean? We ran the same distance."

Earning Freedom

"True, but you've only been running for a few months and you knocked out a marathon. I've been running for longer than 20 years. I don't even feel tired."

"Then run another one."

"That's what I was thinking," I said. "I'm going to."

"Are you nuts? I was only kidding," he tells me. "You've got to let your body heal."

I shrug. "Yeah, I don't think so. I don't even feel as if I've done anything. Next time, I'm going to run a double marathon."

"You're crazy."

"Seriously, I can do it. I could totally do it."

"When?"

"I was thinking that I'll run it on Wednesday."

"On Wednesday of this week? That's ridiculous."

"Do you want to run it with me?" I ask him.

"No, I don't. I'm not running 52 miles. Don't you think that's a little excessive?"

"I can do it."

"Then go for it."

On Wednesday, May 11th, I wake early and I'm eager to set out for the run. I have a plan. I'll start at 6:00, when the track opens, and I'll run for four hours. By 10:00 I'll knock out the first 24 miles. Then I'll return to the housing unit for the census count. After that clears, I'll return to the track and run another 16 miles, bringing me to 40 miles. At the slow pace I intend to run, I expect that stretch will last about three hours. Then I'll return to the housing unit for the afternoon census and a shower. I'll go back to the track after the count and knock out the final 12.4 miles.

"You're a maniac." Greg meets me on the track when I'm on the final stretch. Temperatures are still in the 90s and he passes me a bottle of Gatorade.

"I've got this," I tell him. "Only one more mile."

It takes me nine hours and 40 minutes, but I finish, reaching my goal.

"What're you going to do next?" Greg asks.

"I thought about that during the run," I tell him. "I've got three marathons in now. By the end of this year, I'll run 50 marathons."

He laughs. "There's something wrong with you," he says. "You're crazy."

"I'm going to do it."

* * * * * * *

It's December 31st, 2011 and I'm now in the Atwater federal prison camp, with 8,909 days of prison behind me. As far as exercise goals are concerned, it's been an extraordinary year. My fitness log shows that it's been 1,114 days since I've taken a day off from running. During that stretch, I've logged 10,773 miles. Over the course of 2011, the log shows that I ran 4,073 miles, including 55 marathon distances, 98,500 pushups, with 857.3 total hours of exercise. I intend to push myself harder in 2012.

Carole and I transferred to Atwater on October 3, knowing that it would be our last prison town as I prepare for my release to the San Francisco Bay area. As a privately run facility, the Taft camp could not handle the complicated issues of parole and extended halfway house possibilities. When authorities determined that a Bureau of Prisons facility should oversee my return to society, I asked for Atwater. Carole settled a few miles away in Merced and she has a job as a registered nurse at Mercy Medical Center, her second job in a major hospital. We're counting down the days, expecting that my case manager will provide some guidance with regard to my release date soon.

I expect this system to release me before Halloween, but to keep my mind from dwelling on that which is beyond my ability to control, I work toward some clearly defined goals. The first is helping my friend Andris Pukke (pronounced 'On-dris Puck-y'). Like Lee and Greg, Andris built an awesome business. He launched a credit counseling and debt consolidation company from his living room while advancing through his senior year at the University of Maryland. Under Andris' leadership, that company, branded as Ameridebt, grew to more than 250,000 customers. It became so profitable that Bear Sterns offered to purchase it for more than $100,000,000 before Andris celebrated his 35th birthday. I spend several hours each day with Andris, asking questions that help me write his biography.

Andris' story strengthens my resolve to write about lessons I've learned from exceptional businessmen. Many business leaders served time alongside me despite their never having had any inclination that decisions they were making could expose them to troubles with the law. Speaking and writing about what I've learned could bring more awareness to the dangers of doing business in America today. Indeed, people I've met in prison convince me that business decisions can lead to imprisonment, even when there isn't any criminal intent or efforts to self-enrich at the expense of others. Prosecution of white-collar crime is the new frontier of America's criminal justice system, and I have some unique insight that can help others understand the subject.

Andris is the fourth man I met in prison who has built a hugely successful business. In working with him to write his story, I'm able to push out thoughts about my imminent release. It's important now, during these final months, to focus on work. Otherwise, the combination of excitement and anticipation could derail me. As it always has, work and focus on goals carries me through.

Andris is released on March 30, 2012. That's it. He is the last friend I expect to make in prison. I'll serve the rest of this time alone, expecting that I'll walk out of here before October.

* * * * * * *

It's Wednesday, April 18, 2012 and I received the most amazing book during mail call. It's so impressive, *The Oxford Handbook of Sentencing and Corrections*, edited by Professor Joan Petersilia, who is the Adelbert H. Sweet Professor of Law at Stanford Law School, and Kevin R. Reitz, who is the James Annenberg La Vea Professor of Criminal Procedure at the University of Minnesota Law School. The 764-page book includes contributions from many authors who wrote individual chapters on various subjects pertaining to sentencing and corrections in America's massive prison system. My face beams with pride when I turn to chapter 25 and I see the words I wrote more than three years ago, describing the life I've lived since 1987.

I don't know how to describe the honor I feel that Professor Petersilia invited me to write about my experiences. I'm a prisoner, after all, and yet by including my work I'm in the company of some of the world's leading scholars who hold distinguished positions in some of the world's leading universities. To show my appreciation, I will read each chapter and publish a review to describe what I learned from those who contributed.

There isn't anyone here with whom I can share my joy, but inside, I feel a liberating gratification, giving me a sense that some meaning has come from this long journey. It's a journey that is coming to an end, as I have news that I'm scheduled to transition from the Atwater federal prison camp to the San Francisco halfway house on August 13, 2012.

* * * * * * *

It's July 1, 2012, the last full month that I'm going to serve in federal prison. I have 9,091 days of prison behind me, only 44 days of prison ahead. From the beginning I've been exercising very hard, but I've been waiting for this month for decades, always intending to exercise harder during my final month than ever before. After all, it's the last full month in my life that I'll have to focus exclusively on exercise. I'm determined to run 500 miles during the month. In addition, I'll do 10,000 pushups and 4,000 dips. The intense workout will quell this steady surge of anticipation that has been building for months.

Carole has already made the move to Lee's guesthouse and she secured a job at a Bay area hospital. As crazy as it may sound, I know that my life is one of many blessings, but more than anything else, I cherish the relationship I've built with my wife. We're both indescribably excited about the prospects of building our lives together. Despite the love, enthusiasm, and anticipation inside of me, however, I have a measure of anxiety as well.

For 25 years I've been a prisoner, living in the midst of men, strangers. Privacy has not been a part of my life. I don't know how to eat with metal silverware or off of ceramic plates. I've not had a drink from a glass since 1987, nor have I taken a shower without wearing flip-flops. We're in our 10ᵗʰ year of marriage, but my wife and I have only known each other under the bright lights of prison visiting rooms, always under the watchful eyes of vigilant prison guards.

I don't have any idea about the magnitude of change that is about to come my way, but I know that it's coming. Running these long distances helps to dissipate the anxiety, but I can't help thinking about how I'll react to the changes that are about to come. I don't worry about earning a living or financial matters, as I've prepared well for those challenges.

My anxieties are of a more primal nature. For instance, I dwell for hours at a time about how I'm going to muster the courage to poop in front of my wife. Will she kick me out of bed if she hears me pass gas? I don't have any idea on how I'm going to handle these complexities of domesticity, but I know that I can count on Carole to help me. She just doesn't yet know the worries that I have.

I wonder what's going through *her* mind. For years she's lived as a prisoner's wife, with visiting rooms being our living room, bedroom, and kitchen. She has been very protective of her time with me, and yet it has been only an abbreviated time. Now, in a matter of days, all of that will change.

Carole has begun making purchases to ease my initial transition. She bought us matching iPhones, clothing and hygiene supplies that I'm going to need. We're coordinating events with family, as my sisters, mother, and grandmother want to visit. They've been waiting for 25 years to welcome me home, but my release is complicated by three factors:

1. I'm being released to San Francisco and my family lives in other cities;
2. I'm not really going home, but to a halfway house; and
3. I don't know what restrictions the halfway house is going to place on me.

With all of those complications, I'm asking my mom and sisters to let me spend the initial weeks with Carole. Before receiving visits, I need to settle with her and understand more about this transition into society and what it truly means to live as a husband. I want to receive my driver's license, to begin reporting to work, and to complete whatever demands the halfway house makes upon residents as a condition of increased liberties. I expect that I'll need 90 days to settle.

* * * * * * *

It's 2:00 am on Monday, August 13, 2012. Today is the day, the 9,135th day that I'm waking on a prison rack. It's also the last. I climb down and dress in my exercise gear. I take my cup of instant coffee and walk into the center of the housing unit, where I sit alone in the dark. It's been 25 years and two days since my arrest, and in a few short hours I'm scheduled to walk outside of these fences. Why, I wonder, does society equate this particular amount of time with the concept of justice? In what ways did the quarter century I served contribute to community safety?

As I look around and see all the other prisoners sleeping, the only answer I can come up with is that society wanted to punish me for the laws I broke when I was in my early 20s. I'm now 48 and I don't even remember much about those crimes, as the length of time that I served gradually squeezed those details out of my memory and consciousness. The punishment felt severe with my arrest and trial and sentencing. But as the weeks turned into months, and the months turned into years, I turned all of my attention toward those three principled steps that were going to guide me through my journey:

1. I made a commitment to educate myself;
2. I made a commitment to contribute to society in measurable ways; and
3. I made a commitment to build a strong support network.

That strategy, I hoped, would help redeem the bad decisions of my reckless youth and help me reconcile with society. As the years passed, however, I lost sight of the fact that

427

society was punishing me. Prison became the only life that I knew. Is a man still being punished if he doesn't even know it?

By the time I earned my master's degree in 1995, I felt as ready to live as a contributing member of society as I ever would. That was 17 years ago, but our system of justice didn't have a mechanism in place to encourage individuals to work toward earning freedom. As Shakespeare suggested in his play *A Merchant from Venice*, the system wanted its pound of flesh. Regardless of what efforts an individual made to atone, in our system of justice, all that mattered was the turning of a sufficient number of calendar pages.

As of today, 300 calendar pages have turned since my initial arrest. And in a few more hours, I'm going to walk outside of these gates, where I'll see Carole waiting.

It's 4:00 am and I begin my exercise, first with strength training, knocking out 50 sets of pushups. Then I begin my run. In July I set a goal of running 500 miles. With focus and persistence I blasted through that goal, hitting 700 miles that included eight back-to-back marathons during the month.

I've now exercised for 1,340 days without a single day of rest, but what new routines will begin tomorrow? Many years ago I read *What Got You Here Won't Get You There*, a book by Marshall Goldsmith, a business strategist. The book made an impression on me then, and it seems particularly relevant to me now, as I finish running my 12th and final mile around a prison track. I'm opening my mind to the reality that I'm going to have to change the rigid and precise tactics that have carried me through prison. But I'll never relinquish my commitment to living a principled, deliberate, strategic life. I don't know how I'm going to have to change, but I'm open to the changes that will come when I walk outside of these prison gates.

* * * * * * *

It's 7:00 am and I'm walking alone, steadying my thoughts. I tried to use the telephone but my account has been disabled, confirming that my time in prison is ending. I see a long line of men waiting to enter the chow hall for breakfast and I feel the many eyes upon me; I feel their energy, good wishes from them, but I need this time alone. I walk into the chapel for solitude and I pray in gratitude, thanking God for protecting me through the journey, asking for guidance as I take the next steps home.

"Michael Santos," I hear the announcement. "Number 16377-004. Report with all your property to the rear gate."

I'm carrying my copy of *The Oxford Handbook of Sentencing and Corrections*, but I've given everything else away. I leave the camp and walk toward the gate at the rear of the penitentiary. A guard comes toward me from inside the gate and he crosses through. He calls me forward and asks a few questions to confirm my identity, and it's as simple as that.

We walk through a processing area and I see that it's 8:48, which is, coincidentally, the same number as the criminal code for the crime I committed. Another guard fingerprints and photographs me. Two other guards ask me more questions to confirm my identity. And that's it. We walk through penitentiary corridors, and across an area that leads me into a lobby.

I turn right around a corner, where I meet other guards. They hand over funds from my commissary account and authorize me to cross over to the other side, where Carole, my lovely wife waits with tears flowing down her cheeks. I walk out of the penitentiary and step into her loving embrace.

At last, at last.

Photos

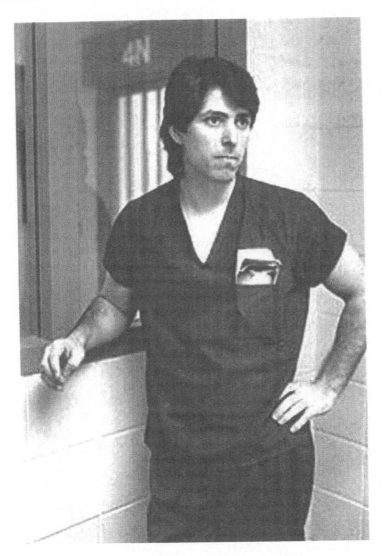

Michael Santos
Pierce County Jail
1987

**Michael Santos
Mercer University Graduation
USP Atlanta
1992**

Michael Santos
Mercer University Graduation
USP Atlanta
1992

**Michael Santos with
Dr. R. Bruce and Carolyn McPherson
FCI McKean
1994**

**Michael Santos with
Dr. R. Bruce McPherson
FCI Fort Dix
1998**

**Michael Santos with
Dr. George Cole
Fort Dix, NJ
2000**

Michael Santos with the Axelrod/Zachary Family
From left: Tristan Axelrod, Carol Zachary,
(Michael) Zachary Axelrod, Jon Axelrod
Fort Dix, NJ
2002

**Michael Santos with
Bob Brennan
Fort Dix, NJ
2003**

Michael and Carole Santos
Wedding Day
Fort Dix, NJ
June 24, 2003

**Michael Santos with
Lee Nobmann
Taft Camp
2011**

**Michael Santos with
Greg Reyes
Taft Camp
2011**

Michael and Carole Santos
Taft Camp
2011

**Michael and Carole Santos
Atwater Camp
2011**

Michael and Carole Santos
Atwater Camp
2012

Michael and Carole Santos
San Francisco, CA
August 13, 2012

Michael Santos
San Francisco, CA
August 31, 2012